POLITICAL CULTURE
IN CONTEMPORARY BRITAIN

Political Culture
in Contemporary Britain

*People and Politicians, Principles
and Practice*

WILLIAM L. MILLER,
ANNIS MAY TIMPSON,
AND
MICHAEL LESSNOFF

CLARENDON PRESS · OXFORD
1996

Oxford University Press, Walton Street, Oxford OX2 6DP
Oxford New York
Athens Auckland Bangkok Bombay
Calcutta Cape Town Dar es Salaam Delhi
Florence Hong Kong Istanbul Karachi
Kuala Lumpur Madras Madrid Melbourne
Mexico City Nairobi Paris Singapore
Taipei Tokyo Toronto
and associated companies in
Berlin Ibadan

Oxford is a trade mark of Oxford University Press

Published in the United States
by Oxford University Press Inc., New York

British Library Cataloguing in Publication Data
Data available

Library of Congress Cataloging in Publication Data
Miller, William Lockley, 1943–
Principles and practice : the political culture of people and
politicians in contemporary Britain / William L. Miller, Annis May
Timpson, and Michael Lessnoff.
Includes bibliographical references and index.
1. Political culture—Great Britain. 2. Great Britain—Politics
and government. I. Timpson, Annis May. II. Lessnoff, Michael H.
(Michael Harry) III. Title.
JN231.M55 1996 320.941′09′049—dc20 95–26849
ISBN 0–19–827984–1

1 3 5 7 9 10 8 6 4 2

Typeset by Graphicraft Typesetters Ltd, Hong Kong
Printed in Great Britain
on acid-free paper by
Bookcraft (Bath) Ltd,
Midsomer Norton, Avon

ACKNOWLEDGEMENTS

THE British Rights Study was funded by the Economic and Social Research Council (ESRC) under grant number R00236737. We would like to thank the Council for this grant, the staff of the ESRC who assisted us with its administration, and the Council's anonymous referees for their comments on our research application. The intellectual inspiration came from colleagues who had conducted similar research in Canada: Professors Paul Sniderman (Stanford), Peter Russell and Joseph Fletcher (Toronto), and Philip Tetlock (Berkeley), and from a lecture given by Justice Brennan at Glasgow University.

We were extremely lucky to have had the efficient research assistance of Malcolm Dickson and Morag Brown of Glasgow University, who helped us develop our survey, trained over 120 interviewers, and managed the computer-assisted telephone interviews on which our study is based. Malcolm Dickson also wrote the CATI computer programme. To them and to the students at the University of Glasgow who conducted the interviews many thanks indeed.

Studies like this would never appear without the time, given freely, of the 4,347 local political leaders and members of the public who undertook our long, searching, and challenging interview. These people, like those who helped us in the critical stages of pretesting our questionnaire, must remain unnamed, but certainly not unthanked.

In the course of conducting this study we benefited from the intellectual advice and the practical support of many other colleagues on both sides of the Atlantic. We would particularly like to acknowledge the significant input we received from colleagues at our own universities of Glasgow, Nottingham, and Sussex who gave up their time to comment on our research and provide practical support with the various stages of its development. Elspeth Shaw, Avril Johnston, and Jeanette Berrie provided remarkably prompt secretarial support. We would also like to record our appreciation for the comments received from colleagues who attended the papers we presented at our own universities, at the British Association for Canadian Studies conference in Hull, and at the Universities of Strathclyde, Oxford, Wales, and Stanford.

We should also thank our editors at Oxford University Press for their encouragement—and their patience.

Finally Annis May Timpson would like to record her personal thanks to Michael and Pat Timpson, Ian Read and Vivien Hart for all their support at different stages of this project.

William L. Miller
Annis May Timpson
Michael Lessnoff

Glasgow and Brighton
August 1995

CONTENTS

CONTENTS

PART ONE
Introduction

1

Questions of Rights

OUR aim in this book is to take a wide-ranging look at British views of the proper relationships between government and citizens, and between one citizen and another. We base our study primarily on the British Rights Survey which we carried out in 1992, but, in designing that survey, we intentionally avoided any narrow definition of rights. We sought to uncover attitudes towards a wide range of what people call civil, political, or social rights. And in our title we have used the broad phrase 'political culture' rather than what some may see as a narrower and possibly more legalistic phrase about 'rights'.

However, we shall make no attempt to follow other writers on British political culture by inventing a single word to describe it. Our own work is rather more in the tradition of Herbert McClosky and Alida Brill's *Dimensions of Tolerance*[1] than in that of Almond and Verba's *Civic Culture*.[2] Excessive zeal for simplistic descriptions has produced not only the 'civic culture', but also 'a predominantly allegiant culture'[3] and even 'a fragmented culture'[4] as characterizations of 'The British Political Culture'. We doubt whether it is particularly illuminating even to talk about 'The British Political Culture'—in contrast to 'political culture within Britain', because that culture is neither homogeneous nor uniquely British. On the one hand, we shall look at the variations in political culture across different social and political groups within Britain, focusing especially on the differences between politicians and the general public; on the other, we shall suggest that fundamental aspects of political culture in Britain are not limited to the jurisdiction of British laws and institutions.

RIGHTS AND OBLIGATIONS

Although we accept that 'the notion of human rights has traditionally been less popular amongst lawyers in the UK than it is in other jurisdictions',[5] British political culture is founded upon public perceptions of rights, broadly framed. Geoff Andrews, for example, refers to Charter 88's 'promise of a new *political culture*' (emphasis added)[6] with its demands for a new people's Bill of Rights and its general focus on the language of rights and citizenship. The Conservative government has responded with its own series of Citizen's Charters. Whether or not this represents a particularly new political culture, 'we live in an age in which it has become common for people in democratic societies to invoke the concept of rights in political discourse',[7] and the language of rights and charters is clearly popular right across the political spectrum in contemporary Britain.

Indeed, quite a few people seem to think it has become too popular. In the mid-1990s leading politicians on the left[8] have joined those on the right in alleging that there is 'too much emphasis on rights' in today's Britain. There is, we often hear, too much emphasis on individuals' rights, and not enough on their obligations. On the face of it, this is a puzzling claim, for rights and obligations are to a large degree (though not totally) logically correlative, so that to assert a right is (usually) to assert an obligation also. The classic analysis of rights is due to the American jurist Wesley Hohfeld,[9] who distinguished (as had Jeremy Bentham before him) between rights in the sense of pure absence of obligation ('liberties') and rights that correspond to (others') obligations ('claim-rights'). The latter are politically much the more relevant kind. The clearest example of a Hohfeldian liberty is the natural right said by Hobbes[10] to be enjoyed (or suffered) by all persons in the state of nature (but only there)—the right of all to do all things, a right which leads to or licenses the war of all against all. The rights advocated today are obviously not of this kind, but are more akin to the natural rights defended by Locke—rights derived from and protected by the *law* of nature: thus, for example, each person has a right to life because the law of nature stipulates that no one must injure the life of another, or, otherwise put, all have an *obligation* not to injure the life of another.[11]

In this sense it is not logically possible to overemphasize rights at the expense of obligations. Probably what the critics of rights really have in mind is something quite different: a tendency to overemphasize *our own* rights rather than the rights *of others*, or, in other words, to concentrate unduly on *our own* rights rather than our own obligations. In still other words, their real target is, or ought to be, selfishness—the self-interested exploitation of the vocabulary of rights 'without assuming obligations'.[12] If so, the attack on rights is a confusion and should be directed elsewhere. Rights are not intrinsically more selfish than they are altruistic.

It is possible, however, that this defence of rights will not satisfy the critics. Granted that rights and obligations are correlative, it may be said, preoccupation with rights bespeaks an attitude to life that is too legalistic and too individualistic. Rights are, admittedly, no more my rights than yours:

but some critics would argue that, if we relate to each other purely as right-holders, then something vital to the good life is lacking from our relationship. Concern for others, they would claim, should not be just a matter of respect for their rights; such a concern is too limited, and too calculating (even, some feminists would say, too masculine). Rather, they argue, we should relate to each other in a spirit of solidarity and mutual caring, of readiness to offer help whenever it is needed. Such a spirit binds us together by ties of 'community', without which human life is shallow and even un-natural. A culture of rights, they claim, is a culture of strangers.[13] Humanity cannot live by rights alone.

It is hard not to have some sympathy with this critique, especially when one remembers the absurd litigiousness of the rights-obsessed culture of the USA—a country where social relations sometimes seem to be mediated mainly by lawyers. Nevertheless, the point should not be overstated. However true it is that rights are insufficient, they remain necessary, indeed essential—and the USA, again, with its tradition of constitutionalism in government, including a Bill of Rights, and in modern times a legally en-shrined right of the citizen to freedom of information (which has more than once proved to be the best recourse of investigators into the dubious doings of secretive *British* governments) serves as a reminder of this side of the question.

Anthony H. Birch suggests that 'the language of rights has become more general since 1945 for two quite different reasons'.[14] In the immediate post-war period the 1948 UN Universal Declaration of Human Rights, the 1949 Basic Law of the German Federal Republic, and the 1950 European Conven-tion for the Protection of Human Rights and Fundamental Freedoms all in quick succession 'made it clear that entrenched rights were not necessarily incompatible with a parliamentary system of government'. Then, in the late 1960s, a new kind of radicalism led many on the left 'to change their em-phasis from . . . policies designed to extend state powers [to policies] stress-ing the rights of the individual against the state'. Although debates about the extent to which citizens should be entitled to enjoy these negative liberties, as well as more positive—welfare-based rights—continued well beyond that time, the particular demand for a written bill of rights re-emerged on the left in the late 1980s with the establishment of Charter 88.

There have, then, been repeated calls over the last three decades for Bri-tain to have a written constitution and a Bill of Rights. While some have argued that such instruments should be based on the 1791 US Bill of Rights (which clarifies the rights of the citizen against the state), others have fa-voured the 1982 Canadian model (which entrenches citizens' rights in a way

that does not completely undermine parliamentary government) or called for
the incorporation of the European Convention on Human Rights (an instrument which aims at enforcement of certain of the rights proclaimed in the
UN Declaration of Human Rights[15] of 1948) into English and Scottish law.[16]
Given this debate, it is both timely and appropriate to seek out the opinions
of the British people on these issues.

CATEGORIES OF RIGHTS

In a celebrated lecture at Cambridge University in 1949, T. H. Marshall took
a historical perspective and

divided citizenship into three elements: civil, political, and social . . . Civil rights
came first and were established in something like their modern form before the first
Reform Act was passed in 1832. Political rights came next and their extension was
one of the main features of the nineteenth century . . . Social rights, on the other
hand, sank to vanishing point in the eighteenth and early nineteenth centuries . . . it
was not until the twentieth century that they attained equal partnership with the other
elements of citizenship.[17]

As history, that might have seemed a more controversial claim in Stornoway[18] than in Cambridge, but it did distinguish well between different categories of rights.
    A somewhat similar categorization appeared in the 1948 UN Declaration of
Human Rights, which contains thirty articles. According to Maurice Cranston,
a philosopher well known as a critic of the Declaration, the Commission
charged with its drafting consciously included two different categories of
rights, which it referred to as 'political and civil rights' (detailed in the first
twenty articles of the Declaration) and 'economic and social rights' (in the
remaining ten) respectively. Cranston argued that only the former category
should have been included.[19] More recently, Margaret Thatcher rejected the
notion of economic rights as 'an all too debased rhetoric of fairness and
equality'.[20] Cranston, by contrast, did not deny the existence of economic
and social rights, but he did deny that they are, or can be, *human* rights—
that is, moral rights of all human beings at all times and in all situations.
Cranston offered no definition of the two categories of rights, merely describing the political and civil rights as 'traditional' and the economic and social
rights as 'new', and leaving us to grasp the difference by means of examples.
Thus, political and civil rights include the rights to life, liberty, and security
of person; the right to freedom of movement; the right to a fair trial if

accused of a crime; the right to freedom of peaceful assembly and association; and the right to religious freedom. On the other side, the economic and social rights include the right to social security; the right to work and to protection against unemployment; the right to form and join trade unions; and the right to a standard of living adequate for health and well-being, including food, clothing, housing, medical care, and necessary social services, and including also the right to security in the event of unemployment, sickness, disability, and old age.[21]

Cranston's argument for restricting human rights to the first category only was inept, but the difference between the two categories of rights is real enough (or rather would be, if they were properly formulated). In essence, Cranston offered two arguments. First of all, human rights are rights of paramount importance: social security and the like are desirable, but not paramount in the way that the right to life or the right to a fair trial is. Clearly, this is an absurd argument, since the point of social security is precisely to preserve life. It appears that what Cranston understood by the 'right to life' was the right not to be killed—obviously this right is of precisely equal importance to the right not to starve, and both are more important than the right to (say) freedom of assembly.

Cranston's other (and perhaps main) argument was that a human right is by definition a universal right of all human beings at all times and in all situations, and hence it must be *universally practicable* at all times and in all situations. What is more, the political and civil rights *are* universally practicable, according to Cranston: they 'can be readily secured by legislation', usually fairly simple legislation that 'restrain[s] the government's own executive arm', since they are mostly 'rights against government interference with a man's activities'. On the other hand, the economic and social rights require not only the right laws but also 'great capital wealth', which the governments of poor countries cannot command. In such countries, social security and similar benefits are ideals, not rights.

This argument also will not do. For one thing, some of the so-called economic and social rights require no government command of resources—for example, the right to form and join trade unions, which is in fact an exemplification of the 'civil and political' right to freedom of association. More importantly, the civil and political rights cannot all be readily secured by legislation, nor are they all mainly rights against government interference: for example, the right to life (meaning thereby the right not to be killed) is a right not to be killed by anyone whatever, and it is very difficult—if not impossible—to secure it universally, as a glance at murder statistics will demonstrate. As Raymond Plant has put it, 'do we have to say that because rights come up against the limits of scarcity [of resources] they are not genuine?—a question that would apply equally well to the protection of civil and political rights as to securing social and economic rights.'[22] To a Chancellor of the Exchequer, the police budget and the health-care budget are no different in principle; both are limited by the state's ability to raise taxes, and both reflect potentially unlimited demands which the Chancellor knows will almost certainly be unsatisfied, if not unsatisfiable. Arguably, if the British government were to devote as much economic resources to policing as to the National Health Service, it would not succeed any better in protecting the life of all against murder than it would in protecting their lives against disease. Plant supports T. H. Marshall's low-key but realistic view of social rights: 'what Marshall meant by social rights was not that these would be individually enforceable but that the state had a general duty to provide collective services in fields of health, education and welfare',[23] just as it does in the field of law and order.

Nevertheless, something can be salvaged from the wreckage of Cranston's argument. Undeniably, there is a philosophically significant difference between rights which, in themselves, impose only *negative* duties, or duties of non-interference—duties not to kill, not to interfere with the practice of a religion, not to imprison or otherwise punish without a fair trial, not to obstruct freedom of movement—and duties which impose *positive* obligations to provide economic or other benefits, such as social security or education. Most of the 'political and civil rights' are in the former category, most of the 'economic and social rights' are in the latter. Furthermore, this philosophical distinction corresponds approximately to an ideological one, between 'liberalism' and 'socialism', at least in familiar enough senses of these two ambiguous terms. It is also true that the 'socialist' rights, since they require resources, are not in principle universally practicable, whereas the 'liberal' rights can be universally realized so long as everyone does their (negative) duty (we need not go into the philosophically vexed question whether this is strictly possible, however unlikely). On the other hand, we can take it for granted that the UK is a society wealthy enough to secure economic and social rights for its citizens, if it so chooses, though the level of provision must obviously be constrained by resource limitations. Whether and to what extent it does so choose, or should so choose in the opinion of British citizens, are among the questions that the British Rights Survey set out to answer.

To his two arguments why economic and social rights are not human rights, Cranston later added a third. Unlike the political and civil rights, to possess the economic and social rights it is not sufficient just to be a human being, nor even a human being for whom it is possible to provide the benefits involved. It is necessary also to have *earned* them. Only *deserving* human beings have these rights. To earn or deserve such rights one must have performed some work or service; one then acquires those rights in return for such work or service. Just what work or what service creates what rights Cranston did not specify, and his position as stated is certainly too strong, since it would deprive children and the disabled of a right to basic necessities. Nevertheless a weaker form of Cranston's view is not self-evidently absurd—namely, that in the case of those capable of work or service such work or service is a necessary condition of their having a right to benefits. This idea may underlie the preference held in some quarters for 'workfare' over unconditional welfare provision. To what extent such views are general in British society is an interesting question on which an exercise like the British Rights Survey can throw some light.

SPECIFIC RIGHTS AND SPECIFIC SURVEY QUESTIONS

In his discussion of the 1948 UN Declaration of Human Rights, Maurice Cranston pointed to another difference between the political and civil, and the economic and social rights: the former are much easier to translate into legally binding form, to enshrine in legislation, and thus to make justiciable. In this he is probably right. At any rate, the famous European Convention for the Protection of Human Rights and Fundamental Freedoms, signed in 1950 by the member states of the Council of Europe, which unlike the UN Declaration is a legally enforceable instrument accompanied by appropriate judicial institutions (in particular the European Court of Human Rights at Strasbourg), concerned itself with rights of the political and civil category only. The Strasbourg court has become a significant actor on the European legal and political stage, and one to which British citizens have not infrequently turned for redress. But use of the Strasbourg judicial machinery is slow and expensive, and there have been many calls for the Convention to be incorporated into English and Scottish law as such, and thus made enforceable by British judges directly. These calls testify both to the importance of the rights detailed in the European Convention, and to dissatisfaction with the British Constitution. They do not necessarily mean, however, that the political and civil rights enshrined in the Convention are more important, or considered by the British people to be more important, than the economic and social rights omitted from it. The British Rights Survey aimed to tap opinion about both classes of rights. Let us consider in more detail the relation between these rights and the questions posed in the Survey.

The Right to Life: Article 2 of the European Convention and
Article 3 of the UN Declaration

It is instructive to compare Article 2 of the European Convention and Article 3 of the UN Declaration, both of which proclaim the most fundamental of all human rights, the right to life (the right not to be killed). (The latter deals also with security of the person, presumably the right not to be physically injured.) The UN Declaration is here precisely that—a ringing affirmation without any qualification whatsoever: 'Everyone has the right to life and security of person.' The European Convention (a justiciable legal instrument) is much more complex and circumspect. While at first affirming that 'everyone's right to life shall be protected by law', it goes on to qualify if not contradict that initial affirmation. Intentional deprivation of life is permissible as a punishment for crimes defined by law, or if it is necessary to defend any person from unlawful violence, or to quell a riot or insurrection, or even to effect a lawful arrest or prevent a person lawfully imprisoned from escaping. Some of these qualifications are possibly surprising, others not. The point, however, is that the qualifications illustrate a fundamental fact: real life, unlike mere Declarations, has to deal with, and compromise between, conflicting values. The individual human life may be a value of the first importance, but the maintenance of civil order and the prevention of crime are highly important also. Conflicts arise between these values, and even within them—thus, to defend one human life it may be necessary to end another.

The British Rights Survey was designed to heed this fundamental fact in several ways. In the present instance, we have not directly sought to elicit views on the right to life (probably a fruitless exercise), but have sought opinions on a number of issues relevant to it. Two of these relate to the conflict between the value of different lives—namely, the importance of strong defence forces (to defend our lives by taking theirs, *inter alia*) and the desirability of the death penalty for murder (likewise). Others have relevance to conflicts between the value of human life and other values—for example, the importance of 'strengthening law and order'. Further questions raise the even more fundamental issue: what is a human life? Does it include the life of a human foetus? If so, the issue of abortion—more particularly 'abortion on demand'—is also a question of a conflict between the value of human life and other values. In this case, however, it is likely that those who advocate abortion on demand do not consider a foetus to be a human being in a full sense.

The Right to Liberty: Articles 5 and 6 of the European Convention

Articles 5 and 6 of the European Convention deal with the right to liberty—that is, the right not to be deprived of liberty (imprisoned) except after conviction in a fair and public trial by a competent court. According to Article 6, every accused person is to be presumed innocent until proved guilty. However, other justifications for deprivation of liberty are stated (in Article 5): in order to bring an accused person to trial, to prevent a person from committing an offence, or to prevent the spread of infectious diseases. Persons of unsound mind, alcoholics, drug addicts, and vagrants may also be deprived of liberty. These are contentious matters, some of which were addressed in the British Rights Survey. Questions concerning the importance of 'law and order' and the prevention of crime (see above) are again relevant here, as concerning values that may conflict with the liberty of the subject. Issues of 'due process' also arise in this connection, a number of which have given rise to considerable unease in Britain over the last decade. Thus, for example, we have asked questions about the accused person's 'right to silence' (hallowed by tradition, but now under legislative attack through the Criminal Justice and Public Order Act of 1994) and about the propriety of convicting a person purely on the basis of his or her own confession. We also asked an important general question: is it more important to protect the rights of suspects, or to ensure the safety of our streets, if the two should conflict?

The Rights of Private Life: Articles 8 and 9 of the European Convention

Articles 8 and 9 of the European Convention concern the rights of private life. Article 9 protects the right to religious freedom—that is, freedom to express religious belief in worship, teaching, practice, and observance; Article 8 proclaims the right to respect for private life generally, and for a person's family life, home, and correspondence. Again these rights are not proclaimed in absolute terms—public safety, public order, the protection of health or 'morals' or of the rights or freedoms of others, as well as (in Article 8) national security, are listed as good grounds for limiting them. In view of these qualifications, it is possible to see the two Articles as somewhat akin to John Stuart Mill's famous right to freedom of self-regarding action, whether individual or collective (action, that is, that does not harm or affect anyone other than the person or persons who freely perform it or who freely consent to be affected by it).

The wording of Article 8, however, suggests also a right of non-interference of a rather different kind, that is, a right to non-invasion of the privacy of one's everyday life—including what we have elsewhere termed 'freedom from the press'[24] (or from the media more generally). One might speculate whether eminent persons in Britain—royalty, politicians, bankers, and others —might not be able to seek legal redress under this Article. Not only the media, of course, threaten invasion of private life—it is a particularly interesting fact that, for example, the British secret services are legally entitled to carry out such invasions in ways forbidden to ordinary citizens, including acts that if carried out by ordinary citizens would constitute burglary. This state of affairs may or may not be justified by the qualifications of the right to respect for private life listed in Article 8.

Be that as it may, the survey sought opinions on a number of matters falling within this area. For example, we asked whether religious freedom should apply to all religious groups, no matter how 'strange, fanatical or weird' they might seem to the majority. Another question raises the problem of religions that prescribe cruel methods of animal slaughter. But freedom in private life does not, of course, relate only to religion (a phenomenon not as easy to define, in any case, as might be thought—any practice can be 'religion' if people think so). We also asked about the right to use drugs in ways that do not harm others, together with a similar question about drinking, and also whether the majority have a right to outlaw homosexuality. Other questions relate to invasions of the privacy of politicians and citizens by press and television, and to telephone tapping by the police and security services.

Freedom of Expression, Association, and Assembly: Articles 10 and 11 of the European Convention

Articles 10 and 11 of the European Convention deal with the most 'political' rights (apart from the right to vote)—namely, the rights to freedom of expression, peaceful assembly, and association with others. It is worth mentioning that the right to form and join trade unions is explicitly included in Article 11 as part of freedom of association, and that freedom of expression, as defined in Article 10, includes 'the right to receive and impart information and ideas without interference by public authority'. As usual the rights are not unqualified—national security, public safety, and the prevention of crime are again listed as justifying exceptions. (The British Criminal Justice and Public Order Act of 1994, controversially, takes advantage of these qualifications to put new restrictions on freedom of assembly and of expression.)

Just because these rights are so highly political, it is inevitable that any investigation such as the British Rights Survey will include a large number of questions relating to them. Not that anyone is likely to express outright opposition to these rights—the questions relate to their proper limits, when they have to be balanced against other goods. How important is freedom of speech, set against the danger to society from extremist views? Should the media be free to attack religious or minority groups? To tell lies? To promote racial or religious hatred? To interview supporters of terrorism? Should any political organization ever be banned because of its extreme views? Should all workers have the right to join trade unions, or only those not employed in essential public services? Should political demonstrations be allowed if they cause significant inconvenience to the public, for example, by blocking traffic? Opinions on all these topics were tapped by our survey.

As noted above, Article 10 of the European Convention interprets freedom of expression to include freedom of information—a highly contentious issue in recent British politics. The idea of a Freedom of Information Act on the US model has many supporters, and many opponents. We asked our respondents for their views on this idea, and also some related questions about the public's right to information concerning government plans in various policy areas, in the light of the 'national interest'. The right to information also raises some less obvious questions. Should it be buttressed by a right of journalists to protect the confidentiality of their sources—even if the source has committed a crime? Should it perhaps be overridden on grounds of the public interest in certain cases—for example, in order to prevent the media giving excessive coverage to violence, or publicizing high rates of crime among minority ethnic groups? Or is the public's 'right to know' absolute in these cases? We asked these questions also.

Economic and Social Rights: Articles 22, 23, 25, and 26 of the UN Declaration

The 1948 UN Declaration of Human Rights, unlike the European Convention on Human Rights, is not legally enforceable, and the 'economic and social rights' proclaimed in its later Articles—unlike the 'political and civil rights'—have (with one exception, of which more below) not been enshrined in a justiciable legal instrument comparable to the European Convention.[25] Despite this, they are just as important as the others, and we have sought opinions about them.

For example, according to Article 23, 'everyone has the right to protection against unemployment'. Admittedly, it is not exactly clear what this means, but a possible interpretation is a right of all adults who want one to have a (decently paid?) job. We have asked, in this spirit, whether government has an obligation to ensure that everyone who wants a job can have one. Maurice Cranston, no doubt, might have objected that there can be no such obligation in a free market economy, in which unemployment cannot be eliminated. So we have asked another question that implicitly recognizes this—simply, how important it is to *reduce* unemployment.

This so-called right to protection against unemployment might be interpreted in a different way—not as a right not to be unemployed, but as a right to 'security in the event of unemployment'. The latter is in fact explicitly proclaimed by Article 25 of the UN Declaration, according to which everyone 'has the right to a standard of living adequate for the health and well-being of himself and his family, including (*inter alia*) housing and medical care and necessary social services, and the right to security in the event of unemployment, sickness, disability, widowhood, old age or other lack of livelihood in circumstances beyond his control'. A general 'right to social security' is proclaimed in Article 22. Several questions in our survey touch on these matters. For example, we asked people in general terms how important they think it is to take care of the needy and to provide help for the disabled. We also asked more specific questions about the obligations of government to look after the unfortunate. Does government have an obligation to ensure a decent standard of living for everyone? To ensure adequate housing for everyone? To provide good medical care for everyone? Of course, ensuring for everyone a decent standard of living, adequate housing, and medical care can be achieved, or at least attempted, in various ways. Should the government itself be responsible for providing benefits on a universal basis, or should it only act as a 'safety net' where other sources fail? The importance of this question in an era where resources available for state welfare services are perceived, rightly or wrongly, to be under particular strain needs no emphasis. Accordingly, we asked our respondents whether or not 'state benefits like family allowances' should be paid only to those who really need them. We also asked how important it is to cut taxes.

An area of state provision which gives rise to somewhat different issues is education, which is dealt with in Article 26 of the UN Declaration. According to this Article everyone has the right to education, indeed to free education 'in the elementary stages'; as for higher education, it must be 'equally accessible to all on the basis of merit'. Needless to say, these words are vague: the meaning of 'merit' and, for that matter, 'education' is ambiguous. But we need not trouble about such questions just now. What is perhaps more interesting is another section of the Article, which states that 'parents have a prior right to choose the kind of education that shall be given to their children'. It is also interesting that the right to education, alone of the UN Declaration's 'economic and social' rights, has been declared legally enforceable by the Council of Europe, in a Protocol added to the European Convention on Human Rights in 1952. Not only does Article 2 of this Protocol declare that no one shall be denied the right to education; it also adds that the state must respect the rights of parents 'to ensure such education and teaching in conformity with their own religious and philosophical convictions'. Such a general, unqualified right seems on the face of it absurd, and even highly dangerous. Surprisingly, no qualification to the right is stated in the Protocol. But, be that as it may, it is perhaps a matter for surprise that, so far, apparently, no British Muslim parents have made any use of this Article in their fight to establish state-financed Islamic schools.

In our survey, we asked a number of questions in this area. We asked whether governments have an obligation to ensure equal opportunities for everyone—a goal to which educational provision is, of course, extremely relevant. More explicitly, we asked also if government has an obligation to provide a good education for everyone. Nor did we neglect the rights of parents in regard to the education of their children: two questions asked whether Welsh parents have the right to have their children educated in publicly funded Welsh-speaking schools, and whether Muslim parents have similar rights that their children be educated in publicly funded Muslim schools.

Constitutional Questions

Neither the UN Declaration nor the European Convention has much to say about constitutional questions, except that both call for democracy—the Declaration in Article 21 ('everyone has the right to take part in the government of his country, directly or through freely chosen representatives'), the Convention in the above-mentioned Protocol, Article 3. We did not ask respondents if they favoured democracy as such: it is not a matter of dispute in current British debate. But related questions are more controversial, and we asked, for example, for opinions on proportional representation, devolution of political authority to the nations of Britain and the regions of England, the proper balance of power between local councils and central government, and a Bill of Rights. We sought views, also, on whether the courts should have authority to enforce a Bill of Rights by declaring parliamentary legislation unconstitutional (thus ending that most prized of British constitutional shibboleths, the sovereignty of parliament). And in view of the important role and high profile of the European Convention in relation to the protection of individual rights in the UK, we sought opinions on whether the European Court of Human Rights should 'have the final say' on laws passed by the Westminster parliament, and also on the importance generally of the courts, both British and European, in protecting citizens' rights and liberties. The findings on these questions were particularly interesting.

Women's Rights

In 1967 the UN issued a declaration on women's rights and in 1980 the UN Convention on the Elimination of All Forms of Discrimination against Women was opened for signature and ratification and has since been ratified, with reservations, by Britain.[26] We asked questions about the principle of equality for men and women and about the use of quotas to encourage gender equality in parliamentary representation and employment.

THE BRITISH RIGHTS SURVEY

Public opinion is a notoriously elusive concept and notoriously difficult to measure on such complex and abstract topics as rights and freedoms. All too often opinion polls offer easy, abstract, and apparently cost-free options which appear to win overwhelming support but do not reflect the actual choices that people would make in real-world situations. So we asked about both abstract principles and the application of those principles in practice, in hypothetical scenarios which often involved conflicts of principle.

Three Samples

But what should 'public' opinion mean in this context—the untested views of people who do not often have to make practical decisions on the issues, or the considered opinions of people who have to face the issues regularly? Which 'public' best represents 'public opinion'? The opinions of the informed and involved public may best represent the opinions that the less informed and less involved would have, if only they had to confront the issues more closely or more often. So we investigated public opinion on two levels by using 2,060 interviews with a representative sample of the British electorate and 1,244 interviews with a sample of senior local politicians (mainly leaders of party groups, including Independent groups, on local government councils throughout Britain).[27] We shall refer to these two samples as the 'British public' and 'politicians' respectively. These senior local politicians were chosen as representative of a particularly well informed and experienced group, whose opinions were likely to be influenced by the fact that they would have made policies or taken decisions that might affect the rights and freedoms of ordinary citizens. Together these two samples give us an insight into the complex structure of public opinion in British society.

We shall show that abstract principles are more strongly, and more simply structured amongst politicians than amongst the general public; that abstract principles influence attitudes to rights in particular scenarios more strongly amongst politicians than amongst the general public; that, paradoxically perhaps, politicians are more favourable to citizens' rights than the general public itself; but, at the same time and less paradoxically, even *local* politicians have a 'governing perspective' which makes them more indulgent towards government prerogatives than the general public.

The validity and significance of these differences might be challenged on the grounds that our samples of public and politicians differed in terms of partisanship: our sampling procedure produced proportionately more Liberals in our sample of politicians than in our sample of the general public, simply because a small Liberal Party group of a few councillors and a large Labour or Conservative group each had one leader available for inclusion in the politicians' sample. Now, if the politicians' sample is disproportionately Liberal (with a capital 'L') compared to the public, that alone might make politicians seem more liberal (with a small 'l'). To meet that challenge we have weighted our sample of politicians to have the same voting preferences as our British public sample—effectively down-weighting Liberal politicians and up-weighting Labour politicians slightly and Conservative politicians a little more. Consequently, none of the differences between public and politicians in this volume owes anything to differences in the party balance, since there are none. Weighting in this way is a standard statistical technique, but to any reader who is suspicious of it we should report that without this weighting opinion percentages amongst politicians usually differ by only 1–2 per cent, and never by more than 5 per cent, from the opinion percentages in the unweighted sample of politicians, and this difference never alters our conclusions in any significant way.

Reflecting the proportions in the electorate, 84 per cent of our British public sample lived in England, 6 per cent in Wales, and 10 per cent in Scotland—too few outside England for that sample to provide a basis for reliable comparisons between the nations of Great Britain. So we also interviewed a third sample of 1,255 respondents, representative of the Scottish, adult population (212 of whom were in our British public sample and 1,043 of whom were not) in order to see whether the well-known and long-established social and constitutional differences between Scotland, on the one hand, and England and Wales, on the other, were reflected in a significantly different political culture north and south of the border. It is almost an article of faith amongst those, both within Scotland and outside, who observe and comment upon Scottish politics that the political culture in Scotland is significantly different from that in England and Wales. However, on the basic fundamentals of political culture on which we focus in this study, we have found the differences to be remarkably slight in most (not all) respects. In terms of its fundamental political culture, Scotland does *not* turn out to be a very distinct society after all. (Or, to put the same point in another way: neither does England!) More often than not, therefore, our third sample serves to corroborate the evidence and confirm the findings of our survey of the British public.

    None of these three sets of interviews should be dismissed as a 'snap poll' of unconsidered opinions. Individual interviews averaged over forty-five minutes in length in order to research opinion in depth. Interviewing for the British public and local politicians' samples was spread over a ten-month period from November 1991 to August 1992 to avoid findings based upon transient emotional reactions to particular current events. The extra 1,043 interviews which formed the bulk of the Scottish public sample were carried out over the summer and autumn of 1992 and completed by November 1992. Despite the extended interviewing period all reported party percentages of 1992 general election votes (not current voting preferences) in the British public sample were within 2 per cent of the actual 1992 general election figures, and in the Scottish public sample within 3 per cent of the actual figures.

The CATI Method

All our interviews were carried out using our own very flexible version of the CATI technique (Computer Assisted Telephone Interviewing). Our questionnaire was so much more complex than usual that it could not have been administered without CATI. One critical feature was that many questions appeared in several variant forms. For some questions there were only two variants, for others as many as a dozen. When the computer controlling the interview reached a particular question it used a random-number generator to decide which one of the several versions of that question it would display on the screen. The interviewer read out the question as it appeared and the computer recorded on its disk which variant of the question was used on that occasion along with the answer given by the interviewee. There were fifty such references to the random-number generator in each interview.

This system of randomly varying question wording had several advantages. First, it allowed us to research more questions than even a high-pressure forty-five-minute telephone interview would normally allow, because each interview contained only one variant of each question. Secondly, because the different variants were randomly assigned to interviews, any differences in the answers could be attributed to variations in the wording (subject to the usual caveats about sampling error). To take one example, we asked about employment quotas:

Do you think the law should require [large private companies/the government and civil service] to hire a fixed percentage of [women/blacks and Asians/disabled people] or should [women/blacks and Asians/disabled people] get no special treatment?

This question involved two references to the random-number generator: first to decide whether the question should ask about private companies or government employment; and, second, to decide whether it should ask about gender, race, or disability. This system allows us to compare support for employment quotas for different social groups and in different sectors of employment. That could be done in a conventional interview by asking all variants of the question, but, in addition to taking six times as long, that approach could generate spurious consistency between answers to one variant and another since people could feel under social and psychological pressure to give consistent answers. But, since each interview with our randomized CATI method used only one variant of the question, no one we interviewed could have felt under any pressure, logical or psychological, to give consistent answers about employment quotas for different social groups. Our strategy eliminates this potentially significant source of spurious consistency as well as researching opinion about several different kinds of employment quota in the time taken by a single question.

Let us take one more example. As part of a battery of agree/disagree questions we asked:

Newspapers which get hold of confidential government documents about [defence/economic/health service] plans should not be allowed to publish them [(null)/because publication might damage our national interests]. Agree/disagree? Strongly or not?

This question came in six different versions depending upon whether the question asked about defence, economic, or health plans; and upon whether it did or did not add the argument that publication 'might damage our national interests'. Again, with all the usual caveats about sampling errors, we can attribute differences in the answers to differences in question wording. We can see how far support for censorship depends upon the topic (defence, economic, or health plans); how much it depends upon an explicit reference to the 'national interests'; and how much it depends upon the interaction between the two, i.e. how much influence references to the national interest have in different topic areas.

We shall use this system of controlled variations in question wording to show that appeals to rational arguments are effective; that appeals to authority are less effective; that it is easier to influence the opinions of the public than those of politicians; and indeed that there is occasional evidence of politicians actually reacting against attempts to pressure them towards certain viewpoints.

But we shall start, in the next chapter, with a simple account of the attitudes of the British, and Scottish, public towards fundamental principles of civil, political, and social rights.

NOTES

1. Herbert McClosky and Alida Brill, *Dimensions of Tolerance: What Americans Believe about Civil Liberties* (New York: Russell Sage Foundation, 1983).
2. Gabriel Almond and Sidney Verba, *The Civic Culture: Political Attitudes and Democracy in Five Nations* (Princeton: Princeton University Press, 1963); see also Gabriel Almond and Sidney Verba (eds.), *The Civic Culture Revisited* (Boston: Little, Brown, 1980).
3. Philip Norton, *The British Polity* (London: Longman, 1984), 34.
4. Anthony H. Birch, *The British System of Government* (7th edn. London: Allen & Unwin, 1986), 18.
5. Tom Mullen, 'Constitutional Protection of Human Rights', in Tom Campbell, David Goldberg, Sheila McLean, and Tom Mullen (eds.), *Human Rights: From Rhetoric to Reality* (Oxford: Basil Blackwell, 1986), 15–36, at 15.
•6. Geoff Andrews, 'Universal Principles', in Geoff Andrews (ed.), *Citizenship* (London: Lawrence & Wishart, 1991), 212–18, at 214.
7. Anthony H. Birch, *The Concepts and Theories of Modern Democracy* (London: Routledge, 1993), 113.
8. See e.g. the article by Tony Blair, *Herald*, 28 Apr. 1995, p. 15.
9. Wesley Hohfeld, *Fundamental Legal Conceptions* (New Haven: Yale University Press, 1923).
10. Thomas Hobbes, *Leviathan*, (London: Penguin, 1974) ch. 14.
11. John Locke, *Essay Concerning Civil Government*, in *Locke's Two Treatises of Government*, ed. Peter Lazlett (Cambridge: CUP, 1988), 265–428, ch. 2, sects. 6, 7.

12. Amitai Etzioni, *The Spirit of Community: The Reinvention of American Society* (New York: Simon & Schuster, 1993), 9.

13. Rights are criticised from a communitarian point of view by Mary Ann Glendon, *Rights Talk: The Impoverishment of Political Discourse* (New York: The Free Press, 1991). Feminist critics of rights include Carol Gilligan. *In a Different Voice: Psychological Theory and Women's Development* (Cambridge, Mass: Harvard UP, 1982) and Seyla Benhabib, "The Generalised and Concrete Other" in Elizabeth Frazer et al. (eds) *Ethics: A Feminist Reader* (Oxford: Blackwell, 1992).

14. Birch, *The Concepts and Theories of Modern Democracy*, 113.

15. Printed in D. D. Raphael (ed.), *Political Theory and the Rights of Man* (London: Macmillan, 1967), 143–8.

16. Council of Europe, *European Convention on Human Rights: Collected Texts* (7th edn., Strasbourg: Council of Europe, 1971).

17. Reprinted in T. H. Marshall and Tom Bottomore, *Citizenship and Social Class* (London: Pluto Press, 1992), 17. Vivien Hart argues that Marshall's time sequence for the development of different kinds of rights 'may not only be a historical fact, but a practical necessity' (Vivien Hart, 'The Right to a Fair Wage: American Experience and the European Social Charter', in Vivien Hart and Shannon C. Stimson (eds.), *Writing a National Identity: Political, Economic and Cultural Perspectives on the Written Constitution* (Manchester: Manchester University Press, 1993), 107). In somewhat convoluted language, Giovanni Sartori also argues that it is also a logical sequence: '[negative] political freedom is the *sine qua non* of all the positive liberty-equalities' (Giovanni Sartori, *The Theory of Democracy Revisited* (Chatham, NJ: Chatham House, 1987), 391.

18. See I. M. M. MacPhail, *The Crofters' War* (Stornoway: Acair, 1989), and more especially the earlier Iain Fraser Grigor *Mightier than a Lord* (Stornoway: Acair, 1979), for detailed accounts of crofters' claims that their civil—as well as political and social—rights were abused in much of the nineteenth century.

19. Maurice Cranston, 'Human Rights, Real and Supposed', and 'Human Rights: A Reply to Professor Raphael', in Raphael (ed.), *Political Theory and the Rights of Man*, 43–53, 95–100.

20. Quoted in Kenneth Hoover and Raymond Plant, *Conservative Capitalism in Britain and the United States* (London: Routledge, 1989), 52.

21. For a detailed case for how such rights might be applied in contemporary Britain, see Commission on Social Justice (Chair: Sir Gordon Borrie), *Social Justice—Strategies for National Renewal* (London: Vintage, 1994). Its central theme is that 'we must recognise that although not all inequalities are unjust . . . unjust inequalities should be reduced and where possible eliminated' (p. 18).

22. Raymond Plant, 'Social Rights and the Reconstruction of Welfare', in Andrews (ed.), *Citizenship*, 50–64, at 57.

23. Ibid.

24. William L. Miller, Annis May Timpson, and Michael Lessnoff, 'Freedom From the Press', in J. Hayward (ed.), *Elitism, Populism and European Politics* (Oxford: Oxford University Press, 1996), 67–87.

25. In 1966 the UN General Assembly adopted an International Covenant on Economic,

Social and Cultural Rights (in addition to an International Covenant on Political and Civil Rights). These Covenants, however, lack enforcement mechanisms comparable to the European Court of Human Rights.

26. For an extended discussion, see Noreen Burrows, 'International Law and Human Rights: The Case of Human Rights', in Campbell, Goldberg, McLean, and Mullen (eds.), *Human Rights*, 80–98.

27. The British Rights Study was funded by the Economic and Social Research Council (ESRC) and directed by William L. Miller, Annis May Timpson, and Michael Lessnoff, with Malcolm Dickson and Morag Brown as principal Research Assistants.

PART TWO
Public Attitudes

2

Principles and Sympathies

IN particular concrete circumstances people may be forced to choose between specific courses of action. They may have to decide whether an extremist party should be banned at a particular time; whether large private companies should be required to hire fixed percentages of women and ethnic minorities; or whether the police should be allowed to tap telephones and, if so, in what circumstances. The public have opinions on such specific questions. But they also have opinions about more general principles such as generalized attitudes to authority, tolerance, or equality. And furthermore, the public also have very general sympathies and antipathies towards different groups in society irrespective of the particular issues in which they may be involved.

In a rational world these general principles and sympathies would be explicit and self-conscious, and would clearly determine individuals' opinions on specific practical issues. But in the real world many people may not have clear guiding principles on which to act. Even if they do, they may be unable to articulate them or else find that they are unable to stick to these principles in all circumstances. People might, for example, declare their support for the principle of free speech or declare themselves free of any antipathy towards religious minorities, yet prove unable to support the idea of a member of a minority religious sect teaching in their child's school.

None the less, we did investigate explicit, self-conscious commitment to general principles amongst the public. Indeed, we asked over fifty questions that bear on general or abstract principles and over thirty about sympathies or antipathies. Although we carried out some exploratory factor analyses of this large set of questions to help inform our judgements, we have grouped them into a set of thirteen 'micro-principles' and six 'micro-sympathies' primarily on the basis of their apparent meaning.

In this chapter we examine the public's commitment to these micro-principles, and in the next chapter we will see how the public's commitment to these micro-principles compares with that of local politicians. Then, in later chapters we shall look at the extent to which these micro-principles exhibit a degree of internal coherence, the extent to which they can be further grouped into a very few 'macro-principles', and the extent to which they influence practical choices in specific circumstances.

FOUR QUESTION FORMATS

Before we review the micro-principles themselves, we should clarify the questions we used. Our questions about principles fell into one of the following four formats:

1. *Agree/disagree.* Here we used a fairly standard 'five-point scale' for answers: 'strongly agree, agree, neither, disagree, strongly disagree'—plus, of course, 'don't know/won't answer, etc.'. Respondents were invited to say whether they agreed or disagreed 'strongly', though this invitation was not repeated after each such question.
2. *Yes/no.* Here we also used a 'five-point scale' of 'yes, qualified yes, neither, qualified no, no'—plus 'don't know/won't answer, etc.'. Respondents were not invited to qualify their answers, but if they spontaneously indicated any doubts, restrictions or qualifications instead of giving a straightforward 'yes' or 'no', our interviewers noted the fact.
3. *Choice of alternatives.* Here we used a 'three-point scale' for answers: 'alternative A, neither/bit of both, alternative B'—plus 'don't know/won't answer, etc.'.
4. *Marks out of ten.* These consisted simply of a mark between zero and ten—plus 'don't know/won't answer, etc.'.

For simplicity, in this chapter, we have excluded all 'don't know' and 'neither' answers, and we have usually taken no account of the strength of agree/disagree answers, or of whether yes/no answers were 'qualified' or not. Thus, for those with an opinion, we can calculate the percentages who agreed, who answered 'yes', or who took the first alternative (and the corresponding percentages who disagreed, who answered 'no', or who took the second alternative are just 100 per cent minus these figures). Similarly, for those with an opinion on marks-out-of-ten questions, we can calculate the average (mean) mark. That will keep our presentation as simple as possible and it suppresses very little of importance. The numbers of answers of 'don't know, etc.' were seldom large or interesting but, where they were, we shall draw special attention to them. When we move on to more complex correlation, multiple regression, and factor analyses in later chapters, however, we reassign such 'missing values' as 'don't know, etc.' to the mid-point of their appropriate scale in order to retain all respondents in the analysis, and we may sometimes retain our full five-point (or eleven-point) scales with all their shades of meaning.

TABLE 2.1. *Respect for authority*

	British public	(Scottish public)
Importance of		
respect for authority	8.2	(8.2)
law and order	8.6	(8.8)
defence	6.7	(6.6)
Strong government (v. chaos)	38	(36)

Notes: Figures outside parentheses are for our British sample of 2,060 respondents. Figures in parentheses are for our sample of 1,255 people living in Scotland.

In the tables of this and the next chapter, figures without decimal points are percentages; figures with decimal points are average 'marks out of ten'.

PRINCIPLES

We shall begin with a range of micro-principles that seem to reflect attitudes towards what Cranston called 'political and civil rights'; then move on through attitudes towards social conformity and tolerance; and finally look at attitudes towards micro-principles that seem to reflect what Cranston called 'economic and social rights'.

Respect for Authority

We asked our respondents to give a number between zero and ten to indicate the importance they attached to various aspects of civic life, including several that bear upon respect for authority. The public gave an average mark of 8.2 to 'respect for authority'—the wording that comes closest to the general idea of this first micro-principle, 8.6 to 'strengthening law and order', and 6.7 to 'maintaining strong defence forces'. The lower level of priority given to strong defence forces may reflect the end of the Cold War era, but the levels of priority given to respect for unspecified 'authority' and for strengthening law and order were very high indeed.

Other questions, however, tempered this finding. When we asked whether people agreed or disagreed with the proposition that 'the only alternative to strong government is disorder and chaos', only 38 per cent of those with an opinion agreed (Table 2.1).[1]

In this and subsequent tables, we have included the results from our special sample of people living in Scotland. On the very few occasions where the views in our Scottish sample differ significantly from those in our British sample, we shall draw attention to the difference and attempt to explain it. But otherwise we shall restrict our comments to the British figures. Surprisingly perhaps, basic principles in Scotland proved so very similar to those in Britain as a whole that the main function of our Scottish sample is to confirm the findings about British public opinion with a second sample. We develop this point in Chapter 11.

Limited Government

Amongst the classic principles of liberal democracy is the need to limit and constrain government,[2] to outlaw arbitrary action by government or its agents, and to ensure that all organs of the state operate through carefully laid down procedures—what is known in the USA as 'due process'. Although, in law, British government is based upon the principle of sovereignty which is diametrically opposed to the principle of limited government, it is claimed that, in practice, British governments behave as if they were bound by this aspect of the US Constitution. Speaking in 1819, Simon Bolivar referred to the 'republican features' of British government: 'can a political system be labelled a monarchy when it recognizes popular sovereignty, *division and balance of powers*, civil liberty, freedom of conscience and of press, and all that is politically sublime?' (emphasis added).[3] Some of those who lived under it at that time did not regard the British system of government as 'sublime', and would have recognized Bolivar's speech as a description of their ambitions rather than of 1819 realities.[4] Be that as it may, those US legal concepts owed much to British political theorists, and current public opinion in Britain now seems more in keeping with US than British law. The principle of limited government seems to be fairly well supported by public opinion in Britain, though more in terms of high politics than in terms of 'due process'.

We put one of two opposing propositions to randomly selected halves of our respondents. We asked the first half whether 'constitutional checks and balances are important to make sure that a government doesn't become too dictatorial and ignore other viewpoints'; and the second whether 'it is important for a government to be able to take decisive action without looking over its shoulder all the time'. These are not quite opposite sides of the same coin: the differences are important and we shall discuss them in a later chapter. However, when we combined answers to these two questions, we found that 58 per cent of the public either *agreed* on the importance of constitutional checks and balances, or *disagreed* with the need for government to be free to take decisive action without undue restriction. In short, even on a very

TABLE 2.2. *Limited government and due process*

	British public (%)	(Scottish public) (%)
Support		
checks and balances	58	(60)
external control of police	78	(79)
right to silence	43	(40)
suspects' rights	14	(12)

stringent test, we found majority support in Britain for the US constitutional concept of government limited by checks and balances. If we had not combined these two questions, and focused only upon the version that explicitly mentioned 'checks and balances', our conclusion would have appeared much stronger, but we felt it right to examine public reactions to the alternative slogan of 'decisive action' before reaching a balanced conclusion (Table 2.2).

The public gave even more support to the principle of holding the police accountable for their actions: 78 per cent agreed that 'the police need to be subject to strong external control in order to protect civil liberties'. However, public support for external control of the police did not imply a very strict attitude to due process. Lord Thomson's Committee on Criminal Procedure in Scotland recommended an increase in police powers after noting 'a conflict between the public interest in the detection and suppression of crime on the one hand, and the interest of the individual citizen in freedom from interference by the police on the other'.[5] Similarly we found the public tilting strongly towards the suppression of crime when asked to choose which was more important 'in dealing with mugging and other serious street crime— to protect the rights of suspects, or to stop such crimes and make the streets safe even if we sometimes have to violate suspects' rights': only 14 per cent opted to give priority to protecting suspects' rights.

The right to silence won more support, but still only minority support, from the public. Of all the 'due-process rights' this is the one most familiar to the public: 'the media, and particularly police dramas on television, have brought the Miranda principle of the right to remain silent to the attention of the mass public with greater frequency than any other due process rights.'[6] The British public also watch those American police dramas and, while we could not expect them to recognize the name of the plaintiff in the Supreme Court case (Miranda) nor think it of any importance anyway, we could expect them to have noticed the issue of principle. Moreover, there was a steady stream of well-publicized miscarriages of justice in Britain itself, involving false confessions as well as false evidence, that came back to the Appeal Court for long overdue acquittals in the period 1989–92—the years just before and during our survey.[7]

The Royal Commission on Criminal Procedure in England and Wales noted two arguments, which it called the 'utilitarian' and 'libertarian' arguments, for maintaining the right to silence both for suspects in the police station or for the accused in court:

the right to silence must be judged not only as a means to the goal of achieving a reliable verdict [the utilitarian argument], but also, and equally important, for its coherence with a liberal understanding of how free persons, including suspects in the police station, at all stages ought to be treated . . . [and] what the individual's relationship to government ought to be in a free democratic society [the libertarian argument].[8]

However, it based its own conclusion on the utilitarian argument. Since then, the principle has been weakened and undermined by recent provisions in the Criminal Justice Act (1994). That seems to reflect public opinion. When we asked whether 'a person charged with a crime should have the right to refuse to answer questions in court, without it being held against them', only 43 per cent backed the right to silence. Overwhelming public acceptance of the need for external control of the police did not mean the public were either 'soft' on suspects or very strict in their adherence to the principles of 'due process'.

The Right to Know

Britain has long been seen as a secretive society in which citizens have not enjoyed free access to information about themselves or about the actions of their government and its bureaucracy.[9] The debate about official secrecy intensified in the mid-1980s when a jury refused to convict the senior civil servant Clive Ponting, who had been charged with revealing secret information about the government's policy during the Falklands War. The idea that citizens should have more information about themselves and about both public and private organizations that affect their lives was put forward with renewed vigour in the late 1980s and early 1990s by the newly formed Charter 88 lobby and stimulated—if not satisfied—by Prime Minister John Major's backing for the Citizen's Charter concept.

We found no ambiguities about public support for the general principle of citizens' right to know. There was strong support for freedom of information,

TABLE 2.3. *The right to know*

	British public (%)	(Scottish public) (%)
Support, with or without reservations		
right to know about self	97	(97)
right to know about government plans	91	(93)
right to know about factory	97	(98)
Support, without reservations		
right to know about self	93	(94)
right to know about government plans	83	(86)
right to know about factory	93	(95)

and in forms that went well beyond those included in John Major's 'Citizen's Charter'. Over 90 per cent agreed that people should have a general right to know the facts about each of the following:

- information about themselves (for example, their own medical records and credit ratings)?
- the government's plans?
- private business activities that might affect the health of people who live near the company's factory?.

Glasnost was exceedingly popular in all its forms. None the less, the public were less insistent on their right to know about government plans (91 per cent), and more insistent on their right to know about their own records or about the activities of companies which might endanger the health of nearby residents (97 per cent). Because all these figures are so high, it is worth distinguishing those who qualified their support for a right to know in some way from those who expressed no reservations. Even if we exclude those who expressed reservations, however, support for a right to know was very high, though the gap between support for a right to know about government plans and about other matters widened from 6 per cent to 10 per cent (Table 2.3).

The Right to Freedom of Speech

Attitudes towards the principle of freedom of speech revealed the powerful effect of catching the right slogan. When asked for a number out of ten to indicate the importance they placed upon 'guaranteeing everyone the right to free speech', people responded with numbers that averaged a massive 9.2

TABLE 2.4. *The right to freedom of speech*

	British public	(Scottish public)
Importance of free speech	9.2	(9.2)
Disagree that free speech not worth it	64	(64)
Not ban extreme political organizations	55	(53)

Note: See note 2 to Table 2.1.

out of ten. We also put the question in tougher forms, however. Only 64 per cent indicated their firm support for free speech by *disagreeing* with the proposition that 'free speech is just not worth it if it means we have to put up with the danger to society from extremist views'. And only 55 per cent took the side of free speech by either *agreeing* that 'we should never ban any political organization whatever its views', or *disagreeing* with the opposite proposition that 'political organizations with extreme views should be banned'. (As usual, each version of this question about banning political organizations was put to a randomly selected half of the sample). None the less, answers to the toughest of these questions still showed majority commitment to the principle of free speech, even when the question was so phrased as to encourage people to reject that principle (Table 2.4).

Rights of Protest and Rebellion

The principle of protest, resistance, and rebellion has long been recognized even in pre-democratic and non-democratic theories of governance. The Huguenot tract *Vindiciae contra tyrannos* published in Paris in 1579 referred to an implied contract between 'king and subjects': 'which requires the people to obey faithfully, and the king to govern lawfully . . . if the prince fails to keep his promise, the people are exempt from obedience'.[10] And the terms of that contract could not be determined purely by ruler and people: from the Calvinist perspective of the *Vindiciae*, 'God is himself a contractor.'[11] The ideas of the *Vindiciae* soon escaped the constraints of their Calvinistic authors, but, even in a more secular age, the concept of a third contractor remains—perhaps now depersonalized into a concept of 'natural justice', 'proper conduct', 'human rights', or, in an expression currently popular in Eastern Europe, 'normal' government.[12] Most liberal constitutions now accept that citizens have a right to protest. The German constitution even includes an explicit right to rebel in certain circumstances: 'All Germans shall have the right to resist any person or persons seeking to abolish that constitutional order, should no other remedy be possible.'[13] That does not require the resistance to have majority, or even any, public support: the 'third contractor' is the liberal democratic constitution of the republic itself.

Adam Smith took the pragmatic view that, 'whenever the confusion which must arise on the overthrow of the established government is less than the mischief of allowing it to continue, then resistance is proper and allowable'.[14] But what had always been remarkable, he claimed, was the reluctance of subjects to rebel: 'that kings are the servants of the people, to be obeyed, resisted, deposed, or punished as the public convenience may require, is the doctrine of reason and philosophy; but it is not the doctrine of Nature.'[15]

We asked a wide variety of questions about the right to protest. Our computer-assisted interviewing technique allowed us to ask randomly selected thirds of the sample whether they agreed with one variant of the following statement: 'If people wish to protest against [something/a government action they strongly oppose/a law they feel is really unjust and harmful], they should have the right to hold protest marches and demonstrations.' Combining the responses to these different variants of the question, we found that 84 per cent agreed with the variant of the proposition that was put to them. That indicated overwhelming support, in the abstract at least, for the right to demonstrate and march in protest. In practice, as we shall see in later chapters, public support for protest demonstrations could be much less. But, while it would be a logical error to assume that the high level of support for the principle will automatically translate into practice, we would be guilty of precisely the same logical error if we interpreted the much lower levels of support for the practice of protest as an accurate guide to the level of support for the principle. An imperfect link between principle and practice invalidates inferences in both directions equally.

In principle, the right to strike also won overwhelming public support: 77 per cent agreed with the statement. '[All workers, even those in essential public services like the Ambulance Service or the Fire Brigade/Workers who do not work in essential public services] should have the right to strike.' A randomly selected half sample was asked each variant. Naturally, support was higher than 77 per cent if essential workers were excluded, and lower if they were included, but that is the overall figure.

Finally, we also asked: 'Suppose parliament passed a law you considered unjust, immoral, or cruel. Would you still be morally bound to obey it?' Almost half said they would not. On this measure public support for the principle of protest and rebellion seemed the least, but this measure came closer to rebellion than to protest. It is perhaps more remarkable that half the

TABLE 2.5. *Rights to protest and rebel*

	British public (%)	(Scottish public) (%)
Right to demonstrate	84	(86)
Right to strike	77	(81)
Not obey unjust law	49	(48)

public rejected the moral authority of parliament and felt under no moral obligation to obey an unjust law, than that much larger numbers would support the right of others to march in protest against it.

Once again let us stress that we are measuring principles, not practice. Of course, our finding does not mean that half the public would actually rebel against an unjust law. Parry, Moyser, and Day concluded from their British Political Participation Study that 'political protest in Britain is typical of most other western democracies in involving a very small proportion of the citizenry'.[16] Although our study found more evidence of protest activity than Parry, Moyser, and Day (our survey, unlike theirs, was conducted after the poll-tax fiasco at the end of the 1980s), we would not disagree with their general conclusion. Fear of the tax collector and the courts can ensure compliance even with a morally discredited law, but only compliance under duress. Altogether, our findings indicate very strong public support for the principle of protest, in both its conventional and less conventional forms (Table 2.5).

Conformity to Traditional Values

We now move to a somewhat different range of principles—more social and less political, more private and in many respects more personal. Like principles of authority, principles of conformity concern liberty, freedom, and control. But conformity relates to control exercised by society and tradition rather than by government. In Britain, at least, conformity is expressed in support for traditional values, opposition to social equality and equal rights for minority groups, and, indeed, in general intolerance.

At the most general level we asked people for numbers out of ten to indicate how much importance they attached to 'preserving traditional ideas of right and wrong' and to 'following God's will'. These questions were designed to tap the fundamental basis for many people's internal self-imposed wish to conform, and perhaps also the basis for the conformity they would inflict upon others. At the same time they were not perfect indicators of all

TABLE 2.6. *Respect for traditional values*

	British public (marks/10)	(Scottish public) (marks/10)
Importance of		
traditional ideas of right and wrong	8.0	(8.1)
following God's will	5.7	(5.9)

kinds of conformity. They do have conservative and religious overtones, and it would be wrong to pretend otherwise.

We found a remarkably high level of commitment to traditional values, however. People responded with an average of 8.0 out of ten for the importance, to them, of 'preserving traditional ideas of right and wrong' and a lower, but still surprisingly high, 5.7 for the importance of 'following God's will'—much higher figures than might be predicted from the hard facts of the public's church attendance or their actual social and moral behaviour. None the less these answers express the ambitions—if not the personal achievements—of the public (Table 2.6). Once again, we need to stress that, even when the public's principles fail to determine their behaviour, we must beware of assuming the converse: that their behaviour must determine their principles. It does not.

Tolerance

John L. Sullivan and his colleagues have argued that it is impossible to 'tolerate' anything of which we fully approve,[17] because the question of tolerance only arises when we are faced with something we believe to be wrong, immoral, or even dangerous. In Bernard Crick's words: 'toleration need not imply the absence of prejudice, but only its constraint and moderation.'[18] Tolerance, like intolerance, presupposes a clear moral position; tolerance of diversity is an empty phrase if we are comfortable with diversity; tolerance implies acceptance of discomfort.

But in one of the most sophisticated statistical analyses of attitudes to toleration, Paul M. Sniderman and his colleagues note that 'it is not true that people must dislike a group in order to be intolerant of it',[19] and they report evidence that Americans with racist attitudes were *less* tolerant of free speech *even for racist agitators* than were those without racist attitudes: racists were so generally intolerant of free speech that they were *intolerant even towards other racists*.[20] So perhaps we have to dislike something or someone in order to tolerate them (as distinct from approving of them), but we can be *intol-*erant even towards those we like!

Susan Mendus highlights another problem. She distinguishes 'toleration in the weak sense' meaning toleration of something we dislike, from 'toleration in the strong sense' meaning toleration of something we feel is morally wrong. She claims that 'the most problematic cases of toleration are those in which what is tolerated is believed to be morally wrong (not merely disliked), and where it is held that there are no compensating virtues associated with the thing tolerated'.[21]

We asked people to give a number out of ten for the importance they attached to 'tolerating different beliefs and lifestyles'. Superficially, they seemed exceedingly tolerant, with an average of 7.2 out of ten, but that question failed to distinguish between approval and tolerance. When tolerance was linked to morality we found that a majority took the intolerant side: 53 per cent agreed that 'we should not tolerate people whose ideas are morally wrong', and 91 per cent agreed that it was 'very important to protect children and young people from wild or immoral ideas'.

Surprisingly, perhaps, for a late-twentieth-century public in a long-established liberal democracy, interviewed well before the establishment of the 1995 Nolan Inquiry on *S*tandards in Public Life, 65 per cent said that 'upholding morality' was one of the duties of government. Traditionally, of course, one of the duties of the State has been to define and uphold morality, and monarchs either submitted to the judgements of the Church or claimed the right to be its head. In England, though not in Scotland or Wales, that tradition continues in law, no less—but no more—absurdly than in the past.

But although this indicates that people felt a strong urge to uphold morality, and protect children from immoral ideas, they proved reluctant to use coercion to enforce their own views on the rest of the community. Their views were not, in fact, medieval. Susan Mendus produces two reasons for tolerating in law what we denounce as immoral. First, 'in the liberal scheme of things the answer . . . [is that] an autonomous agent . . . should be allowed to do what is morally wrong', especially if it conforms to John Stuart Mill's 'no harm principle' of not harming anyone else. This, of course, assumes that something *can actually be morally wrong* even though it harms no one else—a dubious proposition, except perhaps in the case of harm to non-human creatures or, in some people's opinion, the environment. Mendus prefers a second reason, however: 'a specifically socialist answer to the problem . . . [is] the larger desire to secure a sense of belonging for all . . . to create a society in which people can identify their good with the good of others.'[22] Thus even 'toleration in the strong sense' can be justified either on

TABLE 2.7. *Tolerance and intolerance*

	British public	(Scottish public)
Tolerance		
Importance of tolerating different beliefs and lifestyles	7.2	(7.4)
Intolerance		
Protect children from immoral ideas	91	(93)
Not tolerate morally wrong	53	(50)
Morals should equal laws	46	(48)
Enforce community standards	29	(26)
Government has responsibility to uphold morality	65	(67)
No religious freedom for weird	28	(29)

Note: See note 2 to Table 2.1.

grounds of liberty—as respect for the freedom of the individual; or alternatively on grounds of equality—as recognition of equal citizenship for minorities; or, more instrumentally, on grounds of community, as a means of buying a minority's loyalty to the wider community. Lord Percy gives a fourth justification for 'the axiom that personal ethics cannot be directly translated into civilized law':[23] 'the compulsory rules which [man] has devised for general enforcement upon himself and his neighbours have never been more than a selection from the vast repertory of human duty and aspiration . . . [and] the very fact of selecting them for general enforcement inevitably changes their character, usually for the worse.'[24] For these or other reasons many people were unwilling to use the law even against what they denounced as immoral, thereby displaying support for Mendus's 'toleration in the strong sense' (Table 2.7).

Only 46 per cent agreed that 'if something is morally wrong, then it should be made illegal' or disagreed with the alternative proposition that 'even though something may be morally wrong, it should not necessarily be made illegal'. (A randomly selected half sample was asked each variant.) Indeed, when asked to weigh community norms against individual standards and choose between the propositions that 'our laws should aim to enforce the community's standards of right and wrong' and 'our laws should aim to protect a citizen's right to live by any moral standard he or she chooses provided this does no harm to other people', only 29 per cent chose to enforce community standards—though the proviso about doing 'no harm to other

TABLE 2.8. *Equal rights*

	British public	(Scottish public)
Importance of		
ethnic protection	7.3	(7.8)
gender equality	8.2	(8.5)
homosexual equality	6.0	(6.0)
Equal rights not gone far enough	73	(78)

Note: See note 2 Table 2.1.

people' was a very important qualification, albeit one that John Stuart Mill and his followers would have insisted upon including in the question. (We investigate the influence of Mill's proviso on public opinion in Chapter 7, Table 7.7.)

Similarly, only 28 per cent took the side of coercion by agreeing that 'religious freedom should not apply to religious groups that the majority of people consider strange, fanatical, or weird' or disagreeing with the alternative proposition that 'religious freedom should apply to all religious groups, even those that the majority of people consider strange, fanatical, or weird'. (A randomly selected half sample was asked each variant of this question.)

Equal Rights

There was widespread support for equal rights: 73 per cent either agreed that 'we have not gone far enough in pushing equal rights in this country' or disagreed with the alternative proposition that 'we have gone too far in pushing equal rights in this country'. (A randomly selected half sample was asked each variant of this question.) Moreover, this general sentiment held up, albeit to different degrees, when contextualized in terms of ensuring equal rights for different groups of citizens. When people were asked for a number out of ten to indicate the importance they attached to 'guaranteeing equality between men and women', their answers averaged 8.2; for the importance of 'protecting ethnic and racial minorities' they averaged 7.3; but for 'guaranteeing equal rights for homosexuals' they averaged only 6.0. This indicates very strong support for gender equality, moderately high support for the rights of ethnic and racial minorities, and weaker but still positive support for the equal treatment of heterosexuals and homosexuals (Table 2.8).

There are many possible explanations for the lower level of support for 'guaranteeing equal rights for homosexuals', but, unlike women or ethnic and racial minorities, homosexuals are not protected by a specific law against discrimination and a state-funded agency to oversee its implementation,[25] and this lack of legal support may well have affected public opinion.

Economic Equality

Principles of community concern equality and fraternity, the sense of being 'members one of another'. Unlike principles of authority or conformity, they are about help and assistance, rather than control and coercion. They may or may not concern government. Attitudes towards social equality enshrined in the phrase 'equal rights' may reflect attitudes to conformity as well as attitudes to community, attitudes to deviance as well as attitudes to welfare. But attitudes towards economic equality very clearly express principles of community.

We considered attitudes to questions of economic equality within a much broader range of questions about the extent of government responsibilities for different aspects of social and economic welfare. We asked: 'Here are a number of things which many people think are very desirable goals but, at the same time, many people feel that it is not the responsibility of government to provide them. Do *you* think each of the following should, or should not, be the *government*'s responsibility?'

Our question explicitly invited people to distinguish between 'desirable goals' and 'government responsibilities', yet there was almost unanimous agreement that government had a responsibility to provide 'good education for everyone' and 'good medical care for everyone'; 91 per cent also held government responsible for ensuring 'adequate housing for everyone' and 'equal opportunities for everyone'.[26] Rather less, 77 and 78 per cent respectively, held government responsible for ensuring 'a decent standard of living for everyone' and 'that everyone who wants a job can have one'. By contrast, only 51 per cent held government responsible for 'evening out differences in wealth between people'.[27] Obviously the public were split right down the middle on equalizing wealth, but were overwhelmingly of the opinion that government had a duty to ensure good standards of education, housing, health care, living standards, and job opportunities for all.

Attitudes to economic equality provided the clearest example of Scottish distinctiveness in matters of principle. On most indicators of economic equality —and it is important to limit this comment to specifically 'economic' equality, since it did not apply so much to equal rights—Scottish opinion was a little more egalitarian. And on the key aspect of economic equality on which opinion throughout Britain was so divided—holding government responsible

Public Attitudes

TABLE 2.9. *Economic equality*

	British public (%)	(Scottish public) (%)
Government has responsibility for		
equal wealth	51	(63)
equal opportunities	91	(93)
living standards	77	(86)
jobs	78	(84)
housing	91	(95)
education	99	(98)
health care	98	(99)

for 'evening out differences in wealth between people'—Scots were 12 per cent more egalitarian than the British as a whole (Table 2.9).

Self-Reliance

There was strong public support for self-reliance when that concept was viewed in isolation. When people were asked for a number out of ten to indicate the importance they placed upon 'self-reliance, having everybody stand on their own two feet', their answers averaged 7.9; for the importance of 'emphasizing individual achievements', their answers average 7.0. While there is no logical conflict between personal self-reliance and a concern for others, the idea of preaching self-reliance to others has been more popular with politicians of the right than of the left. Hoover and Plant refer to 'Mrs Thatcher's interest in Victorian Values which she sees as centring on the qualities of self-reliance and [personal] independence'.[28]

On the other hand, opinion was evenly divided on whether there was a need for more emphasis on rights or on duties: 50 per cent agreed that 'in Britain today, there is too much emphasis on citizens' rights and not enough on citizens' duties' or disagreed with the opposite proposition. (A randomly selected half sample was asked each variant of the question.) However, it must be noted that the interpretation of these views in the present context is not entirely straightforward. Support for citizens' rights rather than their duties can be and often is called (and castigated as) individualism; but it is certainly not the same kind of individualism as support for self-reliance, indeed it is almost the opposite of it; calls for the upholding of citizens' rights are calls for state action (to protect and benefit citizens). Two conclusions follow. First, the concept of (unqualified) individualism, popular though

TABLE 2.10. *Self-reliance*

	British public	(Scottish public)
Importance of		
self-reliance	7.9	(7.6)
individual achievements	7.0	(6.9)
For individual goals (v. common goals)	44	(44)
Not too much emphasis on individual interests	33	(28)
Too much emphasis on rights (v. duties)	50	(44)

Note: See note 2 to Table 2.1.

it is in political discourse, is more or less useless, since it embraces such opposite values. Second, support for citizens' rights should certainly not be interpreted as support for self-reliance, but rather the reverse.

But what of support for citizens' duties rather than their rights? Although the language of duties has long been popular with right-wing politicians, it has recently been adopted by those on the social democratic left. In his first ever speech as Leader to the Labour Party Conference in October 1994, Tony Blair emphasized the importance of balancing respect for citizens' rights with a recognition of citizens' duties.[29] This shows the political ambiguity of the concept. Right-wing support for citizens' duties rather than rights is perfectly compatible with support for self-reliance and is likely to be combined with it, whereas this is less likely in the case of left-wingers, who are more likely to be thinking of duties to help the unfortunate. But in either case, obviously, support for citizens' duties reflects a relatively strong concept of community.

Support for self-reliance was clearly much less strong when counterpoised against community than when viewed in isolation. When asked to decide whether 'ideally, society should be like a unified body pursuing a common goal' or 'a collection of people independently pursuing their own goals', only 44 per cent opted for the individualistic alternative. And when asked whether 'in Britain today, too much emphasis is placed on individual interests at the expense of the community's interest', only 33 per cent took the individualistic position by disagreeing. Thus, when forced to choose between explicit statements of self-reliance and community, a majority took a position that sharply distinguished them from Margaret Thatcher's infamous claim that 'there is no such thing as society' and came down in favour of community, despite their respect for self-reliance (Table 2.10).

TABLE 2.11. *Caring*

	British public (marks/10)	(Scottish public) (marks/10)
Importance of		
help for the disabled	9.3	(9.5)
reducing unemployment	8.9	(9.3)
taking care of the needy	8.7	(8.9)

Caring

Indeed, if their prescription of self-reliance is aimed at the respondents themselves, concern for others may be a higher form of that kind of self-reliance. Despite their emphasis on self-reliance, there was strong support for helping the disadvantaged and for tackling one of the prime causes of dependence and poverty—unemployment. When asked for numbers to indicate the importance they attached to 'taking care of the needy', answers averaged 8.7; for 'reducing unemployment' it was 8.9; and for 'providing help for the disabled' the average rose to 9.3 out of ten (Table 2.11).

Wealth Creation

At the same time the public also placed considerable importance upon three objectives—economic growth, low inflation, and tax cuts—which are often depicted by right-wing politicians as competing alternatives to economic equality or caring, though left-wing think-tanks such as the Institute for Public Policy Research (IPPR) have disagreed on both ideological and empirical grounds. What these three apparently disparate objectives have in common, however, is that for many people they relate to economic success rather than economic distribution, a concern for the 'size of the cake' rather than the way the cake is cut and distributed, and a lack of concern for the casualties of economic change. Amongst the public, the importance of 'cutting taxes' got an average rating of 6.5, 'holding down inflation' got 8.2, and 'achieving economic growth' 8.4. None the less, these ratings are lower and, in the case of 'cutting taxes' very much lower, than the ratings given to helping the unemployed, the needy, or the disabled (Table 2.12).

Protection

In addition there was near unanimous agreement that government had a responsibility to provide protection for its citizens by 'fighting pollution'

TABLE 2.12. *Wealth creation*

	British public (marks/10)	(Scottish public) (marks/10)
Importance of		
holding down inflation	8.2	(8.1)
cutting taxes	6.5	(7.0)
achieving economic growth	8.4	(8.5)

TABLE 2.13. *Protection*

	British public (%)	(Scottish public) (%)
Government has duty to protect citizens		
against crime	93	(94)
against business	78	(77)
against pollution	95	(94)

(95 per cent) and ensuring 'that citizens are safe from crime' (93 per cent). Unlike the duty of government to provide social welfare and a measure of economic equality, these are the classic duties of government which are accepted by liberals as well as socialists. An overwhelming majority, 78 per cent, also held government responsible for providing additional protection by ensuring 'that big business treats its customers with fairness and consideration', which would have pleased Adam Smith if not all of his more enthusiastic followers (Table 2.13).

SYMPATHIES

We turn now from principles to sympathies and antipathies towards various groups and institutions in society. These sympathies are logically but not always empirically distinguishable from principles. Indeed, despite appearances, to some extent they may be just another way of measuring principles: the difference between sympathy for the poor and support for the principle of 'caring' is not great, though other sympathies may be more clearly distinguishable from principles. Like general principles, sympathies guide opinion on transient or specific issues in politics. They can also combine with principles to influence choices in practical concrete situations. It is easier to support a practical demonstration of free speech if we not only support the principle of free speech but are also sympathetic towards the group which is exercising that right.

We are particularly interested in sympathies for those who claim rights of different kinds, for the establishment which legitimates such claims, and for those who enforce the implementation of accepted rights, or who forcibly resist attempts to implement rejected rights.

Sympathies and Antipathies towards Citizen Groups

Political activists claim both political and social rights. We asked people about their sympathy for eleven different groups of citizens that are politically active in Britain. Most were explicitly linked with political activity, though, for some, the link with political activism was only implicit. Respondents were asked to give a 'mark out of ten to show how much you like each group. If you like a group, give it a score above five; the more you like it the higher the score. If you dislike a group, give it a score less than five; the less you like it, the lower the score.' In descending order, they gave average marks of 7.2 to 'environmental campaigners like Greenpeace', indicating positive sympathy for Greenpeace; a marginally positive rating of 5.5 to 'animal-rights activists'; and a technically neutral rating of 4.9 to 'feminists'. But there was a clear antipathy towards other social groups, particularly towards social groups that could be identified on the basis of sexuality, race, or religion—'gays and lesbians' scored 4.1, 'black activists' 2.5, and 'Muslim activists' only 2.2.

There was also a degree of antipathy towards 'communists', who scored 3.5, and even greater antipathy towards political groups associated with militancy or violence: 'Militant Tendency supporters' scored 2.3, 'National Front supporters' 1.8, 'people who sympathize with Protestant terrorists in Northern Ireland' 1.5, and 'IRA sympathizers' a mere 1.2. We took care not to ask how much people liked or disliked terrorists themselves, or even how much they liked members of the National Front or the Militant Tendency—only how much they liked or disliked these groups' supporters or sympathizers— and even these were heartily disliked. Given the strength of feeling against these groups, it is reasonable to suppose that they could expect little public sympathy when they claimed even generally accepted rights of free speech, association, or assembly (Table 2.14).

In later chapters we shall take sympathy scores for the two terrorist groups' sympathizers, and towards the National Front and Militant Tendency—one

Principles and Sympathies

45

TABLE 2.14. *Sympathy scores for citizen groups*

	British public (marks/10)	(Scottish public) (marks/10)
Greenpeace	7.2	(7.0)
Animal-rights activists	5.5	(5.7)
Feminists	4.9	(4.9)
Gays and lesbians	4.1	(3.9)
Communists	3.5	(3.8)
Black activists	2.5	(2.6)
Militant Tendency supporters	2.3	(2.5)
Muslim activists	2.2	(2.2)
NF supporters	1.8	(1.7)
Protestant terrorist sympathizers	1.5	(1.5)
IRA sympathizers	1.2	(1.2)

on the militant right, the other on the militant left—as indicators of attitudes towards 'militants'; and sympathy scores for the other seven groups as indicators of attitudes towards 'activists'. Very obviously, the two groups of racial activists—black activists and Muslim activists—are on the borderline between 'activists' and 'militants' in terms of public sympathies, if nothing else. Though the level of overall public sympathy towards them suggests they could be placed with the militants, exploratory factor analyses provided no very strong indication that they should be put in one category or the other. Given that we had described both groups as 'activists' in the question we put to respondents, and also because we wanted to keep the 'militants' category' small and balanced between pairs of opposing militants (so that public attitudes towards them would reflect attitudes towards their militancy rather than towards their position on the political spectrum), we decided to place Muslim and black activists in the 'activists' category'.

Social Prejudice

Other questions in our survey provide measures of sympathy, antipathy, or even prejudice towards broad social categories that are less frequently defined, in Britain, as politically active groups. But we felt it was important to gain some sense of public feelings towards these categories of people, given that this may influence peoples' attitudes towards the practice of certain civil and political rights if these broader social groups are involved.

We looked in particular at attitudes towards women, immigrants, and the poor. On women, we asked:

[1.] By their nature, men are more suited than women to do senior jobs in business and government. Agree/disagree, etc.?

[2.] Which comes closer to your view? Women should be:
  • satisfied to stay at home and have families;
  • encouraged to have careers of their own?

Overt sexism was relatively low: only 16 per cent agreed that 'by their nature, men are more suited than women to do senior jobs in business and government'; and even less felt that 'women should be satisfied to stay at home and have families' rather than 'be encouraged to have careers of their own', though about a fifth of respondents volunteered the view that it was up to individual women to decide for themselves. Both these figures are very low, indicating very little explicit prejudice against women in the workplace or, at the least, a widespread awareness that it was no longer culturally acceptable to express such prejudice openly.

But by contrast, and whatever the pressures towards 'political correctness', people expressed highly critical attitudes towards the cultural distinctiveness of immigrants and, implicitly perhaps, towards racial or ethnic minorities: 66 per cent agreed that 'immigrants to Britain should try harder to be more like other British people'. The British, it seems, are not at ease with the idea of multiculturalism. Indeed, this finding suggests that most Britons, in their desire to encourage immigrants to become British, are guilty of what Charles Taylor has termed 'the politics of *mis*recognition'.[30]

There was more open prejudice against the poor than against women, though people were less willing to criticize the poor than immigrants. Charles Murray laments the fact that, 'as Britain entered the 1960s . . . [the] distinction between honest and dishonest poor people [was] softened . . . other popular [Victorian] labels were "undeserving, unrespectable, depraved, debased, disreputable, or feckless" poor'.[31] On the other hand, Adam Smith declared that 'laws and government may be considered . . . as a combination of the rich to oppress the poor, and preserve for themselves the inequality of goods'[32]—probably *not* Margaret Thatcher's favourite quotation from her favourite economic theorist, but not an unusual point of view. We tried to express both the Charles Murray and the Adam Smith perspective in the question: 'The poor are poor because [they don't try hard enough to get ahead/the wealthy and powerful keep them poor]. Agree/disagree, etc.?'

Judged by the fact that only 29 per cent (and only 23 per cent in Scotland)

TABLE 2.15. *Antipathy towards the socially disadvantaged*

	British public (%)	(Scottish public) (%)
Men are better at senior jobs	16	(14)
Women should stay at home	10	(9)
Immigrants should try harder	66	(58)
Poor don't try hard enough	29	(23)

TABLE 2.16. *Confidence in the political system*

	British public	(Scottish public)
Back-bench MPs protect rights	5.7	(5.4)
Local councils protect rights	5.6	(5.6)
Majority not often wrong	52	(47)
Trust most politicians	33	(30)

Note: See note 2 to Table 2.1.

agreed that 'the poor are poor because they don't try hard enough to get ahead' or disagreed with the alternative proposition that 'the poor are poor because the wealthy and powerful keep them poor', only a minority viewed the poor as 'feckless'. Still, that does indicate some degree of antipathy towards the poor (Table 2.15).

Confidence in the Established Political System

Although 90 per cent said that 'generally speaking', most people they came in contact with were 'trustworthy' rather than 'untrustworthy', trust in politicians was low: only 33 per cent agreed that 'most politicians can be trusted to do what they think is best for the country'. And when asked for a 'mark out of ten to indicate how much you feel citizens' rights and liberties are protected' by various institutions, they gave 'back-bench MPs in parliament' only a lukewarm 5.7 and 'local-government councils' only 5.6. Indeed the public seemed to have more confidence in the nebulous concept of 'the majority' than in politicians: only 48 per cent felt that 'the majority is often wrong'. We shall use trust and confidence in these four—politicians in general, MPs, local government, and the 'majority'—as an indication of confidence in the established political system (Table 2.16).

TABLE 2.17. *Confidence in civil institutions*

	British public (marks/10)	(Scottish public) (marks/10)
Citizens' rights protected by		
tabloids	3.9	(3.8)
broadsheets	6.3	(6.3)
television	6.3	(6.6)
trade unions	6.0	(6.3)
churches	5.8	(6.2)

Confidence in Civil Institutions

The press, television, trade unions, and churches constitute some of the most significant institutions in 'civil society'. They have an ambiguous status with regard to civil and political liberties. They claim liberties for themselves but they also defend, and sometimes infringe, the liberties of others. They are at once part of the establishment, and yet natural critics or even opponents of it. Interestingly, the public gave television and the quality press slightly higher marks than local councils or back-bench MPs for protecting their liberties: 6.3 for television, 6.3 for 'quality newspapers like the [*Telegraph/ Guardian*]'—though only 3.9 for 'tabloid newspapers like the [*Sun/Daily Mirror*]'. (In each case a randomly selected half sample was asked about the right-leaning paper and the other half about the left-leaning paper.)

Although trade-union membership and church attendance have dropped significantly in recent years, British people still saw these institutions as significant guardians of civil liberties. 'Trade unions' scored 6.0 and 'churches' 5.8. Again, both scores were fractionally higher than those given to elected representatives at national or local level.

There was a slight tendency for Scots to be a little more critical of the established political system, but a little more favourable to civil institutions, than other Britons (Table 2.17).

Confidence in the Judicial System

The judicial system, comprising courts, judges, and police, is at the heart of our traditional system of law enforcement. It has an authoritarian, conservative (with a small 'c'), 'top-down' image which is justified by the weight of history despite the exceptional occasions when it has acted against established authority. We asked the public to give us marks out of ten for how

TABLE 2.18. *Confidence in the judicial system*

	British public	(Scottish public)
British courts protect rights	6.5	(6.5)
Judges fair	6.0	(5.9)
Police fair	6.2	(6.4)
British government reducing rights	52	(62)
Police/security services protect rights	72	(72)

Note: See note 2 to Table 2.1.

much they thought their rights and liberties were protected by British courts. The answers averaged 6.5 out of ten. We also asked for a 'mark out of ten to indicate how you would rate the fairness and impartiality of British judges' and similarly 'the fairness and impartiality of the police'. On average the fairness and impartiality of judges was rated at 6.0 and of the police at 6.2 out of ten. Although that indicated no more than a moderate degree of confidence in the judicial system, it suggested that the public felt their rights and liberties were better protected by courts and judges than by either national or local politicians.

In the aftermath of the 1984–5 Miners' Strike, Tony Gifford and others complained that 'Freedom under Mrs Thatcher's government has been predominantly the freedom of those who have money to make more. Many other freedoms have been diminished. The freedom to organize and demonstrate for better conditions of life has been chipped away by sweeping police powers and heavy police methods.'[33] Peter Thornton expressed his view in the title of his short but detailed book, *Decade of Decline: Civil Liberties in the Thatcher Years.*[34]

To find out how widespread that perception was by 1991–2, we asked: 'On balance, British governments have been [reducing/increasing] the rights and liberties of British citizens in recent years. Agree/disagree, etc.?' Just over half the British public, and 10 per cent more in Scotland, agreed that recent governments had been reducing the rights and liberties of British citizens (or disagreed with the proposition that governments had been increasing them). Whatever the perceived trend, a substantial though not overwhelming majority, 72 per cent, either agreed that, 'on the whole, the [police/security services] protect our liberties more than they harm them' or disagreed with the opposite proposition. Like the ratings for 'fairness and impartiality', this indicated a moderate degree of confidence in the judicial system, but no more (Table 2.18).

TABLE 2.19. *Confidence in the enforcers of rights*

	British public	(Scottish public)
Government regulation is not harmful	34	(32)
Trust experts	33	(31)
Social workers do not have too much power	45	(38)
Social workers are fair	6.2	(5.9)
EOC/CRE protect rights	6.7	(7.0)
European courts protect rights	6.3	(6.4)

Note: See note 2 to Table 2.1.

Confidence in the Enforcers of Rights

Since the 1960s, in addition to the traditional agencies of the judicial system, a variety of agencies have been set up specifically and exclusively to enforce and promote the rights of citizens. On average, people gave 'bodies like the Equal Opportunities Commission or the Commission for Racial Equality' 6.7 marks out of ten for protecting their liberties, and 'European courts', which to most respondents probably meant the European Court of Human Rights, 6.3 out of ten. Although they were looked upon more favourably than either national or local politicians, these new institutions scored no better than the traditional judicial system (Table 2.19).

The public seemed to trust their own experience and intuition more than that of professional experts. Although people gave social workers 6.2 out of ten for 'fairness and impartiality', 55 per cent felt that 'social workers have too much power to interfere with people's lives'. In Scotland, where social workers' behaviour in the alleged, but unproven, Orkney child-abuse case attracted a deluge of criticism during our survey,[35] fully 62 per cent felt 'social workers have too much power'. More generally, two-thirds agreed with the proposition that 'I'll put my trust in the practical experience of ordinary people rather than the theories of experts and intellectuals'; and a similar number agreed that 'Government regulation of business usually does more harm than good'.

None of this indicates great enthusiasm for what is sometimes called the 'rights industry', and much of it indicates a degree of public suspicion about experts, regulators, and others who make a business of trying to help.

CONCLUSION

How should we summarize commitment to principle in contemporary Britain? We have found a disregard for the rights of suspects and a strong emphasis on respect for authority, coupled with equally strong commitments to limited and controlled government. We have also uncovered strong, even bitter antagonism towards extremists, coupled with strong support for the rights to speak out, to demonstrate, and to strike. Britons currently place a strong emphasis on the importance of traditional ideas of right and wrong, but, ironically, they also manifest equally strong resistance to the idea of enforcing community standards. We found a very balanced division of opinion on whether government should attempt to even out differences in wealth and income, coupled with a very strong welfare ethic. People coupled sympathy for peaceable claimants (the poor but not militants, immigrants but not black or Muslim activists) with a lukewarm attitude towards quasi-judicial rights enforcement and a strong suspicion of administrative enforcement of rights. It is a complex but not incoherent pattern.

Somewhat surprisingly, we have shown that principles do *not* in general reflect differences in the historical, political, constitutional, or legal context in different parts of Britain, which suggests that they derive from sources that are either more personal, or more international, or both.

As a first step towards investigating the factors that do influence principles we shall begin by comparing the views of the governed with the views of those who are more closely involved in the process of government.

NOTES

1. On this question, for example, 96% did have an opinion. In order to avoid making our presentation of findings excessively long-winded, we shall routinely exclude those with no opinion unless they are particularly numerous on a particular question, or otherwise worthy of special attention.
2. Amongst the most famous statements of this principle is Baron de Montesquieu, 'Of the Laws which Establish Political Liberty with Regard to the Constitution', in Philip Norton (ed.), *Legislatures* (Oxford: Oxford University Press, 1990), 23–35.
3. Simon Bolivar, *Angostura Address Feb. 19th 1819*, trans. Lewis Bertrand, repr. in Arend Lijphart (ed.), *Parliamentary versus Presidential Government* (Oxford: Oxford University Press, 1992), 98.
4. At much the same time, just one year later, the Scottish lawyer Francis Jeffrey, later a judge of the Court of Session, wrote: 'I am very much ashamed of the Commons

... the practical question upon which every man should be making up his mind is whether he is for tyranny or revolution' (quoted in Peter Berresford Ellis and Seumas Mac a'Ghobhainn, *The Scottish Insurrection of 1820* (London: Pluto Press, 1989), 280).

5. Committee on Criminal Procedure in Scotland, Cmnd 6218 (1975), quoted in Gerry Maher, 'Human Rights and the Criminal Process, in Tom Campbell, David Goldberg, Sheila McLean, and Tom Mullen (eds.), *Human Rights: From Rhetoric to Reality* (Oxford: Basil Blackwell, 1986), 197–222, at 204.

6. Herbert McClosky and Alida Brill, *Dimensions of Tolerance: What Americans Believe about Civil Liberties* (New York: Russell Sage Foundation, 1983), 159.

7. For a list of some of the more prominent cases, see the section on opinion trends at the end of Ch. 4; for another short review, see also Bill Coxall and Lynton Robins, *Contemporary British Politics* (London: Macmillan, 1994), 452–3.

8. Royal Commission on Criminal Procedure in England and Wales. Cmnd 8092 (1981), quoted in Maher, 'Human Rights and the Criminal Process', 206. For a further discussion of the right to silence in contemporary Britain, see K. D. Ewing and C. A. Gearty, *Freedom under Thatcher: Civil Liberties in Modern Britain* (Oxford: Oxford University Press, 1990), 34–43.

9. See Lord Armstrong, 'The Case for Confidentiality in Government', in William L. Miller (ed.), *Alternatives to Freedom: Arguments and Opinions* (London: Longman, 1995) 47–63, for a powerful defence of 'confidentiality in government'.

10. Michael Lessnoff, *Social Contract* (London: Macmillan, 1986), 32.

11. Ibid. 33.

12. And not just in Eastern Europe. Dennis Kavanagh refers to a 'political culture . . . [defining] certain forms of political behaviour and institutions as "normal" and others as "abnormal" ' (Dennis Kavanagh, *British Politics: Continuities and Change* (Oxford: Oxford University Press, 1989), 46).

13. Paragraph 4 of Article 20, inserted in 1968, see Elmar M. Hucko, *The Democratic Tradition* (Oxford: Berg, 1987), 202.

14. Adam Smith, quoted in Donald Winch, *Adam Smith's Politics: An Essay in Historiographic Revision* (Cambridge: Cambridge University Press, 1979), 55.

15. Adam Smith, quoted in ibid. 54.

16. Geraint Parry, George Moyser, and Neil Day, *Political Participation and Democracy in Britain* (Cambridge: Cambridge University Press, 1992), 46.

17. John L. Sullivan, James Pierson, and George E. Marcus, *Political Tolerance and American Democracy* (Chicago: University of Chicago Press, 1982, 1989).

18. Bernard Crick, quoted in ibid., 4.

19. Paul M. Sniderman, Richard A. Brody, and Philip E. Tetlock, *Reasoning and Choice: Explorations in Political Psychology* (Cambridge: Cambridge University Press, 1991), 135. The same sentence appeared earlier in Paul M. Sniderman, Philip E. Tetlock, James M. Glover, Donald Philip Green, and Michael Hout, 'Principle, Tolerance and the American Mass Public', *British Journal of Political Science*, 19 (1989), 25–45, at 41.

20. Sniderman, Brody, and Tetlock, *Reasoning and Choice*, 278.

21. Susan Mendus, *Toleration and the Limits of Liberalism* (London: Macmillan, 1989),

18. The classic British texts on toleration are John Locke, *A Letter Concerning Toleration*, ed. J. Tully (Indianapolis: Hackett, 1983), and John Stuart Mill, *On Liberty*, ed. G. Himmmelfarb (London: Penguin, 1978).

22. Mendus, *Toleration and the Limits of Liberalism*, 161–2. Bhikhu Parekh, 'Cultural Diversity and Liberal Democracy', in David Beetham (ed.), *Defining and Measuring Democracy* (London: Sage, 1994), 199–221, at 214–15, where he distinguishes the 'autonomy principle', the 'no harm principle', and the 'fundamental or core values of the society' as three bases for defining the limits of toleration.

23. Lord Percy of Newcastle, *The Heresy of Democracy* (London: Eyre & Spottiswood, 1954), 114.

24. Ibid. 113.

25. Malcolm Hurwitt and Peter Thornton, *Civil Liberty: The Liberty/NCCL Guide* (4th edn., London: Penguin, 1989), 215.

26. For an illuminating discussion of the misleading slogan of 'equality of opportunity', see Kenneth Hoover and Raymond Plant, *Conservative Capitalism in Britain and the United States* (London: Routledge, 1989), 218–21.

27. This is considerably less than the 72% who said government 'definitely' or 'probably' had a responsibility for 'reducing income differences between rich and poor' reported by Peter Taylor-Gooby, but his question used the emotive words 'rich and poor', it allowed the answer 'probably', and it was not preceded by an introduction designed to distinguish desirable aims from government responsibilities. See Peter Taylor-Gooby, 'Citizenship and Welfare', in Roger Jowell, Sharon Witherspoon, and Lindsay Brook (eds.), *British Social Attitudes: The 1987 Report* (Aldershot: Gower, 1987), 1–28.

28. Hoover and Plant, *Conservative Capitalism in Britain and the United States*, 70–1.

29. Tony Blair, Speech to the Labour Party Conference, Blackpool, 4 Oct. 1994. Cf. the speech by the Prime Minister of Quebec, Jacques Parizeau ('Modern Quebec and its Quest for Sovereignty', Royal Institute of International Affairs, Chatham House, London, 5 July 1995), in which he claimed that the citizens of Quebec would prefer to have a 'Charter of Rights and Obligations' to replace their current 'Charter of Rights and Freedoms'.

30. Charles Taylor, 'The Politics of Recognition', in Amy Gutman (ed.), *Multiculturalism and the Politics of Recognition* (Princeton: Princeton University Press, 1992), 25.

31. Charles Murray, *The Emerging British Underclass* (London: Institute of Economic Affairs, 1990), 2.

32. Adam Smith, quoted in Winch, *Adam Smith's Politics*, 58.

33. Tony Gifford, *Where's the Justice: A Manifesto for Law Reform* (London: Penguin, 1986), 113.

34. Peter Thornton, *Decade of Decline: Civil Liberties in the Thatcher Years* (London: National Council for Civil Liberties, 1989).

35. The Orkney scandal hit the headlines in the first week of March 1991, following a dawn raid at the end of February by police and social workers in which children were seized from their homes. The *Guardian* carried at least forty-four news stories about the affair between then and October 1992, when Lord Clyde's highly critical report was published, and the tabloids used it and similar cases as a basis for outspoken

attacks on the alleged dictatorial behaviour of social workers. So child-abuse/social-worker scandals were much in the news throughout the fieldwork for our survey. See e.g. Peter Heatherington, 'Social Workers Failed to Stop and Think about Raid', *Guardian*, 28 Oct. 1992, p. 3.

3

The Governing Perspective

How do the views of politicians compare with those of the people? To answer this question we interviewed a sample of 1,244 politicians simultaneously with our survey of the public, asking them all the questions we put to the public plus a few extra questions about their role and experience in politics. We set out to interview the leader of each political group on each local government council throughout Britain—including the leaders of Independent groups as well as those who led Conservative, Labour, Liberal, Nationalist, and other party groups. Since groups have to notify their existence to the Chief Executive of the council, we were able to get a definitive list of such groups from chief executives. In the few councils where there were no groups at all, we set out to interview the Chair and Vice-Chair of the council. In the event we succeeded in interviewing 86 per cent of the leaders or chairs on our target list. They represent an intermediate stratum of the 'political class' in Britain.

Most elected politicians are local: there are approximately 25,000 elected local government councillors compared to only 651 MPs. And group leaders on local councils are quite senior politicians, deeply involved in government, albeit mainly executive government rather than legislative government. Indeed they have a great deal more experience of the opportunities and pressures of day-to-day government than most MPs. Unlike most MPs, they are not just politicians whose task is either to make up their own minds or obey the party whip, but political *leaders*, who have to organize, administer, mobilize consent, and keep some semblance of unity and purpose within their political group. Moreover, they often make crucial decisions about the maintenance of civil and political liberties in their own locality. They have responsibility for overseeing local party policy, be it on the installation of surveillance cameras in shopping centres and housing estates, the financial resources available to the police, the criteria for acceptance of planning applications, and the extent to which old people are cared for in their community. In Scotland they have the sole responsibility for giving, or withholding, permission for public marches and demonstrations. In sum, they have 'professional' reasons for thinking deeply about citizens' rights and liberties.

FOUR THEORIES

The *theory of democratic élitism* argues that the democratic process selects, encourages, and promotes talented and tolerant politicians with an above-average commitment to civil and political rights. Populist theories of democracy advocate mass involvement in decision-making through such devices as referendums. The theory of democratic élitism, however, argues that democracies will be more liberal—as well as more stable and efficient—if popular political participation is restricted to periodic elections in which the less tolerant and capable masses are given a chance to choose between competing, but tolerant and capable, governing élites.[1] We are concerned here not with all the ramifications of this theory, but with the question of whether elected politicians are more likely than their electorates to have a strong commitment to civil and political rights, however.

The theory argues that, in order to win enough support within parties to get nominated, and then within the electorate to get elected, successful candidates for elective office need to display an unusual degree of flexibility, tolerance, and concern for the interests of ordinary citizens—unlike leaders and officials who gain office either through a military *coup* or through bureaucratic promotion. So the theory of democratic élitism posits that the elective process is a selection procedure that 'filters out' the inflexible and intolerant.

But the democratic process moulds as well as selects: once elected, democratic politicians, in the American phrase, 'have to go along to get along'. To be successful, politicians in a democratic system have to compromise and accommodate, they have to respect the interests and concerns of colleagues and rivals whose views they do not themselves fully share. If these characteristics do not come naturally, the democratic politician has to learn them or face failure, defeat, or exclusion.

The end result, according to this theory of democratic élitism, is that successful politicians in a representative democracy are more liberal, more tolerant, more willing to compromise, and more concerned about the rights and liberties of citizens than even the citizens themselves:

This portrait of the élites and the masses indicates that the survival of the democratic system does not depend upon a consensus that penetrates every level of society. It is apparently not necessary that most people commit themselves to democracy; all that is necessary is that they fail to commit themselves actively to an anti-democratic system . . . The apathy of the masses acts to counterbalance the radically conservative and potentially irrational nature of their values.[2]

This theory, developed as it was in the wake of Nazism and during the rise of McCarthyism, claims that liberal democracy is not safe in the hands of the people. It is vigorously criticized by Peter Bachrach, who argues that the theory of democratic élitism 'is grounded upon a profound distrust of the majority of ordinary men and women, and a reliance upon the established élites to maintain the values of civility and the "rules of the game" of democracy . . . while embracing liberalism it rejects . . . the major tenet of classical democratic theory—belief and confidence in the people'.[3] Suspicion of the people has a long pedigree, however: 'all the [ancient] Greek philosophers and historians whose writings have survived . . . depicted [democracy] as government by the ignorant or government by the poor.'[4]

Partly overlapping with this theory of democratic élitism, but also challenging it, is the *theory of participation*. Participation theories are diametrically opposed to theories of democratic élitism in their prescriptions. Participation theorists would maximize the degree of mass involvement in the governing process, while democratic élitists would minimize it. And participation theorists would extend the sphere of political participation right to the heart of the workplace, while democratic élitists would confine it to the centres of government. As Carole Pateman notes: 'the theory of participatory democracy stands or falls on two hypotheses: the educative function of participation and the crucial role of industry.'[5]

Yet, while participation theorists and democratic élitists are poles apart in their ideas about the proper sphere of politics, they both argue that participation has an 'educative' effect, and one that increases commitment to civil rights and liberties. While democratic élitists argue that the democratic process encourages tolerance amongst political leaders engaged in a 'competitive struggle for the people's vote',[6] the theory of participation argues that simple participation in politics—whatever the level and whatever the basis or origins of that participation—forces participators to confront issues, and encourages them to think things through—at least a little more than they otherwise would do. People who are active in public affairs, whether they be elected politicians or not, are 'called upon . . . to weigh interests not [their] own; to be guided . . . by another rule than [their] private partialities'.[7] And as well as bringing participants into contact with other participants, participation also reminds them of how various policy initiatives have progressed in the past. All of this encourages both restraint and moderation and discourages purely expressive 'knee-jerk' reactions. Sentiments such as 'hang them all' or 'nuke the lot of them' are much more likely to be heard in social conversations amongst the disenfranchised and disaffected than in local council chambers, cabinet rooms, or defence committees. Power, it is argued

by participation theorists, breeds responsibility: 'only direct political participation . . . is a completely successful form of civic education for democracy
. . . of course, when participation is neutered by being separated from power,
then civic action will be only a game.'[8]

But there are alternative theories which predict just the opposite. The
theory of activism argues that political activists are almost always extremists.[9] Only those with extreme political views have enough motivation to put
in the enormous amount of time and effort that political activism entails, and
usually for so little personal reward. Their extremism lies not in their political policies themselves but in their degree of personal commitment to them.
Those who are utterly certain that they are right and that others are wrong
are the ones who will be driven to political action. For a few that may mean
a lifetime devoted to violent or illegal revolutionary activity. For many more
it may mean joining a pressure group or a political party.

It would be surprising, indeed, if Conservative activists were not more
committed to right-wing policies than Conservative voters, or Labour activists were not more committed to left-wing policies than Labour voters. Indeed Downsian[10] theories of party policy often postulate a tension between
the relatively extreme views of those inside the party and the relatively
moderate views of the party's marginal voters who are so necessary to its
electoral success. Surprising though it may be, however, recent surveys by
Paul Whiteley, Patrick Seyd, and Jeremy Richardson of opinion amongst
party members and activists in Britain suggest that they are not particularly
extreme in terms of policy: 'the view that Conservative activists are all right-
wing extremists is *not* supported by the evidence . . . [Conservative] activists
are to the *left* of non-activists';[11] and 'there are no major differences of
opinion between [Conservative] members and [Conservative] voters'.[12] Patrick
Seyd and Paul Whiteley reached similar conclusions about Labour Party
members and activists.[13] None the less, despite those overall conclusions,
party members usually held more intense opinions—even if not usually
more extreme opinions. Labour members also differed sharply from their
voters on attitudes towards nationalization, and—perhaps more relevant to
our discussion of political culture—Conservative members differed sharply
from their voters on stricter laws against trade unions (by 13 per cent) and
the death penalty (by 20 per cent).[14]

Commitment to extreme policies may or may not have implications for
civil and political liberties. Conceivably the extreme policy may be extremely liberal, extremely tolerant. But extreme commitment to any policy,
it might be argued, is psychologically incompatible with tolerance and respect for the views and rights of others. So the theory of political activism

implies that the very enthusiasm which drives people to become so active and involved in politics that they ultimately rise to become political leaders is also likely to make them intolerant and aggressive towards others.

Finally, there is the *theory of political corruption*, so memorably expressed in Lord Acton's words: 'Power tends to corrupt, and absolute power corrupts absolutely. Great men are almost always bad men.'[15] Happily we do not live in a country where great men or women can easily wield absolute power, but, at any level and to any degree, the claim that 'power tends to corrupt' cannot be lightly cast aside. We are not concerned with financial corruption, though disclosures in Italy, Japan, the former communist bloc, and much closer to home serve as a reminder that those with political power are often tempted to turn it to financial advantage. What is relevant here is the possibility that power may corrupt attitudes toward ordinary citizens' rights and liberties. Lord Acton, a devout but deeply troubled Catholic, wrote his memorable phrase in an attack on what he regarded as the papacy's abuse of power, both spiritual and temporal.[16] What citizens may regard as a despairing cry from the heart may appear to those in power as a simple challenge to their authority, an outbreak of disorder, or a step towards chaos. Conversely, what governors may regard as efficient and effective administration may appear to citizens as an unacceptable diminution of their rights and liberties. So the theory of political corruption implies that those in power will be less tolerant of the rights of citizens and more tolerant of the prerogatives of governors and government, less sympathetic to the needs and aspirations of citizens and more sympathetic to the problems of governing.

All of these theories—democratic élitism, participation, activism, and political corruption—are plausible. No doubt the forces that they postulate are all at work to a greater or lesser degree. What matters is the balance of these forces. When everything is taken into account, are politicians more tolerant of citizens' rights, as the theories of both democratic élitism and political participation imply? Or are they less tolerant of citizens' rights, as the theories of activism and corruption imply? Our baseline for measuring the balance of these forces must be the opinions of citizens themselves.

A METHODOLOGY FOR COMPARISON

Before we proceed to an empirical comparison of the principles of politicians and the public, however, we need to consider whether our sample design might unduly affect our conclusions. Our sample of the general public was designed to be representative of the electorate. No other choice would be appropriate. But our survey of politicians was designed to represent the leaders of political groups on all local councils—irrespective of whether their political groups were large or small, and irrespective of whether the populations of their local authority areas were large or small. One consequence is that our sample of politicians contains approximately equal numbers of Conservative, Labour, and Liberal Democrat politicians—as defined by their *parliamentary* voting preferences. (Because of the number of Independent group leaders, it would be inappropriate for comparative purposes to categorize their partisanship by their *local*-government party label.) Now if Liberal Democrats have distinctive views on citizens' rights—and they do—then the differences in the party balance between our sample of politicians and the electorate might, by itself, produce differences in attitudes to citizens' rights: a sample of politicians skewed towards Liberals (with a capital 'L') might be skewed towards liberals (with a small 'l'). So, to make our comparisons between politicians and people more valid, we have weighted our sample of politicians so as to make the proportions of politicians with Conservative, Labour, and Liberal voting preferences (for a parliamentary election) the same as the corresponding proportions in the electorate. Effectively that means down-weighting Liberal politicians and up-weighting Conservative politicians, eliminating the over-representation (relative to the electorate) of Liberal politicians and the under-representation of Conservative politicians.

Of course, even after this adjustment, our sample of politicians remains more male, more middle aged, and better educated than the electorate. They remain socially unrepresentative even when we have weighted them to be (party) politically representative. In this chapter we look at differences of opinion between the general public and our weighted sample of politicians. Those differences of opinion cannot be attributed to *party* differences, but we leave to a later chapter the question of whether they reflect nothing more than *social* differences. However, even if the distinctive political culture of politicians merely reflected the biases in their social backgrounds (which, in fact, they do not), the cultural differences between people and politicians would still be important—explaining them would not explain them away.

PRINCIPLES

We turn now to examine politicians' commitments to the thirteen micro-principles and six micro-sympathies that we considered in Chapter 2. In each case we shall compare the extent of politicians' commitment with that of our British public sample.

TABLE 3.1. *Respect for authority*

	Politicians	Difference from public
Importance of		
respect for authority	7.5	−0.7
law and order	8.0	−0.6
defence	6.5	−0.2
Strong government (v. chaos)	27	−11

Notes: In this chapter, all comparisons are between samples of 1,244 British politicians and 2,060 members of the British public. We have made no use of our special sample of Scotland here.

See note 2 to Table 2.1.

Respect for Authority

Although there were only small differences between politicians and the public on questions of respect for authority, strengthening law and order, and maintaining strong defence forces, politicians were 11 per cent less willing to agree that 'the only alternative to strong government is disorder and chaos'. And by all our measures, politicians had *less* respect for authority than the general public (Table 3.1).

Limited Government

Conversely, politicians were 6 per cent more committed than the public to the general idea of limited government, as indicated by their agreeing that 'constitutional checks and balances are important to make sure that a government doesn't become too dictatorial and ignore other viewpoints', or disagreeing with the alternative that 'it is important for a government to be able to take decisive action without looking over its shoulder all the time'.

And politicians differed even more from the public on limiting and constraining the actions of more junior officials. They were 13 per cent more inclined than the public to uphold an accused person's 'right to silence' in court; and 18 per cent more inclined than the public to give priority to suspects' rights rather than cut corners to clamp down on street crime (Table 3.2).

The Right to Know

The public was already so supportive of a citizen's 'right to know' that politicians could scarcely give it any more support—though they certainly

Public Attitudes

TABLE 3.2. *Limited government and due process*

	Politicians (%)	Difference from public (%)
Support		
checks and balances	64	+6
external control of police	78	0
right to silence	56	+13
suspects' rights	32	+18

TABLE 3.3. *The right to know*

	Politicians (%)	Difference from public (%)
Support, with or without reservations		
right to know about self	98	+1
right to know about government plans	92	+1
right to know about factory	98	+1
Support, without reservations		
right to know about self	94	+1
right to know about government plans	83	0
right to know about factory	94	+1

gave it no less. But, interestingly, politicians' support for freedom of information followed an identical pattern to that of the public—less support for a right to know about government plans, and up to 11 per cent more support for the right to know about their own records or about the activities of companies which might endanger the health of nearby residents (Table 3.3).

The Right to Freedom of Speech

There were big differences between the opinions of public and politicians on freedom of speech. While these did not show up on our question about the importance of 'guaranteeing everyone the right to free speech'—which attracted almost universal support—politicians were 24 per cent less willing than the public to agree that 'free speech is just not worth it if it means we have to put up with the danger to society from extremist views', and 13 per cent less willing than the public to ban extreme political organizations (Table 3.4).

TABLE 3.4. *The right to freedom of speech*

	Politicians	Difference from public
Importance of free speech	9.4	+0.2
Disagree that free speech not worth it	88	+24
Not ban extreme political organizations	68	+13

Note: See note 2 to Table 2.1.

TABLE 3.5. *Rights to protest and rebel*

	Politicians (%)	Difference from public (%)
Right to demonstrate	90	+6
Right to strike	77	0
Not obey unjust law	34	−15

Rights of Protest and Rebellion

Consistent with these less authoritarian attitudes, politicians gave 6 per cent more support than even the public (90 per cent compared to 84 per cent) to the general principle of the right to hold protest marches and demonstrations.

Yet, although politicians had generally less authoritarian attitudes than the public, at the same time they were more law-abiding and more inclined to advocate self-restraint. Politicians gave no more support to the 'right to strike' than the public. And they were 15 per cent more likely than the public to agree that they would be 'morally bound to obey' even an 'unjust, immoral, or cruel' law passed by parliament. Only a third of politicians, in contrast to half the public, were willing to disregard an 'unjust, immoral, or cruel' law.

Attitudes towards protest and rebellion provide the first indication of a distinctively 'governing perspective' amongst politicians which appears to combine greater support for citizens' liberties, including rights to peaceful and non-disruptive protest, with greater opposition to law-breaking and rebellion (Table 3.5).[17]

Conformity to Traditional Values

Politicians placed slightly less importance than the public—but only slightly less—on 'preserving traditional ideas of right and wrong' or 'following God's will' (Table 3.6).

TABLE 3.6.   *Respect for traditional values*

	Politicians (marks/10)	Difference from public (marks/10)
Importance of		
traditional ideas of right and wrong	7.6	−0.4
following God's will	5.0	−0.7

Tolerance

On the question of toleration, however, there were substantial differences between politicians and the public. With the exception of 'enforcing community standards', which was relatively unpopular with both people and politicians, and protecting children and young people from 'wild and immoral ideas', which was widely supported by both, all our measures of toleration showed politicians to be substantially more tolerant than the general public.

By over one point (on a ten-point scale) politicians placed more importance on 'tolerating different beliefs and lifestyles'. Politicians were 10 per cent more in favour of extending religious freedom to religious groups that were thought to be 'strange, fanatical, and weird'; they were 12 per cent less inclined to say government had a duty to uphold morality (foreshadowing one of the spectacular controversies of 1994—the Conservative leader's 'Back to Basics' campaign); 18 per cent more willing to tolerate people whose ideas were 'morally wrong'; and 22 per cent less willing to agree that 'if something is morally wrong, then it should be made illegal'. Without doubt, politicians were more tolerant than the public, and less willing to demand moral conformity from citizens than were citizens themselves (Table 3.7).

Equal Rights

There were smaller differences between the public and politicians on equal rights: politicians were marginally less favourable to gender equality, but proved more favourable than the public to homosexual/heterosexual equality and, more especially, to ethnic equality (Table 3.8).

Economic Equality

On many aspects of economic equality also, differences between the public and politicians were slight, but there were exceptions. These exceptions concerned whether government had a duty to ensure 'a decent standard of

TABLE 3.7. *Tolerance and intolerance*

	Politicians	Difference from public
Tolerance		
Importance of tolerating different beliefs and lifestyles	8.3	+1.1
Intolerance		
Protect children from immoral ideas	87	−4
Not tolerate morally wrong	35	−18
Morals should equal laws	24	−22
Enforce community standards	29	0
Government has responsibility to uphold morality	53	−12
No religious freedom for weird	18	−10

Note: See note 2 to Table 2.1.

TABLE 3.8. *Equal rights*

	Politicians	Difference from public
Importance of		
ethnic protection	8.0	+0.7
gender equality	7.9	−0.3
homosexual equality	6.3	+0.3
Equal rights not gone far enough	73	0

Note: See note 2 to Table 2.1.

living for everyone' and 'that everyone who wants a job can have one'. Politicians were 6 per cent more inclined than the public to say government had a responsibility for living standards, yet, at the same time, politicians were 13 per cent less willing than the public to say government had a duty to ensure full employment. Thus politicians were either more realistic or more defeatist—depending upon your viewpoint—but, on balance, they were neither more nor less favourable to economic equality than the public (Table 3.9).

Self-Reliance

Politicians were more inclined than the public to emphasize a caring community with collective goals. Politicians also put less emphasis on individual achievements, and much less on 'self-reliance'—giving it a full 1.5 points

TABLE 3.9. *Economic equality*

	Politicians (%)	Difference from public (%)
Government has responsibility for		
equal wealth	52	+1
equal opportunities	92	+1
living standards	83	+6
jobs	65	−13
housing	90	−1
education	98	−1
health care	99	+1

TABLE 3.10. *Self-reliance*

	Politicians	Difference from public
Importance of		
self-reliance	6.4	−1.5
individual achievements	6.4	−0.6
For individual goals (v. common goals)	35	−9
Not too much emphasis on individual interests	37	+4
Too much emphasis on rights (v. duties)	55	+5

Note: See note 2 to Table 2.1.

less than the public on a ten-point scale; and politicians were 9 per cent more likely than the public to see the ideal society as a 'unified body pursuing a common goal' rather than a mere collection of individuals.

At the same time they were very slightly more inclined to complain that there was 'too much emphasis on citizens' rights and not enough on citizens' duties' in Britain today but very slightly less inclined than the public to complain that there was 'too much emphasis . . . on individual interests at the expense of the community's interest' in Britain today—though neither of these differences exceeded 5 per cent (Table 3.10).

Caring

Support for helping the needy, the unemployed, and the disabled ran at very high, and almost identical, levels amongst both politicians and the public (Table 3.11).

TABLE 3.11. *Caring*

	Politicians (marks/10)	Difference from public (marks/10)
Importance of		
help for the disabled	9.1	−0.2
reducing unemployment	8.6	−0.3
taking care of the needy	8.9	+0.2

TABLE 3.12. *Wealth creation*

	Politicians (marks/10)	Difference from public (marks/10)
Importance of		
holding down inflation	7.5	−0.7
cutting taxes	4.7	−1.8
achieving economic growth	8.0	−0.4

Wealth Creation

On the other hand, politicians gave less priority to economic growth and keeping down inflation and *very* much less priority to keeping down taxes. Politicians gave only 4.7 points out of ten to the importance of keeping down taxes, whereas the public gave it 6.5 out of ten—clear evidence that the governing perspective undoubtedly included special recognition that adequate levels of taxation were necessary to ensure the provision of public services (Table 3.12).

Protection

On all aspects of protection—against crime, big business, or pollution—the differences between politicians and the public proved negligible. They were almost unanimous in agreeing that government had a duty to fight crime and pollution. And three-quarters of both the public and politicians agreed that government had a duty to ensure that business treated its consumers fairly.

TABLE 3.13. *Protection*

	Politicians (%)	Difference from public (%)
Government has duty to protect citizens		
against crime	96	+3
against business	76	−2
against pollution	96	+1

SYMPATHIES

Just as politicians tended to be less authoritarian but more law-abiding than the public in principle, we found that politicians were also more sympathetic than the public towards the socially disadvantaged and even towards political activists but, at the same time, less sympathetic than the public towards militants of various kinds.

Sympathies and Antipathies towards Citizen Groups

When asked for marks out of ten to indicate how much they liked various groups of activists, politicians were more favourable than the public to black activists, communists, and Muslim activists; but less favourable than the public to environmental campaigners 'like Greenpeace' and especially to National Front supporters and animal-rights activists.

   Amongst politicians, antipathy was clearly greatest towards the balanced set of four groups we propose to use for our indicator of 'antipathy towards militants'—the two groups of terrorist sympathizers, and supporters of Militant Tendency or the National Front. While the two groups of racial/ethnic activists remained less popular than any of the remaining groups, politicians (unlike the public) clearly had less antipathy towards them than towards the four groups we shall use for our 'antipathy-towards-militants' indicator (Table 3.14).

Social Prejudice

Compared to the public, politicians were neither more nor less prejudiced against the poor, but slightly less prejudiced against women, and very much less prejudiced against immigrants. Only 49 per cent of politicians, compared to 66 per cent of the public, agreed that 'immigrants to Britain should try harder to be more like other British people' (Table 3.15).

TABLE 3.14. *Sympathy scores for citizen groups*

	Politicians (marks/10)	Difference from public (marks/10)
Black activists	3.4	+0.9
Communists	4.3	+0.8
Muslim activists	2.7	+0.5
IRA sympathizers	1.4	+0.2
Feminists	5.0	+0.1
Gays and lesbians	4.2	+0.1
Militant Tendency supporters	2.1	−0.2
Protestant terrorist sympathizers	1.2	−0.3
Greenpeace	6.8	−0.4
NF supporters	1.0	−0.8
Animal-rights activists	4.5	−1.0

Note: Listed in order of differences between the British public and politicians.

TABLE 3.15. *Antipathy towards the socially disadvantaged*

	Politicians (%)	Difference from public (%)
Men are better at senior jobs	8	−8
Women should stay at home	7	−3
Immigrants should try harder	49	−17
Poor don't try hard enough	30	+1

Confidence in the Established Political System

As we might expect, politicians and the public had markedly different views about politicians themselves. Local-government leaders rated both MPs and local councils—but especially local councils—more highly than the public on the extent to which they protected 'citizens' rights and liberties'. Local political leaders gave local councils 6.9 out of ten while the public gave them only 5.6, and there was a huge difference in answers to the question about whether 'most politicians can be trusted to do what they think is best for the country': only 33 per cent of the public, but 58 per cent of politicians, agreed to that. It would seem that the politicians had rather more faith in the theories of democratic élitism than the public.

Public Attitudes

Table 3.16. *Confidence in the political system*

	Politicians	Difference from public
Majority not often wrong	40	−12
Trust most politicians	58	+25
Back-bench MPs protect rights	6.6	+0.9
Local councils protect rights	6.9	+1.3

Note: See note 2 to Table 2.1.

We conceptualized the nebulous 'majority' as an aspect of the establishment. In an adversarial democracy, that is not unreasonable. But, although other aspects of the establishment won greater approval from politicians than from the public, that was not true for 'the majority'. Only 40 per cent of politicians, compared to 52 per cent of the public, disagreed with the proposition that 'the majority is often wrong'. Thus, in a very old tradition traceable right back through James Madison's classic statement in *The Federalist Papers*,[18] politicians were even more suspicious of 'the majority' than were the people. If we could validly identify 'politicians' with our sample of political leaders, and 'the majority' with our sample of the public, these results about 'trust in politicians' and 'the majority is often wrong' would suggest a degree of mutual wariness between people and politicians (Table 3.16).

Confidence in Civil Institutions

Differences between people and politicians in their evaluation of other aspects of civil society—notably television, the press, trade unions, and the churches—were slight. But, with the exception of the tabloid press, which they viewed with even more disdain than the public, politicians were slightly better disposed than the public to the idea that these institutions protected civil liberties (Table 3.17).

Confidence in the Judicial System

Differences between people and politicians in their attitudes towards the judicial system were slight, except that 9 per cent more of the politicians felt that recent governments had been reducing rights and liberties in Britain. Despite that perception of trend, politicians were slightly more inclined to agree that the police/security services did more to protect our liberties than to harm them, and politicians gave very slightly more marks than the public

TABLE 3.17. *Confidence in civil institutions*

	Politicians (marks/10)	Difference from public (marks/10)
Citizens' rights protected by		
tabloids	3.6	−0.3
broadsheets	6.7	+0.4
television	6.5	+0.2
trade unions	6.5	+0.5
churches	5.9	+0.1

TABLE 3.18. *Confidence in the judicial system*

	Politicians	Difference from public
British government reducing rights	61	+9
Police/security services protect rights	74	+2
Judges fair	6.4	+0.4
Police fair	6.4	+0.2
British courts protect rights	6.5	0.0

Note: See note 2 to Table 2.1.

to the police and judges for fairness and impartiality. Politicians and the public gave British courts identical marks for protecting citizens' rights and liberties (Table 3.18).

Confidence in the Enforcers of Rights

However, politicians' attitudes towards government intervention and regulation in economic and social matters were noticeably different from those of the public. Politicians were 16 per cent less willing than the public to agree that 'government regulation of business usually does more harm than good', and 13 per cent less willing to accept that 'social workers have too much power to interfere with people's lives'. At the same time, however, they were 7 per cent less willing to put their trust in 'the theories of experts and intellectuals' rather than 'the practical experience of ordinary people'. While there were some noticeable discrepancies between the public and politicians in these three areas, there was virtually no disagreement between them when rating bodies like the Equal Opportunities Commission, the Commission for

TABLE 3.19. *Confidence in the enforcers of rights*

	Politicians	Difference from public
Government regulation is not harmful	50	+16
Social workers do not have too much power	58	+13
Trust experts	26	−7
Social workers are fair	6.6	+0.4
EOC/CRE protect rights	6.5	−0.2
European courts protect rights	6.6	+0.3

Note: See note 2 to Table 2.1.

Racial Equality, or the European courts in terms of their contribution towards defending citizens' rights and liberties (Table 3.19).

THE GOVERNING PERSPECTIVE

Our findings fail to provide unqualified support for any of the four theories we outlined at the start of this chapter. Instead, we need a new and slightly more complex *theory of democratic governance*. Different aspects of our findings suggest that politicians are simultaneously more committed to citizens' rights and more deferential to, or have greater confidence in, government. On the one hand, politicians are more committed to due process, free speech, and toleration of moral deviance amongst the citizenry; and they are more sympathetic to women and ethnic minorities. But, at the same time, their greater confidence in government is expressed in their attitudes to politicians, social workers, and government regulation; and their greater deference to government is expressed in the way that they feel morally bound to obey even unjust laws.

So the democratic governing perspective comprises both a special commitment to citizens' rights and a more confident and relaxed attitude towards the prerogatives of government.

We went on to consider whether this 'governing perspective' divided politicians one from another, as well as distinguishing politicians as a whole from the general public. We asked all our political leaders whether they saw themselves as 'on the side of the parties or groups which control your council' or 'in opposition' to them, or neither. Because different parties were in control in different councils, the partisan differences between those 'in control' and 'in opposition' were not large. But to eliminate partisan influences,

TABLE 3.20. *The governing perspective amongst politicians*

	Politicians in control (%)	Politicians in opposition (%)	Effect of being in control (%)
Resistance to authority			
For suspects' rights	30	35	−5
Disagree that free speech not worth it	89	90	−1
Not obey unjust law	30	38	−8
Conformity			
Not tolerate morally wrong	31	35	−4
Morals should equal laws	18	25	−7
Sympathies and confidence			
Immigrants should try harder	48	45	+3
Trust most politicians	61	56	+5
Government regulation is not harmful	49	51	−2

Note: For this table only, politicians in control and in opposition have been reweighted so as to have the same (parliamentary) party preferences as each other, and as the public.

for this analysis (and only for this analysis) we reweighted each set of politicians by parliamentary party preference, so that, after this reweighting, those in control, those in opposition, and those on the cross-benches all had the same party preferences as each other—and as the public. Thus any differences of opinion that remained could not be attributed to party differences.

In many respects local politicians who were in control locally did not differ from those who were in opposition locally. But some small differences did emerge. Politicians in control were more tolerant of moral deviation than those in opposition, just as politicians were generally when compared to the public—though only by a maximum of 7 per cent. Similarly, politicians in control had a stronger governing perspective than those in opposition, in that they were more willing to trust politicians and felt more morally bound to obey an unjust law—though only by 8 per cent more than politicians in opposition. Again the difference between politicians in control and those in opposition runs in the same direction as the difference between politicians as a whole and the public at large (Table 3.20).

These differences suggest that those opinions which most distinguished politicians from the public also divided politicians in control from those in opposition. However, the differences between politicians in control and those in opposition were relatively small and occasionally ran in the reverse direction. In broad terms, therefore, the governing perspective appeared to distinguish politicians from the public more than it distinguished politicians in office from those in opposition.

CONCLUSION

The general conclusion of US studies of democratic élitism in the 1950s was that, while masses and élites agreed on libertarian principles, which they overwhelmingly supported, they diverged on libertarian practice, which they both supported much less anyway. In practice then support for civil liberties was always less than in principle, but particularly so amongst the masses.[19]

However, the conclusion that élites and masses agreed even on principles was based upon 'soft' questions that reflected conventions of 'political correctness' rather than firm commitment to principle—questions such as: 'I believe in free speech for all no matter what their views might be'; 'Nobody has a right to tell another person what he should and should not read'; 'You can't really be sure whether an opinion is true or not unless people are free to argue against it'; 'No matter what a person's political beliefs are, he is entitled to the same legal rights and protection as anyone else.'[20] No wonder they found overwhelming support for such libertarian principles amongst both élites and the masses.

This chapter has been restricted to an analysis of principle, but it has been based upon survey questions that attempted to measure real commitment to principle rather than knee-jerk responses to familiar, acceptable, or even 'politically correct' slogans. So, if we take our questions on the principle of free speech, for example, we not only asked our respondents what they thought about the importance of 'guaranteeing everyone the right to free speech', but also got them to consider whether 'free speech is just not worth it if it means we have to put up with the danger to society from extremist views'.

Some of our findings significantly strengthen the conclusions of the earliest US studies of democratic élitism, because they reveal differences between politicians and the public *even on questions of principle*. On principles of respect for authority and traditional values, wealth creation, tolerance, limited government, free speech, and self-reliance we found that politicians were substantially more liberal than the public—though on egalitarian principles politicians hardly differed from the public.

However, some of our other findings seriously undermine the theory of democratic élitism. In particular, we found that politicians were significantly *less liberal than the public* on the principles of protest and rebellion—and that reverses the conclusions of those early US studies. It also confirms some of the scepticism expressed about those studies at the time:

We should not necessarily assume that our freedoms are safe in the hands of the élites . . . The failure of the élite to defend the right to demonstrate against the war in Vietnam is not a unique example of the failure of élites to support civil liberties. The career of Senator Joseph McCarthy, and the response of élites to his career, is another example of the failure of élites to respond to a challenge to the system.[21]

We also found differences between the public and politicians in terms of sympathies and confidence. In keeping with their relatively liberal principles, politicians were relatively sympathetic to women and immigrants. However, the greatest difference between the public and politicians was a striking 25 per cent difference in the amount of confidence in politicians. While that lends some support to the participation theorists' claim that participation in policy-making increases people's confidence in the political institutions that affect their daily lives, it also lends credence to Vivien Hart's claim that 'the long held élitist suspicion that the people are a threat to democracy has long been matched by the perception of the people, less elegantly expressed but as well-founded, that the élites are a threat to democracy'.[22]

So far we have compared politicians and the public only with respect to broad general principles. Throughout subsequent chapters we shall analyse the opinions of the public and politicians in parallel to uncover further differences. In the next chapter, we turn to consider whether politicians have more coherent structures of principle than the public, and then, in the following chapter, we shall ask whether they connect their principles with practice more closely than the citizens they are elected to represent.

NOTES

1. Joseph A. Schumpeter, *Capitalism, Socialism and Democracy* (London: Allen & Unwin, 1942), 269–72, is considered the *locus classicus* of the theory of democratic élitism, though not of all the elements of it that we discuss.
2. Thomas R. Dye and L. Harmon Zeigler, *The Irony of Democracy: An Uncommon Introduction to American Politics* (Belmont, Calif.: Wadsworth, 1970 edn.), 137–9.
3. Peter Bachrach, *The Theory of Democratic Élitism: A Critique* (London: London University Press, 1967), 93–4.
4. Anthony H. Birch, *The Concepts and Theories of Modern Democracy* (London: Routledge, 1993), 45.

5. Carole Pateman, *Participation and Democratic Theory* (Cambridge: Cambridge University Press, 1970), 44.
6. Schumpeter, *Capitalism, Socialism and Democracy*, 269.
7. John Stuart Mill, *Representative Government* (Everyman Edition; London: Dent, 1972), 217.
8. Benjamin R. Barber, *Strong Democracy: Participatory Politics for a New Age* (Berkeley and Los Angeles: University of California Press, 1984), 235–6.
9. Giovanni Sartori, *The Theory of Democracy Revisited* (Chatham, NJ: Chatham House, 1987), 118.
10. Anthony Downs, *An Economic Theory of Democracy* (New York: Harper, 1957).
11. Paul Whiteley, Patrick Seyd, and Jeremy Richardson, *True Blues: The Politics of Conservative Party Membership* (Oxford: Oxford University Press, 1994), 121.
12. Ibid. 64.
13. Patrick Seyd and Paul Whiteley, *Labour's Grass Roots: The Politics of Party Membership* (Oxford: Oxford University Press, 1992), 217–18.
14. Whiteley, Seyd, and Richardson, *True Blues*, 65.
15. Lord Acton, quoted in J. M. and M. J. Cohen, *Penguin Dictionary of Quotations* (London: Penguin, 1981), 1.
16. Hugh Trevor-Roper, 'Introduction', to *Lord Acton's Lectures in Modern History* (London: Fontana, 1960), 13.
17. Herbert McClosky and Alida Brill, *Dimensions of Tolerance: What Americans Believe about Civil Liberties* (New York: Russell Sage Foundation, 1983), 110, found that, despite their élite's general tendency to be much more liberal than their public, on the issue of 'obeying a law that conflicts with conscience' their élites were only 2 per cent less insistent on obedience than their public, and their 'legal élite' sample was slightly more insistent on obedience than the public. Our own findings are consistent with this, but stronger.
18. James Madison, 'Number X: The Same Subject Continued', in James Madison, Alexander Hamilton, and John Jay, *The Federalist Papers* (London: Penguin, 1987), 122–8, at 125.
19. Dye and Zeigler, *The Irony of Democracy*, 129–30; Herbert McClosky, 'Consensus and Ideology in American Politics', *American Political Science Review*, 58 (1964), 361–82; McClosky and Brill, *Dimensions of Tolerance*, 48–9.
20. All four questions come from McClosky, 'Consensus and Ideology', reproduced in Dye and Zeigler, *The Irony of Democracy*, 129.
21. Dye and Zeigler, *The Irony of Democracy*, 139.
22. Vivien Hart, *Distrust and Democracy: Political Distrust in Britain and America* (Cambridge: Cambridge University Press, 1978), 208.

PART THREE
Coherence

4

Dimensions of Principle and Sympathy

ALTHOUGH we reviewed answers to many detailed questions about principles in the two preceding chapters, we have no reason to suppose that people have quite so many principles. While answers to our individual questions may elicit shades and subtleties of meaning, it is very likely that a few broad dimensions of principle underlie the answers to all these questions. At the extreme, it is possible that people might be guided by just two opposing principles like liberty and authority, constituting a single dimension of principle (with authoritarians being automatically anti-libertarian and vice versa). Similarly people might have only one dimension of sympathy or antipathy: for or against political activists and social claimants, for example (with those sympathetic to activists and claimants being automatically antipathetic towards the political and judicial establishment). But it is also possible that the structures of opinion are more complex than that.

In fact, answers to our many questions of principle probably do reflect many different aspects of principle, but aspects of principle that are more or less loosely tied together. If this is the case, we need to know *how closely* they are tied together, and whether there is one general underlying dimension of principle, or several different dimensions, that tie them together. We shall use factor analysis to help us decide, first of all, how many—or how few—general dimensions of principle underlie our many particular questions of principle; and, secondly, how closely or loosely individual questions of principle depend upon more general dimensions of principle.

Factor analysis is often used more for the first of these purposes than for the second. Indeed, there is a tendency amongst factor analysts to treat anything that is not general as merely random, but we do not wish to be so dismissive. We recognize that general dimensions of principle fail to provide perfect predictions of answers to particular questions about principle, in part because of the random element in people's replies to short questions fired at them in rapid succession—but only in part. As we have explored the answers given by our respondents, we have been struck by the interpretability and rationality of the 'unique' elements of answers to particular questions of principle which do *not* reflect general underlying dimensions of principle. We shall draw attention to some of these 'unique' elements in later chapters where appropriate, but in this chapter we shall focus on those elements of principle which our many individual questions have in common.

We shall also pursue our comparison of people and politicians to find out whether politicians have the same structure of general principles as the public. Although, in the last chapter, we found many similarities and some differences between politicians and the public in their levels of commitment to various principles, that tells us nothing about the differences, if any, in their *structures* of principle—in the extent to which different principles 'hang together' amongst politicians and the public. It would be surprising if the public and politicians proved to have fundamentally different structures of principle. After all, democratic politicians emerge from the same society as the people. Furthermore, if they wish to stay in office, they must keep in touch with public opinion. And, conversely, the public may look to politicians to articulate their own half-formulated opinions, to raise issues, to argue cases, to provide political cues, and to give structure, meaning, and interpretability to political ideas. Democracy is an interactive, two-way process of opinion formation. There is no reason, therefore, to expect a difference in the fundamental structure of principle and prejudice held by people and politicians. But, given their greater experience, their greater involvement with political issues, and their greater commitment to a party—with all the explicit guidance provided by their chosen party's history and ideology—politicians could be expected to have a stronger ideology, a simpler, clearer, more powerful structure of principle. In short, we would expect politicians' responses to different questions of principle to be more coherent, better organized, less random, more meaningful than the responses of the general public. So, while the structure of politicians' principles should be fundamentally similar to that of the people, it should be simpler, clearer, and less obscured by random answers to half-understood or seldom-considered questions—a sharper, more focused version of the same thing. We shall see.

MACRO- AND MICRO-PRINCIPLES

In earlier chapters we grouped our many questions about principle (fifty-one in all) under thirteen broad headings such as 'respect for authority', 'limited government', and 'the right to know'. This grouping was based primarily upon the wording of the questions, which had originally been formulated to provide multiple indicators of these far less, but still quite numerous 'micro-principles', as we have called them. At the margin, the fine-tuning of this grouping was influenced by a variety of exploratory factor analyses of opinion in our three separate samples—the British public, local politicians, and the Scottish public—but the basis for it remained ultimately a matter of judgement.

We shall examine the elements of that hierarchy for both internal and external coherence. By *internal coherence* we mean the extent to which answers to the individual questions grouped into one of the thirteen micro-principles do indeed hang together in the way that we might expect and thus jointly provide a more reliable indicator of that micro-principle. By *external coherence* we mean the extent to which these thirteen micro-principles themselves, now measured by relatively reliable indicators, can be grouped into an even broader, simpler structure with just a very few dimensions or 'macro-principles'.

We are well aware that each stage of this two-stage[1] simplification process not only averages out random influences upon answers to the original fifty-one questions, but also suppresses some significant shades of meaning. None the less, at some cost in terms of nuance and subtlety, it does help to reveal the basic structure underlying public opinion.

There is a difference of emphasis between the two stages. At the first stage in this two-stage procedure we are hoping primarily to reduce, though not completely to eliminate, the obscuring fog of semi-random answers to half-understood, ill-considered, or even ill-framed questions. At the second stage we hope primarily to discover how far the thirteen micro-principles, each of them now measured as well as our data permit, reflect attitudes towards a very few, very broad, underlying macro-principles.

We shall then look at the structure of sympathies, antipathies, and prejudices in a similar way.

STANDARD NUMERICAL CODES

Questions about principles fell into one of four formats: 'agree/disagree' questions, 'yes/no' questions, a request for 'marks out of ten', or a choice between two alternatives. For the analyses in this chapter, we have assigned the following numerical values to these answers in order to place all answers on scales that ranged from plus 100 through zero to minus 100 as follows:

Answers to *agree/disagree* questions were assigned values:

+100 strongly agree
+50 agree
0 neither, or don't know
−50 disagree
−100 strongly disagree

Similarly, answers to *yes/no* questions were assigned values:

+100 yes
+50 qualified yes
0 neither or don't know
−50 qualified no
−100 no

Answers to *choice-of-alternatives* questions were assigned values:

+70 alternative A
0 neither or don't know
−70 alternative B

since there was no indication of strength of feeling about the choice.

And answers to *marks-out-of-ten* questions were assigned values:

+100 for 10/10 marks	−20 for 4/10 marks
+80 9/10	−40 3/10
+60 8/10	−60 2/10
+40 7/10	−80 1/10
+20 6/10	−100 0/10

0 for 5/10 or don't know.

All of these assignments were arbitrary, and clearly other assignments might have been equally justifiable. For example, 'yes' and 'no' might have been assigned plus and minus 50, like 'agree' and 'disagree', with plus and minus 25 for 'qualified yes' and 'qualified no'. And our 'choice of alternatives' might have been assigned plus and minus 100, plus and minus 50, or plus and minus 75. However, with the assignments we have chosen, zero always indicates the neutral or don't-know response, plus and minus 100 indicate relatively strong positive or negative responses where we have a five-point scale, plus and minus 50 indicate relatively weak positive and negative responses where we have a five-point scale, and plus and minus 70 indicate positive and negative responses where the scale does not stretch to five points. More complex numerical assignments could be devised, taking into account the spread of answers to each individual question, and might be preferable on purely statistical grounds—though they would need to take account of the different spread of answers to the same question in our three different samples,—but the simple assignments we have chosen are statistically adequate, easy to understand, and easy to justify without appeal to abstruse statistical argument.

Having made these numerical assignments, we then reversed the sign (interchanging positive and negative responses) for some questions in order to get all the indicators associated with one of the thirteen micro-principles to point, arithmetically, in the same logical direction. For example, commitment to the right to speak out was indicated by disagreement (not agreement) with the proposition 'Free speech is just not worth it if it means we have to put up with the danger to society from extremist views'.

Where randomization was used to present a proposition, in two opposing forms, to randomly selected half samples—so that agreement with one form was (more or less roughly) equivalent to disagreement with the other—the numerical values assigned to answers were reversed in sign for one random half sample but not the other. For example, when we asked randomly selected half samples whether 'We [have gone too far/have not gone far enough] in pushing equal rights in this country', we take disagreement with the first proposition as equivalent to agreement with the second. This approach not only simplifies the statistical computations but also makes the tables easier to read, because all indicators of any one micro-principle now run in the same logical direction.

Ideally each micro-principle should be measured by a range of indicators which, in the original questionnaire, pointed in different directions—or were individually based upon two opposite wordings put to random half samples —in order to avoid positivity-bias. That was not always practical, although we have come much nearer to achieving this goal than is usual in survey research.

INTERNAL COHERENCE

In order to assess the internal coherence of each micro-principle we apply correlation, factor, and reliability analyses. The correlation analysis checks that all the indicators of a micro-principle are positively intercorrelated. In terms of logic and meaning they appear, to us, to point in the same direction once they have been numerically coded as described in the previous section. So we expect people who tend towards high positive scores on one indicator to have relatively high scores on all other indicators of the same micro-principle. But occasionally the pattern of public opinion contradicts our expectations and this, of course, deserves particular attention.

The factor analysis tells us, first of all, whether the indicators of a particular micro-principle seem to reflect just one, or more than one, underlying factor: whether, for example, there is a strong statistical case for subdividing our 'attitudes-to-economic-equality' micro-principle into attitudes towards two different aspects of economic equality. Secondly, it tells us how much of the variation associated with these indicators can be attributed to, or 'explained by', the underlying factor or factors. The usual criterion for deciding how many factors underlie a set of indicators is known as *Kaiser's criterion*. That criterion recognizes any factor that explains as much as a single indicator which, pathologically, happens to be totally uncorrelated with any of the other indicators. We regard that as an excessively weak criterion. In particular, we prefer to recognize more than one factor only when the second and subsequent factors explain more than 1.5 times that minimal amount. (Such factors are said to have *eigenvalues* that exceed 1.5.) None the less we shall draw attention to any second factors that meet Kaiser's weaker criterion but not our stronger one.

Finally we compute a summary measure of each micro-principle by averaging the values of the indicators associated with it. We assess the reliability of this overall measure using *Cronbach's alpha* which can be interpreted as the squared correlation between this summary measure based upon the available questions in our survey, and a more comprehensive measure based upon averaging answers over all possible questions relevant to the same principle in an infinitely long interview. Crudely stated, *alpha* is thus the squared correlation between our measure of a micro-principle and a perfect measure of that same micro-principle.

If the indicators all have the same variance as each other, then one formula for *alpha* is:

$$alpha = 1 - \{[1 - r]/[1 + (k - 1)r]\}$$

where there are k indicators, with an average intercorrelation of r.

From this formula it is obvious that *alpha* approaches an upper limit of 1.0 either when the average intercorrelation (r) between the indicators is very high (approaching 1.0)—making the numerator $[1 - r]$ approximate zero—or when the number of indicators (k) is high—making the denominator $[1 + (k - 1)r]$ very large. The basic idea of reliability analysis is that of cancelling random errors. Even though several indicators of a micro-principle may be individually corrupted and obscured by random answers to half-understood or ill-considered questions, averaging out across the different indicators cancels out the randomness and allows the meaning to emerge. The average indicator will be more reliable if the randomness in the original indicators is small (i.e. r is high) or—and this is the useful point—if the number of indicators that are averaged together (i.e. k) is large.

However, reliability analysis assumes that, apart from randomly inaccurate answers, the different indicators really do measure the same micro-principle.

There is no point in averaging out the answers to questions that measure fundamentally different things. So there is an inevitable tension between the wish to put together a large number of indicators, thereby improving the accuracy of measurement, and the need to keep truly different things separate. Hence, in part, our grouping of fifty-one questions into thirteen micro-principles giving an average of four indicators per principle. Fewer micro-principles would have given more indicators per principle but would have involved averaging-out answers to questions that seemed only distantly related to each other. Even so, the *alpha* coefficients will suggest that some of our summary measures of micro-principles are based upon rather disparate sets of indicators.

We have not chosen to maximize the reliability coefficients, *alpha*. The *alphas* presented here could have been improved, though usually only slightly, in two ways. First, by scaling each indicator to have equal variance before averaging across indicators. Our standard scaling of indicator values onto a +/–100 scale goes most of the way towards achieving this in a simple way, however. Second, the *alphas* could have been increased by eliminating from each micro-principle any indicator which was relatively uncorrelated with other indicators of the same micro-principle. We have chosen not to maximize the *alphas* in these ways for two reasons. The reliability gains that could be achieved in practice were usually very marginal. More important, we wished to use the same definitions of micro-principles in each of our three different samples—the British public, the politicians, and the Scottish public. Adjusting definitions by standardizing variances, or dropping particular indicators, would have changed the definitions and even the meanings of the micro-principles affected, and would have changed those meanings in different ways in each of the three different samples, thereby destroying comparability. So both for simplicity and uniformity we have accepted slightly, but only slightly, less optimal reliabilities than our data would permit.

MICRO-PRINCIPLES

We begin by assessing the internal coherence of each of the thirteen micro-principles discussed in Chapters 2 and 3. After that we shall go on to investigate their external coherence, or dimensionality.

Respect for Authority

Five of our micro-principles related to different aspects of authority: respect for authority, limited government, the right to know, the right to freedom of

TABLE 4.1. *Respect for authority*

	Politicians	British public	(Scottish public)

Importance of
  respect for authority
  law and order
  defence
Strong government (v. chaos)			

% explained by factor(s)	58% F1	52% F1	(49% F1)
Alpha	0.73	0.62	(0.58)

Notes: '58% F1' means that the first factor explained 58% of the variation in the indicators.
   The lack of an F2 or F3, etc., means that not more than one factor met our criterion for
recognizing a factor (i.e. had an eigenvalue exceeding 1.5).
   But note that we always report the first factor, however little variation it explains.
   Alpha is Cronbach's *alpha*, as defined in the text.

speech, and the right to protest and rebellion. Within each of these micro-principles all indicators were positively intercorrelated and factor analysis, even by Kaiser's weak criterion, recognized only one underlying factor behind each micro-principle.

Our measures of respect for authority proved to be the most internally coherent. A single factor explained over half the variation in its four indicators, and the reliability coefficient *alpha* was 0.73 amongst politicians and 0.62 amongst the public. Both public and politicians clearly saw interconnections between the importance of 'respect for authority', 'strengthening law and order', or 'maintaining strong defence forces' and the idea that 'the only alternative to strong government is disorder and chaos' (Table 4.1).

Limited Government

The distinction between politicians and the public was particularly marked on attitudes to limited government, however, as was the distinction between the Scots and others. Amongst politicians *alpha* was 0.53, while amongst the British public it was only 0.32, and amongst Scots only a very weak 0.19. Clearly, politicians found it easier to make the interconnections amongst attitudes to 'checks and balances', 'external control of the police', the 'right to silence', and 'the rights of suspects', and Scots found it more difficult. We have the sense that our measures triangulated the elusive concept of limited government without getting as close as we would have wished (Table 4.2).

TABLE 4.2. *Limited government and due process*

	Politicians	British public	(Scottish public)
Support checks and balance external control of police right to silence suspects' rights			
% explained by factor(s)	43% F1	33% F1	(30% F1)
Alpha	0.53	0.32	(0.19)

TABLE 4.3. *The right to know*

	Politicians	British public	(Scottish public)
Support, with or without reservations right to know about self right to know about government plans right to know about factory			
% explained by factor(s)	46% F1	42% F1	(41% F1)
Alpha	0.37	0.29	(0.25)

The Right to Know

Our measure of the right to know was also less reliable than we would have wished. The underlying factor explained less than half the variation in the indicators and the *alpha* coefficients were only 0.37 amongst politicians and a mere 0.29 amongst the public. There was near universal support for the right to know principle and indicators failed to discriminate well between those who were more committed to a general, topic free, right to know and those who were less committed—though the views of politicians were slightly more internally coherent than those of the public (Table 4.3).

The Right to Freedom of Speech

Similarly with our measure of the right to freedom of speech. The underlying factor explained only two-fifths of the total variation in the indicators and the *alpha* coefficient was a mere 0.27 amongst both politicians and the public. One reason for that was the near universal support for the importance

TABLE 4.4. *The right to freedom of speech*

	Politicians	British public	(Scottish public)
Importance of free speech			
Disagree that free speech not worth it			
Not ban extreme political organizations			
% explained by factor(s)	42% F1	41% F1	(40% F1)
Alpha	0.27	0.27	(0.25)

TABLE 4.5. *Rights to protest and rebel*

	Politicians	British public	(Scottish public)
Right to demonstrate			
Right to strike			
Not obey unjust law			
% explained by factor(s)	50% F1	43% F1	(45% F1)
Alpha	0.44	0.28	(0.31)

of 'free speech for all'. When support is universal, an indicator fails to discriminate between those who are more committed to a principle and those who are less committed. Correlation, factor, and reliability analyses inevitably focus attention upon divisive principles rather than those which are universally accepted (Table 4.4).

Rights of Protest and Rebellion

As on attitudes to limited government, there was a marked distinction between politicians and the public on rights of protest and rebellion. Amongst politicians the *alpha* coefficient was 0.44 but amongst the public only 0.28. Politicians were somewhat more able than the public to see the interconnections amongst attitudes to demonstrations, strikes, and disobeying unjust laws (Table 4.5).

If we look back across the whole range of micro-principles associated with different aspects of authority, it is evident that, with the exception of attitudes to free speech, where politicians and the public both showed a low level of internal coherence, the answers given by politicians were nearly always more internally coherent than those of the public. And, with the

TABLE 4.6. *Respect for traditional values*

	Politicians	British public	(Scottish public)
Importance of traditional ideas of right and wrong following God's will			
% explained by factor(s)	71% F1	71% F1	(70% F1)
Alpha	0.54	0.55	(0.52)

interesting exception of attitudes to rights of protest and rebellion, the answers given by our additional Scottish sample were always a little less internally coherent than those of the British public at large.

Conformity to Traditional Values

Although we had only two indicators of respect for traditional values, they were sufficiently highly correlated to give reliability coefficients of 0.54 amongst politicians, and 0.55 amongst the public. Here the public had no more difficulty than politicians in seeing the interconnections (Table 4.6).

Tolerance

Our micro-principle of tolerance was more complex, however. The seven indicators were positively intercorrelated and, by our criteria, revealed only one underlying factor. However, by Kaiser's criterion there was just, but only just, evidence of two underlying factors. The second factor scraped past Kaiser's criterion with eigenvalues of 1.05 amongst politicians and 1.07 amongst the public. A varimax-rotated two-factor analysis revealed that the same pair of factors emerged amongst both politicians and people. The first factor—which might be described as 'tolerance of immorality'—focused upon (disagreement with) four indicators:

1. what is 'morally wrong' should be 'illegal';
2. 'we should not tolerate people who are morally wrong';
3. 'it is very important to protect children and young people from wild and immoral ideals';
4. 'the government has a responsibility to for 'upholding morality';

and the second—which might be described as 'tolerance of diversity'—focused upon two:

TABLE 4.7.   *Tolerance*

	Politicians	British public	(Scottish public)
Different beliefs and lifestyles important			
Not protect children from immoral ideas			
Tolerate morally wrong			
Morals should not equal laws			
Not enforce community standards			
No government responsibility to uphold morality			
Religious freedom even for weird			
% explained by factor(s)	32% F1	26% F1	(26% F1)
Alpha	0.63	0.50	(0.50)

1. 'religious freedom should apply to all religious groups, even those that the majority regard as strange, fanatical, or weird';
2. it is important to tolerate 'different beliefs and lifestyles'.

While this distinction does have some plausibility, the eigenvalues of the second factor were only very slightly greater than 1.0, making the statistical case for distinguishing between varieties of tolerance rather weak.

Averaging over all seven indicators of tolerance produced reliability coefficients of 0.63 amongst politicians and not a great deal less, 0.50, amongst the public (Table 4.7).

Equal Rights

Our four indicators of equal rights were strongly intercorrelated, revealed only one underlying factor, and produced high *alphas* of 0.76 amongst politicians and 0.64 amongst the public. Again, the public found relatively little difficulty in seeing the interconnections here (Table 4.8).

Economic Equality

Although the *alpha* coefficients for economic equality were high at 0.70 amongst politicians and 0.64 amongst the public, that partly reflected the fact that we used as many as seven indicators of attitudes towards economic equality. All the indicators correlated positively, but factor analyses revealed two factors according to Kaiser's criterion (though not ours) amongst both politicians and public. The eigenvalues were 1.20 (amongst politicians), and 1.11 (amongst the public) respectively.

TABLE 4.8. *Equal rights*

	Politicians	British public	(Scottish public)
Importance of			
ethnic protection			
gender equality			
homosexual equality			
Equal rights not gone far enough			
% explained by factor(s)	60% F1	49% F1	(49% F1)
Alpha	0.76	0.64	(0.61)

Amongst both politicians and the public the same two factors emerged. The first focused upon government responsibilities for ensuring:

• a more even distribution of wealth
• a decent standard of living for everyone
• a job for everyone that wants one;

and the second upon government responsibilities for ensuring:

• good education for everyone
• good medical care for everyone.

At first sight it might seem plausible to call these an 'equality-of-wealth' factor, and an 'equality-of-opportunity' factor. Unfortunately, one of the indicators included in our set of seven explicitly asked whether government has a responsibility for ensuring 'equal opportunities for everyone', and it loaded more heavily onto the first factor ('equality of wealth') than the second (tentatively described as an 'equality-of-opportunity' factor). This happened in all three samples—politicians, British public, and Scots, and particularly so amongst the public, whether in Britain as a whole or in Scotland—which undermines the notion that the public can clearly distinguish between 'equality of wealth' and 'equality of opportunity'—a conclusion reinforced by the relatively small eigenvalues for the second factor amongst the public in Britain as a whole (1.11) and amongst the Scots (1.09). To a very large extent, therefore, the public regard 'equality of wealth' and 'equality of opportunity' as merely two facets of a general concept of equality which they do not find easy to separate, despite the sophistry of party propaganda.

It would be more plausible to suggest a distinction between 'equality of wealth' (as a label for the first factor) and 'equality of welfare' (as a label

TABLE 4.9. *Economic equality*

	Politicians	British public	(Scottish public)
Government has responsibility for			
equal wealth			
equal opportunities			
living standards			
jobs			
housing			
education			
health care			
% explained by factor(s)	39% F1	33% F1	(32% F1)
Alpha	0.70	0.64	(0.59)

TABLE 4.10. *Self-reliance*

	Politicians	British public	(Scottish public)
Importance of			
self-reliance			
individual achievements			
For individual goals (v. common goals)			
Not too much emphasis on			
individual interests			
Too much emphasis on rights			
(v. duties)			
% explained by factor(s)	40% F1	27% F1	(28% F1)
Alpha	0.61	0.25	(0.21)

for the second factor), or between 'equality of market-based consumption' and 'equality of social provision', but the statistical basis for such a division is not very compelling (Table 4.9).

Self-Reliance

The indicators of self-reliance as shown in Table 4.10 were positively intercorrelated—though it is important to notice that, while the first four emphasize individual self-reliance, individual achievements, individual interests, and individual goals, the fifth is critical of rights and stresses the importance of duties by agreement with the proposition that 'In Britain today, there is too much emphasis on citizens' rights and not enough on citizens' duties'. Amongst politicians they reflected a single factor and produced a reasonably high *alpha* coefficient of 0.61. However, amongst the public the patterns of correlation were more complex: three factors met Kaiser's criterion (though none met ours) and the *alpha* coefficient was only 0.25. It is possible that the language of self-reliance proved too abstract for the public to grasp, or— a rather different explanation—that the public failed to make interconnections that were conventional (whether they were rational or not) amongst politicians (Table 4.10).

The factor analysis of attitudes amongst the public suggested that they could see a link:

1. between emphasizing the importance of self-reliance and individual achievements, and
2. between individual interests and individual goals, but that
3. they had difficulty combining self-reliance/individual achievement with individual interests/goals, and
4. they were also reluctant to combine either of these with an emphasis on the concept of 'citizens' duties',

thus producing three factors which we might label individual achievements, interests, and responsibilities. As we have noted, these factors only emerge when we apply the relatively weak Kaiser criterion and are therefore not statistically imperative, but the distinctions make some sense conceptually.

Politicians were more ready than the public to combine an emphasis on (or rejection of) individual achievements, interests, and responsibilities into a single factor. This also makes some conceptual sense, in so far as high evaluation of individual achievement and support for individuals' interests make up a coherent package of 'right-wing individualism', while a stress on individual responsibilities (rather than rights) might be called 'right-wing anti-individualism'. However, as we noted in Chapter 2, stress on individual duties above rights can also be given a left-wing interpretation. Perhaps in the late 1990s, as leading left-wing politicians such as Tony Blair put more stress on individual duties and responsibilities without accepting the primacy of individual interests over community interest, the conventional connections between these different concepts of self-reliance will be broken even amongst politicians.[2]

TABLE 4.11. *Caring*

	Politicians	British public	(Scottish public)
Importance of help for the disabled reducing unemployment taking care of the needy			
% explained by factor(s)	65% F1	58% F1	(53% F1)
Alpha	0.73	0.62	(0.54)

Caring

Our indicators of caring correlated positively, the factor analysis revealed a powerful single factor, and the *alpha* coefficients were high: 0.73 amongst politicians, and 0.62 amongst the public (Table 4.11).

Wealth Creation

Similarly, our indicators of wealth creation correlated positively, the factor analysis revealed a powerful single factor, and the *alpha* coefficients were high: 0.72 amongst politicians, and 0.65 amongst the public. It is difficult to find an entirely satisfactory name for this constellation of opinions, though they clearly do correlate relatively well with each other amongst both politicians and the public. The intercorrelation suggests a 'dash-for-growth' perspective that puts more priority on creating wealth (the importance of 'achieving economic growth') than on distributing it widely or fairly (the importance of 'cutting taxes'). It would be wrong to assume that respondents necessarily saw wealth creation and growth as a special benefit to themselves personally, and thus equate this micro-principle simply with selfishness, however. On balance, that may be true, but even caring left-wing politicians have sometimes become convinced that growth solves more problems than redistribution (Table 4.12).

Protection

The intercorrelations between indicators of protection were positive and the factor analysis revealed a single factor but the *alpha* coefficients were low at 0.25 amongst politicians and 0.31 amongst the public, no doubt partly because of the near universal feeling that government had a duty to protect

TABLE 4.12. *Wealth creation*

	Politicians	British public	(Scottish public)

Importance of
  holding down inflation
  cutting taxes
  achieving economic growth			

% explained by factor(s)	65% F1	61% F1	(62% F1)
Alpha	0.72	0.65	(0.67)

TABLE 4.13. *Protection*

	Politicians	British public	(Scottish public)

Government has duty to protect citizens
  against crime
  against business
  against pollution			

% explained by factor(s)	41% F1	43% F1	(45% F1)
Alpha	0.25	0.31	(0.38)

citizens against crime and pollution, but also to some extent because protection against crime, pollution, and big-business was a rather heterogeneous combination, and further because there were only three indicators available. None the less, it is worth noting that, most unusually, the internal coherence was highest amongst the Scots and lowest amongst politicians (Table 4.13).

MACRO-DIMENSIONS OF PRINCIPLE

We can usefully calculate each respondent's score on each micro-principle by averaging their scores on the indicators of that micro-principle; so that scores range from a minimum of minus 100 where, for example, a respondent disagreed strongly with every indicator of the principle up to plus 100 where a respondent agreed strongly with every indicator. Then we can subject the thirteen micro-principles themselves to a factor analysis using our criterion of a minimum eigenvalue of 1.5.

Two, and Only Two, Macro-Dimensions of Principle

The factor analysis reveals two macro-dimensions of principle which together explain 52 per cent of the variation in micro-principles amongst
politicians, and 40 per cent amongst the public. The patterns of factor loadings
are remarkably similar amongst people and politicians. The usual varimax-
rotation procedure produces a first factor focused upon (in order of their
closeness to the factor):

- respect for authority
- conformity to traditional values
- tolerance
- wealth creation
- limited government
- the right to freedom of speech

and a second focused upon:

- economic equality
- caring
- equal rights
- protection
- the right to know

while both factors reflect the other two micro-principles, self-reliance and
rights of protest and rebellion.

Since the early studies by Eysenck in the 1950s,[3] it has been repeatedly
suggested that British political attitudes fall along two dimensions, an 'economic left/right' dimension and a 'libertarian/authoritarian' dimension—
that is, confusingly, sometimes also described as 'left/right'. Heath, Jowell,
and Curtice suggested something similar in their 1983[4] and 1987[5] election
studies. In the limited sense that we also detect two, and only two, general
dimensions underlying British political culture, our findings were broadly
consistent with these earlier insights.

But, of course, the details matter. In their earlier text, Heath and his associates used public attitudes to a single question about the nationalization/
privatization of industry to define 'the main east–west axis representing class
values', and another about attitudes to nuclear disarmament to define a 'north–
south [axis] representing liberal values'. Two questions (certainly *these* two
questions) are insufficient to carry the weight of such concepts as an 'axis
representing class values' and an 'axis representing liberal values'.

In their later text, Heath and his colleagues used a dozen questions, some oriented to general principle, others to current issues, to define a 'left-right scale' and a 'liberal–authoritarian scale' by means of factor analysis. Their 'left–right scale' was a mix of socialism and egalitarianism—based on questions about nationalization, redistribution, and cash for the NHS; by contrast, their 'liberal–authoritarian scale' was based on questions about the death penalty, sex on film, and abortion under the NHS, but also on questions about equal opportunities for blacks, Asians, and women.

Our own survey and factor analysis grouped equal rights with other aspects of equality, rather than with principles of liberty and authority, which seemed more logical, though we recognized some hints of logical ambiguity about that particular micro-principle.

We shall deal with social influences upon principle in a later chapter, but we should note at this point that the social pattern of support for the principles defined by our factor analysis is *not* the same as that found by Heath and his associates for theirs. Our two factors are *not* equivalent, therefore, to just any other set of two factors supposedly underlying public opinion in Britain. The details are important.

Our two general dimensions are best described as dimensions of:

1. *liberty* (versus authority and conformity)
2. *equality* (versus a hard and uncaring acceptance of inequality).

It is important to stress that we found only two, not three or more, general macro-dimensions of principle.[6] While a third factor would just meet Kaiser's weak criterion, its eigenvalue would be only 1.19 in the British public sample, 1.16 in the Scottish sample, and a mere 1.08 in the politicians' sample and would increase the percentage of variation explained by only 8 or 9 per cent. A. H. Halsey asserts 'that Liberty, Equality and Fraternity are the three fundamental values in terms of which societies are to be judged . . . [and] simultaneous maximizing of them is not possible',[7] but we really did not uncover *three* such fundamental dimensions of public opinion. Even if we used Kaiser's weak criterion and accepted a three-factor solution, it would not resolve into factors that could be labelled 'liberty', 'equality', and 'fraternity'. It would be relatively unstable and variable across our three samples but would tend to divide authority, traditional values, and wealth creation combined with caring, on the one hand, from intolerance, and opposition to freedom of speech and equal rights, on the other—that is, it would divide attitudes towards liberty into dimensions of authority and conformity. But, as we have said, the statistical imperative is very weak and the three-factor solution is more interesting for what it is not than for what it is. Indeed, it is possible that fraternity really is not a 'fundamental value', as

A. H. Halsey supposed, but an amalgam of liberty and equality that combines the tolerance aspect of liberty with the caring aspect of equality. Or perhaps it is just a rhetorical device prompted by a subconscious need to have three elements, a trinity, in a good slogan.

At the same time, we need to stress that there were two general dimensions, not one, especially amongst the public though less obviously amongst politicians. Members of the public who supported the principle of equality were *not* much more or less likely to support the principle of liberty: the two dimensions were fairly independent (technically, indeed, they must be exactly independent if we use an orthogonal factor-analysis procedure such as varimax).

Cross-Dimension Micro-Principles

This macro-factor analysis separates most—but not all—of our micro-principles fairly unambiguously into those associated with the dimension of liberty and those associated with the dimension of equality. Perhaps the more interesting of the two ambiguously classified micro-principles is support for rights of protest and rebellion. That micro-principle is clearly tied to both liberty and equality. For the public it is slightly more closely tied to the macro-principle of equality, but for politicians it is more closely tied to the macro-principle of liberty. Rights of protest and rebellion are, of course, a matter of self-interest for ordinary citizens, but a matter of altruistic concession for power-holders. Citizens assert their right to protest, while governments and politicians concede it. Public and politicians look at protest from opposite perspectives (Table 4.14).

The Correlation between Liberty and Equality amongst Politicians and the Public

At the start of this chapter we speculated that the structure of politicians' attitudes might be simpler and more powerful—in short more clearly ideological —than that of the people. It was clearly more powerful: the two-dimensional structure explained 52 per cent of the variation in politicians' attitudes to principles, but only 40 per cent of the variation in the public's.[8]

But is it a more simple pattern as well as a more powerful one? Again the answer is 'yes'. Amongst the public, two dimensions of almost equal power explained 22 per cent and 18 per cent of the variation respectively. Of course, this refers to the top two orthogonal dimensions which were extracted initially and not to the two dimensions subsequently produced by the

TABLE 4.14. *Dimensions of principle*

	Politicians		British public (Scottish public)	
	F1	F2	F1	F2
	(% variation explained by factors before rotation)			
	38%	+14%	22% (22%)	+18% (+16%)
	Liberty	Equality	Liberty	Equality
	(Factor loadings (×100) after varimax rotation)			
Micro-principles tied more to liberty				
Respect for authority	−85	.	−78 (−78)	. (.)
Respect for traditional values	−79	.	−72 (−72)	. (.)
Wealth creation	−76	.	−67 (−68)	. (.)
Tolerance	+73	.	+67 (+65)	. (.)
Limited government	+62	.	. (.)	. (.)
Right to free speech	.	.	. (.)	. (.)
Micro-principles tied to both liberty and equality				
Rights of protest and rebellion	+52	+49	. (.)	+54 (+54)
Self-reliance	−51	−52	. (.)	. (.)
Micro-principles tied more to equality				
Economic equality	.	+77	. (.)	+73 (+70)
Caring	.	+76	. (.)	+68 (+59)
Equal rights	.	+70	. (.)	+67 (+68)
Protection	.	+59	. (.)	. (.)
Right to know	.	.	. (.)	. (.)

Notes: Factor loadings less than 0.45 have been replaced by full points.

Within each factor, micro-principles have been listed in descending order of their loadings on the factor within the politicians' sample; but note that, within the British public sample, tolerance loaded very slightly more than wealth creation on the liberty factor.

varimax rotation; so the 22 per cent should not be identified with liberty nor the 18 per cent with equality. But it remains true that the macro-structure of the public's principles was most certainly two dimensional and that any attempt to represent it by a single dimension would involve massive distortion and misrepresentation.

Not so with politicians, however. Amongst politicians, the first dimension explained almost three times as much as the second: 38 per cent as against 14 per cent. Again we need to repeat—with perhaps greater emphasis—that this refers to the factors extracted initially, not to the varimax rotations; so this very powerful 'first dimension' was not liberty, and the relatively weak 'second dimension' was not equality. But it remains true that the structure of politicians' principles could be represented by a single composite dimension with far less distortion or misrepresentation than could the structure of the public's principles. For politicians, that single powerful dimension would be a left–right dimension that incorporated elements both of liberty and of equality. Amongst politicians, unlike the public, only a small minority combined a love of equality with above-average respect for authority.

Another way of detecting this distinction between the structures of the public's and the politicians' principles is to use an oblique factor analysis such as the SPSS OBLIMIN routine. Compared to the usual orthogonal varimax method of factor analysis, oblique factor analyses relate each microprinciple more closely to one, and only one, general dimension. They reduce the ambiguity involved in linking particular micro-principles to general dimensions of principle (technically they 'simplify the factor pattern matrix'), but, in so doing, they produce general factors which may themselves be correlated. Amongst politicians, an oblique factor analysis produced two factors—liberty and equality—which correlated at 0.29, confirming the fairly strong tendency amongst politicians either to support both liberty and equality, or to oppose both. Amongst the British public, by contrast, an oblique factor analysis again produced two factors—liberty and equality—which were also positively correlated, but at only 0.11 (and at only 0.09 in Scotland). Thus, amongst the public, the positive link between liberty and equality was much weaker than amongst politicians, and these two general dimensions come close to being independent of each other.

We can reach the same finding without using anything more advanced than a correlation coefficient. Suppose we take three of the four microprinciples most closely tied to the first dimension (liberty)—respect for authority, traditional values, and tolerance[9]—reverse the signs of the first two to make all three point in the same (pro-liberty) direction, and then average each respondent's score on all three to get a simple measure of their commitment to liberty. Similarly, we can take the three micro-principles most closely tied to the second dimension (equality)—economic equality, caring, and equal rights—and average each respondent's score on these three to give a simple measure of their commitment to equality. In this very simple way we can confirm the conclusions that emerged from our oblique factor analysis, since these simple measures of liberty and equality—which we shall use extensively in later chapters—correlate at 0.32 amongst politicians, but only at a negligible 0.02 amongst the British public (and a slightly negative but also negligible −0.05 in Scotland).

David Held has drawn attention to 'The New Polarization of Democratic Ideals'[10] between 'Legal Democracy' centred on 'maintaining liberty',[11] and 'Participatory Democracy' centred on 'an equal right to self-development', 'a concern for collective problems', and 'a redistribution of material resources'.[12] At the rhetorical level that may be so, but, despite all the rhetoric of right-wing politicians, neither public nor politicians saw liberty and equality as opposing concepts, and politicians saw them as positively related.[13] Our findings are consistent with those of Herbert McClosky and Alida Brill, who found a positive correlation, larger amongst élites than amongst the mass public, between their scales of support for 'civil liberties' and those for 'economic liberalism',[14] though their definition of economic liberalism was much narrower than our equality, while their concept of civil liberties included some aspects of our equality. They also found a strong correlation, very much stronger amongst their élites than their mass public sample, between their civil liberties scale and a 'general equality' scale based upon agreement with propositions about non-specific equality—'all people are equally worthy and deserve equal treatment', 'make everyone as equal as possible', etc.[15]

Giovanni Sartori claims that 'the relationship between equality and freedom is a love–hate relationship . . . equality can either be the best complement of freedom or its worst enemy',[16] though elsewhere he refers to 'the liberty–equality dyad'.[17] Our findings suggest that British politicians tended to see liberty and equality as a 'dyad', while to the public they were locked in a more ambiguous 'love–hate relationship' but were certainly not exclusive alternatives (Table 4.15).

A table of correlations between the three components of these measures of liberty and equality provides even more insight. It shows there was a strong tendency for politicians who scored low on respect for authority, traditional values, or intolerance to score high on economic equality or equal rights; but there was some tendency for politicians who were more committed to traditional values to be the very ones who were more committed to caring

TABLE 4.15. *Correlations between selected micro-principles*

	Politicians			British public (Scottish public)		
	Anti-authority (r × 100)	Anti-traditional values (r × 100)	Tolerance (r × 100)	Anti-authority (r × 100)	Anti-traditional values (r × 100)	Tolerance (r × 100)
Economic equality	+39	+19	+14	. (.)	. (.)	. (−14)
Caring	.	−11	.	−18 (−25)	−30 (−34)	. (−12)
Equal rights	+43	+30	+41	+13 (−10)	. (.)	+31 (+28)

Note: Correlations less than 0.10 have been replaced by full points.

—a link that owed something to religiosity, and that reduced the correlation between liberty and equality. Amongst the public this pattern was even more striking.

So what we have found here is that some aspects of equality—namely, those associated with the micro-principle of caring—had a special appeal to those who supported authority while others had a special appeal to those who opposed authority. Whether the macro-principles of liberty and equality remained uncorrelated depended upon the relative power of these opposing appeals. Amongst the public they almost cancelled each other out, while amongst politicians the aspects of equality that appealed to those who opposed authority outweighed the aspects of equality that appealed to those who supported authority.

Comparative Scores of Politicians and the Public on Principles

We can usefully calculate the average score of the public and of politicians on each macro- and micro-principle. Recall that scores can range from a minimum of minus 100 where, for example, a respondent disagrees strongly with every indicator of the principle up to plus 100 where a respondent agrees strongly with every indicator. Politicians had an average liberty score of minus 12 and the public an average of minus 25. So on that macro-principle, politicians were 13 points (on a 200-point scale) more committed to liberty than the public. Both the public and politicians had an average equality score of 55. So on that macro-principle, there was no difference between politicians and the public. In sharp contrast to the politicians, what distinguished Scots from the British public was a greater concern not for liberty, but for equality: they scored exactly the same as the British public on liberty, but 6 points higher on equality. None the less, it is worth noting that the difference between politicians and the public on liberty was about twice as great as the difference between the Scots and others on equality.

Politicians differed by at least 10 points from the public on all of the first-dimension (liberty) principles, but on none of the others, neither the second-dimension (equality) principles nor the two cross-dimension principles of self-reliance and the right to protest. Compared to the public, politicians were substantially more committed to liberty but neither more nor less committed to equality. Scots never differed by as much as 10 points from the British public on any principle, though they differed most (by 7 points) on economic equality (Table 4.16).

TABLE 4.16. *Macro- and micro-principles, average scores*

	Politicians (scores)	British public (scores)	(Scottish public) (scores)
Liberty	−12	−25	(−25)
Equality	55	55	(61)
Respect for authority	27	39	(39)
Respect for traditional values	26	37	(39)
Wealth creation	34	53	(58)
Tolerance	18	3	(2)
Limited government	14	1	(1)
Right to speak out	53	35	(34)
Right to protest and rebel	25	31	(35)
Self-reliance	4	13	(9)
Economic equality	45	46	(53)
Caring	77	79	(84)
Equal rights	44	40	(45)
Protection	54	53	(52)
Right to know	89	87	(90)

Notes: Liberty = average of authority, traditional values, and tolerance, with the signs of the first two reversed.

Equality = average of economic equality, caring, and equal rights.

MICRO-SYMPATHIES

The same approach can be applied to sympathies and prejudices as to principles: we shall look first at the internal coherence of each of the micro-sympathies, and then at their external coherence.

Sympathies for Activists and Minorities

Sympathies or antipathies towards the seven groups we have labelled activists correlated positively and produced high *alphas* of 0.86 and 0.77 amongst politicians and the public respectively. Amongst politicians only one factor emerged, but amongst the public a second factor just squeezed past Kaiser's criterion (but not ours) with an eigenvalue of 1.09. Varimax rotation suggested one factor focused upon black activists, Muslim activists, and communists; and a second factor focused upon environmental campaigners and animal-rights activists. While that distinction has an immediate plausibility —attitudes towards traditional minority racial or ideological movements, on

TABLE 4.17. *Sympathies for activists and minorities*

	Politicians	British public	(Scottish public)
Gays and lesbians			
Greenpeace			
Animal-rights activists			
Communists			
Feminists			
Muslim activists			
Black activists			
% explained by factor(s)	54% F1	42% F1	(42% F1)
Alpha	0.86	0.77	(0.76)

the one hand, and towards new-politics or 'post-materialist' groups, on the other—the statistical basis for it is slight since the eigenvalue was so low, and there is little statistical necessity to distinguish different dimensions of sympathy for activists (Table 4.17).

Sympathies for Militants

While some activist groups have used militant tactics to make their claims known, the four groups we have classified as militants form a balanced set of two opposed pairs, and all of them have a militant ideology and a history of using militant, violent, or terrorist tactics to make their demands known. Given that they do comprise two pairs of opposed groups, it is all the more surprising that antipathies towards these four different groups of militants were also positively intercorrelated. This means, for example, that antipathy towards IRA sympathizers and towards Protestant terrorist sympathizers was not bipolar: those who showed the most intense dislike towards the one also tended to dislike the other intensely. Amongst the public and politicians alike, dislike of terrorists in general far outweighed the differences in their attitudes towards the particular political causes espoused by particular terrorists. Factor analysis revealed only one factor underlying antipathy towards all four kinds of militant, and averaging across attitudes to all four produced *alpha* coefficients of 0.73 amongst politicians and 0.72 amongst the public (Table 4.18).

Sympathy for the Socially Disadvantaged

Grouping the poor, immigrants, and women together as objects of social prejudice is—in one sense—very crude indeed: they are a very heterogeneous

TABLE 4.18. *Sympathies for militants*

	Politicians	British public	(Scottish public)
NF supporters			
Militant Tendency supporters			
IRA sympathizers			
Protestant terrorist sympathizers			
% explained by factor(s)	56% F1	55% F1	(52% F1)
Alpha	0.73	0.72	(0.69)

TABLE 4.19. *Sympathy for the socially disadvantaged*

	Politicians	British public	(Scottish public)
Disagree with			
men better at senior jobs			
immigrants should try harder			
poor don't try hard			
% explained by factor(s)	52% F1	41% F1	(41% F1)
Alpha	0.54	0.28	(0.25)

set of citizens. But it makes sense if we are trying to distil an essence of social prejudice that is not highly dependent upon particular objects of social prejudice. Sympathy for these three groups was positively correlated, and averaging all three produced a moderately high *alpha* of 0.54 amongst politicians, though a much lower one of 0.28 amongst the public. Politicians, at least, had a general sense of social sympathy or prejudice that transcended particular objects of prejudice (Table 4.19).

Confidence in the Established Political System

Our four indicators of confidence in the established political system correlated positively amongst politicians. But amongst the public, confidence in 'the majority' (themselves perhaps) was negatively correlated, if only very slightly, with confidence in 'politicians'. Factor analysis revealed only one factor amongst politicians. It suggested a second factor on Kaiser's criterion (not ours) amongst the public, but since this second factor had an eigenvalue of only 1.03 we shall ignore it. Averaging across the four indicators produced fairly weak *alphas* of 0.42 amongst politicians and 0.37 amongst the public (Table 4.20).

TABLE 4.20. *Confidence in the political system*

	Politicians	British public	(Scottish public)
Back-bench MPs protect rights			
Local councils protect rights			
Majority not often wrong			
Trust most politicians			
% explained by factor(s)	42% F1	40% F1	(41% F1)
Alpha	0.42	0.37	(0.38)

TABLE 4.21. *Confidence in civil institutions*

	Politicians	British public	(Scottish public)
Citizens' rights protected by			
tabloids			
broadsheets			
television			
trade unions			
churches			
% explained by factor(s)	39% F1	39% F1	(39% F1)
Alpha	0.58	0.61	(0.59)

Confidence in Civil Institutions

Indicators of confidence in the institutions of civil society included three questions about the mass media, and two about trade unions or churches. Not surprisingly, factor analysis on Kaiser's criterion (but not ours) divided these five indicators into the media questions versus the rest, but our interest lay in civil society more generally, not just in the media. All five indicators were positively correlated, and averaging across them produced *alpha* co- efficients of 0.58 and 0.61 amongst politicians and the public respectively (Table 4.21).

Confidence in the Judicial System

Our four indicators of confidence in the judicial system correlated positively, factor analysis revealed only one factor, and averaging produced high *alphas* of 0.77 amongst politicians and 0.69 amongst the public (Table 4.22).

Coherence

TABLE 4.22. *Confidence in the judicial system*

	Politicians	British public	(Scottish public)
British courts protect rights			
Judges fair			
Police fair			
Police/security services protect rights			
% explained by factor(s)	62% F1	54% F1	(52% F1)
Alpha	0.77	0.69	(0.66)

TABLE 4.23. *Confidence in the enforcers of rights*

	Politicians	British public	(Scottish public)
Government regulation is not harmful			
Trust experts			
Social workers do not have too much power			
Social workers are fair			
EOC/CRE protect rights			
European courts protect rights			
% explained by factor(s)	39% F1	31% F1	(29% F1)
Alpha	0.65	0.52	(0.46)

Confidence in the Enforcers of Rights

Our six indicators of confidence in the rights industry correlated positively and produced *alphas* of 0.65 and 0.52 amongst politicians and public respectively. However, factor analysis according to Kaiser's criterion (but not ours) revealed second factors with eigenvalues of 1.05 and 1.17 amongst politicians and public respectively. While these are statistically small enough to ignore, it is worth noting that the same two factors emerged amongst both politicians and public. The first focused upon European courts and the Equal Opportunities Commission/Commission for Racial Equality; the second upon the power of social workers and the harmfulness of government regulation. They distinguish, therefore, between judicial and administrative approaches to the implementation or enforcement of civil rights, and, of course, between rights-enforcement agencies that are clearly institutionalized and those that are not. However, as with the other minor distinctions we have identified, although plausible they are not statistically imperative (Table 4.23).

MACRO-DIMENSIONS OF SYMPATHY

Factor analysis of our seven types of micro-sympathy revealed two factors which explained 61 per cent of the variation amongst politicians and 55 per cent amongst the public. After varimax rotation the first dimension grouped together social prejudice with sympathy for activists and militants; while the second grouped together confidence in the established political system and in civil institutions. The first dimension might therefore be labelled 'sympathy towards claimants' and the second 'confidence in political and civil institutions' (Table 4.24).

Amongst politicians, confidence in the rights industry (the 'enforcers of rights') correlated more with the claimants' dimension than with the institutions' dimension. However, it was the other way round amongst the public, where confidence in the rights industry correlated more with the institutions' dimension. So, while politicians seemed to regard the rights industry as a set of agencies that put pressure on our political system, the public seemed to regard it as part of the political system itself. Both perspectives have some justification, and seem particularly appropriate to political leaders and ordinary citizens respectively.

Comparative Scores of Politicians and the Public on Sympathies

We calculated average scores on sympathies and confidence in the same way as we calculated average scores on micro-principles. Thus, a respondent would get a sympathy score of minus 100 if they strongly agreed with every adverse statement (or gave marks of zero out of ten for how much they liked each of the groups involved); and plus 100 if they strongly disagreed with every adverse statement (or gave marks of ten out of ten for how much they liked each of the groups involved).

Overall, both public and politicians were sympathetic to the socially disadvantaged (women, immigrants, and the poor), but somewhat unsympathetic towards activists, and very unsympathetic towards militants. Compared to the British public as a whole, Scots scored 10 points higher on sympathy for the socially disadvantaged, and politicians 12 points higher. But Scots were no more sympathetic than the British public as a whole towards militants, and politicians were 6 points less sympathetic. Attitudes towards activists differed little between our three samples (Table 4.25).

Politicians had more confidence in all kinds of institutions than the public generally. The difference was least on confidence in civil institutions and the judicial system, slightly more on confidence in the rights industry, and by far

TABLE 4.24. *Dimensions of sympathy and confidence*

	Politicians		British public (Scottish public)	
	F1	F2	F1	F2
(% variation explained by factors before rotation)				
	37%	24%	29% (28%)	26% (24%)
	Claimants	Institutions	Claimants	Institutions
(Factor loadings (×100) after varimax rotation)				
Micro-principles tied more to claimants				
Sympathy for activists	+89	.	+87 (+86)	(.)
Sympathy for socially disadvantaged	+77	.	+62 (+59)	(.)
Sympathy for militants	+55	.	+68 (+63)	(.)
Micro-principles tied to both claimants and institutions				
Confidence in rights industry	+71	.	(.)	+60 (+58)
Confidence in judicial system	−53	+57	(.)	+70 (+70)
Micro-principles tied more to institutions				
Confidence in civil institutions	.	+79	(.)	+71 (+64)
Confidence in established political system	.	+80	(.)	+78 (+79)

Note: Factor loadings less than 0.45 have been replaced by full points.

TABLE 4.25. *Sympathy and confidence, average scores*

	Politicians (scores)	British public (scores)	(Scottish public) (scores)
Sympathy for socially disadvantaged	30	18	(28)
Sympathy for activists	−12	−14	(−13)
Sympathy for militants	−71	−65	(−65)
Confidence in rights industry	11	5	(4)
Confidence in judicial system	28	24	(25)
Confidence in civil institutions	17	13	(16)
Confidence in established political system	17	1	(3)

the greatest—fully 16 points—on confidence in political institutions. It was not altogether a surprise to find that politicians had more confidence than the public in political institutions and, at only a 16-point difference on a 200-point scale, the estrangement between people and politicians could have been much worse.

THE CORRELATION BETWEEN SYMPATHIES AND PRINCIPLES

It is easier to draw a logical than an empirical distinction between sympathies and principles, but not that easy even in logic. There is an undeniable relationship between principle and prejudice. Logically, adherence to principles such as respect for authority should prejudice people in favour of institutions of enforcement and against groups of citizens who would challenge the established order: respect for authority implies respect for 'the authorities'.[18] Conversely, emotional reactions towards institutions and citizen groups can be generalized, abstracted, and reformulated as principles (Table 4.26).

Correlations between sympathies and principles were much higher amongst politicians than amongst the public, reflecting the usual pattern of greater coherence of opinion amongst politicians. Amongst both the public and politicians, however, the strongest correlations linked commitments to liberty and equality with sympathy for social groups and political activists, and with antipathy towards the judicial system.

With one exception, correlations with commitments to liberty and equality ran in the same direction, though they differed in strength. Sympathy towards

TABLE 4.26. *Sympathy and principle, correlations*

	Politicians		British public (Scottish public)			
	Liberty (r × 100)	Equality (r × 100)	Liberty (r × 100)		Equality (r × 100)	
Sympathy for socially disadvantaged	58	56	35	(32)	39	(34)
Sympathy for activists	53	62	37	(31)	46	(41)
Sympathy for militants	20	16	14	(.)	15	(.)
Confidence in the rights industry	39	53	14	(13)	23	(13)
Confidence in the judicial system	−54	−37	−32	(−26)	−16	(.)
Confidence in the political system	−33	.	−22	(−16)	.	(.)
Confidence in civil institutions	−23	18	−24	(−25)	19	(16)

Note: Correlations less than 0.10 have been replaced by full points.

militants correlated more with the principle of liberty, sympathy towards activists and confidence in the rights industry correlated more with the principle of equality, and sympathy for the socially disadvantaged about the same with both—but all four correlated positively with commitments to both liberty and equality; while confidence in the political and judicial system correlated negatively with both, but especially with the principle of liberty.

The one exception was confidence in civil institutions—a mixed bag of the press, television, trade unions, and churches. That correlated *positively* with equality but *negatively* with liberty. To explore why that occurred we correlated the principles of liberty and equality with each of these indicators of confidence in civil institutions separately. Confidence in trade unions correlated positively with both principles, but very much more strongly with equality: amongst the British public the correlations were 0.05 with liberty but 0.31 with equality. Conversely, confidence in tabloid newspapers correlated negatively with the principle of Liberty ($r = -0.20$) but not at all with equality. And correlations with confidence in the churches mirrored those with civil institutions as a whole: confidence in the churches correlated negatively with the principle of Liberty ($r = -0.35$) but positively with the principle of Equality ($r = +0.16$). In turn, that negative correlation between confidence in the churches and the principle of Liberty was not unreasonable, since our index of Liberty was based in part on the rejection of traditional and religious values.

THE STABILITY OF PRINCIPLES AND SYMPATHIES

If we really have uncovered elements of opinion that can properly be dignified with the label 'principles' as distinct from attitudes towards the merely transient issues and personalities of day-to-day politics, then we should expect them to show a degree of stability, at least in the short-to-medium term. Of course, people are free to change their principles and their sympathies, or even to reform their characters. But the justification for describing some of their opinions as principles is not just that they constitute general frameworks for guiding opinion on other matters, but also that these frameworks are relatively stable and change slowly or infrequently, if at all. If so-called principles did change rapidly, then we would, at the least, be inclined to describe them as 'lightly held principles', if 'principles' at all.

But politics takes place in time and, as time moves on, the people as a whole are exposed to a whole range of transient issues, be they, for example, the ups and downs of the economy, nationally televised scandals, or the antics of political activists designed to draw national attention to their particular concerns. Of course some individuals may pay more attention to these national events than others, but some events may come close to impinging upon almost everyone at a particular time. If that is so, then we should expect to find trends in perceptions and opinions, though less change in fundamental values.

Since our survey was not based upon a panel of respondents, each interviewed on more than one occasion, we cannot determine whether individuals changed their minds on principles or on transient issues. But since our interviewing was spread out over a lengthy period, and we made an attempt to randomize the selection of respondents for interview at any one time, we can investigate aggregate trends in opinion on values and issues.

Our interviewing was spread over the best part of a year from October 1991 onwards. For budgetary and operational reasons, interviews with our Scottish booster sample were mainly compressed into the closing months of that period. The heavy pressures on politicians around the time of the parliamentary general election in April 1992 and the local-government elections in May of the same year also disrupted our uniformly spread schedule of interviews with them. But in our main sample of the British public we tried, and largely succeeded, in randomizing our selection of respondents with respect to time as well as space. Any one week of these interviews thus constituted an approximately random subsample of our full sample of the British public. Random though it might be, however, a single week's sample would be too small to provide reliable estimates of public opinion. So we have divided the British public sample roughly into four quarters, centred on the most influential political event that occurred during our interviewing, namely the general election of 9 April 1992. By dividing our sample at 9 February, 9 April, and 9 June we obtain three subsamples of approximately 460 interviews each, plus a somewhat larger one of about 650 in the period 9 February–9 April, just prior to the election. In terms of education, age, and class these subsamples proved to be very similar to each other, and no adjustments were necessary to make them more socially comparable (Table 4.27).

Divided in this way, our sample of the British public shows the Conservatives drawing slightly ahead of Labour in the quarter before the election, and well ahead of Labour immediately after it—the familiar post-election 'honeymoon effect'. Trends in economic optimism were even more dramatic: in our survey, the percentage who expected the national economy to get better exceeded the number who expected it to get worse by 17 per cent in the first two subsamples and doubled to 39 per cent after the election, before economic optimism collapsed in our fourth subsample, and the number of pessimists

TABLE 4.27. *Short-term trends* (British public only)

	to 9 Feb.	9 Feb.–9 Ap.	9 Ap.–9 June	after 9 June
Vote preference: % Con. – % Lab	−1	2	9	13
Econ optimism: % better – % worse	17	17	39	−7
Commitment to liberty (scores)	−26	−23	−26	−23
Commitment to equality (scores)	54	54	55	55
Confidence in the judicial system (scores)	28	25	23	20

then exceeded the number of optimists by 7 per cent. As we know from other surveys, support for the newly re-elected government collapsed soon after-wards. Our evidence is consistent with a pattern of economic and political euphoria that peaked shortly after the election in April, and then collapsed progressively during the summer.

It is worth emphasizing these sharp trends in economic optimism just in order to contrast them with the almost complete lack of trend in all of our indicators of principles. On our 200-point scale, from minus 100 to plus 100, only two of our indicators of micro-principles varied by as much as 5 points, another two by 4 points, four by 3 points, and four by 2 or less. While the Conservative lead in vote preferences and net economic optimism (both of them also measured on a 200-point scale) varied by 14 points and 46 points respectively, our measure of commitment to liberty varied by only 3 points and our measure of commitment to equality by only one point. These are negligible variations. The contrast between the sharp trends in economic optimism and party perferences, on the one hand, and the stability of our measures of prin-ciple, on the other, provides some reassurance that we have succeeded in measuring more enduring aspects of public opinion that could provide guid-ing frameworks for opinion on more specific and more transient issues.

It might be reasonable to expect more movement in sympathies than in principles, since sympathies could be affected by the well-publicized be-haviour of the groups, individuals, or institutions that were the objects of sympathy. But in the event, the only noteworthy change we detected was an 8-point decline in confidence in the judicial system. Throughout the 1980s there was mounting evidence of police misconduct, and 'sometimes, it seemed, [juries] acquitted defendants merely to show disapproval of police con-duct'.[19] There was certainly a steady stream of well-publicized miscarriages of justice, most involving false confessions or false evidence, that reached a conclusion around the time of our survey.[20] Such was the concern in official circles about the conduct of the police and security services that the 1984 Police and Criminal Evidence Act (PACE) brought in some limited new safeguards against fabricated evidence and involuntary confessions (while retaining 'conviction on confession', in principle), but many of the cases that had resulted in conviction before 1984 now came up before the Appeal Court. The Guildford Four had been released in 1989, well before our sur-vey, but the Birmingham Six were released in March 1991, the Maguire Seven in June 1991, the Tottenham Three in November 1991, and Judith Ward in May 1992, while the campaign against the conviction of the Bridgewater Four[21] continued. Stefan Kiszko, jailed for murder in 1976 on his own confession, was released on bail in December 1991 and cleared in

February 1992 on the clearest possible scientific evidence—which had been available at the time of his trial. No one date is particularly significant in this unhappy sequence, not least because each of these cases received wide publicity for months before and after the Appeal Court verdict, but there was a cumulating sense that the system had been found wanting, and the public were unlikely to take as much notice of the very limited 1984 PACE reforms as of the continuing evidence of injustice—old injustice originating from the 1970s that was now being admitted perhaps, but all the more disgraceful for that; there could never be adequate compensation for sixteen hard and un-deserved years in jail.

The trend was even more marked in some of the indicators on which our measure of confidence in the judicial system was based: there was, for example, an increase from 21 per cent in the first quarter to 38 per cent in the third quarter in the number of people who agreed that the security services did 'more to harm our liberties than to protect them'; perceptions of the police moved in the same direction though to a slightly lesser extent. Several of the highly publicized scandals about the treatment of alleged terrorists during the period of our interviews involved Appeal Court hearings that exposed illegal police action against alleged terrorists. Technically they were 'police', but police acting in a security-service role rather than in a normal civilian-policing role.

Conversely, over the same period there was a gradual increase in the num-bers willing to permit interviews with apologists for terrorism in Northern Ireland, foreshadowing a later government decision to lift the government's ban on broadcasting such interviews, undubbed, on radio or television.

However, despite a long string of scandals about the private lives of senior politicians and members of the Royal Family, there was little evidence of any clear trend of opinion about press intrusions into private lives. Through-out our survey, people drew a clear distinction between the lives of ordinary people and senior politicians—and perhaps, by extension, the Royal Family —but no very clear trends emerged. Opinion did seem to harden, briefly, against the press when it focused upon revelations about Paddy Ashdown's affair with a former secretary, but it became even more supportive after-wards than it had been before.

CONCLUSION

We have found two, but only two, broad macro-principles—liberty and equal-ity—that seem to underlie more specific micro-principles. Commitment to liberty reflected tolerance, and lack of deference towards authority or traditional values. Commitment to equality reflected support for economic equality, equal rights, and caring. Both macro-principles reflected support for rights of protest and rebellion, and an aversion to preaching self-reliance to others.

Although analysts often define broad macro-principles in a way that ensures they must be uncorrelated with each other, we chose not to do that. We found that commitments to liberty and equality were, in fact, uncorrelated amongst the public but that they were positively correlated amongst politicians. (In later chapters we shall find these two macro-principles were correlated amongst some sections of the public also.) Partly because of that, the principles of politicians were much more coherent than those of the public. Indeed a single combined 'liberty-and-equality' factor could explain almost as much of the variation in politicians' principles as two separate factors could explain amongst the public.

Commitment to liberty correlated strongly with sympathy towards political activists and the socially disadvantaged; and with a lack of confidence in the judicial system and civil institutions. Commitment to equality correlated even more strongly with sympathy towards political activists and the socially disadvantaged; but less strongly with a lack of confidence in the judicial system and positively with confidence in civil institutions.

Over the year during which we carried out our interviews, we found no trends in commitment to liberty or equality. We might expect fundamental principles to remain stable at least over that period of time. By contrast we found a gradual erosion of confidence in the judicial system, large changes in voting intentions, and huge fluctuations in economic optimism. The contrast between the stability of principles and the variability of perceptions was striking.

In this chapter we hope we have developed convincing measures of fundamental principles. In the chapters that follow we shall look at the consequences of commitment to these principles—at how they affect decisions on practical issues; and at their causes—at the influence of social background and personal experience on commitment to both macro- and micro-principles.

NOTES

1. A similar two-stage procedure was used by Herbert McClosky and Alida Brill, *Dimensions of Tolerance: What Americans Believe about Civil Liberties* (New York:

Russell Sage Foundation, 1983), 479; and by Geraint Parry, George Moyser, and Neil Day, *Political Participation and Democracy in Britain* (Cambridge: Cambridge University Press, 1992), 59.

2. See Amitai Etzioni, *The Spirit of Community: The Reinvention of American Society* (New York: Simon & Schuster, 1993), reputedly a favourite of the 'New Labour' leadership.

3. H. Eysenck, *The Psychology of Politics* (London: Routledge & Kegan Paul, 1951).

4. Anthony Heath, Roger Jowell, and John Curtice, *How Britain Votes* (Oxford: Pergamon, 1985), 116–21—a section titled 'A Two-Dimensional View of the Electorate'.

5. Anthony Heath *et al.*, *Understanding Political Change: The British Voter 1964– 1987* (Oxford: Pergamon, 1991), 174–5.

6. Anthony Heath ('Do People Have Consistent Attitudes?', in Roger Jowell, Sharon Witherspoon, and Lindsay Brook (eds.), *British Social Attitudes: The 1986 Report* (Aldershot: Gower, 1986), 1–16) found five factors—economic equality, sexual liberty, political liberty, conservation, and defence—but these were more akin to our micro-principles than our macro-dimensions of principle.

7. A. H. Halsey, *Change in British Society* (2nd edn., Oxford: Oxford University Press, 1981), 160.

8. McClosky and Brill, *Dimensions of Tolerance*, 479, carried out a factor analysis of 'civil liberties subscales'—roughly equivalent to our micro-principles, and also found higher proportions of variation explained amongst élites than the mass public. Their analysis produced a single factor, not two, but their focus was restricted to something roughly equivalent to our macro-principle of liberty, and excluded our macro-principle of equality.

9. We have chosen tolerance rather than wealth creation because its link to the first dimension, liberty, is more self-evident even if slightly less statistical. In fact, tolerance did load slightly more strongly than wealth creation on the liberty factor in the British public sample, though slightly less than wealth creation in the politicians' and Scots' samples.

10. David Held, 'The New Polarization of Democratic Ideals', in *Models of Democracy* (Oxford: Blackwell, 1987), ch. 8.

11. Ibid. 252.

12. Ibid. 262.

13. For a strong argument that these principles are naturally correlated, see Roy Hattersley, 'Through Equality to Liberty', in William L. Miller (ed.), *Alternatives to Freedom: Arguments and Opinions* (London: Longman, 1995), 133–50.

14. McClosky and Brill, *Dimensions of Tolerance*, 256.

15. Ibid. 328.

16. Giovanni Sartori, *The Theory of Democracy Revisited* (Chatham, NJ: Chatham House, 1987), 340.

17. Ibid. 390.

18. But not always. See e.g. the lament of Vasilii Shulgin, a member of the last Tsarist Duma, who had a great respect for the Tsarist system but not for the incumbent Tsar: 'How terrible it is to have an autocracy without an autocrat' (Vasilii V. Shulgin, *The*

Years: Memoirs of a Member of the Russian Duma, trans. Tanya Davis (New York: Hippocrene Books, 1984), 260). The parallels with contemporary attitudes towards the British Royal Family are painfully obvious.

19. Peter Thornton, *Decade of Decline: Civil Liberties in the Thatcher Years* (London: National Council for Civil Liberties, 1989), 53.

20. See e.g. Bill Coxall and Lynton Robins, *Contemporary British Politics* (London: Macmillan, 1994), 452–3.

21. Paul Foot, *Murder at the Farm: Who Killed Carl Bridgewater* (London: Penguin, 1988).

5

The Practice of Principle

THE *practice* of rights is supremely important, particularly to those who seek or enjoy rights, but also to those who would grant or defend the rights of others. Practice tests commitment to principle.

Indeed, practice gives meaning to principle; it 'interprets' principle. People are not always put to the test: they may not have the power or the occasion to put their principles into practice. But we can ask them to think themselves into particular scenarios and to confront, in their imagination at least, the dilemmas of decision in those specific circumstances.

In this chapter we ask how far practice is consistent with principle. We test the British public's and politicians' commitments to the practice of liberty and equality by reviewing the decisions they would make in a variety of situations, all of which have occurred, or could well occur in Britain. It will soon become apparent that even a decision about the simplest of scenarios may involve the exercise of more than one principle, and these principles may themselves be in conflict. For that reason if for no other, any single principle will fail to determine practical decisions completely.[1] However, our evidence suggests that principles are, none the less, strong influences upon decisions in specific practical scenarios.

Our comparison of people and politicians in Chapter 3 showed that politicians generally paid more lip-service to principles of citizens' rights than did citizens themselves. Now we ask whether politicians would also give more support to citizens' rights than citizens themselves *in practical situations*. At the same time, in Chapter 3, we noted an exception—or rather a paradox: that politicians also paid more lip-service to the principle of obedience to the law, even to 'unjust, immoral, or cruel' laws. That seemed to indicate a peculiarly 'governing perspective'. So we shall also seek to find out how far this 'governing perspective' is actually manifest in practice.

In Chapter 4 we found that politicians had a more simple and coherent structure to their principles than the public. Two factors explained 52 per cent of the variation in micro-principles amongst politicians, but only 40 per cent amongst the public; and, even more strikingly, a single factor explained 38 per cent amongst politicians, but only 22 per cent amongst the public. Is the same true of the coherence between principles and practice? Do principles exert more influence upon the practical decisions of politicians than upon those of the public?

We shall also ask: which principles—which micro-principles and which macro-principles—have the most influence on practical decisions? Superficially, we might expect that commitment to liberty and its associated micro-principles would exert the greater influence upon practical decisions about the negative rights of civil and political liberties—those that concern freedom of expression, freedom to protest, freedom of association, freedom of information, freedom of lifestyle, and powers to uphold the law or defend the state; while commitment to equality and its associated micro-principles would exert the greater influence upon practical decisions about positive social rights—equality in political life, equality in social life, welfare, and protection. But it is even more difficult to disentangle the positive and negative in practice than it is in principle.

The reasons for asserting a practical civil liberty, a specific restriction on government action, may not be that we object to that government action in principle, but that we do not trust government officials to act on that issue with sufficient regard to equality of treatment for different individuals or categories of citizen. Howard Zinn connects equality not merely with positive rights but with classic negative rights when he claims that 'the distribution of information to the public is a function of power and wealth';[2] 'the [Vietnam] draft . . . discriminates against the poor, the uneducated, the young';[3] 'at every stage of the judicial process . . . the poor person is treated worse than the rich, the black worse than the white, the politically or personally odd character worse than the orthodox';[4] and 'like money, freedom of expression is available to all in America, but in widely varying quantities'.[5] In practice even issues of negative liberty may become issues of equality. So we shall not be too surprised if we find that commitment to equality affects opinion on issues of liberty, and vice versa.

FREEDOM OF EXPRESSION

In practice, freedom of speech is not just the freedom to grumble to family, friends, workmates, or casual acquaintances but the freedom to teach, to publish, to demonstrate, to address public meetings—in short, to speak out in ways that command attention.[6]

The principle of free speech wins widespread support, but how far are people willing to permit the exercise of this freedom by others, especially if they do not approve of the things others wish to express? Defending the liberties of a group we like is close to being an act of self-interest, and is certainly an act of approval, rather than an act of tolerance. As Sullivan, Pierson, and Marcus have argued,[7] we cannot tolerate a group we like: we can only be said to tolerate a group if we dislike it but defend it. It follows that the greater our dislike for any particular group, the greater the tolerance we show when we defend that group's liberties.

As a criterion for judging whether, and to what extent, people are tolerant, there are problems in applying the methods of Sullivan and his colleagues, since everyone is likely to be intolerant of some groups or actions: almost everyone has his or her private hit-list. George Will, for example, argues that 'there are political purposes for protecting free speech, and some speech is incompatible with those purposes . . . there is no such thing as an amoral constitution, neutral regarding all possible outcomes'.[8] However, we sought to identify active groups in British politics which would strain, but not necessarily break, the tolerance of our respondents. We began by presenting them with a list of groups, emphasizing that these were groups 'which some people like but others dislike' and asking them to give a mark out of ten to show how much they liked or disliked each group. We told our respondents that 'if you like a group give it a score above five; the more you like it, the higher the score. If you dislike a group, give it a score less than five; the less you like it, the lower the score.' We have already used the answers to this battery of questions to measure sympathy and antipathy towards activists, minorities, and militants. They were:

- gays and lesbians
- environmental campaigners like Greenpeace
- animal-rights activists
- communists
- feminists
- National Front supporters
- muslim activists
- Militant Tendency supporters
- IRA sympathizers
- people who sympathize with Protestant terrorists in Northern Ireland
- black activists.

The particular groups on the list are not important at this stage, because we used the eleven sympathy/antipathy scores to identify, for each respondent, that one single group which they liked least—their 'Most Disliked Group' or MDG. (We excluded those very few people who gave scores of 5 or more to all the groups, indicating no antipathy towards any of them. And where

a respondent displayed an equally high level of antipathy towards several
groups, the computer randomly selected one for use as the MDG.) Our
eleven groups ran the gamut of the ideological spectrum and, although the
MDG chosen from this restricted list was not the same as the group—from
an unrestricted list—that might have inspired the greatest antipathy, it does
provide some basis for measuring tolerance. Barnum and Sullivan have shown
that party and ideology do have a great effect upon which groups particular
people dislike most (left-wingers dislike right-wing groups and vice versa[9]),
but within our wide range of groups, most respondents could find some
group they heartily disliked.

We then asked people four questions to assess the extent to which they
would tolerate their MDG. The first two focused on social and domestic life,
the other two on freedom of expression. We asked whether people agreed or
disagreed with each of following propositions about their MDG:

- I would be unhappy if a [MDG] moved in next door to me.
- I would be unhappy if a child of mine became emotionally involved with a
  [MDG].
- [MDG]s should not be allowed to make public speeches in my locality.
- [MDG]s should not be allowed to teach in publicly funded schools.

(The computer controlling the interview automatically substituted the actual
name of the interviewee's most disliked group for the letters [MDG] in each
of these questions.)

Our results suggest that both the public and their political leaders distinguish sharply between the domestic sphere and the public sphere. Three-
quarters of both public and politicians said they would be unhappy to have
their MDG living next door and significantly more would be unhappy to
have their children emotionally entangled with their MDG. But these high
levels of personal antipathy, even animosity, contrasted strongly with their
much greater willingness to allow MDGs to make speeches in their locality
or teach children in state schools. Commitment to the practice of free speech
can override personal and social antipathy.

However, although the public and politicians responded in a similar fashion to questions about the more personal aspects of tolerance, they differed
significantly on the degree to which they would allow their MDG to speak
out or teach. Although just under half the public would ban members of their
MDG from making speeches in their locality, less than a third of politicians
would do so; and two-thirds of the public, compared to just under half the
politicians, would ban MDGs from teaching in publicly funded schools. It is

TABLE 5.1. *Freedom of expression for MDG*

	Politicians (%)	British public (%)	(Scottish public) (%)
Not next door	72	73	(73)
Not with my children	89	86	(89)
Ban speeches	29	44	(50)
Ban teaching	47	67	(69)

also important to note that these differences between the public and politicians on freedom of speech occurred despite the similarity in their reactions to the prospect of MDGs living next door or becoming emotionally involved with their children. Politicians drew an even sharper distinction than the public between the domestic and civic domains (Table 5.1).

We also asked people to tell us whether 'you regard [MDG] as dangerous, or merely unpleasant?', and if dangerous, 'very dangerous or just a bit dangerous?' Amongst both politicians and the public, about two-fifths said their MDG was 'merely unpleasant', a quarter said 'a bit dangerous', and a third said 'very dangerous'.

The practical tolerance of both politicians and the public clearly depended upon the extent and severity of the perceived threat from their MDG as well as on the distinction between domestic and civil domains. The public were 21 per cent more unhappy at living next to a 'very dangerous' MDG than a 'merely unpleasant' one, 12 per cent more unhappy at their children getting involved with a 'very dangerous' MDG, 33 per cent more willing to ban speeches by a 'very dangerous' MDG, and 26 per cent more willing to ban a 'very dangerous' MDG from school teaching. Amongst politicians the corresponding differences were 23 per cent, 13 per cent, 32 per cent, and 41 per cent. So amongst both politicians and the public the extent of the perceived threat had more effect upon practical tolerance in the civil domain than in the domestic domain.

A large majority of politicians would let the 'merely unpleasant' teach, and a large majority of both politicians and the public would let the 'merely unpleasant' make speeches in their locality. Tolerance for 'very dangerous' MDGs was much lower, however: two-thirds of the public and half the politicians would ban them from making speeches, and around three-quarters of both would ban them from teaching. But perhaps the degree to which people would let even 'very dangerous' MDGs make public speeches—limited though it was—is more remarkable than anything else (Table 5.2).

TABLE 5.2. *Dangerous or merely unpleasant MDGs*

	Politicians			British public (Scottish public)		
	Merely unpleasant (%)	A bit dangerous (%)	Very dangerous (%)	Merely unpleasant (%)	A bit dangerous (%)	Very dangerous (%)
Category distribution	41	27	32	44 (44)	25 (25)	31 (32)
Not next door	63	73	86	65 (63)	78 (74)	86 (87)
Not with my children	83	92	96	81 (82)	91 (94)	93 (95)
Ban speeches	17	30	49	32 (39)	47 (46)	65 (72)
Ban teaching	30	50	71	56 (57)	73 (74)	82 (88)

In principle, freedom of speech implies freedom to publish, but the extent to which journalists, academics, clerics, or others should be allowed in practice to express themselves freely in print or on television is a highly contentious matter—certainly so in contemporary Britain where controversies such as those surrounding the publication of *Spycatcher*, the *Satanic Verses*, critiques of Christian doctrine, and scandals about the Royal Family or leading politicians have abounded over the last decade.

As these examples demonstrate, some disputed issues of press freedom concern public access to information, while others primarily concern freedom of expression. Let us leave questions about freedom of information to a later section of this chapter, and concentrate here on freedom of expression: on the freedom of writers rather than the freedom of readers. We asked a series of questions designed to map out some of the limits to public tolerance of free expression in the press and in broadcasting. First, we asked:

Some people think there should be no restrictions on what can be published in books and newspapers or screened on television, but others disagree. For each of the following please say whether you think it should be [allowed on television *without any restrictions*, or *restricted*, for example, to late night viewing, or *banned* from television altogether/allowed in newspapers *without any restrictions*, or *restricted*, for example, to books, or *banned* from publication altogether.]

- pictures of extreme violence?
- abusive attacks on [the Christian religion/minority religions such as the Muslim or Hindu religion]?
- lies and distortions of the truth?

Around one-third of both the public and politicians opted for a complete ban on violent pictures and abuse of religion. Varying the question wording to focus on television or books and newspapers had no effect on average. However, the public, and more especially the politicians, distinguished sharply between abusive attacks on Christianity and minority religions: the public were about 12 per cent more willing to ban attacks on minority religions than on Christianity, and politicians were about 26 per cent more willing to do so. So politicians were more tolerant than the public towards attacks on Christianity, but less tolerant than the public towards attacks on minority religions. This may reflect their sense of representing citizens from a broad range of ethnic groups, not just the one to which they feel they belong personally.

We touched on the question of religious attacks in another question when we asked: 'Do you think it should be against the law to write or speak in a

Coherence

TABLE 5.3. *Freedom to publish abusive, sensational, or biased material*

	Politicians (%)	British public (%)	(Scottish public) (%)
Ban racial/religious incitement	75	64	(66)
racial	80	70	(72)
religious	69	58	(61)
Ban violent pictures	33	32	(30)
Ban religious abuse	35	38	(42)
of Christianity	22	32	(36)
of minority religions	48	44	(48)
Ban lies	75	77	(77)
Ban sensational crime coverage	32	44	(45)
Equal coverage of parties on TV	42	77	(74)

way that promotes [racial/religious] hatred?' Both the public and politicians were 12 per cent more inclined to ban racial incitement than religious incitement. That difference was reflected in the law: the 1986 Public Order Act made it an offence even to possess material that was abusive or insulting in circumstances likely to stir up racial hatred where 'racial' was defined to include colour, nationality, citizenship, or ethnic origin but *not* religion.[10] However, taking race and religion together, 75 per cent of politicians and 64 per cent of the public would ban publication of anything that promoted racial or religious hatred.

We should recall, at this point, how in Chapter 3 we found that politicians were significantly more committed than the public to the principle of free speech. So their greater readiness to defend some aspects of the practical expression of free speech is not surprising; but it makes their greater readiness to ban other aspects of the practical expression of free speech all the more remarkable. And the point is reinforced by our use of two very different questions about racial/religious attacks. Politicians' willingness to ban abuse of racial or religious minorities may be explained by their greater commitment to the principle of ethnic equality, however (see Chapter 3). It seems clear that politicians faced a conflict of principle on practical issues that linked free speech and the protection of racial/religious minorities. When this conflict was not present, they reacted very differently (Table 5.3).

Support for a ban on publication of 'lies and distortions' was widespread amongst both the public and politicians—77 per cent amongst the public and 75 per cent amongst politicians. There is a liberal argument in defence of free speech that we should combat lies and distortions by publishing the truth rather than by a legal or administrative ban. But that view clearly failed to sway public opinion. One reason is that lies and distortions are more than a matter of free expression; they corrupt the free flow of information and, as we shall see later in this chapter, that offends politicians even more than the public—hence the willingness of politicians to support a ban on lies and distortion just as strongly as the public. Tam Dalyell's lengthily titled book *Misrule: How Mrs Thatcher has Misled Parliament from the Sinking of the Belgrano to the Wright Affair* illustrates the indignation of one politician who feels that lies and distortions have indeed been used to corrupt the flow of information. 'This is not a matter of honest policy differences . . . this is about deceit . . . this Government was deceiving Parliament, press and people about their real policy.'[11] Dalyell details alleged government lies and distortions over the sinking of the Belgrano, the sale of Westland helicopters, conflict with Libya, the coal strike, the BBC's *Secret Society* series, and Peter Wright's *Spycatcher*. Paddy Hillyard and Janie Percy-Smith claim more generally that 'the official information that we are given by politicians and civil servants is incomplete, highly partial and in many cases deliberately intended to mislead'.[12]

We tackled other issues affecting the freedom of the press in two very different ways. First we asked:

Heavy television and press coverage of dramatic crimes like murders or terrorist incidents should be banned [(null)/because it may encourage others to commit more crimes/because, later on, it may prevent an accused person getting a fair trial]. Agree/disagree?

We then asked a question 'about ways of ensuring fair competition between the main parties, Conservative, Labour and Liberal Democrat':

Consider the amount of coverage these three parties get on television. Should it be *exactly the same* amount for each party, or should it reflect the *size of vote* each party got in the last election, or should it depend upon *how newsworthy* each party is at the time?

Once again there were substantial differences between the public and politicians. But this time—and in sharp contrast to our question on promoting racial/religious hatred—the politicians gave more support than the public to the practice of press freedom. Only 32 per cent of politicians would ban sensational crime coverage, while 44 per cent of the public would do so (combining, as usual, the answers to our three versions of the crime-coverage question). Similarly, only 42 per cent of politicians but 77 per cent of the public would restrict the freedom of journalists by demanding exactly equal coverage of the three main parties, irrespective of their newsworthiness —an issue that is debated every time there is a general election.

FREEDOM TO PROTEST

Britain has a long history of protest demonstrations and marches, but in British law there are 'no recognized rights of meeting or procession'[13] and 'rights of peaceful meeting and protest attract little legal concern in terms of their social value in a democratic society; instead attention is invariably centred upon public order aspects, or the effect upon the rights of other non-protesting citizens'.[14] Under the 1986 Public Order Act 'the sole precondition [for bans on meetings and processions in England and Wales was] that the police "reasonably believe" that there may be "serious damage to property" or "serious disruption" or "intimidation" '.[15]

Something of this was reflected in public opinion. We turned the issue of freedom to speak about religion on its head by asking how far people would tolerate various groups disrupting traffic with a demonstration or procession: 'Should a [political protest group/religious group/group organizing a town's festival or gala] be allowed to hold a parade that blocks town-centre traffic for two hours?' On average, only 44 per cent of politicians but 63 per cent of the public would ban such disruption. At the same time, both were most tolerant of a town gala and least tolerant of religious processions: for example, only 46 per cent of the public would ban a disruptive town gala but 73 per cent would ban a similarly disruptive religious procession. So, although we found in earlier chapters that very few people—only 16 per cent of the public and 10 per cent of politicians—were opposed in principle to the idea of protest marches and demonstrations, they proved very much less tolerant in practice. Moreover, the small difference in principle between public and politicians widened to a chasm in practice.

Interestingly, both public and politicians were much more tolerant of situations where there was a potential for public disorder rather than the certainty of inconvenience. We asked: 'If there is a real possibility that a [political demonstration/football match] may lead to public disorder or even a riot, should it be banned in advance or should the authorities make special arrangements to deal with trouble but allow it to go ahead?' Only a third would ban such events even where there was a real possibility of public disorder, though both public and politicians were more willing to ban political demonstrations than football matches—11 per cent more amongst the public and 18 per cent amongst politicians. Football riots were clearly seen as somehow less threatening than political riots.

We put the question of riots and demonstrations in a more exclusively political context by asking how people ought to behave if they disapproved of government policy on taxation. We asked:

If people don't like the government's decisions about [income tax or VAT/local-government taxes], they can vote against it at the next election, but they should not [refuse to pay a tax they don't like/hold disorderly demonstrations and riots to force the government to change its tax decisions/physically attack officials who are trying to collect the tax/hold protest rallies and demonstrations to oppose the tax]. Agree/disagree?

Opposition to the collection of taxes has a long and distinguished history in Britain and has, at one time or another, been used by all parts of the political spectrum.[16] When framing this question we had in mind not only the widespread opposition to the poll tax in the late 1980s and early 1990s, but also many earlier protests against taxation. These included refusals by religious Nonconformists to pay taxes that subsidized church schools, attempts by Quakers to protest the payment of taxes that supported weapons manufacture and deployment, tax strikes by Welsh-language enthusiasts, and refusal to pay taxes by those who supported the House of Lords' vote against Lloyd George's 'People's Budget' of 1910—a vote which, they claimed, destroyed any legal basis for taxation (though the courts at the time took a more pragmatic view of the matter and enforced payment). But, despite these celebrated historical precedents—and the more recent experience of massive, disruptive, illegal, and often violent resistance to the poll tax—three-quarters of both the public and politicians agreed that resistance to taxation should be confined to the ballot box.

Although neither the public nor politicians made any distinction between resistance to national taxes (income tax and VAT) and local-government taxes, they drew very sharp distinctions between the four modes of resistance mentioned in alternative variants of the question. There was almost unanimous agreement that people should not attack tax collectors, less but still overwhelming condemnation of refusal to pay, and strong opposition to riots and disorderly demonstrations, but majority support for protest rallies and demonstrations providing force or violence was not mentioned (Table 5.4).

TABLE 5.4. *Freedom to protest in practice*

	Politicians (%)	British public (%)	(Scottish public) (%)
Ban protest/gala procession	44	63	(66)
political protest	48	71	(70)
religious	54	73	(78)
town gala	28	46	(50)
Ban potential political/football riot	31	37	(40)
political demonstration	40	43	(50)
football match	22	32	(30)
Resist tax but not	75	75	(70)
refuse to pay	94	86	(78)
riot	76	74	(66)
attack officials	100	94	(96)
demonstrate	30	43	(36)

Politicians were substantially more sympathetic than the public to protest rallies, but less sympathetic than the public towards refusals to pay, or towards riots, or attacks on tax collectors; so they were more sympathetic than the public to peaceful protest yet less sympathetic than the public to violence or disruption. Thus our complex randomized question revealed a practical example of politicians' combination of a more liberal attitude towards peaceable protest with a more deferential attitude towards the law—a view which might be summed up in the slogan 'protest but obey'. Their greater commitment to liberty was expressed in their greater support for peaceful protests against taxation, while their 'governing perspective', which we discovered in Chapter 3 and which made politicians more committed in principle to obeying unjust laws, was reflected in their greater opposition to illegal methods of resisting taxation.

FREEDOM OF ASSOCIATION

Practical questions of free speech, free expression, and protest shade into questions of free association. Without the freedom to combine together to put their case, articulate their discontents, and protest against injustice, freedom for individuals may have only limited practical consequences. Amongst the classic practical implementations of the freedom to associate with others is the freedom to join a trade union and the right to go on strike[17]—activities that were banned in Britain under the notorious 'Combination Acts' of 1800, 1825, and 1859, and only removed from the conspiracy law by the 1875 Conspiracy and Protection of Property Act. The right to belong to a trade union was not conceded in Britain without a long and bitter struggle and has never been accepted without qualification. It exists under International Labour Organization (ILO) Conventions 87, 98, and 151 amongst others, but 'removal of trade union membership from workers at Government Communications Headquarters [was] . . . a direct attack on the core of that right'.[18] In October 1988 the British government dismissed civilian workers at GCHQ, its intelligence-gathering centre at Cheltenham, for belonging to a union. It was the first time this century that British government employees had been sacked for belonging to a trade union. The government argued that membership of a trade union and the possibility of strike action constituted a threat to national security but it rejected the trade-union offer of a 'no-strike' agreement.[19]

Despite this view of the British government, we found that almost everyone else in Britain supported both the right to join a trade union as well as the right to refuse to do so.[20] Moreover, support for the right to join a trade union was unaffected by whether it was applied to essential public services or not (Table 5.5). We asked:

[1.] Should workers have the right to *refuse* to join a trade union if they do not want to join one?

[2.] Should [all workers, even those in essential public services like the Ambulance Service or the Fire Brigade/workers who do not work in essential public services]

- have the right to join a trade union if they wish?
- have the right to strike?

However, public support for the right to strike was a good deal less than for the right to belong to a trade union. While only 5 per cent of the British public and 3 per cent of politicians opposed the right to belong to a trade union, almost a quarter of both the British public and politicians opposed the right to strike (combining answers to the variants of the question that included and excluded essential service workers). And although there was almost universal support for the right of workers in essential public services to join a union, support for the right to strike was much lower for workers in essential public services than it was for workers in other areas. Amongst the British public, 18 per cent more would ban strikes by essential workers

TABLE 5.5. *Freedom of association in practice*

	Politicians (%)	British public (%)	(Scottish public) (%)
Against right to join trade union	3	5	(4)
including essential public services	4	6	(4)
excluding essential public services	2	4	(5)
Against right to refuse to join trade union	3	3	(3)
Against right to strike	23	23	(19)
including essential public services	35	32	(23)
excluding essential public services	10	14	(14)

than by non-essential workers, and amongst politicians 25 per cent more. Yet even when asked the variant of the question that specifically included workers in essential services, only a third of both the public and politicians opposed their right to strike. Interestingly, in Scotland the figure was much lower: only 23 per cent opposed the right to strike even for workers in essential services.

The Influence of Principle on Issues of Free Expression, Protest, and Association

Superficially, we may seem to have uncovered a gross contradiction between principle and practice. In Chapters 2 and 3 we found people gave very high marks out of ten for the importance to them of 'guaranteeing everyone the right to free speech', a large majority supported the principle of free speech even if that meant tolerating 'extremist views', and an overwhelming majority supported—in principle—the right of angry citizens to protest and demonstrate. Yet now we find majority support for censorship in some circumstances, and a large majority against allowing any political demonstration that might disrupt traffic for an hour or two. It might appear that attitudes to practice contradict attitudes to principle.

The contradiction, however, is more apparent than real. No single principle can ever be absolute. It should be obvious that, whatever our commitment to the principle of free speech, some expressions or modes of expression can be so offensive to our other principles that we would willingly ban them. There can, therefore, be no logical connection between the absolute level of support for a particular principle and the absolute level of support for corresponding decisions in practice: absolute levels simply cannot contradict each other, however different they may be.

But there should at least be a correlation between principle and practice: those who declare more support for a certain principle should, in logic, be more willing than others to take the appropriate side in corresponding practical decisions. This forms the basis for our assessment of the influence which principle has upon practice. Following our approach in Chapter 4, we can construct a measure of commitment to liberty by averaging scores on three of the four micro-principles most closely tied to the first dimension (liberty) uncovered in our factor analysis—(rejection of) authority, (rejection of) traditional values, and tolerance; and construct a measure of commitment to equality by averaging scores on the three micro-principles most closely tied to the second dimension (equality)—economic equality, caring, and equal rights. Using these we can calculate how far practical decisions correlate with the principles of liberty and equality.

In addition, to gauge the overall influence on a practical decision of several principles working in combination, we can use the multiple correlation coefficient from a multiple regression based upon all of the thirteen micro-principles defined in Chapter 4. For this purpose we have used SPSS stepwise multiple regression, which also highlights the particular principles that have most influence. (Where the influence of principle was so weak that no regression passed the default criteria for stepwise regression, our tables show the multiple correlation as zero, though a multiple correlation based upon a complete multiple regression would usually be slightly but not significantly above that.)

Our expectation in using this approach was that on practical issues of liberty we would find a higher correlation with our measure of commitment to liberty than with our measure of commitment to equality, and conversely. Usually, but not always, that proved to be the case. And, of course, the multiple correlation based upon the stepwise multiple regression using up to thirteen micro-principles must necessarily be greater than the simple bivariate correlation with either liberty or equality, though not necessarily by much.

Applying this approach to practical issues of freedom of expression, protest and association produced several broad findings:

1. Many of the correlations were high, which indicated a strong influence of principle. Amongst politicians, for example, acceptance of peaceful demonstrations against an unpopular tax correlated at 0.55 with our battery of principles and acceptance of a political protest that blocked

traffic correlated at 0.54. Amongst the public these correlations were both 0.42. So principle does matter, at least for some decisions.

2. The correlations were usually a little higher, and sometimes much higher, amongst politicians than amongst the public. For example, on the issue of banning their MDG from teaching in state-funded schools, the multiple correlation with our battery of principles ran at 0.35 amongst politicians but only 0.20 amongst the public. So principles seemed to influence the decisions of politicians more than the public.

3. The correlations were very variable. For both politicians and the public, correlations with our battery of principles were relatively high on issues about banning various kinds of protest, but relatively low on the issue of banning racial or religious incitement. So our battery of principles seemed to influence some decisions far more than others.

4. Amongst the public, practical decisions on free expression usually correlated with commitment to liberty but showed little or no correlation with commitment to equality—as we might expect. Amongst politicians, however, practical decisions on free expression tended to correlate strongly with both liberty and equality.

5. As we discovered in Chapter 4, the basic principles of liberty and equality were themselves uncorrelated amongst the public but strongly (and positively) linked with each other amongst politicians. So for politicians it is inevitably more difficult to separate out the influence of these two principles, and what often appears as a qualitative distinction amongst the public usually becomes a quantitative difference only amongst politicians. None the less, amongst politicians as well as the public, commitment to liberty correlated more strongly than commitment to equality with most practical issues of free expression except for the right to join a trade union or take part in a strike.

6. None the less, amongst the public attitudes towards the right to join a trade union, though apparently an issue of liberty, correlated exclusively with commitment to equality; and attitudes towards the right to strike also correlated far more with an abstract commitment to equality than with an abstract commitment to liberty. And there was also a hint of evidence to suggest that attitudes towards banning racial incitement correlated more strongly with commitment to equality than to liberty— and, even more unusually, that it was the egalitarians who were more inclined to place restrictions on freedom of expression in this case. McClosky and Brill note that their

concept of 'civil rights' [similar to, but not the same as, our measure of equality] is distinguishable from 'civil liberties' [similar to, but not the same as, our measure of liberty] principally in its emphasis on equality . . . although [they] reinforce each other, they are sometimes in conflict. Civil rights organizations have been known, in the name of equality, to propose the censorship of publications that preach race hatred or that openly express prejudice against Catholics, Jews, women, homosexuals, or others . . . the domains of freedom and equality, of civil liberties and civil rights, are not always or in all respects compatible.'[21]

Our findings echo that conclusion here.

Why are some correlations so much higher than others? Why does our battery of principles appear to influence some decisions so much more than others? The differences do not seem to be accidental, and they provide deeper insights into the connection between principle and practice.

For example, principle had very little influence upon whether people were unhappy at the thought of their MDG moving in next door or becoming emotionally involved with their children. Irrespective of principle, *social* intolerance towards people's MDG was strong. But principle had a moderately strong influence upon their *political* toleration of their MDG: principle influenced whether they would ban members of their MDG from teaching in state schools or making speeches in their locality. And that is as it should be: political principle should influence political tolerance, but places us under no obligation to be happy about our children's emotional involvement with groups we heartily detest (Table 5.6).

Principle had some influence, but a fairly weak influence, upon attitudes towards a ban on racial/religious incitement and abuse of minority religions but a much stronger influence upon attitudes towards a ban on abuse of Christianity. Similarly, principle had only a moderate influence upon attitudes towards disruption of traffic by a town gala, but a strong influence upon attitudes towards similar disruption by a political demonstration or religious procession; a moderate influence upon attitudes towards banning a potentially riotous football match, but a strong influence upon attitudes towards banning a potentially riotous political demonstration; little or no influence upon attitudes towards attacking tax collectors but a moderately strong influence upon attitudes towards refusal-to-pay, and a very strong influence upon attitudes towards peaceful protest demonstrations against tax; and, finally, a stronger influence upon attitudes towards banning trade unions or strikes in essential services than in the workplace generally. (These same patterns of correlations occurred amongst the public as amongst politicians, though usually at a somewhat lower level.)

Again, these differences are explicable. Practical issues that evoked a broad consensus necessarily did not show a pattern of opinion dictated by

TABLE 5.6. *Correlations between principle and practice on freedom of expression, protest, and association*

	Politicians			British public (Scottish public)		
	Liberty (r × 100)	Equality (r × 100)	Multiple (r × 100)	Liberty (r × 100)	Equality (r × 100)	Multiple (r × 100)
Not next door	·	·	·	· (−)	· ( )	· (10)
Not with my children	·	·	·	· (−)	· ( )	· (10)
Ban speeches	−22	·	29	−22 (−25)	· ( )	29 (34)
Ban teaching	−31	−15	35	−17 (−18)	· ( )	20 (27)
Ban racial/religious incitement	·	·	15	· (−)	· ( )	10 (17)
racial	·	15	20	−15 (−)	· (17)	12 (22)
religious	·	·	17	· (−)	· ( )	16 (15)
Ban violent pictures	−19	·	22	−22 (−21)	· ( )	25 (24)
Ban religious abuse	−26	·	30	−21 (−27)	· ( )	25 (30)
of Christianity	−41	·	46	−31 (−38)	· ( )	36 (44)
of minority religions	−14	·	18	−13 (−15)	· ( )	22 (16)
Ban lies	−24	·	31	−27 (−26)	· ( )	14 (14)
Ban sensational crime coverage	−35	·	39	· ( )	· ( )	32 (28)
Equal TV for parties	−12	12	23	· ( )	12 (13)	18 (16)
Ban protest/gala procession	−34	−28	42	−27 (−24)	−13 (−13)	33 (29)
political protest	−42	−37	54	−34 (−31)	· ( )	42 (44)
religious	−40	−30	48	−27 (−18)	· ( )	35 (22)
town gala	−20	−18	25	−22 (−26)	· ( )	29 (25)

Ban potential riot	-30	36	-19 (-20)	-12 ( )	28 (26)
if political demonstration	-37	44	-31 (-23)	-13 ( )	40 (35)
if football match	-21	27	-16 (-16)	-11 ( )	17 (15)
Resist tax but not	-23	27	-19 (-20)	-10 ( )	26 (26)
refuse to pay	-20	26	-17 ( )	-12 ( )	31 (38)
riot	-36	43	-26 (-36)	-14 (-22)	34 (49)
attack officials	.	.	. ( )	-12 (-13)	17 (26)
demonstrate	-45	55	-33 (-30)	-14 (-15)	42 (38)
Against right to join trade union	-15	32	-24 ( )	-17 (-15)	27 (28)
including essential public services	-20	39	-27 ( )	-21 (-18)	32 (32)
excluding essential public services	-10	26	-20 ( )	-12 (-12)	25 (24)
Right to refuse to join trade union	.	-22	-11 ( )	. ( )	-15 (-13)
Against right to strike	-30	n.r.	-15 ( )	-28 (-23)	n.r. n.r.
including essential public services	-39	n.r.	-17 ( )	-33 (-25)	n.r. n.r.
excluding essential public services	-23	n.r.	-13 (-14)	-23 (-22)	n.r. n.r.

Notes: Measures of liberty and equality defined as in the text, and more fully in Chapter 4, each being an average of three micro-principles. In the liberty and equality columns, negative signs indicate that a proposition has less support amongst those who are committed to liberty or equality. Multiple correlation coefficients do not have a sign, of course. They are based upon stepwise multiple regressions in which all thirteen micro-principles could be used if sufficiently predictive.

n.r. = not relevant, since the 'right to strike' forms part of our measure of the protest principle and hence the multiple correlation would be spuriously high.

Correlations less than 0.10 have been replaced by full points.

divisions of principle. When sharp divisions over issues of practice did occur, there was more scope for principle—or, more accurately, divisions over matters of principle—to have a powerful effect. Town galas were generally popular, physical attacks on tax collectors were universally condemned, and the right to trade-union membership in non-essential services universally approved. On these matters, people with different principles were broadly in agreement. But opinion was more evenly divided on attitudes to political marches, or peaceful demonstrations against taxes, and these divisions of opinion on practical issues did reflect divisions of principle more closely. When the consensus over practice is broken, therefore, principle helps to decide who will break away from it.

As well as measuring the combined predictive power of all the micro-principles taken together, stepwise regression also identified which micro-principle appeared to have the most influence. Surprisingly perhaps, since the practical decisions at issue concerned freedom of expression and association, our micro-principles of right to free speech and rights of protest and rebellion were less powerfully predictive than respect for authority, traditional values, and economic equality. These three were, however, amongst the key principles most closely tied to the broad underlying dimensions of principle which we found in Chapter 4. Respect for traditional values was the most effective predictor of attitudes towards banning violent pictures, religious abuse, lies, and sensational crime coverage—though respect for authority was not far behind. Respect for authority was the most powerful predictor of attitudes towards banning disruptive processions, potential riots, and resistance to an unpopular tax. Conversely, while economic equality had very little predictive influence over the various issues of publication, it had some on issues of public order, and was the best predictor of attitudes towards issues that concerned trade unions and strikes.

Authoritarians versus Liberals

Another way of looking at the influence of principle upon practice is simply to contrast the practical decisions of those who have different principles. It has the added advantage of showing what statistical correlations mean in terms of percentage support for practical decisions, though it would be an impossibly long-winded way of presenting the bulk of our findings.

Respect for authority was the core micro-principle in the first dimension of principle uncovered in Chapter 4. We can divide both public and politicians roughly into half, according to whether they have above- or below-average respect for authority. We define that average level of respect for authority as the score on our respect for authority principle that lies midway between the mean scores amongst public and politicians. (Using the point midway between the median scores would make hardly any difference here.) Since politicians had rather less respect for authority than the public, 56 per cent of politicians fall into our below-average category while 60 per cent of the public fall into our above-average category. None the less that leaves adequately large numbers of both public and politicians in each category yet makes the dividing-point the same for both public and politicians. For brevity, let us use the terms 'authoritarians' and 'liberals' in this section for those with above- and below-average respect for authority.

Earlier in this chapter we found that our measures of principle correlated much more strongly with attitudes towards the abuse of Christianity than with attitudes towards the abuse of minority religions. The reason for that is now clear. Amongst politicians, above-average respect for authority more than doubled support for a ban on the abuse of Christianity—raising it quite dramatically from 24 per cent (amongst the liberals) to 59 per cent (amongst the authoritarians). By contrast, support for a ban on the abuse of minority religions only went up from an already very high 74 per cent (amongst the more liberal politicians) to 82 per cent (amongst the more authoritarian). Indeed, support for a ban on the abuse of minority religions was so high generally that an above-average respect for authority could do little to raise it further—hence the low correlation. Conversely, however, while authoritarians showed high opposition to abuse of any religion, liberals were fairly willing to tolerate abuse of Christianity, the majority religion in Britain, but very unwilling to tolerate abuse of minority religions: which may suggest that they see this abuse more in terms of racial discrimination than in terms of religious discrimination or may, of course, simply reflect liberals' instinctive sympathies for minorities and the oppressed (Table 5.7).[22]

Members of the public who had above- and below-average respect for authority proved to be almost identical to similarly authoritarian (or liberal) politicians in terms of their support for a ban on the abuse of minority religions: 75 per cent of the liberal members of the public and 82 per cent of the authoritarians supported such a ban. Their support for a ban on abusive attacks on Christianity, however, was different from that of politicians, even though it went in the same direction, with 46 per cent of the liberals and 67 per cent of the authoritarians supporting such a ban. Liberal members of the public especially were less liberal in practice than politicians with the same liberal principles.

Again amongst politicians, 68 per cent of authoritarians but only 33 per cent of liberals would ban a political demonstration that blocked traffic,

TABLE 5.7. *Support for freedom of expression in practice,
by liberals and authoritarians*

	Politicians		British public (Scottish public)	
	Liberals (%)	Authoritarians (%)	Liberals (%)	Authoritarians (%)
Category distribution	*56*	*44*	*40 (41)*	*60 (59)*
Not next door	71	73	73 (74)	73 (72)
Not with my children	88	91	85 (87)	87 (90)
Ban speeches	22	39	35 (38)	50 (59)
Ban teaching	34	62	60 (62)	71 (75)
Ban racial/religious incitement	75	74	61 (68)	67 (66)
racial	83	78	72 (75)	69 (70)
religious	68	70	50 (61)	64 (62)
Ban violent pictures	76	87	72 (69)	86 (82)
Ban religious abuse	51	71	61 (59)	75 (81)
of Christianity	24	59	46 (42)	67 (78)
of minority religions	74	82	75 (73)	82 (84)
Ban lies	83	92	88 (89)	91 (87)
Ban sensational crime coverage	21	46	33 (34)	51 (53)
Equal TV coverage	41	46	75 (71)	80 (79)

Note: Liberals and authoritarians defined as in the text.

while—in the case of politicians—there was no majority of either liberals or authoritarians for banning an equally disruptive town gala. So liberal politicians opposed any ban on disruptive processions, while their authoritarian colleagues were more discriminating and would ban a disruptive political or religious demonstration, but not a disruptive town gala. Hence respect for authority correlated much more with attitudes towards a disruptive political or religious demonstration, than with attitudes towards a disruptive town gala.

Both liberal and authoritarian politicians were very opposed to a refusal to pay taxes (over 90 per cent), and almost totally opposed to attacks on tax collectors (over 99 per cent). But while they were agreed on opposition to those extreme forms of protest, liberals and authoritarians differed by 28 per cent in their opposition to riotous demonstrations against tax, and by a massive

TABLE 5.8. *Support for freedom to protest in practice,
by liberals and authoritarians*

	Politicians		British public (Scottish public)	
	Liberals (%)	Authoritarians (%)	Liberals (%)	Authoritarians (%)
Category distribution	*56*	*44*	*40 (41)*	*60 (59)*
Ban protest/gala procession	30	60	50 (55)	71 (73)
political protest	33	68	56 (52)	82 (81)
religious	38	73	62 (73)	80 (81)
town gala	21	38	36 (40)	53 (57)
Ban potential political/football riot political	19	46	26 (32)	44 (45)
demonstration	26	57	26 (42)	54 (56)
football match	14	33	27 (23)	35 (35)
Resist tax but not	65	87	66 (59)	80 (77)
refuse to pay	90	99	81 (74)	89 (81)
riot	63	91	63 (44)	81 (83)
attack officials	99	100	96 (95)	93 (97)
demonstrate	11	55	22 (21)	57 (46)

44 per cent in their opposition to peaceful demonstrations against tax (Table 5.8).

Unlike the Conservative government in Britain, only a handful of even the more authoritarian politicians would deny workers the right to join trade unions, whether or not those workers were employed in essential public services. But liberals and authoritarians differed more on banning strikes, especially in essential public services: 57 per cent of authoritarian politicians but only 18 per cent of liberal politicians would ban them. Hence respect for authority correlated much more strongly with the right for workers in essential services to strike than it did with their right to join a trade union.

So differences between liberal and authoritarian politicians in their percentage support for practical decisions were very large indeed. And while they were noticeably smaller amongst the public than amongst politicians, they were still frequently of the order of 20 per cent (Table 5.9).

Moreover, these percentage differences would have been considerably

TABLE 5.9. *Support for freedom of association in practice, by liberals and authoritarians*

	Politicians		British public (Scottish public)	
	Liberals (%)	Authoritarians (%)	Liberals (%)	Authoritarians (%)
Category distribution	56	44	40 (41)	60 (59)
Against right to join trade union	1	6	3 (3)	6 (5)
including essential public services	1	8	4 (3)	7 (4)
excluding essential public services	1	4	3 (4)	5 (6)
Against right to refuse to join trade union	3	3	3 (3)	4 (4)
Against right to strike	11	39	16 (15)	28 (21)
including essential public services	18	57	24 (22)	38 (24)
excluding essential public services	4	19	9 (7)	17 (18)

TABLE 5.10.   *Support for a ban on a disruptive demonstration or gala,*
by four levels of respect for authority

	Politicians (%)	British public (%)	(Scottish public) (%)
Amongst those whose respect for authority falls into the			
lowest quartile	23	42	(46)
second quartile	43	58	(62)
third quartile	53	68	(68)
highest quartile	66	74	(79)

Note: Quartile cut points were defined as the points mid-way between the quartile points for the British public and politicians' samples. Thus the same cut-points were used for each of the three samples, though, of course, rather more of the politicians fall into the lower quartiles, and rather more of the public into the higher quartiles as defined here.

larger still if, instead of dividing people into just two groups, with above- and below-average respect for authority, we had divided them into a wider range of groups with greater differences on principle. For example, politicians who were simply *above and below average* on respect for authority differed by 30 per cent in their willingness to ban disruptive demonstrations or galas, but those in the *top and bottom quartiles* on respect for authority differed by 43 per cent; amongst the public the corresponding figures were 21 per cent and 32 per cent.

Principle does matter; it matters a great deal; and where it appears not to matter the explanation is usually that a tidal wave of sympathy (for the right of workers to join trade unions, for example) or a tidal wave of revulsion (against violence, for example) drives liberals and authoritarians together on a limited range of specific issues (Table 5.10).

FREEDOM OF INFORMATION

While some issues of censorship and press freedom reflect principles of free expression, others are more closely related to freedom of information—the public's so-called 'right to know'.[23] We looked into this second aspect of press freedom in a number of ways. First we asked our respondents whether they thought that each of the following:

should be [*allowed* on television without any restrictions, or restricted, for example, to late night viewing, or *banned* from television altogether/*allowed* in newspapers without any restrictions, or *restricted*, for example, to books, or *banned* from publication altogether]:

- interviews with supporters of [IRA terrorists/Protestant terrorists in Northern Ireland]?
- stories that intrude into [ordinary people's/leading politicians'] private lives?

Combining answers to the television and press versions of these questions, we found that just over half the public supported a ban on intrusions into people's private lives and just under half supported a ban on interviews with supporters of terrorists. In both cases, politicians gave roughly 10 per cent less support to a ban than did the public.

Throughout the period spanned by our surveys, the issue of press intrusions into private lives was hotly debated. In July 1989 the government set up an official inquiry under Sir David Calcutt into the issue. Six years and several official and unofficial inquiries later the government published its White Paper *Privacy and Media Intrusion: The Government's Response* in July 1995.[24] That White Paper finally recommended against the introduction of new criminal offences to prevent such press intrusions into private lives, but only after the industry's own Press Complaints Commission had appointed a former government minister as its chairman. Interestingly, the government minister, Virginia Bottomley, declared that 'the government would prefer to see a self-regulatory process than to introduce a law which would create more problems than it is designed to solve',[25] while her backbenchers and the chief opposition spokesman expressed disappointment at the lack of proposals for more restrictive new laws.

We found that both the public and politicians were 21 per cent more willing to ban intrusions into the lives of ordinary people than into the lives of leading politicians. Indeed, while a majority would ban intrusions into the lives of ordinary people, a majority would permit press intrusions into the lives of leading politicians. Politicians were less willing than the public to ban press intrusions into private lives and, to their credit, they took that relatively liberal view irrespective of whether the intrusions were into ordinary people's lives or into politicians' lives: their principles outweighed their personal interests.

In 1988 the then Home Secretary, Douglas Hurd, issued an order to both the BBC and IBA under the 1981 Broadcasting Act, banning the broadcast of any person 'representing or purporting to represent' a list of organizations

TABLE 5.11. *Freedom of information in practice*

	Politicians (%)	British public (%)	(Scottish public) (%)
Ban interviews with terrorists	37	48	(54)
IRA	38	50	(57)
Protestant terrorists	37	45	(52)
Ban intrusions into private lives	45	54	(51)
of ordinary people	56	64	(64)
of leading politicians	34	43	(38)
Ban publication of confidential documents	46	58	(53)
defence plans	62	76	(66)
economic plans	44	51	(51)
health plans	31	47	(40)
Ban publication of black crime rates	23	40	(42)

that included the then *illegal* IRA and UVF, and the then *legal* UDA and Sinn Fein.[26] The broadcasters responded by screening interviews in which they used actors to 'voice-over' silent film using the words, and even the accents, of the original interviewees. As the Peace Process has developed, the ban has been lifted, but it was in place throughout the period of our surveys. It had the support of just under half the public though only just over a third of politicians. Neither the public nor politicians distinguished between IRA and Protestant terrorists in this connection. Both the public and politicians were marginally *more* inclined to ban interviews with terrorists than they were to ban intrusions into the private lives of *leading politicians*, though much *less* inclined to ban interviews with terrorists than press intrusions into the lives of *ordinary citizens* (Table 5.11).

British governments have long been obsessed by the supposed need for secrecy.[27] The notorious Section Two of the 1911 Official Secrets Act was so draconian that it eventually became almost impossible to get juries to take it seriously: 'it [was] difficult to defend a statutory provision which in theory at any rate [made] it a criminal offence to tell an outsider what [was] on the menu in the office staff canteen.'[28] The new Official Secrets Act 1989 followed Margaret Thatcher's general philosophy of reducing the role of government but increasing its authority over the domain that it retained. Thus the range of items designated as secret was reduced but the Act's approach towards the remaining government secrets was uncompromising. Under the

1989 Act newspapers which published government secrets could not defend themselves in court by claiming 'prior publication elsewhere' or that the 'public interest' in publication should take priority over the government's interest in secrecy, since both these classic arguments for publication were explicitly rejected in the Act.[29]

To get the public's view on government secrets, we asked whether: 'Newspapers which get hold of confidential government documents about [defence/economic/health service] plans should *not* be allowed to publish them [(null)/because publications might damage our national interests]. Agree/disagree?' And we found that, in these circumstances, politicians backed freedom of information more than the public: only 46 per cent of politicians but 58 per cent of the public would ban publication of confidential government plans. However, both the public and politicians were around 30 per cent more willing to ban publication of confidential defence plans than confidential health service plans.

Finally we asked whether: 'Newspapers should be banned from publishing research showing very high rates of crime among blacks [(null)/ because this may encourage prejudice against them]. Agree/disagree?' This produced another significant difference between the public and politicians: 40 per cent of the public but only 23 per cent of politicians agreed to such a ban.

As on practical decisions about freedom of expression, principles exerted a very strong influence upon these practical decisions about freedom of information. The multiple correlation between our battery of micro-principles and attitudes towards banning interviews with terrorists or publication of confidential government documents ran as high as 0.65 amongst politicians and 0.48 amongst the general public. There were smaller but still quite strong correlations with attitudes towards banning intrusions into private lives or the publication of black crime rates. We also found evidence that principles had a slightly—but only slightly—stronger influence upon attitudes towards banning interviews with supporters of the IRA than with Protestant terrorists (Table 5.12).

On all these practical issues concerning freedom of information, correlations with commitment to liberty were stronger than with commitment to equality, though, as before, the distinction between the influence of these two principles was less clear amongst politicians, particularly on the issue of publishing confidential government documents. And, although the correlations with equality were very weak, it is significant none the less that it was the egalitarians who were the *least* willing to defend press intrusions into the lives of ordinary people or the publication of black crime rates, although

TABLE 5.12. *Correlations between principle and practice on freedom of information*

	Politicians			British public (Scottish public)		
	Liberty (r × 100)	Equality (r × 100)	Multiple (r × 100)	Liberty (r × 100)	Equality (r × 100)	Multiple (r × 100)
Ban interviews with terrorists	-57	-28	62	-33 (-32)	-10 (.)	42 (43)
IRA	-58	-35	65	-39 (-37)	-11 (.)	48 (52)
Protestant terrorists	-56	-21	60	-26 (-27)	. (.)	38 (39)
Ban intrusions into private lives	-26	.	32	-22 (-22)	. (.)	25 (25)
of ordinary people	-23	.	30	-22 (-29)	. (.)	28 (35)
of leading politicians	-31	.	35	-23 (-20)	. (.)	27 (23)
Ban publication of confidential documents	-46	-39	55	-29 (-29)	-13 (-14)	36 (36)
defence plans	-45	-39	57	-33 (-27)	-19 (-20)	42 (38)
economic plans	-53	-40	59	-28 (-27)	-14 (-18)	38 (39)
health plans	-47	-44	58	-29 (-31)	. (-10)	38 (39)
Ban publication of black crime rates	-26	.	34	-25 (-22)	14 (.)	32 (30)

Note: Correlations less than 0.10 have been replaced by full points.

they were by far the most willing to defend interviews with apologists for terrorism or the publication of confidential government documents.

Amongst individual micro-principles, respect for authority and traditional values were particularly influential once again. Both exerted an influence in the same direction, but, of the two, respect for authority had the greater influence upon attitudes towards banning interviews with terrorists or the publication of government secrets, while adherence to traditional values had the greater influence upon attitudes towards banning publication of black crime rates or press intrusions into private lives.

FREEDOM OF LIFESTYLE

In Chapters 2 and 3 we found a high level of commitment in principle to toleration of 'different beliefs and lifestyles', a division of opinion on whether laws should reflect morals, and a large majority against enforcing community standards. Politicians had an even higher respect than the public for tolerating different beliefs and lifestyles; they opposed the enforcement of community standards; and they were massively opposed to the idea of translating morals into laws.[30]

But, in Bhikhu Parekh's words, 'no society can tolerate every practice'.[31] We asked specific questions about drink (by implication, alcoholic), drugs, abortion, AIDS tests, homosexual activity, and ritual slaughter. Across this range of issues, it was only on attitudes towards AIDS tests that politicians were much more tolerant than the public. Indeed, on some other issues, such as restricting drugs, politicians proved to be slightly less tolerant than the public in practice. Despite their clear differences on principle, we found that in practice there was little difference between the public and politicians on most issues relating to morals and lifestyle.

We asked whether 'People should be allowed to [take whatever drugs/ drink as much as] they like [(null)/provided they do not harm or behave offensively to other people]'. While on average, just over half the politicians and just under half the public would put limits on people's intake of drugs or alcohol, their answers depended very much on whether the question referred to drink or drugs. Although only a quarter of both groups would restrict consumption of alcohol, a significant majority—79 per cent of politicians and 69 per cent of the public—would limit the intake of drugs. Politicians and the public had very similar (and fairly permissive) attitudes to drink, but politicians proved to be 10 per cent more restrictive than the public in their attitude to drugs, despite their much greater commitment in principle to tolerating deviant lifestyles (Table 5.13).

TABLE 5.13. *Freedom of lifestyle in practice*

	Politicians (%)	British public (%)	(Scottish public) (%)
Limit drugs/drink	51	46	(48)
drugs	79	69	(72)
drink	25	24	(25)
Abortion morally wrong	46	46	(54)
IF RIGHT: free on NHS	82	72	(79)
IF WRONG: make illegal	41	42	(50)
Compulsory AIDS tests	55	70	(71)
for cooks	47	60	(61)
for surgeons	62	81	(81)
Accept ban on homosexuality	18	16	(20)
Want ban on homosexuality	14	20	(24)
Accept ban on ritual slaughter	71	71	(65)
Want ban on ritual slaughter	72	78	(80)

We phrased our question on abortion in a way that would allow us to explore the extent to which people would tolerate different lifestyles. Specifically, we asked: 'Suppose that a woman decides to have an abortion *for no other reason* than that she does not wish to have the child. Then, in this particular case, would she be morally right or morally wrong to have an abortion?' If the response was that such an abortion would be morally right, we then asked: 'Should she be able to get an abortion free on the NHS or should she have to pay for it?' On the other hand, if the initial response was that the abortion would be morally wrong, we then asked: 'Irrespective of your personal views do you think that the *law* should forbid such an abortion?'

Just under half of both politicians and the public said an abortion would be morally wrong in these circumstances, but only two-fifths of those who said it would be wrong (about one-fifth of all interviewees, therefore) went on to say that it should be made illegal. So there was no difference between politicians and the public in their tolerance of abortion.

Amongst those who said it would be morally right, 72 per cent of the public and 82 per cent of politicians said she should 'be able to get an abortion free on the NHS' rather than having to pay for it herself—but that is not evidence of greater tolerance amongst politicians so much as a greater commitment to publicly financed welfare.

On attitudes towards AIDS tests, politicians were clearly more tolerant than the public, however. We asked: 'Should [people who cook for restaurants or schools/surgeons and dentists] be required to take a test to prove that they have not been infected by the virus which causes AIDS?' Fully 70 per cent of the public but only 55 per cent of politicians backed such tests. However, both the public and politicians were more inclined to impose AIDS tests on surgeons than on cooks: amongst the public 21 per cent more would do so, and amongst politicians 15 per cent more.

Elsewhere in the interview we asked: 'Suppose [the majority/parliament/ the government] wanted to make homosexuality a crime. Should they be able to do so even though the ban would reduce the freedom of individuals to do what they want? And do you, yourself, favour such a ban?' Less than a fifth of the British public or politicians would either accept or advocate such a ban. In Scotland exactly a fifth said they would accept a ban and just under a quarter said they would advocate one. Although marginally more politicians than the public—18 per cent as opposed to 16 per cent—said they would accept a ban on homosexuality, less of the politicians than the public —14 per cent as opposed to 20 per cent—actually favoured such a ban.

Using a similar format of question, we asked: 'Suppose [the majority/ parliament/the government] wanted to ban the ritual slaughter of animals by cruel methods, even if it was part of a religious tradition. Should they be able to do so? And do you, yourself, favour such a ban?' An overwhelming majority of around three-quarters of both the public and politicians would accept, and advocate, a ban on such methods of slaughter. As Jeremy Paxman noted during the 1995 demonstrations against the export of live calves, concern for animals is deeply rooted in British culture.[32] Certainly we found that it far outweighed religious tolerance.

That recalls the response we discussed in Chapter 2 to our question about sympathies for various potentially unpopular groups of activists, minorities, or militants. Out of eleven groups only two received a score that indicated positive sympathy—'environmental campaigners like Greenpeace' and 'animal-rights activists'. We also found in Chapter 3 that politicians had more sympathy than the public for activists representing religious minorities, but much less sympathy than the public for animal-rights activists; and, consistent with that, we also found the public slightly more willing than politicians—78 per cent compared to 72 per cent—to ban such methods of slaughter.

So the high level of public tolerance for the principle of 'tolerating different beliefs and lifestyles', and the large majority which opposed the principle of enforcing community standards, translated into very diverse levels of tolerance in practice: fairly widespread tolerance of unlimited drinking and homosexuality was combined with equally widespread intolerance of drug-taking and cruel methods of ritual slaughter. An even division of opinion about the morality of 'abortion on demand' was combined with a marked reluctance to make it illegal. There was occasional slight evidence of greater practical tolerance amongst politicians, but, in general, their greater commitment to the principle of tolerance for a variety of lifestyles did *not* translate into much greater tolerance in practice—a very significant *lack* of difference, where a greater difference might have been expected (Table 5.14).

On the other hand, attitudes towards practical issues of lifestyle did correlate with principle, both amongst politicians and the public. While the overall level of practical tolerance varied sharply according to the specific issue involved, on each issue, those politicians or members of the public who had expressed the greatest commitment to tolerance-in-principle were the ones who tended to display the greatest tolerance-in-practice.

General principles correlated very weakly with attitudes towards cruel methods of ritual slaughter, but more strongly with issues of drugs, abortion, AIDS testing, and homosexuality. Commitment to liberty correlated very strongly with opposition to AIDS test for cooks, though somewhat less strongly with opposition to AIDS tests for surgeons. Similarly, commitment to liberty correlated fairly strongly with attitudes towards drugs but not with attitudes towards alcohol. And, as might be expected, opinion on all these issues hardly correlated with commitment to equality. But opposition to a ban on homosexuality correlated almost equally well with commitments to liberty and equality (though, amongst politicians only, and only with respect to advocating a ban, the correlation was markedly higher with liberty than with equality).

Different aspects of the abortion issue correlated with different principles in an obviously rational way, most clearly so amongst the public. Commitment to liberty correlated with the view that abortion on demand was morally right. Even amongst those who thought abortion on demand was morally wrong, commitment to liberty correlated with the view that it should not be legally banned. Neither of these views was influenced by commitment to equality. But amongst those who felt abortion on demand was morally right, it was commitment to equality, rather than to liberty, which made them support free access to NHS facilities for abortion.

Three of our thirteen micro-principles had a particularly strong influence upon attitudes to lifestyle issues, but these were not the same three principles as those which correlated most strongly with attitudes to the practice of other aspects of freedom such as free speech. The principles that correlated most

TABLE 5.14. *Correlations between principles and practice on freedom of lifestyle*

	Politicians			British public (Scottish public)		
	Liberty (r × 100)	Equality (r × 100)	Multiple (r × 100)	Liberty (r × 100)	Equality (r × 100)	Multiple (r × 100)
Limit drugs/drink	−13	·	19	−14 (−13)	· ( )	17 (20)
drugs	−21	·	21	−22 (−19)	· ( )	23 (26)
drink	−11	·	21	· (−11)	· ( )	18 (23)
Abortion morally wrong	−14	·	21	−17 (−17)	· ( )	23 (22)
IF RIGHT: free on NHS	−24	−29	32	· (−10)	−17 ( )	18 (19)
IF WRONG: make illegal	−18	·	24	−23 (−26)	· ( )	27 (32)
Compulsory AIDS tests	−38	−13	40	−28 (−29)	· ( )	33 (34)
for cooks	−47	−17	50	−35 (−33)	−15 ( )	41 (37)
for surgeons	−31	−11	35	−20 (−23)	· ( )	26 (34)
Accept ban on homosexuality	−26	−27	35	−23 (−26)	−24 (−27)	40 (46)
Want ban on homosexuality	−36	−26	47	−26 (−31)	−23 (−25)	44 (50)
Accept ban on ritual slaughter	·	·	14	· (11)	· ( )	11 (14)
Want ban on ritual slaughter	−11	·	17	· (·)	· ( )	· (·)

Note: Correlations less than 0.10 have been replaced by full points.

with lifestyle issues were traditional values, tolerance, and equal rights. Traditional values had by far the most influence upon attitudes towards the *morality* of abortion but, very significantly, not on attitudes towards whether an immoral abortion should then be made *illegal*. Reasonably enough, it was tolerance that had the greatest influence upon whether an immoral abortion should be made illegal. Tolerance and traditional values vied with each other for the most influence upon attitudes to a ban on drug-taking and excessive drinking, or towards compulsory AIDS tests. Tolerance and equal rights were both strong influences upon attitudes towards a ban on homosexuality, though our composite measure of the equal-rights principle did include an explicit question about homosexuals which makes the size of that correlation somewhat less impressive.

POWERS TO UPHOLD THE LAW

Despite greater deference to the principle of obeying the law amongst politicians than amongst the public, when it came to practical issues of law enforcement and criminal-justice procedure, it was politicians who tilted more towards the rights of the accused and less towards the powers of law enforcement.[33]

On some questions we found no difference between the public and politicians and overwhelming support for one side of the issue. When we asked whether social workers should 'have the right to take a child away from its parents if [(null)/there are allegations that] the parents regularly ill treat the child?' 87 per cent of both the British public and politicians agreed (and only marginally less in Scotland), despite a series of notorious scandals in Britain about social workers' decisions to remove children from their families during the months preceding the survey.[34] At the same time, almost 90 per cent of both public and politicians agreed that 'courts should not convict people purely on the basis of a confession [(null)/ because people sometimes confess to things they haven't done/because people are sometimes put under so much pressure they confess to things they have not done]'. A series of false convictions based on extorted or faked confessions had been exposed and condemned in the months before and during the survey (Table 5.15).[35]

Opinion was more divided, and differences between public and politicians greater, on other issues of law enforcement. While those who respect authority may wish to protect the confidentiality of government information, those who respect the liberty of citizens may wish to protect the confidentiality of others, especially of opposition politicians, journalists, the clergy,

TABLE 5.15. *Support for practical measures to uphold the law*

	Politicians (%)	British public (%)	(Scottish public) (%)
Convict on confession	11	12	(11)
Support death penalty	26	50	(53)
Remove child	87	87	(85)
Reveal sources	27	40	(41)
journalists	39	47	(43)
clergy	16	34	(40)
Random searches in mall	30	46	(44)
drugs	32	48	(48)
theft	28	43	(41)
guards	30	43	(46)
police	40	54	(50)
owners	19	40	(37)
shoppers	27	43	(41)
workers	32	48	(48)

or professional advisers.[36] Under Article 47 of the Basic Law of Germany '[parliamentary] deputies may refuse to give evidence concerning persons who have confided facts to them in their capacity as deputies . . . [and] no seizure of documents shall be permissible'.[37] In the view of those who framed the German Constitution, democracy requires that MPs' sources be protected. Similarly, can journalists obtain the access they need to report on events and conditions of public concern without sometimes refusing to co-operate in specific acts of law enforcement? Television news organizations, especially the BBC and ITN, normally resist demands to pass video-tapes to the authorities unless and until they are put under extreme duress by the courts. On the other hand, governments tend to be more concerned with enforcing the law than protecting journalists and their sources. As Prime Minister Margaret Thatcher expressed her view very plainly on one occasion, either 'one was on the side of justice in these matters or one was on the side of terrorism'.[38] It is easy to understand how prime ministers weighed down by the burdens of office might take that view. But what of the public and what of less pressured politicians outside central government?

We asked: 'If a person consults a [journalist/clergyman] in confidence, and confesses to a crime, do you think that a court should be able to force the [journalist/clergyman] to reveal the name of that person?' Our question touched on both the traditional church view of the 'privacy of the confessional' and the modern dilemma facing investigative journalists concerned with political terrorism as well as organized crime. Although 40 per cent of the public said the clergy or journalists should reveal the identity of someone who had told them, in confidence, about a crime he or she had committed, only 27 per cent of politicians agreed.

McClosky and Brill had found American élites more willing than their public to force journalists to reveal their sources, but their question included a bizarre suggestion that forcing journalists to reveal sources 'is justified when the names of the sources are necessary *for a fair trial*' (emphasis added), which perhaps weighed heavily with American élites.[39] We certainly found no evidence of such a governing perspective on the issue of revealing sources; on the contrary, British politicians were notably pro-citizen and anti-authority on this issue.

Both the public and politicians were substantially more inclined to allow courts to force journalists, rather than clergy, to reveal their sources, however (the public by 13 per cent, and politicians by 23 per cent)—interesting evidence of respect for the sanctity of the church in a secular age (or, some would say, of a superstitious hangover from the past).

The 1984 Police and Criminal Evidence Act (PACE) granted extended stop-and-search powers to the police, 'amidst a formidable array of new police powers'[40] and a 'token [extension of suspects'] rights'. None the less, the public were even more willing to approve random searches than politicians. We asked: 'In the case where there is concern about [illegal drug use/ shoplifting] in a shopping centre, do you think that a [security guard/police officer/shop owner] should have the right to make random searches of the bags carried by [shoppers/people who work in that shopping centre]?' Overall, 46 per cent of the public but only 30 per cent of politicians approved of random searches in these circumstances. It made little difference whether the searches were of shoppers or workers, nor whether they were for drugs or for shoplifting; on the other hand, both the public and politicians were particularly willing to concede the right of search to the police, and particularly unwilling to concede it to shop owners—by a margin of 14 per cent amongst the public and 21 per cent amongst politicians.

However, the largest difference between the public and politicians was on the death penalty. We asked: '[Given that parliament has repeatedly voted against the death penalty/In order to clamp down on rising crime and violence], do you think Britain should reintroduce the death penalty for murder, or keep things as they are?' In our survey, 50 per cent of the public supported the reintroduction of the death penalty. Other surveys have found more public support for the death penalty[41] though ours put the question in the midst of a relatively sophisticated dialogue about civil rights. Even so, there was a sharp contrast between the views of the public and those of politicians: only 26 per cent of politicians supported the reintroduction of the death penalty (Table 5.16).

Principle had a strong influence upon attitudes towards the death penalty —a multiple correlation of 0.54 amongst politicians and 0.39 amongst the public; and principle also had a moderate influence upon all other issues of law enforcement except for the powers of social workers to remove children from their families. The micro-principles of respect for authority and limited government had a particularly strong influence—in opposite directions, of course.

Attitudes towards random searches correlated more with commitment to liberty than to equality. Much more surprisingly, our survey shows that opposition to conviction-on-confession, opposition to the death penalty, and refusal to name sources correlated with commitment to equality as well as with commitment to liberty. Formally, of course, these are all issues of liberty, but we know that in practice it is the poor and those without the right connections who get convicted and executed in disproportionate numbers. So, in practice, issues of law enforcement often are issues of equality as well as being issues of liberty or authority.[42]

POWERS TO DEFEND THE STATE

Compared to the public, politicians were much more willing to limit the powers of the state and to defend the rights of citizens in matters of ordinary crime. But when state security was threatened, politicians were no longer, in practice, any more liberal than the public. Then politicians—even the local politicians interviewed in our survey—were actually *more* willing than the public to concede power to the authorities. The difference of opinion between politicians and public on state security was never large, but it was striking because it ran in the opposite direction to the usual differences between public and politicians.

We asked: 'If there is a genuine national emergency, is it all right to suspend some of our usual civil rights?' On this initial question, 80 per cent of politicians as against 78 per cent of the public agreed to the suspension of civil rights. The difference of 2 per cent is trivial, and could easily be explained away as a sampling quirk. But on most questions about civil rights we should have expected a substantial difference between public and

TABLE 5.16. *Correlations between principles and practice on powers to uphold the law*

	Politicians			British public (Scottish public)		
	Liberty (r × 100)	Equality (r × 100)	Multiple (r × 100)	Liberty (r × 100)	Equality (r × 100)	Multiple (r × 100)
Convict on confession	-22	-25	32	-13 (.)	. (.)	20 (14)
Support death penalty	-42	-40	54	-28 (-27)	-17 (-16)	39 (41)
Remove child	.	11	14	. (.)	. (.)	11 (16)
Reveal sources	-16	-20	28	. (-12)	. (.)	18 (18)
journalists	-24	-28	33	. (-11)	-15 (-14)	21 (24)
clergy	.	-11	26	. (-13)	. (.)	20 (22)
Random searches in mall	-24	-18	31	-17 (-19)	. (.)	23 (22)
drugs	-30	-17	34	-22 (-21)	. (.)	30 (26)
theft	-18	-18	30	-12 (-16)	. (.)	17 (19)
guards	-22	-15	29	-21 (-25)	. (.)	30 (26)
police	-26	-19	31	-16 (-14)	. (.)	23 (24)
owners	-25	-18	35	-15 (-17)	. (.)	19 (24)
shoppers	-25	-18	30	-18 (-16)	. (-13)	26 (24)
workers	-22	-17	30	-17 (-21)	. (.)	22 (22)

Note: Correlations of less than 0.10 have been replaced by full points.

politicians—and one which ran in the opposite direction. That is what makes this numerically trivial difference politically significant. At the very least it is another case of 'the dog that did not bark' to which Sherlock Holmes drew attention. It is evidence that the governing perspective—which we uncovered in Chapter 3—may operate in practice as well as in principle.[43]

If our respondents agreed to the suspension of civil rights in times of national emergency (which most of them did), we went on to ask: 'Would [widespread terrorism/widespread public disorder/widespread attacks on minority ethnic or racial groups/an economic crisis caused by strikes in important industries] be sufficient to justify suspending some of our usual civil rights?' Examples of such action in Britain at the time of our survey included the Prevention of Terrorism Act, passed annually since the Birmingham bomb outrages of 1974 (Table 5.17).

Amongst those who agreed that it was all right to suspend civil rights in an emergency, two-thirds (on average) accepted the particular justification offered, though the four different justifications naturally attracted greatly differing levels of support. Terrorism was the most persuasive justification and strikes the least persuasive—by a margin of 34 per cent amongst the public and an even larger margin of 48 per cent amongst politicians. Indeed, our detailed scenarios revealed a further twist in the complex web of opinion on security matters: politicians were more willing than the public to suspend civil rights in order to combat terrorism, yet less willing than the British public (at least outside Scotland) to do so merely in order to end economically damaging strikes.

We went on to examine attitudes towards one of the particular rights that might be suspended—the right of privacy.[44] Ewing and Gearty have claimed that 'the practice of telephone tapping in Britain is a symptom of the deep-rooted problems facing civil liberties in this country . . . the matter is now regulated by statute . . . yet the statute authorizes interception on wider grounds than those previously acknowledged . . . [and] unauthorized tapping may continue [with no mechanism of control] except the police'.[45] Peter Thornton quoted allegations of over 30,000 phone taps per year in Britain.[46]

We asked:

In order to combat [crime, should the police/terrorism, should the security services/ the spread of dangerous and undemocratic ideas, should the security services] ever be allowed to [tap phones/inspect people's bank accounts]?

IF YES: Should the [police/security services] themselves decide when to do this, or should they get permission each time from a judge?

TABLE 5.17. *Practical measures to defend the state*

	Politicians (%)	British public (%)	(Scottish public) (%)
OK to suspend rights in emergency	80	78	(74)
IF YES: Justified in order to combat	63	66	(62)
terrorism	84	79	(79)
disorder	73	75	(76)
attacks on minorities	59	62	(58)
strikes	36	45	(35)
Allow phone taps, bank inspections	54	48	(42)
phone taps	57	54	(49)
bank inspections	52	42	(35)
to combat crime	57	47	(45)
to combat terrorism	67	59	(50)
to combat dangerous ideas	40	38	(30)
IF YES TO PHONE TAPS, ETC:			
require permission from judge	94	86	(86)
price worth paying	93	93	(95)

ALSO IF YES: If you discovered the [police/security services] had done it to you, would you no longer feel it should be allowed, or would you feel it was just part of the price to be paid by law-abiding citizens for their protection?

Once again, politicians were more willing than the public, if only slightly so, to concede power to the authorities: 54 per cent of politicians compared to only 48 per cent of the public would concede these powers of surveillance.[47] But at the same time, amongst those who did accept state surveillance, an even higher proportion of politicians, 94 per cent compared to 86 per cent of the public, said that the prior permission of a judge should be sought in each case of surveillance. This is significant because one reason why politicians support government prerogatives more than the public may be their conviction that such prerogatives will not be misused, that there are sufficient internal checks to prevent arbitrary government action.

There was slightly more support for phone taps than for inspections of bank accounts, especially amongst the public. Motivations mattered far more than methods, however: there was most approval for surveillance to combat terrorism and least for surveillance to combat the spread of dangerous ideas

—by a margin of 21 per cent amongst the public and 27 per cent amongst politicians. Perhaps that reflected 1990s concerns over the bush fires of endemic terrorism in contrast to 1950s concerns over the Cold War and the struggle against communism, but it meant there was a substantial majority *against* state surveillance to combat dangerous ideas, yet a substantial majority *in favour* of surveillance to combat terrorism (Table 5.18).

Principles had a strong influence upon politicians' attitudes to emergency powers, though much less upon public attitudes—the multiple correlations were 0.45 and 0.22 respectively. In particular, principles had considerably more influence upon politicians' attitudes to the use of emergency powers to combat terrorism, disorder, or strikes than upon those of the public. At the same time, principles completely failed to influence politicians' attitudes to the use of emergency powers to protect ethnic minorities, while they did have some influence amongst the public. So, amongst politicians at least, sympathy for ethnic minorities and the itch to use emergency powers seldom coincided. We found earlier that politicians were unusually willing to protect ethnic minorities by banning racial or religious abuse, but not, it now seems, by going as far as imposing emergency powers.

Opposition to the idea of suspending civil rights in an emergency correlated with commitments to both liberty and equality; and so did opposition to all the justifications for emergency powers except for the use of emergency powers to combat attacks upon minorities. Commitment to liberty had no effect at all on attitudes towards the use of emergency powers to protect ethnic minorities, and, most unusually, commitment to equality actually *increased* support for this application of authoritarian methods.

Opposition to surveillance aimed at combating crime or terrorism correlated almost exclusively with commitment to equality. On the other hand, opposition to surveillance aimed at combating the spread of dangerous ideas correlated with commitments to both liberty and equality, as did more subtle questions about the need for judicial authorization, or an unwillingness to accept being placed under surveillance themselves. This suggests that the main reason for opposing surveillance aimed at crime and terrorism, like that for opposing other crime-prevention measures, is the fear that it will be applied inequitably rather than public concern that it is intrinsically illiberal.

EQUALITY IN POLITICAL LIFE

So far we have looked at attitudes to practical issues which seemed to be issues of liberty rather than of equality, on the surface at least. In the event,

TABLE 5.18. *Correlations between principles and practice on defending the state*

	Politicians			British public (Scottish public)		
	Liberty (r × 100)	Equality (r × 100)	Multiple (r × 100)	Liberty (r × 100)	Equality (r × 100)	Multiple (r × 100)
OK to suspend rights in emergency	-36	-31	45	-12 (.)	-15 (-11)	22 (20)
IF YES: Justified in order to combat						
terrorism	-18	-18	25	-15 (-12)	.	22 (17)
disorder	-19	-26	33	-12 (-14)	.	23 (22)
attacks on minorities	.	10	36	-17 (-10)	11	29 (16)
strikes	-36	-33	47	-24 (-23)	. (-26)	23 (33)
						34 (36)
Allow phone taps, bank inspections	.	-29	30	.	-17	26 (18)
phone taps	-13	-30	35	.	-14	24 (19)
bank inspections	.	-28	29	.	-20 (-10)	30 (22)
to combat crime	.	-22	26	(11)	-24 (-12)	29 (33)
to combat terrorism	.	-33	34	.	-17	28 (23)
to combat dangerous ideas	-20	-33	37	.	-13	22 (.)
IF YES TO PHONE TAPS, ETC:						
require permission from judge	16	13	24	(10)	.	15 (18)
price worth paying	-22	-17	27	.	(-11)	13 (18)

Note: Correlations less than 0.10 have been replaced by full points.

we found that opinion on some of those issues, especially those affecting the rights of trade unions, the right to strike, and the suppression of crime, was influenced by commitments to equality as well as to liberty. Now, however, we turn to issues which appear, even on the surface, to be issues of equality rather than of liberty, but it will not be entirely surprising if we find that commitment to liberty has a bearing on at least some aspects of these egalitarian issues.

We used a variety of scenarios to examine attitudes towards the practice of equality in the spheres of political and social life which touched on issues about elections and voting, education, employment, and health care.

We asked three sets of questions about equality in political life. First, we asked: 'Should citizens of Commonwealth countries like [Canada and Australia/Nigeria and India] be allowed to vote in British elections if they are living in Britain at the time? And how about people from European Community countries?' We intentionally chose one pair of Commonwealth countries that are still predominantly populated by whites, and one pair that are predominantly black or Asian, but no interviewee was ever asked about both. Consequently this provided a relatively unobtrusive indicator of comparative attitudes to black and white Commonwealth citizens. However, since none of our respondents was ever presented with all four countries, they may not have thought of these pairs of countries in terms of their ethnic or racial composition. Indeed, our measure may have been so unobtrusive as to be effectively invisible.

Just over two-fifths would concede voting rights to Commonwealth citizens and fractionally less to European Community citizens. We had expected that the first part of the question might reveal well-hidden racist tendencies, by showing stronger support for Canadians and Australians rather than Nigerians and Indians being allowed to vote in Britain. But our results showed the reverse: a slim majority would concede voting rights to Commonwealth citizens from the predominantly black and Asian countries, whereas only a minority of both the public and politicians would allow citizens of predominantly white Canada and Australia to vote in British elections—and the difference in attitude to black/Asian and white countries was quite large, a margin of 12 per cent amongst the public and 25 per cent amongst politicians.

We examined the issue of race and political equality more directly by linking it to a broader question about whether we need more women or ethnic and racial minorities as representatives in parliament. The political parties in Britain are currently taking some internal measures, such as all-female short lists for parliamentary candidatures, to increase the numbers of women and minorities in parliament, but there have been very few proposals to do so by law. The most politically credible has been the Scottish 'Woman's Claim of Right', which demands equal representation (by law) for men and women in a Scottish parliament or assembly, along with a raft of operational differences from the Westminster parliament, all designed to open participation to a broad range of women.[48]

We asked: 'Is it important to have more [women/ethnic or racial minority] MPs in parliament?' and, if the respondent replied that it was important, we asked two further questions: 'Ideally, should the proportion of [women/ethnic or racial minority] MPs in parliament be as large as in the country as a whole? And should the law be changed to ensure more [women/ethnic or racial minority] MPs?' Two-thirds of the public and three-quarters of politicians agreed it was important to have a more socially proportional parliament; and two-thirds of those who did agree opted for strict proportionality. Politicians drew little distinction between gender and race, but the public were 17 per cent more favourable to gender equality than to racial equality, and 20 per cent more inclined to opt for strict proportionality when the issue concerned gender rather than race.

The third part of the question, which asked whether the law should be changed, produced the greatest difference of opinion between the public and politicians, however. Amongst those who stressed the importance of more social proportionality in parliament, half the public but only one-fifth of politicians advocated changing the law to achieve it. Of course, the politicians we interviewed—male or female, black or white—had all achieved their leading position as a result of open competition, and might therefore be predisposed to defend existing arrangements, but it is equally possible that they were simply less inclined to use such regulatory interventions and coercive legislation (Table 5.19).

Although support for the proportional representation of women and minorities was quite high, there was a lot less support for what has traditionally been meant by the phrase 'proportional representation'—namely, a level of party representation in parliament that would be in proportion to party shares of the vote. We asked: 'Consider how the electoral system affects the three main parties. Should the proportion of seats for each party in the House of Commons be the same as its proportion of votes in the election, or should MPs be elected the way they are now?' Only 51 per cent of the public and 43 per cent of politicians opted for party proportionality.

Principles had a strong influence upon attitudes towards the practice of equality in political life. Amongst politicians, the multiple correlation between principles and support for racial quotas in parliament reached a remarkably

TABLE 5.19. *The practice of equality in political life*

	Politicians (%)	British public (%)	(Scottish public) (%)
Commonwealth franchise	42	45	(41)
for Canadians and Australians	30	39	(33)
for Nigerians and Indians	55	51	(50)
European franchise	41	39	(36)
Support more women/minorities in parliament	73	68	(70)
women	77	76	(76)
ethnic or racial minorities	70	59	(64)
IF FOR MORE WOMEN/MINORITIES:			
strictly proportional	67	67	(65)
change law	19	47	(51)
Support party PR	43	51	(53)

high 0.61, and, although they were lower amongst the public, they still reached as high as 0.41 on support for racial quotas in parliament.

Any explicit or even implicit reference to race seemed to trigger the application of principle. Principles had more influence upon support for racial quotas than gender quotas, and more influence upon support for the voting rights (in Britain) of Nigerian and Indian citizens than of Canadian and Australian citizens.

As might be expected, support for gender or ethnic quotas in parliament, and for Nigerian and Indian voting rights in Britain, all correlated much better with commitment to equality than to liberty, though support for party proportionality in parliament correlated at about the same level with both principles. The most influential micro-principles were equal rights and economic equality, and, of the two, equal rights had more influence than economic equality (Table 5.20).

EQUALITY IN SOCIAL LIFE

Although a number of British feminist theorists have become increasingly concerned about women's restricted experience of citizenship,[49] political equality, even in parliaments and cabinets, does not guarantee social equality.[50] Hilary Wainwright notes that 'The Norwegian Parliament, for instance,

TABLE 5.20. Correlations between principles and practice in political life

	Politicians			British public (Scottish public)		
	Liberty (r × 100)	Equality (r × 100)	Multiple (r × 100)	Liberty (r × 100)	Equality (r × 100)	Multiple (r × 100)
Commonwealth franchise	14	19	25	. (10)	16 (11)	17 (16)
for Canadians and Australians	11	.	15	. ( )	12 ( )	14 ( )
for Nigerians and Indians	16	29	35	. (14)	20 (18)	24 (27)
European franchise	28	22	35	. ( )	16 (14)	19 (19)
Support more women/minorities in parliament	32	51	56	. (10)	28 (29)	32 (33)
women	31	45	52	. ( )	20 (28)	26 (31)
ethnic or racial minorities	34	56	61	15 (15)	33 (30)	41 (37)
IF FOR MORE WOMEN/MINORITIES:						
strictly proportional	31	31	41	11 (12)	13 (16)	20 (23)
change law	12	23	25	-10 (-20)	23 (13)	36 (36)
Support party PR	41	39	53	21 (24)	15 ( )	33 (32)

Note: Correlations less than 0.10 have been replaced by full points.

is made up of over 40 per cent women and, between 1986–89 over a third of the cabinet were women, including the Prime Minister; yet Norway has one of the most gender segregated occupational structures in Western Europe and child-care provisions are amongst the lowest.'[51]

An uncompromising case for the use of quotas in social life was put by Justice Thurgood Marshall in his judgment on the celebrated case of *Bakke* v. *The University of California*: 'It is unnecessary in 20th century America to have individual negros demonstrate that they have been victims of racial discrimination; the racism of our society has been so pervasive that none, *regardless of wealth or position*, has managed to escape' (emphasis added).[52] American opinion has shifted since that time,[53] and the British—with or without justification—seem to feel less collective guilt about their past, and consequently less need for collective reparation. Wendy McElroy puts the case against quotas just as uncompromisingly as Justice Marshall put the case in favour: 'The preferential treatment of women in employment is nothing less than a frontal attack on the rights of the individual . . . it runs against the sense that every individual has the right to the fruit of whatever talent or resource he or she possesses.'[54]

In any event, British attitudes towards the use of quotas in the sphere of employment were even less favourable than they had proved to be in the parliamentary context. We asked: 'Do you think the law should require [large private companies/the government and civil service] to hire a fixed percentage of [women/blacks and Asians/disabled people] or should [women/ blacks and Asians/disabled people] get no special treatment?' About two-fifths backed the concept of employment quotas. Interestingly, people drew no distinction between private- and public-sector employment, but very sharp distinctions between the groups who might benefit. Large majorities *in favour* of quotas to help the disabled were accompanied by large majorities *against* quotas for women or ethnic minorities. Politicians were a little more opposed to gender quotas than ethnic quotas, while the public were a little more opposed to ethnic quotas than to gender quotas; but both were opposed by at least three-quarters of the public and of politicians.

It might appear that there was a great deal more opposition to gender and ethnic quotas in the sphere of employment (even public-sector employment) than in the sphere of parliamentary representation. However, our question about job quotas was framed in terms of legislation, and *changing the law* to achieve more representation for women and minorities in parliament was also unpopular, not quite so unpopular with the public but even more unpopular with politicians than legislation to enforce job quotas.

Minorities may want more than formal equality, particularly in the cultural matters. Bhikhu Parekh claims that the 'widespread belief that British society is made up of self-determining individuals and cannot tolerate self-conscious communities is fundamentally mistaken',[55] and quotes with approval 'cases [in which] a person's cultural background made a difference to his or her treatment by the courts . . . departures from the norm of formal equality were made in different ways and guises, showing how to reconcile the apparently conflicting demands of uniformity and diversity'.[56] In her review of the 'communitarian critics of liberalism', Amy Gutman points out that,

whereas the good society of the old critics [of the 1960s] was one of collective property ownership and equal political power, the good society of the new critics [of the 1980s] is one of settled traditions and established identities . . . the new critics are [for example] inclined to defend the efforts of local communities to ban offensive activities in the name of preserving the community's *way of life and the values that sustain it*.[57] (emphasis added)

a switch from economic communitarianism to cultural communitarianism, and a switch of emphasis from 'formal equality' to 'special recognition'.

Of course, communitarian critics of liberalism often focus on locally or even nationally dominant communities rather than minority communities, but their arguments often apply equally well to both. The critical distinction is not between majority and minority communities as such, but between voluntary communities that permit easy and practical 'exit' without imposing onerous penalties and those that do not—though communitarians often fail to appreciate this distinction. Our questions focused upon the facilitation of cultural diversity within Britain. Emigration is not an easy option. Our questions therefore focus on the issue of imposing uniformity within the British national (more strictly, 'state') community, and the freedom and encouragement given to minority communities within it. They did not investigate the issue of whether minority communities should be given coercive powers over their own members or over those who live near them. The issue of freedom to choose Welsh-language education is very different, for example, from the issue of imposing Welsh-language education on all residents in an area. Indeed these two issues place the Welsh language in the roles of oppressed and oppressor respectively. We deal with the first issue, but not with the second.

On minority education we asked: 'Should [parents who live in Wales/ Muslim parents] have the right to have their children educated in publicly funded [Welsh-speaking/Muslim religious] schools if they wish?' On average, about three-quarters supported the idea of minority schools, but there was 32 per cent more support for Welsh than for Muslim schools.

We also asked directly:

Should there be any religious teaching in publicly funded schools in Britain?

IF YES: Should it be mainly Christian, or should it treat all the major religions equally?

IF CHRISTIAN: Should it be mainly Christian, even in schools where the majority of children come from non-Christian families?

Four-fifths of the British public and politicians backed religious teaching in publicly funded schools, though support was substantially lower—only 68 per cent—in Scotland where religion is a more sensitive issue. However, in all three of our samples, the majority of those who did support religious teaching in state schools wanted all major religions treated equally. Superficially that seems to conflict with our earlier results about differences between attitudes towards the abuse of different religions, where we found that people discriminated positively in favour of minority religions. But, in fact, it is entirely consistent with our earlier findings because raising the educational status of minority religions to equality with Christianity is another exercise in positive discrimination, entirely consistent with our earlier finding that there was greater willingness to ban abuse of minority religions.

Amongst the minority who wanted religious education *and* wanted it to be to be mainly Christian, half insisted on Christian teaching even where the parents were not Christian—though they constituted a very small minority of the population as a whole.

Turning from equality in education to equality in health care, we asked: 'Suppose [the majority of people in this country/parliament/the government] wanted to ban private medicine, in order to make health services the same for rich and poor. Should they be able to do so even though the ban would reduce the freedom of individuals to do what they want? And would you, yourself, favour such a ban?' Roughly a third would accept a ban, and a similar number would advocate such a ban. Such aggressive opposition to private health care was noticeably stronger in Scotland, where 40 per cent would accept the right of 'the majority, parliament, or the government' to impose such a ban and even more, 47 per cent, would themselves advocate one (Table 5.21).

Principles had a strong influence upon attitudes towards the practice of equality in social life, as they had on equality in political life. Amongst politicians, the multiple correlation with principles was 0.43 on support for religious education, 0.46 on whether major religions should be treated equally

TABLE 5.21. *The practice of equality in social life*

	Politicians (%)	British public (%)	(Scottish public) (%)
Employment quotas	42	42	(42)
in private firms	42	41	(42)
in government employment	43	42	(42)
for women	18	23	(20)
for blacks & Asians	24	15	(19)
for the disabled	84	85	(86)
Welsh/Muslim schools	71	76	(77)
Welsh	88	92	(91)
Muslim	53	60	(62)
Support religious education	79	80	(68)
IF YES: treat major religions equally	61	72	(82)
IF CHRISTIAN: even for non-Christians	47	53	(55)
Accept ban on private medicine	38	35	(40)
Want ban on private medicine	32	37	(47)

in schools, 0.50 on employment quotas for blacks and Asians, and 0.47 on the suppression of private medicine. Amongst the public, multiple correlations with principles were lower, but reached 0.35 on support for equal treatment of major religions in schools and 0.32 on the suppression of private medicine.

With one very notable exception, attitudes to these issues of equality in social life correlated better with commitment to equality than to liberty. That one exception, where opinion correlated almost exclusively with commitment to liberty rather than to equality, was on the basic issue of religious teaching in state-funded schools and it is an exception that makes good sense. Attitudes to the supplementary question of whether any such teaching should then treat the major religions equally correlated much more strongly with commitment to equality rather than to liberty, however.

According to Giovanni Sartori, 'the freedom seeker's formula is not "unequal opportunities to become equal" but "equal opportunities to become unequal"'.[58] If so, commitment to liberty should correlate with opposition to job quotas. Amongst the public, support for liberty correlated with *opposition* to job quotas for women and the disabled, though with *support* for job quotas for ethnic minorities. A multiple regression, taking account of support for both liberty and equality, reduced the apparent influence of liberty on support for ethnic job quotas to less than our standard threshold level of 0.10, without eliminating it completely, however. That is broadly in line with Sartori's theoretical assertion. But support for liberty correlated with support for all kinds of job quotas amongst politicians. Of course, support for liberty and equality were closely connected amongst politicians; so a multiple regression, controlling for equality, made a considerable difference to the apparent influence of liberty on politicians' support for job quotas. Once we took account of equality, we found no link at all, amongst politicians, between liberty and support for disabled job quotas; but support for liberty still had a strong influence upon support for gender and especially racial job quotas. 'Freedom-seeking' politicians simply failed to behave as Sartori said they should.

Again, the most influential micro-principles were equal rights and economic equality. Of the two, equal rights had the greater influence on the issues of equal treatment of all major religions in schools and employment quotas for women and ethnic or racial minorities; while economic equality had the greater influence on support for a ban on private medicine and on employment quotas for the disabled. This difference between the relative influence of different micro-principles on the issues of job quotas for women, ethnic minorities, and the disabled is particularly illuminating and helps to explain why job quotas for the disabled won so much more support than those for women and ethnic or racial minorities (Table 5.22).

Support for religious education in state schools was influenced primarily by the traditional values micro-principle, as might reasonably be expected, since it included a question about 'following God's will'. Yet opinion on the supplementary issues of whether it should be mainly Christian and, if so, whether this should still be so even when the parents were mainly non-Christian was influenced primarily by the principle of equal rights, not traditional values—again a rational pattern.

WELFARE AND PROTECTION

At the time of our survey, politicians of all parties were remarkably optimistic about the state of public finances—wrongly, as it later turned out. But wrong though they later proved to be, it did not seem odd, at the time of our survey, to ask: 'If the government found that it had a surplus of cash available, which should it do: cut taxes or increase spending on public services?' In those happy circumstances, 76 per cent of the public and 81 per cent of

TABLE 5.22. *Correlations between principles and practice on equality in social life*

	Politicians			British public (Scottish public)		
	Liberty (r × 100)	Equality (r × 100)	Multiple (r × 100)	Liberty (r × 100)	Equality (r × 100)	Multiple (r × 100)
Employment quotas	18	26	30	(·)	15 (13)	16 (18)
in private firms	21	24	30	(·)	14 (14)	18 (23)
in government employment	15	28	31	(·)	15 (13)	16 (17)
for women	25	29	36	−10	25 (12)	27 (21)
for blacks & Asians	39	40	50	12	18 (17)	23 (18)
for the disabled	11	34	41	−12 (−15)	12 (17)	20 (28)
Welsh/Muslim schools	·	17	21	(·)	17 (16)	17 (20)
Welsh	·	21	26	(·)	13 (15)	16 (22)
Muslim	·	14	23	(·)	22 (18)	24 (23)
Support religious education	−40	−14	43	−26 (−20)	· (·)	32 (24)
IF YES: treat major religions equally	22	41	46	15 (14)	29 (23)	35 (31)
IF CHRISTIAN: even for non-Christians	−26	−20	31	−12 (−15)	−16 (−12)	20 (25)
Accept ban on private medicine	18	28	33	(·)	14 (·)	25 (25)
Want ban on private medicine	17	38	47	(·)	21 (18)	32 (30)

Note: Correlations less than 0.10 have been replaced by full points.

politicians said they would prefer to improve public services rather than cut taxes.

That did not imply an irresponsible attitude towards expenditure, however, since a majority of politicians and two-thirds of the public backed a modern equivalent of the means test by agreeing that 'State benefits like family allowances should be paid only to those who really need them'. In their attempt to make means-testing respectable once again, Goodin and Le Grand have reiterated the simplistic and subversive tautology that 'the more the non-poor benefit, the less redistributive (or, hence, egalitarian) the impact of the welfare state will be'[59]—subversive because it attempts to turn egalitarians against the basic principles of universal free schooling, universal free access to the NHS, and most of the other achievements of Britain's post-war socialist government, simplistic because it ignores the distortions, the stigmatizing, and the inefficiencies caused by means-testing, and the difficult but essential task of building and maintaining the broader political support necessary to sustain mechanisms that, *inter alia*, help the poor. None the less, their views clearly had majority support.

Similarly, support for public services did not imply an over-indulgent attitude towards those who provided them. We asked: 'Suppose [an NHS doctor or hospital/a private doctor or private hospital outside the NHS] makes a serious mistake in treating a patient. In these circumstances, should the patient get financial compensation, or just be regarded as unfortunate?' Fully 95 per cent demanded financial compensation, and they drew no distinction between the NHS and private health care companies. We also asked: 'Suppose that [British Rail/British Gas/British Telecom/an Electricity Company] provides a particularly poor service to one of its customers by failing to meet its advertised standards. Should the customer get financial compensation or just be regarded as unfortunate?' There was rather less support for compensation in these circumstances, though still over four-fifths. It is probably significant that people took a relatively sympathetic attitude towards the still publicly owned British Rail and a relatively unsympathetic attitude towards the recently privatized gas and electricity utilities. Amongst the public, for example, 25 per cent more demanded compensation from electricity companies than from British Rail; amongst politicians, the difference was lower, but still 17 per cent (Table 5.23).

Principles had little influence upon attitudes towards compensation for poor business service or for medical errors. Even our protection principle failed to correlate highly with attitudes to compensation. But principles had a strong influence upon attitudes towards the tax-versus-services issue, with a multiple correlation of 0.31 amongst the public and 0.61 amongst politicians.

TABLE 5.23. *Welfare and protection in practice*

	Politicians (%)	British public (%)	(Scottish public) (%)
Against means tests	44	36	(40)
For increased services, not tax cuts	81	76	(71)
Compensation for medical mistakes	96	95	(93)
NHS	97	94	(93)
in private medicine	95	95	(93)
Compensation for poor service	88	82	(81)
by British Rail	75	66	(68)
by British Gas	95	86	(87)
by British Telecom	91	94	(82)
by an electricity company	92	91	(87)

The relationship between principles and attitudes to means-testing was unique: the multiple correlation was a high 0.50 amongst politicians but a negligible 0.09 amongst the public. It was usual for principles to exert more influence amongst politicians than amongst the public, but not anywhere near that much more. It is possible that the public simply missed the point of this question, and that a vigorous public debate upon the issue would encourage them to connect it to their principles to a much greater extent than they did when we interviewed them.

Amongst politicians, both equal-rights and economic-equality micro-principles correlated fairly strongly with politicians' attitudes to means-testing and the tax-versus-services issue, economic equality somewhat more strongly than equal rights. But neither of these equality principles correlated with the public's attitudes to these issues. Amongst the public, the multiple correlation of 0.31 between principles and the tax-versus-services issue was mainly based upon a correlation of 0.24 between that issue and the wealth-creation micro-principle—and our composite measure of that micro-principle included a question about holding down taxes, which makes that correlation less impressive (Table 5.24).

CONCLUSION

In this chapter we have uncovered some strong links between the principles that people adopt and the actions that they would take in particular scenarios.

TABLE 5.24. *Correlations between principles and practice on welfare and protection*

	Politicians			British public (Scottish public)		
	Liberty (r × 100)	Equality (r × 100)	Multiple (r × 100)	Liberty (r × 100)	Equality (r × 100)	Multiple (r × 100)
Against means tests	36	39	50	. (.)	. (.)	. (16)
For increased services, not tax cuts	34	50	61	12 (19)	10 (10)	31 (36)
Compensation for medical mistakes	.	.	12	. (.)	. (.)	. (18)
NHS	14	10	15	. (.)	. (.)	. (24)
in private medicine	.	.	.	. (.)	10 (.)	12 (22)
Compensation for poor service	.	.	.	. (.)	. (.)	. (19)
by British Rail	.	.	15	. (.)	. (11)	. (27)
by British Gas	.	14	16	. (.)	. (13)	. (13)
by British Telecom	.	.	.	. (.)	13 (.)	16 (29)
by an electricity company	.	20	20	. (.)	. (.)	17 (14)

Note: Correlations less than 0.10 have been replaced by full points.

In general, our results show the strong—and discriminating—influence that principle had on practice. We found that the extent to which politicians and the public were committed to our broad principles of liberty and equality clearly affected the decisions they made when confronted with specific scenarios that conjured up issues about freedom (to speak, protest, pursue particular lifestyles, or break the law) and equality (be this social, political, or economic in nature). Those who were more committed to liberty or equality in principle were indeed more committed to it in practice.

And that applied to groups as well as to individuals. In particular, politicians' greater commitment to the principle of liberty was reflected in a greater commitment to liberty in practice—usually, though not always. The apparent exceptions are perhaps more interesting than the general rule. We reported in Chapter 3 that politicians had a higher commitment to free speech than the general public; but, when pushed to reconsider this commitment in the context of banning abusive attacks on minority religions, politicians, in fact, proved to be much less committed to this aspect of free speech than the public. Similarly, although politicians claimed to have greater respect than the public for the principle of tolerating different beliefs and lifestyles, when pushed to consider practical issues about homosexuality, abortion on demand, or alcohol and drug abuse, they proved to have very similar outlooks to their electors. These findings are somewhat similar to those of McClosky and Brill, who found that, over a wide range of issues of tolerance, American élites and masses differed by between minus 3 per cent and plus 27 per cent—that is to say, their élites (not all of them such *political* élites as ours) ranged from being marginally less tolerant than the public to being very much more tolerant than the public on different issues.[60]

In Chapter 3 we noted that politicians—perhaps because of their governing perspective—showed a greater propensity than the public to demand obedience to the law, even in principle. In this chapter we found their practice reflected this principle when we asked about legal and illegal ways of opposing the poll tax. At the same time, politicians proved much more inclined than the public to protect the rights of the accused when we asked about various agents of the state cracking down on crime. Once again that reflects a greater commitment to strict legality combined with a more liberal attitude towards citizens' rights.

But this chapter was not just concerned with the question of how far politicians and the public put their principles into practice when they confronted issues like censorship, allowing a member of a group they detest to teach in a state school, permitting strikes and political demonstrations, imposing employment quotas, or reintroducing the death penalty. We also tried to estimate how far people's decisions about issues that, in appearance at least, seemed to raise concerns about liberty or equality were actually driven by their levels of commitment to these two broad principles.

We found that the attitudes of both the public and politicians on many issues were indeed more correlated with the apparently more relevant principle. At the same time, however, we found that amongst both politicians and the public (though particularly amongst the politicians) responses to questions—such as those to do with membership of a trade union, strike action, and the suppression of crime—correlated with both liberty and equality. Commitment to equality had effects that spilled over from purely and obviously egalitarian issues to others that had seemed, on the surface, more obviously issues of liberty and authority.

We also looked at how people's decisions on different issues were influenced by their commitment to our micro-principles as well as to the broader macro-principles of liberty and equality. The discriminating influence of different micro-principles was revealed, for example, by the fact that traditional values was the most powerful predictor of support for banning violent pictures, religious abuse, lies, or sensational crime stories, while respect for authority was the most powerful predictor of attitudes towards disruptive processions, potential riots, or resistance to unpopular taxes; by the fact that traditional values was the most powerful predictor of attitudes towards the morality of abortion yet tolerance was the most powerful predictor of whether an immoral abortion should be declared illegal; by the fact that traditional values was the most powerful predictor of whether religion should be taught in schools while equal rights was the most powerful predictor of how it should be taught; and by the fact that equal rights was the most powerful predictor of support for job quotas for women or ethnic minorities while economic equality was the most powerful predictor of support for job quotas for the disabled. The detailed patterns of interconnections between principle and practice revealed a considerable degree of rationality underpinning their complexity.

We have looked in this chapter at how politicians and the public respond when confronted with scenarios that raise issues of rights and freedoms. We turn in the next chapter *from issues to mechanisms*. We ask by what mechanisms, institutions, or processes the public and their politicians would choose to have these civic rights and freedoms protected in contemporary Britain—by traditional civic institutions, by mechanisms proposed by radicals on the left and right of the political spectrum, or by a more populist style of democracy than that associated with our current form of parliamentary government.

And just as we considered in this chapter how attitudes towards issues of rights and freedoms correlated with individuals' commitment to liberty and equality, in the next chapter we shall ask how attitudes towards existing or proposed mechanisms for protecting civic rights in Britain are shaped by those two macro-principles.

NOTES

1. For impressive statistical evidence that the gap between principle and practice is often evidence of conflicting principles rather than insincerity, see Paul M. Sniderman, Richard A. Brody, and Philip E. Tetlock, *Reasoning and Choice: Explorations in Political Psychology* (Cambridge: Cambridge University Press, 1991), esp. ch. 4.
2. Howard Zinn, 'How Democratic is America?', in Robert E. DiClerico and Allan S. Hammock (eds.), *Points of View: Readings in American Government and Politics* (Reading, Mass.: Addison Wesley, 1983), 2–14, at 8.
3. Ibid. 9.
4. Ibid.
5. Ibid. 11.
6. For the then current legal position on rights of free expression in Britain, see Malcolm Hurwitt and Peter Thornton, *Civil Liberty: The Liberty/NCCL Guide* (4th edn, London: Penguin, 1989), 28–58.
7. John L. Sullivan, James Pierson, and George E. Marcus, *Political Tolerance and American Democracy* (Chicago: University of Chicago Press, 1982, 1989).
8. George F. Will, 'Nazis: Outside the Constitution', in DiClerico and Hammock (eds.), *Points of View*, 291–3, at 292. For a robust and uncompromising defence of free speech without such limits, see American Civil Liberties Union, 'Why Free Speech for Racists and Totalitarians', also in DiClerico and Hammock (eds.), *Points of View*, 286–90.
9. David G. Barnum and John L. Sullivan ('Attitudinal Tolerance and Political Freedom in Britain', *British Journal of Political Science*, 19 (1989), 136–46) applied the same logic using ten groups: pro-abortionists, anti-abortionists, CND, communists, the Protestant northern Irish Democratic Unionist Party, fascists, freemasons, Militant Tendency, National Front, and republican Sinn Fein.
10. Hurwitt and Thornton, *Civil Liberty*, 207.
11. Tam Dalyell, *Misrule: How Mrs Thatcher has Misled Parliament from the Sinking of the Belgrano to the Wright Affair* (London: Hamish Hamilton, 1987), 29.
12. Paddy Hillyard and Janie Percy-Smith, *The Coercive State: The Decline of Democracy in Britain* (London: Fontana, 1988), 142.
13. Jim Murdoch, 'The Rights of Public Assembly and Procession', in Tom Campbell, David Goldberg, Sheila McLean, and Tom Mullen (eds.), *Human Rights: From Rhetoric to Reality* (Oxford: Basil Blackwell, 1986), 173–96, at 181. On the law concerning rights of protest in Britain more generally, see Hurwitt and Thornton, *Civil Liberty*, 1–27.

14. Murdoch, 'The Rights of Public Assembly and Procession', 179.
15. K. D. Ewing and C. A. Gearty, *Freedom under Thatcher: Civil Liberties in Modern Britain* (Oxford: Oxford University Press, 1990), 119.
16. Indeed it has an analogy even within parliament, where the traditional method of censuring a minister is to move a motion to reduce his or her salary by some trivial amount.
17. For the legal position on rights of workers in Britain in 1989, see Hurwitt and Thornton, *Civil Liberty*, 267–98.
18. Elspeth Attwooll, 'The Right to be a Member of a Trade Union', in Campbell, Goldberg, McLean, and Mullen (eds.), *Human Rights*, 223–49, at 224.
19. Peter Thornton, *Decade of Decline: Civil Liberties in the Thatcher Years* (London: National Council for Civil Liberties, 1989), 85.
20. Although the Acts of 1980, 1982, and 1984 strengthened workers' rights to refuse to join working-class trade unions, there is no such right for professional workers to refuse to join professional associations such as the Law Societies or the British Medical Association. See Attwooll, 'The Right to be a Member of a Trade Union', 239.
21. Herbert McClosky and Alida Brill, *Dimensions of Tolerance: What Americans Believe about Civil Liberties* (New York: Russell Sage Foundation, 1983), 326–7.
22. Note that by using the micro-principle respect for authority rather than the macro-principle liberty as our criterion for dividing people into liberals and authoritarians, our measure of principle does not depend, even to a small degree, on answers to our question about the importance of 'following God's will'. So there is no problem of circularity here.
23. For the then current legal position on the 'right to know' in Britain, see Hurwitt and Thornton, *Civil Liberty*, 72–81.
24. Cmnd. 2918, *Privacy and Media Intrusion: The Government's Response* (London: HMSO, July 1995).
25. *Guardian*, 18 July 1995, p. 5.
26. Ewing and Gearty, *Freedom under Thatcher*, 243.
27. For a detailed history of that obsession, see David Hooper, *Official Secrets: The Use and Abuse of the Act* (London: Secker & Warburg, 1987), which lists and describes a host of official secrets trials from 1833 to 1987.
28. Lord Armstrong, 'The Case for Confidentiality in Government', in William L. Miller (ed.), *Alternatives to Freedom: Arguments and Opinions* (London: Longman, 1995), 47–63, at 48.
29. Ewing and Gearty, *Freedom under Thatcher*, 202–3.
30. For a discussion of the relationship between morals and laws, based in part upon our British Rights Survey, see Senator Daniel Patrick Moynihan, 'Defining Deviancy Down', and William L. Miller, Annis May Timpson, and Michael Lessnoff, 'Public Tolerance of Private Freedom', both in William L. Miller (ed.) *Alternatives to Freedom*, 171–84, 184–208.
31. Bhikhu Parekh, 'Cultural Diversity and Liberal Democracy', in David Beetham (ed.), *Defining and Measuring Democracy* (London: Sage, 1994), 199–221, at 214.
32. Jeremy Paxman, 'The Moral Catch', *Guardian*, 23 Feb. 1995, pp. 2–3.

33. For the then current legal position on the rights of suspects and defendants in Britain, see Hurwitt and Thornton, *Civil Liberty*, 123–73.
34. On the Orkney case, see Ch. 2 n. 35.
35. See the end of Ch. 4 for a list. See also Gerry Conlon, *Proved Innocent—the Story of Gerry Conlon and the Guildford Four* (London: Hamish Hamilton, 1990)—he was imprisoned from 1974 till the end of 1989.
36. Charmingly, the major US study of attitudes to civil liberties asked about protecting the sources of journalists and the confidences given to the clergy—as in our survey—but also the confidences given to psychiatrists. It would make a better anecdote if we could say that Americans wished to protect psychiatrists as much as journalists and the clergy, but they did not. See McClosky and Brill, *Dimensions of Tolerance*, 184.
37. Elmar M. Hucko, *The Democratic Tradition: Four German Constitutions* (Oxford: Berg, 1987), 211.
38. Ewing and Gearty, *Freedom under Thatcher*, 241.
39. McClosky and Brill, *Dimensions of Tolerance*, 66.
40. Thornton, *Civil Liberty*, 44.
41. Ivor Crewe, Neil Day, and Anthony Fox (*The British Electorate 1963–87* (Cambridge: Cambridge University Press, 1991), 408) give figures ranging from 63% in 1983 to 82% in 1966.
42. We shall return to this point in Ch. 12.
43. For a study of how British élites treat civil liberties in times of crisis, see Neil Stammers, *Civil Liberties in Britain during the Second World War* (Beckenham: Croom Helm, 1983). He was particularly interested in élite consensus, as expressed in the wartime coalition which existed for a part, but only a part, of the war: 'while it would be difficult to argue that the existence of consensus among the political élite is itself undemocratic, this study has shown that it can be . . . [and] such effects may occur whenever a consensus is formed', whether during wartime or not (p. 236).
44. For the then current legal position on the right to privacy in Britain in 1989, see Hurwitt and Thornton, *Civil Liberty*, 59–71.
45. Ewing and Gearty, *Freedom under Thatcher*, 82–3.
46. Thornton, *Civil Liberty*, 23. Bill Coxall and Lynton Robins (*Contemporary British Politics* (London: Macmillan, 1994)) give a good short review in 'Chapter 18: The Secret State', 333–48, including figures and trends for admitted mail intercepts and phone taps at p. 338.
47. Barnum and Sullivan ('Attitudinal Tolerance and Political Freedom in Britain') found British MPs were very much more tolerant than the public of free speech, etc., for their MDG—by 28% on average—but MPs were none the less 13% more willing than the public to tap the phones of their MDG. Similarly, McClosky and Brill (*Dimensions of Tolerance*, 188) found their élite 4% more favourable to phone taps than their public; and at p. 129 they also found their élites were as much in favour as their public of police infiltrating extremist organizations—despite the tendency for their élites to give more support than their public to civil liberties in general. Joseph F. Fletcher ('Mass and Élite Attitudes about Wiretapping in Canada: Implications for Democratic Theory and Politics', *Public Opinion Quarterly*, 53 (1989), 225–45) found that Canadian élites were more favourable to wire tapping than the public, and

that this was true for each of the four targets of wire tapping permitted under the constitution—wire tapping against suspected subversives, foreign agents, spies, and terrorists.

48. Caroline Ellis, 'Sisters and Citizens', in Geoff Andrews (ed.), *Citizenship* (London: Lawrence & Wishart, 1991), 235–42, at 240–1.

49. See e.g. Ruth Lister, 'Tracing the Contours of Women's Citizenship', *Policy and Politics*, 21 (1993), 3–16; and Anne Phillips, 'Universal Pretensions in Political Thought', in Michèle Barrett and Anne Phillips (eds.), *Destabilizing Theory: Contemporary Feminist Debates* (Cambridge: Polity Press, 1992), ch. 2, pp. 10–30, at 11–12.

50. For the then current legal position on positive and negative discrimination in Britain, see Hurwitt and Thornton, *Civil Liberty*, 193–229.

51. Hilary Wainwright, 'New Forms of Democracy for Socialist Renewal', in David McLellan and Sean Sayers (eds.), *Socialism and Democracy* (London: Macmillan), 70–86, quoted in Ellis, 'Sisters and Citizens', 239.

52. Justice Thurgood Marshall, 'The Case for Racial Quotas', in DiClerico and Hammock (eds.), *Points of View*, 308–14, at 313. For a more recent and wide-ranging discussion by US academic lawyers of affirmative action, see Ellen Frankel Paul, Fred D. Miller Jr., and Jeffrey Paul, *Reassessing Civil Rights* (Oxford: Blackwell, 1991).

53. See e.g. Thomas Sowell, 'Weber and Bakke, and the Presumptions of Affirmative Action', in W. E. Block and M. A. Walker (eds.), *Discrimination, Affirmative Action and Equal Opportunity: An Economic and Social Perspective* (Vancouver: The Fraser Institute, 1981), 37–63.

54. Wendy McElroy, 'Preferential Treatment of Women in Employment', in Caroline Quest (ed.), *Equal Opportunities: A Feminist Fallacy* (London: Institute for Economic Affairs, 1992), 101–14, at 113.

55. Bhikhu Parekh, 'British Citizenship and Cultural Difference', in Andrews (ed.), *Citizenship*, 183–204, at 194.

56. Ibid. 200.

57. Amy Gutman, 'Communitarian Critics of Liberalism', in Shlomo Avineri and Avner de-Shalit (eds.), *Communitarianism and Individualism* (Oxford: Oxford University Press, 1992), 120–36, at 121.

58. Giovanni Sartori, *The Theory of Democracy Revisited* (Chatham, NJ: Chatham House, 1987), 358.

59. Robert E. Goodin and Julian Le Grand, *Not Only the Poor* (London: Allen & Unwin, 1987), 215.

60. McClosky and Brill, *Dimensions of Tolerance*, 89–90.

6

Means and Mechanisms

IN the last chapter we discussed the extent to which people's commitment
to principles influenced the actions they would take when confronted with
specific scenarios that raised practical issues of rights and liberties. In this
chapter we focus upon the institutional mechanisms of liberty and equality
rather than specific issues and policies. Egalitarians may not care too much
about the mechanisms by which they achieve their goals. But liberals care
intensely. Their philosophy is at least as much a philosophy of means as of
ends, if not more so. Their song has got to be: 'It ain't what you do, it's the
way that you do it.' For, as Giovanni Sartori puts it: 'Liberalism is unique . . .
the only engineering of history that endows ends with means.'[1]

Traditionally in Britain we have relied upon the strength of elective democracy and the sturdy institutions of civil society, rather than an entrenched
constitution or Bill of Rights, to provide protection for individuals' rights and
liberties—on parliament, elected local-government councils, trade unions,
churches, a free press, and an independent judiciary. Anthony Birch claims
that

since long before [Britain's] political system was in any sense democratic . . . the
rights of citizens have been established not by the declarations of politicians but by
the decisions of judges . . . one could search the Statute Book in vain for Acts con-
ferring upon citizens the rights of free speech, freedom of association, or freedom
of movement. These rights rest simply on the age-old assumption by British courts
that a citizen is free to do as he likes provided he does not commit any specific
breach of the law.[2]

But in recent years this complacency has been attacked by radicals of all
kinds who allege that existing institutions have failed in that task.[3]

Institutional reformers on the left—Labour, the Liberals, and especially
cross-party bodies like Charter 88—have put forward legal and constitutional proposals that emphasize the need for British citizens to take more
part in political decision-making and to enjoy a broader set of civil and
political rights than they do at present. They call for the devolution of power
to elected assemblies in Scotland, Wales, and the English regions, an elected
House of Lords, a Freedom of Information Act, and a people's Bill of

Rights. Although these proposals are now more closely associated with the left, they have also attracted support from politicians on the right—when they were in opposition at least. Most of Charter 88's proposals from a Bill of Rights embodying the European Convention on Human Rights, to a written constitution, to Scottish devolution and a strengthened House of Lords, were advocated by Lord Hailsham when he was in opposition.[4] We shall use the term 'Charter 88 mechanisms' purely for convenience, nothing more.

On the other side of the political spectrum, 'new-right' Conservatives have emphasized the role of citizens as consumers of services. Margaret Thatcher turned her back on devolution to elected regional assemblies in the late 1970s and offered instead what she called devolution to individual citizens themselves—rights for sitting tenants to purchase their council houses, wider share ownership especially in newly privatized industries, and postal ballots for members of trade unions contemplating industrial action. Conservative Party radicals claimed that, instead of limiting central government by shifting power to other bureaucratic or collective institutions such as courts or elected regional assemblies, they would reduce the role of government at all levels and shift power all the way down to individuals.

Underlying these two approaches is the view of the left that government can and should do good, and the view of the right (or at least of the 'new' right) that government is at best a necessary evil—so that the less it does the better.[5] But there is also a third, more populist view of how to reform the role of citizens in civil society, that would also shift power away from institutions but not to individuals acting alone within a market. It is a view that has been voiced not just by activists involved in a wide range of 'social movements', but also by ordinary citizens who in recent years have taken to the streets in opposition to the poll tax, the criminal justice system, the Child Support Agency, the construction of more motorways, and the export of animal livestock. We shall return to this more populist view later in the chapter, but we begin by assessing support for the mechanisms advocated by Thatcher's Conservative Party and the counter-proposals of Charter 88.

MEANS

We begin by assessing public confidence in traditional mechanisms for the protection of citizens' liberties, and their confidence in new or proposed mechanisms advocated by reformers of the right or left. Later we shall see how attitudes towards principles conditioned people's confidence in different mechanisms.

Traditional Protectors of Citizens' Rights and Liberties

The common ground between left-wing and right-wing radicals is that traditional mechanisms for the protection of individual liberty have failed. We decided to assess public attitudes to a wide range of issues that embraced their alternative approaches. We asked respondents to:

give a mark out of ten to indicate how much you feel citizens rights and liberties are protected by each of the following. Ten indicates something you feel is extremely important for protecting rights and liberties; while zero indicates something you feel does nothing at all to protect them. But remember you can use *any* mark between zero and ten.

There followed a list of seventeen of the protectors of liberty advocated by traditionalists and by reformers on both the left and the right.

Let us start by investigating the extent of public confidence in established mechanisms for protecting civil liberties in Britain. Our list of seventeen possible protectors of citizens' rights and liberties included both long-established institutions:

- back-bench MPs in parliament
- local-government councils
- tabloid newspapers like the [*Sun/Daily Mirror*]
- quality newspapers like the [*Telegraph/Guardian*]
- television
- trade unions
- churches
- British courts

as well as more recently established institutions that have only become important protectors of rights in the post-war years:

- bodies like the Equal Opportunities Commission or the Commission for Racial Equality
- European courts.

We have already used the answers to these questions (along with others) as indicators of confidence in the political system, civil institutions, the judicial system, and the rights industry. At the least, the marks out of ten given for their contribution towards protecting citizens' liberties will provide a base-line against which to judge public attitudes towards the new policies and institutions of radicals and reformers (Table 6.1).

186 *Coherence*

TABLE 6.1. *Established mechanisms for protecting citizens*

	Politicians (marks/10)	British public (marks/10)	(Scottish public) (marks/10)
Political system			
back-bench MPs	6.6	5.7	(5.4)
local-government councils	6.9	5.6	(5.6)
Civil institutions			
tabloids (*Sun/Daily Mirror*)	3.6	3.9	(3.8)
quality papers (*Daily Telegraph/Guardian*)	6.7	6.3	(6.3)
television	6.5	6.3	(6.6)
trade unions	6.5	6.0	(6.3)
churches	5.9	5.8	(6.2)
Judicial system			
British courts	6.5	6.5	(6.5)
Rights enforcers			
EOC/CRE	6.5	6.7	(7.0)
European courts	6.6	6.3	(6.4)

What is immediately apparent from the answers is that politicians and the public they represent had very different ideas about the institutions that do most to protect their rights and liberties. Given the startling gap between the public's and politicians' degree of confidence in elected representatives that we uncovered in Chapter 3, it is not entirely surprising that they have different views about which of these traditional institutions can best protect their rights and freedoms. While politicians accorded the highest marks to the political system (6.6 to MPs and 6.9 to local councils—but then they were, of course, *local*-government politicians), the British public put their faith most strongly in the rights industry and the judicial system (6.5 to British courts, and 6.7 to bodies like the Equal Opportunities Commission and the Commission for Racial Equality), which they placed well above back-bench MPs (only 5.7) and local-government councils (5.6).

Quality newspapers and television also scored better than MPs amongst the public, and just as well as MPs amongst politicians. Amongst quality papers, the left-of-centre *Guardian* got slightly higher marks than the right-of-centre *Daily Telegraph*. The tabloid press, on the other hand, got such low marks that they were probably seen as damaging rather than defending

TABLE 6.2. *Radical mechanisms for protecting citizens*

	Politicians (marks/10)	British public (marks/10)	(Scottish public) (marks/10)
Charter 88 mechanisms			
Bill of Rights	7.6	6.7	(6.5)
Freedom of Information Act	8.2	7.7	(7.9)
elected House of Lords	6.6	6.6	(6.8)
AVERAGE	7.5	7.0	(7.1)
Conservative Party mechanisms			
council-house sales	5.8	6.4	(6.8)
privatization of industries	4.1	4.4	(3.8)
NHS reforms	4.2	4.3	(3.7)
elected school boards	5.6	5.5	(5.1)
AVERAGE	4.9	5.2	(4.9)

citizens' liberties—just 3.9 amongst the public and 3.6 amongst politicians. Interestingly, our results revealed a substantial difference between attitudes towards the right-wing *Sun* (3.3 amongst the public and 2.9 amongst politicians) and the left-wing *Daily Mirror* (4.4 amongst both).

Amongst the public, trade unions and churches scored slightly better than MPs but a little worse than television or the quality press. Courts, whether British or European, scored about as well as the quality press, and bodies like the Equal Opportunities Commission or the Commission for Racial Equality slightly better than the quality press amongst the public, though slightly worse amongst politicians.

Overall, then, there seems to be a passable (more than half marks), though less than enthusiastic, level of confidence in these established defenders of liberty, with the very notable exception of the tabloid part of the press. And amongst the public, there seems a little more confidence in appointed courts or commissions, and in the self-appointed mass media, than in elected MPs and councillors.

Radical Mechanisms for Protecting Citizens' Rights and Liberties

Our list of seventeen potential defenders of citizens' liberties also included recent or proposed innovations (Table 6.2).

- a Bill of Rights, passed by parliament, and enforced by the courts
- a Freedom of Information Act, giving more legal access to government information
- a reformed House of Lords, whose members were elected
- the sale of council houses to sitting tenants
- privatization of nationalized industries
- recent changes in the way the NHS is organized
- the introduction of elected school boards.

The first three of these mechanisms have been strongly advocated by Charter 88[6] and by some Labour and Liberal Democrat politicians, while the remaining four were advocated by the Conservative governments of Margaret Thatcher and John Major and, indeed, were being implemented by the time of our interviews. Though they seem very different from the Charter 88 mechanisms, these Conservative mechanisms were all contained in a Conservative Research Department document titled *Civil Liberties*.[7] Despite appearances, these two sets of mechanisms do address the same issues, though they remind us that politicians in argument often seem to talk past each other rather than meet head on.

Both the public and politicians gave higher marks to all three of the Charter 88 proposals than to all four of the Conservative government reforms. Indeed, only council-house sales scored anywhere near as much as the least popular of the Charter 88 proposals. Privatization of nationalized industries and NHS reorganization scored particularly badly, with ratings of 4.4 and 4.3 respectively, rivalling the dismal scores given to the tabloid press. Averaging across these radical proposals, the Charter 88 proposals scored 7.0 amongst the public, and the new-right Conservative mechanisms only 5.2. Amongst politicians the gap was wider, since the Charter 88 proposals were more popular, and the Conservative mechanisms slightly less popular, than amongst the public generally. If we compare both sets of radical alternatives with the traditional protectors of liberty that we considered in the previous section, the public clearly rated the Charter 88 proposals more highly than traditional mechanisms, and generally regarded the new-right Conservative mechanisms less favourably than traditional mechanisms.

Both the public and their politicians gave their strongest support to the introduction of a Freedom of Information Act: amongst the public this proposal scored 7.7, amongst the politicians 8.2. But their lowest support varied: amongst the public NHS reorganization received the worst rating at 4.3; amongst politicians it was privatization at 4.1.

These differences are so large that many of our respondents—like some of our present readers perhaps—may have simply failed to understand why we included such matters as privatization in a list of potential mechanisms for the defence of liberty. Yet it is important to realize that the Conservative Party saw such reforms as a means of promoting liberty, and not just as a means of encouraging efficiency. Their programme of denationalization and deregulation was intended to lift the oppressive hand of the state from the lives of citizens by reducing the power of bureaucrats, downsizing the state, and restricting government intervention in the market. This, it was argued, would enlarge the freedom of citizens by giving them a choice of services within a competitive market. Indeed, the Conservative mechanisms listed in our table were the rhetorical answer, explicitly given by the Conservative Party in its speeches and publications, to the institutional reforms proposed by radicals in the centre and on the left. As a *Guardian* article on the 1995 Conservative leadership-contender John Redwood noted, his 1988 book *Popular Capitalism* 'was a celebration of private ownership . . . as the avenue to *personal liberation*, economic efficiency and *social justice*' (emphasis added).[8] Around the same time, Mikhail Gorbachev—a distinguished ally of Margaret Thatcher in these matters—also argued that 'the market and private property were important not only in themselves, but also because *they alone could guarantee democracy and human rights*' (emphasis added).[9] Council-house sales and reform of the House of Lords are indeed commensurate in the metric of party rhetoric and political debate.

The Territorial and Non-Territorial Devolution of Power

At the time of the 1979 Referendum on the Scotland Act, shortly before gaining office, Margaret Thatcher offered the Scots 'a better form of devolution' than elected regional or national assemblies. Under her governments, however, this turned out to be nothing more than the 'devolution to the individual' which we have already discussed. But by the time she left office in 1990, devolution to elected bodies in Scotland, Wales, and English regions also, was re-emerging onto the agenda of the left as a mechanism for decentralizing and distributing real power throughout the land. It was no longer the preserve of the mis-named 'Celtic fringe', but was in the Charter 88 programme and advocated by the Commission on Social Justice under the heading of 'Reviving Local Democracy'.[10] We took up this issue by asking respondents whether they would 'support or oppose giving greater powers of self-government to Scotland? Wales? Northern Ireland? London? and regions of England, such as the North-West or South-East?'

Amongst both public and politicians, over three-quarters of those with a

TABLE 6.3. *Territorial devolution*

	Politicians (%)	British public (%)	(Scottish public) (%)
Support more self-government for			
Scotland	75	81	(78)
Wales	72	75	(77)
Northern Ireland	73	75	(76)
London	51	40	(45)
English regions	55	41	(54)

Note: As usual, the percentages are of those with an opinion; larger numbers in England than in Scotland did not have an opinion.

view supported greater self-government for Scotland, Northern Ireland, and Wales. Differences between Scots and others were negligible on these three questions—yet another significant example of 'the dog that did not bark' which needs some emphasis. Throughout Britain, attitudes towards more self-government for Scotland were much the same. Indeed on our figures self-government for Scotland was a few per cent more popular outside Scotland than inside, though Scots have been much more exposed to the arguments against it (as well as in favour of it) over a long period (Table 6.3).

But in sharp contrast, only just over half the politicians and two-fifths of the British public supported greater self-government for London or the English regions. In Scotland there was 5 per cent more support for greater self-government for London and 13 per cent more for the English regions than in Britain as a whole. Although Scots, like people in the rest of Britain, gave most support to self-government for Scotland, what distinguished Scottish opinion most was not an unusually high level of support for greater Scottish self-government, but an unusually high level of support for regional self-government *within England*. Perhaps Scots saw English regional devolution as the necessary condition for the achievement of greater self-government in Scotland. Alternatively, perhaps Scots had come to the conclusion that regional devolution was such a good system of government that they could recommend it to their southerly neighbours. Certainly, both the Scots and the English (who made up 84 per cent of our British sample) were inclined to let each other get on with the business of internal self-government. Attempts by some Conservative Party politicians in England—and perhaps some nationalist politicians in Scotland—to portray the issue of devolution as a 'zero-sum' game could not be further from the perspective of the public,

TABLE 6.4. *Institutions independent of government*

	Politicians (%)	British public (%)	(Scottish public) (%)
TV/press should be more independent	79	75	(73)
Independent control of police/ security services	74	86	(84)
of police	86	90	(88)
of security services	63	82	(81)

who seemed to view the issue as having more to do with good government than with separatism (Table 6.3).

Not only was there considerable support for territorial devolution; there was also overwhelming support for important institutions being independent of government—that is, for functional devolution. We asked whether: '[Television and the press should be more independent of government control/There should be more government control of television and the press]?' Three-quarters of the public and four-fifths of politicians opted for more independence for the media.

Similarly, we asked: 'Who should investigate complaints against the [security services/police] and monitor their activities: [the government/senior members of another police force] or [a committee of MPs/elected local councillors] or an independent outside body?' ('Government' and 'MPs' were used in the question about security services; 'another police force' and 'councillors' in the question about the police.) Fully 86 per cent of the public and 74 per cent of politicians opted for an independent outside body. Support for independent monitoring was higher for the police than for the security services, especially amongst politicians, because 31 per cent of politicians wanted a committee of MPs to monitor the security services. But a huge majority of the public opted for monitoring of both the police and the security services by an independent body and not by elected representatives, whether in local or central government (Table 6.4).

Parliamentary Supremacy

Issues of territorial devolution and political control of broadcasting or the police and security services raise questions of sovereignty and supremacy. The core of Charter 88's critique of the British constitution is its refusal to accept the concept of unlimited sovereignty. In theory, that is vested in a legal fiction known as 'the Crown in parliament'; in practice, in a prime minister, cabinet, and government backed by a majority in the House of Commons. It is difficult to reconcile the concept of parliamentary sovereignty with the idea of an entrenched constitution, or even an entrenched Bill of Rights guarded by the courts, which implies that there is some authority superior even to parliament.

In practice, however, the irreconcilable can be reconciled. The Canadians, for example, built the famous 'notwithstanding' clause into their Charter of Rights and Freedoms, thereby allowing federal and provincial governments to override certain sections of the Charter for a period of up to five years.[11] And elsewhere, constitutional protections are regularly suspended during 'states of emergency'. But there is still a difference between a system in which normal politics revolves around a sovereign constitution and one in which it revolves around a sovereign parliament. The relationship between parliament, on the one hand, and other elected bodies, the courts, or the people themselves, on the other, determines whether citizens' rights and liberties are to be preserved by relying on political competition and the good sense and self-restraint of an all-powerful parliament, or by relying on the checks and balances of widely dispersed power.

In order to look at this issue more closely we asked two questions about using the law—and more especially the courts—to limit parliamentary sovereignty:

[1.] Suppose we had a constitutional Bill of Rights, as some other countries do. If parliament passed a law but the courts said it was unconstitutional, who would have the final say: parliament or the courts?

[2.] Suppose someone in Britain objects to a law passed by parliament and takes the case to the European Court of Human Rights. Who should have the final say: the European court or the British parliament?

The public were fairly evenly divided between parliament and the courts, though they tilted slightly in favour of the European court and against British courts: only 45 per cent said they would let parliament overrule the European court, but 52 per cent would let it overrule British courts. Earlier, of course, we found that, on marks-out-of-ten scales, the public rated European courts slightly lower than British courts, though ahead of MPs. Politicians, however, were firmly in favour of the European court and firmly against British courts in any dispute with parliament: only 41 per cent of them would back parliament against the European court but fully 64 per cent would back parliament against British courts—effectively opting for parliamentary sovereignty within Britain but not within Europe. No doubt many agreed with Paddy Hillyard and Janie Percy-Smith that, within Britain, 'rather than the law operating in such a way as to check state power and uphold "rights", it is used as a resource which has added to the power of the state'.[12] The externality of the European court, or perhaps its established track-record, gave it an authority that British courts could not match. Peter Thornton noted in 1989 that 'in total some 80 UK laws or regulations have been repealed or amended as a result of [European court] proceedings under the European Convention'.[13] It might be argued that our results were biased by use of the European court's full title as a court 'of Human Rights', but that seems very unlikely since the European court was acclaimed by politicians more than the public and, as we shall show in the next chapter, politicians usually held more robust attitudes than the public and were less easily swayed by the addition of such phrases. Politicians were probably swayed by their knowledge of the European court's record, not by its title.

We also considered using the electoral legitimacy of local government (and by implication other elected bodies such as regional or national assemblies) to limit parliamentary sovereignty by asking: 'Suppose a local council wants to do something and gets the support of local people by winning a local [election/referendum] on that issue, but the government is opposed to it. Who should have the final say: the local council or the government?'

We are well aware that there is a theoretical distinction between parliament and government, but equally well aware that there is seldom much of a distinction in practice. The issue of central versus local government had been a major area of confrontation in British politics during the 1980s, when local councils had their revenue-raising powers capped by central government and many troublesome local governments—including the Greater London Council and all the Metropolitan County Councils—were simply abolished by Westminster.[14]

In answer to our question, neither the public nor politicians drew a distinction between the mandate provided by a local *election* and that provided by a local *referendum*: their focus seemed exclusively on the clash between local and central government, and they both backed local government though to varying degrees. Only 23 per cent of the public, but 39 per cent of politicians, backed central government. Still, it is perhaps surprising that the difference was so small and that only a minority of politicians backed parliament. They were local-government politicians, however, and therefore had a very special self-interest in this particular battle with parliament.

TABLE 6.5. *Parliamentary supremacy*

	Politicians (%)	British public (%)	(Scottish public) (%)
Decision should rest with			
central government, not local council	39	23	(20)
parliament, not British courts	64	52	(47)
parliament, not European court	41	45	(40)
parliament, not people in a referendum	67	36	(27)
parliament, not government, to declare emergency	73	67	(66)

None the less, the overall level of support for local rather than central government, taken together with substantial minority support for English regional devolution and overwhelming support for Scots, Welsh, and Northern Irish devolution, indicates a preference for a variety of electorally based mandates and a rejection of unrestricted parliamentary sovereignty over other elected bodies (Table 6.5).

Parliament won more support when contrasted with 'the government'. We recognize that, for most purposes of ordinary discourse, the terms 'parliament' and 'government' are interchangeable. For most people, most of the time, 'government' does not mean the legal fiction of 'the Crown in parliament' but simply the people who sit on the government front bench in the House of Commons; and 'parliament' tends to mean the House of Commons. Since the one exists at the day-to-day pleasure of the other, the distinction between them is often obscure and irrelevant. None the less, there are occasions when the distinction can be usefully made. There are occasions when the government front bench cannot rely upon a secure majority in the House, either because the issues are seen as matters of personal conscience such as abortion, capital punishment, the age of consent for sexual activity, and other moral issues, or because the sense of national crisis is so acute that members feel there is a national interest that transcends ordinary political and party loyalties.

We approached this distinction between government and parliament in two ways. We began by asking:

If there is a genuine national emergency is it all right to suspend some of our usual civil rights?

IF YES: Who should have the power to declare an emergency: parliament or the government alone?

It is the answers to the supplementary question that are relevant here. Even amongst those who accepted a suspension of civil rights, two-thirds of the public and three-quarters of politicians would require parliamentary approval for it: for them, the government's judgement was not enough.

Conversely, however, parliament scored very badly indeed—amongst the public, though not amongst politicians—when contrasted with the people's will expressed through the mechanism of direct democracy. We presented interviewees with the statement: '[Important political issues are too complex to be decided by everyone voting in a referendum and should be left to parliament to decide/It would be better to let the people decide important political issues by everyone voting in a referendum, rather than leaving them to parliament as at present]?' Two-thirds of the public opted for a referendum, while two-thirds of politicians opted for parliament. In the absence of any specific issue, our survey seems to suggest that politicians backed parliament against the people, while the public backed the people against parliament. What is not entirely clear is whether they did so on instrumental or procedural grounds—because they felt their chosen mechanism would lead to better decisions or because it seemed the more democratic alternative.

This raises the issue of justified authority, which we pursued further. We tried to find out whether people would accept the right of 'the majority of people in this country' to overrule their own personal choices—implicitly the equivalent of accepting the verdict of a referendum which had gone against the respondent's own preferences. And we also tried to compare their willingness to be overruled by the majority of people in this country with their willingness to be overruled by parliament, or by the government. To do this we posed three moral dilemmas, in each of which we randomly invoked the authority of government, parliament and (the majority of) the people. We asked:

Suppose [the majority of people in this country/parliament/the government] wanted to ban private medicine, in order to make health services the same for both rich and poor. Should they be able to do so even though the ban would reduce the freedom of individuals to do what they want? And would you, yourself, favour such a ban?

And suppose [the majority/parliament/the government] wanted to ban the ritual slaughter of animals by cruel methods, even if it was part of a religious tradition. Should they be able to do so? And do you, yourself, favour such a ban?

And suppose [the majority/parliament/the government] wanted to make homosexuality a crime. Should they be able to do so even though the ban would reduce the freedom of individuals to do what they want? And do you, yourself, favour such a ban?

   The real test of deference to justified authority is whether those who said that they themselves did *not* favour such a ban would, none the less, accept the right of the majority of people, parliament, or the government, to impose such a ban. Averaging across these three moral questions, we found that the public drew almost no distinction between the authority of government, parliament, and people—though they were 1 or 2 per cent more willing to defer to the majority of people than to parliament or the government. By contrast, politicians drew a modest distinction, according most authority to parliament and least to the people—so that they were 9 per cent more willing to accept such bans by parliament than by referendum.
   What is more striking is that so few of the public would defer to any kind of authority in a country that was once notorious for its deference. Only 23 per cent of politicians would accept the will of parliament on these issues, and much less would accept the judgement of the people or the government. Similarly, only 9 per cent of the public would accept the will of the people, and less would bow to parliament or the government. Huge majorities of those who themselves favoured these bans would accept the rights of the majority of people, parliament, and the government to impose such bans, but that is no evidence for deference. So when two-thirds of the public say they want important issues to be decided in a referendum, and two-thirds of politicians say they would prefer them to be decided by their colleagues in parliament, both may simply be saying they would prefer the issues to be decided 'by people like us' who would hopefully decide the issue 'as we would ourselves'. We have found small minorities who would consciously defend the rights of the majority, parliament, or the government to overrule their own personal views, but they are small indeed. And, while politicians were consistent in being somewhat more willing to defer to parliament than to the majority of people, the public were inconsistent in showing so little inclination to back the majority of people much more than parliament when the decision went against their personal preferences on the issue (Table 6.6).

ENDS AND MEANS

We have investigated public support for a variety of mechanisms to protect citizens' rights and liberties—traditional and radical (Conservative Party and

TABLE 6.6. *Deference to government, parliament, and people*

	Politicians (%)	British public (%)	(Scottish public) (%)
Oppose ban on private medicine/ritual slaughter/homosexuality, but would none the less accept right of			
majority of people	14	9	(10)
parliament	23	7	(8)
government	15	8	(8)
to impose such a ban.			

Charter 88) mechanisms, devolution, and restraints on parliamentary sovereignty. Now we turn to consider how far support for these different mechanisms for protecting rights and liberties reflects our respondents' commitment to the principles of liberty and equality. People with a high commitment to liberty, for example, may well take a different view from those with a high commitment to authority, about the best mechanisms for protecting—and not over-protecting—citizens' rights.

Principles and Protectors of Liberty

Amongst the public, every sizeable correlation between commitment to the principle of liberty and the rating given to any protector of liberty was negative: quite properly, libertarians were almost universally suspicious, though they treated different institutions with varying degrees of suspicion. No mechanism pleased them much; even the ratings given to bodies like the Equal Opportunities Commission or the Commission for Racial Equality were only very slightly correlated (positively) with commitment to liberty. But some traditional mechanisms—such as churches, British courts, and tabloid newspapers—displeased them more than others.

Similarly with attitudes towards the radical mechanisms for protecting liberty: those with a strong commitment to liberty were distinguished not by the high marks they gave to Charter 88 mechanisms but by the low marks they gave to radical Conservative Party mechanisms.

By contrast, commitment to equality correlated positively with high marks for some traditional mechanisms—particularly trade unions, and bodies like the Equal Opportunities Commission or the Commission for Racial Equality. Commitment to equality also correlated with high marks for Charter 88 mechanisms—particularly a Freedom of Information Act and an elected House of Lords. And, to a slightly lesser extent, commitment to equality correlated with low marks for the radical Conservative Party mechanisms.

Interestingly, ratings for civil institutions (television, trade unions, and churches) and the political system (back-bench MPs and local councils) correlated positively with equality but negatively with liberty: egalitarians tended to praise them, but liberals to criticize them (Tables 6.7 and 6.8).

Amongst politicians, by contrast, there were high correlations between both liberty and equality, on the one hand, and the marks given to a wide range of protectors of citizens' rights, on the other. Patterns of correlation were broadly similar to those amongst the public, but they were much larger: amongst politicians, the positive correlations between equality and two of the Charter 88 mechanisms exceeded 0.5, as did the negative correlations between most of the radical Conservative mechanisms and both liberty and equality.

Principles and Devolution

The issue of territorial devolution, or greater self-government for the different national areas and regions within the UK, can be considered either as an issue of liberty, since it involves a degree of freedom from central UK government, or as an issue of equality, since the imbalance between the populations of Scotland, England, Northern Ireland, and Wales inevitably means that central government is primarily English government. We have no wish to join that theoretical debate here, but, amongst both the British and Scottish publics, support for devolution correlated much more with commitment to equality than to liberty; and that was true irrespective of whether the question raised the issue of devolution in the context of Scotland, Northern Ireland, Wales, or the regions of England (Table 6.9).

Amongst politicians, as usual, the distinction between the influence of these two principles was less sharp because these principles were themselves correlated amongst politicians. None the less, even amongst politicians, support for Scottish and Welsh devolution correlated more strongly with commitment to equality than to liberty, while support for devolution to Northern Ireland or the regions of England correlated equally well with commitments to both equality and liberty. In short, therefore, support for devolution was an expression more of fairness and equity than of freedom—a result that confirms our earlier interpretation of support for devolution as reflecting a desire for good government rather than a wish for national separatism.

Commitment to liberty correlated at over 0.2 with the view that the media

TABLE 6.7. *Correlations between support for principles and established mechanisms*

	Politicians			British public (Scottish public)		
	Liberty (r × 100)	Equality (r × 100)	Multiple (r × 100)	Liberty (r × 100)	Equality (r × 100)	Multiple (r × 100)
Political system						
back-bench MPs	−13	.	17	−12 (.)	. (.)	22 (21)
local-government councils	−24	11	34	. (.)	13 (11)	16 (18)
Civil institutions						
tabloids (*Sun/Daily Mirror*)	−30	−18	32	−20 (−21)	. (.)	28 (25)
quality papers (*Daily Telegraph/Guardian*)	−18	.	21	−10 (.)	. (.)	17 (13)
television	.	14	16	−11 (−13)	11 (13)	17 (20)
trade unions	.	44	49	.	31 (26)	38 (32)
churches	−24	21	41	−35 (−36)	16 (11)	43 (44)
Judicial system						
British courts	−43	−23	48	−25 (−21)	. (.)	31 (30)
Rights enforcers						
EOC/CRE	19	55	57	10 (.)	36 (34)	40 (36)
European courts	12	31	34	. (.)	17 (19)	21 (18)

Note: Correlations less than 0.10 have been replaced by full points.

TABLE 6.8. *Correlations between support for principles and radical mechanisms*

	Politicians			British public (Scottish public)		
	Liberty (r × 100)	Equality (r × 100)	Multiple (r × 100)	Liberty (r × 100)	Equality (r × 100)	Multiple (r × 100)
Charter 88 mechanisms						
Bill of Rights	15	39	43	. (.)	10 (10)	19 (26)
Freedom of Information Act	30	53	60	. (.)	28 (26)	34 (37)
elected House of Lords	25	53	57	. (.)	29 (14)	29 (20)
Conservative Party mechanisms						
council-house sales	−53	−38	65	−27 (−30)	. (.)	36 (40)
privatization of industries	−54	−52	74	−25 (−19)	−19 (−19)	47 (43)
NHS reforms	−54	−56	76	−26 (−23)	−24 (−18)	45 (44)
elected school boards	−35	−37	55	−22 (−18)	−11 (.)	33 (35)

Note: Correlations less than 0.10 have been replaced by full points.

TABLE 6.9. *Correlations between support for principles and devolution*

	Politicians			British public (Scottish public)		
	Liberty (r × 100)	Equality (r × 100)	Multiple (r × 100)	Liberty (r × 100)	Equality (r × 100)	Multiple (r × 100)
Support territorial devolution for						
Scotland	39	48	59	11 (.)	24 (21)	31 (31)
Wales	39	46	58	10 (.)	25 (19)	28 (28)
Northern Ireland	30	30	42	13 (11)	18 (18)	25 (28)
London	51	46	64	. (.)	22 (15)	24 (19)
English regions	50	50	66	. (.)	23 (19)	27 (24)
Support functional devolution						
TV/press should be more independent	20	22	26	21 (25)	10 (.)	28 (29)
Independent control of police/security services	.	15	18	. (.)	10 (12)	14 (18)

Note: Correlations less than 0.10 have been replaced by full points.

should be more independent of government, but failed to correlate with demands for independent control of the police and security services.

Principles and Parliamentary Supremacy

Those with a high commitment to liberty were much more inclined to back the European court, but not British courts, against parliament; and to insist that parliamentary approval be required for declarations of emergency. Like those committed to liberty, those with a high commitment to equality were much more inclined to back the European court, but not British courts, against parliament, but egalitarians would go much further in their opposition to parliamentary supremacy: they were also much more inclined to back local-government councils, or the judgement of the people in a referendum, against parliament (Table 6.10).

CONCLUSION

Although in the late 1980s and early 1990s political activists on both the right and the left called for an overhaul of our traditional institutions and mechanisms for protecting rights and liberties in Britain, our results show that the alleged failure of these institutions was *not* a very pressing concern. Indeed, we found that both the public and politicians had a moderately favourable opinion of the traditional mechanisms for defending their rights and liberties. At the same time, however, some calls for reform had a resonance with the public. Both the public and their politicians proved even more favourable to the new mechanisms proposed by Charter 88 than to the traditional mechanisms. Other proposals for reform were unpopular: neither the public nor their politicians ever had better than a neutral opinion of the Conservative Party reforms and usually they had a worse opinion than that.

Both public and politicians alike wanted a new Bill of Rights and a Freedom of Information Act; both supported territorial and non-territorial devolution; and both would back the European court and British local governments against Westminster. However, they differed sharply in their attitudes to direct popular control by means of a referendum. Although this form of direct democracy was supported by a large majority of the public, it was opposed by an equally large majority of politicians. These findings seem to bear out in practice what we established in Chapter 3 when we found that, in principle, politicians had a much higher level of confidence than the public in elected representatives. The governing or non-governing

TABLE 6.10. *Correlations between support for principles and parliamentary supremacy*

	Politicians			British public (Scottish public)		
	Liberty (r × 100)	Equality (r × 100)	Multiple (r × 100)	Liberty (r × 100)	Equality (r × 100)	Multiple (r × 100)
Decision should rest with						
central government, not local council	−16	−33	37	. (10)	−20 (−21)	28 (31)
parliament, not British courts	.	.	.	. (.)	. (.)	10 (16)
parliament, not European court	−40	−44	55	−22 (−14)	−25 (−25)	38 (31)
parliament, not people in a referendum	.	−14	19	. (.)	−17 (−16)	27 (23)
parliament, not government, to declare emergency	29	31	41	16 (16)	. (.)	24 (25)

Note: Correlations less than 0.10 have been replaced by full points.

perspective is not just a matter of principle. It clearly affects opinion about the best institutional means for reaching the desired democratic end.

Opinion on these mechanisms was not, however, solely influenced by whether or not one held political office. It was also influenced—sometimes strongly, and both amongst the public and their politicians—by commitment to the macro-principles of liberty and equality, which both increased support for the reforms proposed by Charter 88 and reduced support for the Conservative mechanisms. Commitments to both liberty and equality also increased support for the European court, though not the British courts, overruling parliament. However, the effects of these commitments differed: equality had more influence than liberty on support for devolution, and for giving priority to local and referendum-based decisions over those of the central government; while liberty had more influence upon a lack of confidence in British courts, churches, the tabloid press, and the Conservative Party mechanisms.

Practical issues and proposals for institutional reform are the stuff of day-to-day political debate. So opinion on these matters is not likely to be either a simple or a stable reflection of attitudes to principle. Politicians argue their case on practical issues by trying to establish—or sometimes by trying to break—the links between day-to-day issues and fundamental principles. To change opinion on a practical issue it is not necessary to change people's basic beliefs and values; it is sufficient to change their perception of the connection between the issue and those basic principles.

In this chapter and the previous one we looked at the influence of commitment to principle over opinion on practical, concrete issues. In the next chapter we turn to look at the impact of argument, not on basic principles, but on opinions about practical issues. Strong arguments may occasionally override the influence of principle; they can always add to it.

NOTES

1. Giovanni Sartori, *The Theory of Democracy Revisited* (Chatham, NJ: Chatham House, 1987), 383.
2. Anthony H. Birch, *The British System of Government* (7th edn., London: Allen & Unwin, 1986), 216.
3. See e.g. Lord Jenkins, 'The Case for a People's Bill of Rights', in William L. Miller (ed.), *Alternatives to Freedom: Arguments and Opinions* (London: Longman, 1995), 21–30.

4. Lord Hailsham, *The Dilemma of Democracy: Diagnosis and Prescription* (London: Collins, 1978).
5. For a classic statement of this perspective, and one that reputedly influenced Margaret Thatcher, see Milton Friedman with the assistance of Rose D. Friedman, *Capitalism and Freedom* (Chicago: University of Chicago Press, 1962; updated edn., 1982).
6. For the text of Charter 88, including demands for an elected House of Lords, a Bill of Rights, and much greater freedom of information, see Geoff Andrews (ed.), *Citizenship* (London: Lawrence & Wishart, 1991), 207–11. Party support was more ambiguous and variable. Labour, for example, was always antagonistic to the House of Lords, but at the 1983 election it proposed to abolish that House, kept mute on the issue in 1987, hinted through its senior spokesmen that it would support an elected House of Lords in 1992, and subsequently seemed to move in favour of abolishing the right of hereditary peers to vote in the House, though retaining their right to speak, and retaining the rights of first-generation peers unchanged.
7. These Conservative Party mechanisms for liberty, along with criticisms of the Charter 88 mechanisms and others, were all included in a briefing document sent to us by the Conservative Research Department: *Civil Liberties* (London: Conservative Research Department, 17 May 1990), though these arguments may well appear in more accessible Conservative Party publications also.
8. Guardian, 27 June 1995.
9. Stephen White, Graeme Gill, and Darrell Slider, *The Politics of Transition: Shaping a Post-Soviet Future* (Cambridge: Cambridge University Press, 1993), 10, quoting an original report in *Pravda*, 19 Aug. 1990.
10. Commission on Social Justice (Chair: Sir Gordon Borrie), *Social Justice—Strategies for National Renewal* (London: Vintage, 1994), 350–60, esp. 354.
11. Peter H. Russell, *Constitutional Odyssey: Can Canadians be a Sovereign People?* (Toronto: Toronto University Press, 1992), 121.
12. Paddy Hillyard and Janie Percy-Smith, *The Coercive State: The Decline of Democracy in Britain* (London: Fontana, 1988), 168.
13. Peter Thornton, *Decade of Decline: Civil Liberties in the Thatcher Years* (London: National Council for Civil Liberties, 1989), 92.
14. For different accounts of the open warfare between British local and central government in the 1980s, see Gerry Stoker, *The Politics of Local Government* (2nd edn., London: Macmillan, 1991); Tony Byrne, *Local Government in Britain* (5th edn., London: Penguin, 1992); William L. Miller, *Irrelevant Elections? The Quality of Local Democracy in Britain* (Oxford: Oxford University Press, 1988); see also William L. Miller, 'Local Elections in Britain', in Lourdes Lopez Nieto (ed.), *Local Elections in Europe* (Barcelona: Institut de Ciencies Politiques i Socials, 1994), 59–84.

PART FOUR
Influences

7

Argument

WHEN expressions of opinion change in response to real changes in the terms of the question, the circumstances, conditions, or stimuli involved, then they indicate a welcome sensitivity and attention to detail on the part of the respondent. It would be unreasonable to hold opinions that took no account of circumstances or conditions, or of the objects of those opinions. For example, it would be irrational to support (or to oppose) all kinds of protests, by all kinds of protesters, in all kinds of circumstances; and irrational to support (or to oppose) all kinds of censorship irrespective of what was to be censored or the circumstances surrounding the act of censorship. In earlier chapters, particularly Chapter 5, we noted the effect of changing question wordings in ways that materially altered the circumstances. We distinguished between parades by political protesters, religious groups, or town galas; between censoring publication of confidential government documents on defence, the economy, or the health service; and between press intrusions into the private lives of ordinary people and leading politicians. We welcomed evidence that people did indeed take account of detailed circumstances. It showed some attention to the details of our questions and a degree of rational response.

At the same time we would doubt the sincerity or the significance of opinions that appeared to change for no good reason at all. For example, if we could alter the expression of opinion by presenting a meaningless, irrelevant, or inappropriate argument—without changing the material circumstances of the question—then we might doubt whether those opinions expressed any reality whatsoever. A change in expressed opinion resulting from trivial changes in the real terms of the question, or in response to the presentation rather than the content of the question, would reveal the power of the interviewer and the malleability, even weak-mindedness—rather than rationality—of the respondent.

But there is a third possibility, somewhat intermediate between these two. It is reasonable to take account of arguments that do have content. They may not change the nature and circumstances of the question but they may present genuinely different perspectives and remind us of different factors that have a bearing on the question, and it would not be an act of weak-mindedness to respond to them. It is, of course, largely a matter of subjective judgement whether a particular argument has genuine content or is merely a trivial rewording. Ultimately readers will have to make that judgement for themselves, but some of the arguments we put to our respondents were intentionally trivial, while others were intended to be full of content and meaning.

In this chapter we shall attempt to discover the power of genuine arguments of different kinds and the sensitivity of the respondent to them, as well as the purely manipulative power of the interview. We shall look at the impact of using arguments without content, of adding arguments that do have content, of presenting alternative and opposed arguments, and of challenging people to change their minds. But we shall not look at the impact of variations in question wording that materially alter the circumstances of the question, since we have covered that topic in earlier chapters.

THE METHODOLOGY OF CATI DIALOGUES

In everyday discussion of complex issues we try out different ways of expressing ideas, phrasing and rephrasing questions until we have a sufficiently accurate and comprehensive understanding of the opinions being expressed: 'So what you mean is . . .', 'In other words, what you are saying is . . .', 'But in such-and-such circumstances, would you still say that . . .', and so on. Similarly, we are used to opinions being expressed in a conditional form: 'In such and such circumstances, I think . . .', 'My view is such and such, but only if certain conditions hold', and so on. We have tried to do the same in our public-opinion interviews.

It would have been impractical to conduct several thousand interviews as entirely unstructured dialogues and difficult if not impossible to have drawn precise conclusions from them even if we had done so. Yet several thousand interviews were necessary if we were to use our sample to represent the public with any degree of statistical accuracy. So, instead of unstructured dialogues, we varied question wordings but limited and controlled the use of alternative wordings using our CATI system. This had advantages as well as disadvantages when compared with unstructured interviews. The disadvantages include the limited range of alternative phrasings—limited often to only two alternatives, though sometimes including as many as a dozen. On the other hand, the limited range of alternatives allows statistical analysis, and the randomization of these alternatives means that effects can be clearly attributed to the wording of particular questions and not confused with the effects of different conversational sequences. In that respect our computer-controlled interviewing system is far better than everyday, unstructured conversations, in which, inevitably, many answers to questions are conditioned by the way the whole conversation has developed up to that point, and therefore cannot be clearly and unambiguously linked to the specific questions themselves.

AGREEABILITY: ARGUMENTS WITHOUT CONTENT

First, let us consider the problem of agreeability, often termed 'positivity bias' by methodologists. It is alleged that respondents develop a rapport with their interviewers and try to please them by giving the expected answer—in particular by simply agreeing to propositions as put to them by the interviewer.[1] Of course, a disagreeable minority may develop some antagonism towards interviewers and be inclined to disagree with any and every proposition put by them. But extremely disagreeable people are likely to refuse to be interviewed at all, and, according to those who fear positivity bias, such persistently disagreeable people are in the minority anyway. So the net effect of agreeability (and disagreeability) should be to increase the percentage who agree to a proposition above the percentage who really have that opinion. Agreeability bias simply reflects the weak-mindedness of respondents. It corrupts the expression of their opinions. It reveals no genuine subtleties.

We put ten agree/disagree questions in both a positive and negative form. If the negative form was a pure logical inversion of the positive form, then, in the absence of any agreeability bias (and any sampling error), the percentage who *disagreed* with the negative form of the question should exactly equal the percentage who *agreed* with the positive form. To put it another way, the sum of the percentages agreeing with the positive and negative forms should come to 100 per cent in the absence of agreeability bias. In so far as there is (net) agreeability bias, this sum should exceed 100 per cent; and if there is a (net) *dis*agreeability bias, a tendency to react against the wording of the question, the sum of those agreeing to the positive and negative versions should come to less than 100 per cent. A simple, yet generalizable, measure of agreeability bias is therefore:

(net) agreeability bias index = (% who agree to positive form
+ % who agree to negative form − 100%)/2

which equals the extent to which the percentage agreeing to the positive version exceeds the percentage who really have that positive opinion (and also equals the extent to which the percentage agreeing with the negative version exceeds the percentage who really have that negative opinion). A negative value for the agreeability bias indicates a bias towards disagreement. The index we have defined can range from plus 50 per cent down to minus 50 per cent.

In any of the three circumstances—no bias, positivity bias, or negativity bias—the best estimate of true, unbiased opinion is given by averaging the percentage who agree to the positive version of the question with the percentage who *dis*agree with the negative version.

However, something other than weak-mindedness can produce non-zero values for the agreeability bias index. If the alternative versions of the proposition are *not mutually exclusive*, then people can quite reasonably agree to both. Suppose we asked for agree/disagree responses to the propositions

$$2 + 2 = 4$$
$$\text{and } 5 + 5 = 10.$$

Then, of course, we should expect 100 per cent agreement to both. And if we, falsely, interpreted these two statements as alternatives we should get an agreeability bias index of plus 50 per cent (the maximum).

Conversely, if the alternatives are *not exhaustive*—that is, if they do not cover all possibilities, and people really do support some third, unmentioned, alternative—then they may reasonably disagree with both of the propositions which are on offer and produce a negative agreeability bias index of up to minus 50 per cent.

We put ten agree/disagree questions which were intended to be exclusive and exhaustive alternatives. Of these, four produced only small measures of agreeability bias amongst both people and politicians. They were:

1. *Equal rights*: 'We [have gone too far/have not gone far enough] in pushing equal rights in this country.'
2. *Police and civil liberties*: 'On the whole the [police/security services] [do more to harm our liberties than to protect them/protect our liberties more than they harm them].' For present purposes, we make no distinction between the police and security services variants, but contrast the random half sample where the proposition alleged 'more harm' versus the random half sample where it alleged 'more protection'.
3. *Religious freedom*: 'Religious freedom should [apply to all religious groups even those/not apply to religious groups] that the majority of people consider strange, fanatical, or weird.'
4. *Press freedom*: '[Television and the press should be more independent of government control/There should be more government control of television and the press.]'

TABLE 7.1. *Neglible agreeability bias*

	Politicians (%)	British public (%)	(Scottish public) (%)
Equal rights gone too far v. not far enough	−4	+1	(+4)
Police/security services harm v. protect liberties	+3	+3	(+4)
Religious freedom for weird groups v. not	0	+6	(+6)
Media should be more v. less independent	−6	+1	(+1)
AVERAGE	−2	+3	(+4)

Note: Definition of effect of agreeability: = (%agree version A + %agree version B − 100%)/2. This equals the bias from a neutral, intermediate viewpoint in the direction of wording pressure. Note that each of the two wordings has this biasing effect, but in opposite directions.

TABLE 7.2. *Agreeability bias amongst people, but not amongst politicians*

	Politicians (%)	British public (%)	(Scottish public) (%)
Rights v. duties	+2	+12	(+11)
Morally wrong should be illegal v. not	+1	+10	(+13)
British governments reducing v. increasing rights	+2	+9	(+10)
AVERAGE	+2	+10	(+11)

Logically, there is a missing 'no-change' option in the equal-rights and press-freedom questions, but otherwise each of these questions was presented in a pair of exclusive and exhaustive alternatives. The agreeability bias index was small for all four questions and for both public and politicians. Overall it indicated a very slight agreeability bias amongst the public (+3 per cent) and an even smaller *dis*agreeability bias amongst politicians—two findings that are reassuring both in general and in detail (Table 7.1).

On three of the ten questions, the public displayed a moderately strong degree of agreeability bias while politicians did not (Table 7.2). These were:

1. *Rights and duties*: 'In Britain today, there is too much emphasis on citizens' [rights and not enough on citizens' duties/duties and not enough on citizens' rights].'

TABLE 7.3.   *Disagreeability bias, or missing alternatives?*

	Politicians (%)	British publish (%)	(Scottish public) (%)
British liberties less v. more than elsewhere	−11	−7	(−6)
Poor don't try v. wealthy keep them poor	−20	−13	(−10)
Ban extreme political organizations v. not	−16	−5	(+2)
AVERAGE	−16	−8	(−5)

2. *Morals and laws*: '[If something is morally wrong, then it should be made illegal/Even though something may be morally wrong, it should not necessarily be made illegal.]'

3. *British rights (trends)*: 'On balance, British governments have been [reducing/increasing] the rights and liberties of British citizens in recent years.'

Logically, once again, there is a missing 'neither' option in the 'rights-and-duties' and 'trends' questions, and perhaps a missing 'sometimes' option in the question on morals and laws. But despite these logically missing options, which would tend to produce a negative agreeability bias, all three questions seemed capable of pushing the general public's expressed opinion about 10 per cent in either direction (which, of course, produces a 20 per cent difference in opinion as measured by answers to the two versions of the question), though the wording had relatively little effect upon politicians. That seems to indicate a degree of malleability amongst the public on these questions at least.

The remaining three of the ten pairs of inverse alternatives produced fairly strong but negative agreeability bias scores, especially amongst politicians, indicating a strong tendency to *dis*agree with both versions of each question (Table 7.3). It seems worth looking at their content for clues as to why that happened. They were:

1. *British rights (comparisons)*: 'On the whole, the rights and liberties enjoyed by British citizens are [less/greater] than those enjoyed by people who live in [America/West European countries like France and Germany/Scandinavian countries like Norway, Denmark, or Sweden].' For present purposes we have ignored the distinction between America,

Europe, and Scandinavia, and contrasted responses to the random half
sample that used the term 'less' with that which used 'greater'.

2. *The poor*: 'The poor are poor because [they don't try hard enough to
get ahead/the wealthy and powerful keep them poor].'

3. *Banning extremists*: '[Political organizations with extreme views should
be banned/We should never ban any political organization whatever its
views.]'

It is easy to suggest missing alternatives for the first two questions—that
British rights are *the same* as elsewhere, and that the poor are just *unfortunate* rather than feckless or oppressed; and missing alternatives tend to generate negative agreeability bias scores. The third question is less obviously
deficient in this way. Among the British public it displays only a small
negative agreeability bias (and amongst our Scottish sample, a slight *positive*
agreeability bias score). The most likely explanation is that some local political leaders, who frequently have to face the issue of banning extremist
political activity in their localities, were very reluctant to ban extremists but
not willing to go so far as to exclude that option in all circumstances. For
them at least, there was an important missing alternative that might be expressed as 'ban only very extreme organizations in particularly dangerous
circumstances'.

What general conclusions can we draw from these ten tests? At most, the
public showed a very small bias towards agreement. Overall the scale of
these effects suggest that agreeability bias, though it may exist amongst the
public, if not amongst politicians, is not sufficiently large to suggest that
they do not have real opinions on the questions put to them. Where the
alternatives used in our questions were not exclusive or exhaustive, agreeability and disagreeability bias scores could be high, but that would reflect
the nature of the questions rather than the malleability or irascibility of the
respondents. However, the agreeability bias on the rights-versus-duties question, the morals-and-laws question, and the increasing-or-decreasing-rights
question seems more likely to result from public malleability when confronted with obscure questions, or at least questions that seemed difficult and
obscure to the general public. It was significant that the politicians did not
display any substantial degree of malleability on these three questions.

Educated Disagreeability

We should also expect that people with higher levels of education might
understand the questions better and therefore show less tendency towards
simple agreeability—and they do. Dividing the public up into those without

TABLE 7.4.   *Agreeability bias by education* (British public only)

	Low education (%)	Medium education (%)	High education (%)
Equal rights gone too far v. not far enough	+4	−1	−1
Police/security services harm v. protect liberties	+3	+3	+3
Religious freedom for weird groups v. not	+10	+5	0
Media should be more v. less independent	+8	+3	−8
Rights v. duties	+19	+9	−4
Morally wrong should be illegal v. not	+15	+8	+4
British governments reducing v. increasing rights	+15	+6	−4
British liberties less v. more than elsewhere	−2	−10	−14
Poor don't try v. wealthy keep them poor	−7	−16	−20
Ban extreme political organizations v. not	+4	−9	−12
AVERAGE	+7	0	−6

educational qualifications, those with school certificates, and those with university or polytechnic qualifications, shows that public agreeability correlated with a lack of formal education. Rightly or wrongly, graduates were less willing to agree, and more willing to disagree, than those without qualifications. That was true on almost every proposition put to them. On average over the ten propositions, those with school certificates had zero agreeability bias scores, and those without qualifications had a positive agreeability bias score of 7 per cent, while graduates had a negative or *dis*agreeability bias score of 6 per cent. Since agreeability bias is measured relative to a hypothetical neutral wording, on average a change in question wording therefore produced an apparent opinion shift of 14 per cent in the direction of the question wording amongst those without educational qualifications, but an apparent opinion shift of 12 per cent in the opposite direction to the question wording amongst graduates. Amongst those without educational qualifications it was possible to shift opinion on such obscure (to them) questions as the rights-versus-duties question by as much as 38 per cent in the direction of the question wording. (Table 7.4 shows that each of the two wordings could shift opinion 19 per cent, in opposite directions.) Conversely, amongst graduates, on a question with such a genuine and blatant missing 'third' alternative as in the question on the causes of poverty, there was an apparent shift *against* the question wording of 40 per cent (20 per cent in opposite directions with each version of the wording).

EXPLICIT ARGUMENTS WITH CONTENT

True agreeability bias is caused by argument without content—that is, by nothing more than positive or negative phrasing. Arguments that include real content should have more effect. We tried three different formats for such arguments, two of which involved prior-argument; the third involves post-argument:

1. *Opposing arguments*: we used alternative wordings that went well beyond mere linguistic inversion.
2. *Added arguments*: we put a proposition both with and without supporting arguments.
3. *Challenges*: after respondents had answered a question, we challenged them to consider changing their minds.

Opposed Arguments

Three questions presented alternative, and opposed, arguments to random half samples. This is quite different from laying out both the arguments before the respondent and asking them to choose between them. We did use that format in many questions but it does not allow us to measure the impact of an argument on opinion. By presenting one side, *and only one side*, of the argument to random half samples we can measure the impact on people's answers of explicitly articulating the arguments. We stress the phrase 'explicitly articulating' because the more alert and interested respondents may have thought up the full range of arguments and counter-arguments on both sides by themselves, in the few seconds between being asked the question and answering it. By explicitly articulating one side of the argument we can be sure that respondents were aware of that side of the argument; but we cannot be quite so certain that they were unaware of the opposite argument just because we did not articulate it.

The three questions which presented opposed arguments to random half samples were:

1. *Decisive government*: '[It is important for a government to be able to take decisive action without looking over its shoulder all the time/ Constitutional checks and balances are important to make sure that a government doesn't become too dictatorial and ignore other viewpoints.] Agree/disagree?'
2. *Referendums*: '[Important political issues are too complex to be decided by everyone voting in a referendum, and should be left to parliament

to decide/It would be better to let the people decide important political issues by everyone voting in a referendum, rather than leaving them to parliament as at present.] Agree/disagree?'

3. *Death penalty*: '[Given that parliament has repeatedly voted against the death penalty/In order to clamp down on rising crime and violence], do you think Britain should reintroduce the death penalty for murder or keep things as they are?'

Certainly these questions include only brief arguments, but they opposed decisive government *versus* checking dictatorial tendencies; the complexity of political issues and the prestige of parliament *versus* the raw will of the people; and the authority of parliament *versus* fears about crime and violence.

It is very significant that parliament's prestige and authority proved totally worthless or even counter-productive. Invoking parliament's name had only the slightest positive effect upon the public, while local political leaders reacted against it. Although a majority of politicians opposed the death penalty, they were actually 4 per cent (twice the 2 per cent effect in either direction, as shown in the table) *more* likely to support it when parliament's name was invoked against it than they were when the argument in favour of the death penalty was used. Similarly, although a large majority of politicians opposed referendums, they were actually 14 per cent (twice the 7 per cent effect in the table) *more* likely to support referendums when parliament's name was invoked against referendums than when the pro-referendum argument was used. On these questions, highly educated members of the public reacted against references to parliament in just the same way as local politicians, and to a slightly greater extent. So these particular examples of explicit arguments failed miserably to shift opinion in their favour (Table 7.5).

On the other hand, a large majority agreed with both propositions about decisive government. Whether that reflects the power of these arguments is less obvious, however. Although it generated an enormously high index of agreeability, the agreeability effect was just as high amongst politicians as amongst the public, and just as high amongst the university educated as amongst those with no educational qualifications. Such patterns are not characteristic of persuasively phrased arguments so much as of a broad consensus that the two propositions were not exclusive alternatives. It seems likely that most people want both decisive *and* constitutionally limited government and simply do not see these as incompatible. We are inclined to agree with them (Table 7.6).

TABLE 7.5. *Effect of opposed arguments*

	Politicians (%)	British public (%)	(Scottish public) (%)
Decisive government	+35	+38	(+34)
Referendums	−7	+4	(+6)
Death penalty	−2	0	(−1)

Note: Definition of effect of opposed arguments: = (%agree with argument A + %agree with argument B − 100%)/2. This equals the bias from a neutral, intermediate viewpoint in the direction of the argument, and is arithmetically the same as our definition of effect of agreeability bias. The difference here is that there is a real meaningful content to the alternative wordings, not just a substitution of positive and negative phrasing. Note that each of the two arguments has this biasing effect, but in opposite directions; so the difference between answers given to the two versions of the question is twice the figure shown in the table.

TABLE 7.6. *Effect of opposed arguments by education* (British public only)

	Low education (%)	Medium education (%)	High education (%)
Decisive government	+34	+37	+33
Referendums	+8	+3	−8
Death penalty	0	+1	−2

Added Arguments

While invoking the authority and prestige of parliament had little effect upon the public, and actually produced an adverse reaction amongst both politicians and well-educated members of the public, our experiments with adding arguments to propositions were more successful at manipulating expressed opinion. We sought agreement with the following propositions:

1. *Conviction on confession*: 'Courts should not convict people purely on the basis of a confession [(null)/because people sometimes confess to things they haven't done/because people are sometimes put under so much pressure they confess to things they have not done].'
2. *The national interest*: 'Newspapers which got hold of confidential government documents about [defence/economic/health service] plans should *not* be allowed to publish them [(null)/because publication might

TABLE 7.7. *Effect of added arguments*

	Politicians (%)	British public (%)	(Scottish public) (%)
Not convict on confession			
confess wrongly v. (null)	+9	+13	(+14)
pressure to confess v. (null)	+9	+14	(+13)
Censor plans: national interests v. (null)	+6	+11	(+16)
when plans are defence plans	+3	+8	(+16)
when plans are economic plans	+17	+18	(+14)
when plans are health plans	−2	+9	(+18)
Censor black crime: prejudice v. (null)	+7	+11	(+15)
Censor crime stories			
encourage crime v. (null)	+2	+16	(+6)
prevent fair trial v. (null)	+20	+22	(+25)
Allow drink/drugs: not harm v. (null)	+22	+21	(+22)
Take child if ill treated: alleged v. (null)	−19	−20	(−21)

Notes: '(null)' indicates the question as worded without any added argument.
Definition of effect of added arguments: = % with argument added − % without argument.

damage our national interests].' For present purposes we focus on the presence or absence of the argument about 'national interests'.

3. *Black crime*: 'Newspapers should be banned from publishing research showing very high rates of crime among blacks [(null)/because this may encourage prejudice against them].'

4. *Sensational crime*: 'Heavy television and press coverage of dramatic crimes like murders or terrorist incidents should be banned [(null)/ because it may encourage others to commit more crimes/because, later on, it may prevent an accused person getting a fair trial].'

Where '(null)' appears it indicates that no argument was added to the question wording. In all these cases, our estimate of the power of argument must necessarily be an underestimate since, even when we did not articulate an argument, some respondents may have had it in mind anyway. But we can at least measure the effect of explicitly articulating these arguments (Table 7.7).

Both the arguments against accepting conviction on confession were

TABLE 7.8.   *Effect of added arguments by education* (British public only)

	Low education (%)	Medium education (%)	High education (%)
Not convict on confession			
confess wrongly v. (null)	+19	+9	+9
pressure to confess v. (null)	+22	+9	+6
Censor plans: national interests v. (null)	+13	+11	+7
Censor black crime: prejudice v. (null)	+7	+14	+10
Censor crime stories			
encourage crime v. (null)	+23	+13	+7
prevent fair trial v. (null)	+23	+21	+21
Allow drink/drugs: not harm v. (null)	+17	+23	+26
Take child if ill treated: alleged v. (null)	−17	−22	−18

versions of the 'utilitarian' argument, used by the 1981 Royal Commission on Criminal Procedure in England and Wales, that 'the risk of false confessions'[2] justified maintaining the suspect's or the accused's right to silence. And both arguments raised opposition to conviction on confession by 9 per cent amongst politicians, by about 14 per cent amongst the public generally, and by about 20 per cent amongst the least educated members of the public.

The argument that sensational crime reporting could prevent a fair trial raised opposition to it by about 21 per cent amongst both politicians and people and proved almost as powerful amongst the best educated as amongst the least. But, in sharp contrast, the argument that crime reporting should be censored to avoid encouraging crime failed to move politicians and had relatively little effect upon well-educated members of the public, though it raised support for censorship by 16 per cent amongst the public generally, and by 23 per cent amongst the least-educated members of the public. It seems clear that different kinds of argument appeal to different kinds of people.

The argument that reporting black crime might encourage racial prejudice had a smaller but more evenly spread effect upon support for censorship (Table 7.8).

Attempts to invoke the national interest against the press had a rather complex effect. Overall, it raised support for censorship by only 6 per cent amongst politicians and 11 per cent amongst the public. It had a greater effect—around 18 per cent—on support for censoring publication of government economic plans; but much less effect upon support for censoring publication of defence plans (which was widely popular) or on support for censoring health-service plans (which was widely *un*popular).

We are particularly interested in the effect of invoking the 'national interest' to justify suppressing publication of health-service plans because we can see no rational connection whatsoever between secrecy in the health service and preservation of any legitimate national interest. In this connection (if not more generally) our use of the term 'national interest' was a fraudulent cover for government convenience and nothing more. Yet the mere mention of this undefined 'national interest' raised support for censorship of health-service plans by 21 per cent amongst the least-educated members of the public. At the same time it had very little effect at all (plus 2 per cent) upon university graduates and even provoked a small adverse reaction amongst politicians. It was a good measure of political gullibility.

In earlier chapters, we have already discussed the extent to which opinion depends upon the detailed circumstances in which practical action might be taken to implement principles. In two questions we added phrases that might either be construed as changing the circumstances or as obliquely advancing an argument. These were:-

1. *Drink and Drugs*: 'People should be allowed to [take whatever drugs/ drink as much as] they like [(null)/provided they do not harm or behave offensively to other people]. Agree/disagree?' Here, we shall ignore the distinction between drink and drugs, which we discussed earlier, and simply contrast the random half samples that did or did not include the qualifying phrase about not harming other people.
2. *Removing children*: 'Should social workers have the right to take a child away from its parents if [(null)/there are allegations that] the parents regularly ill treat their child?'

In the first question the implicit argument is that drink and drugs are a private matter that affect only those that take them. In the second, the implicit argument is that allegations may not be true: the form of the question that omitted the word 'allegations' assumes a degree of certainty that cases such as the notorious Orkney affair do not justify.[3]

Both these obliquely put arguments proved relatively powerful. The additional phrase increased tolerance of drink/drug-taking and decreased support for social workers actions by about 20 per cent amongst both politicians and public. Moreover, both these arguments proved effective right across the education spectrum.

TABLE 7.9. *Effect of challenges*

% willing to consider changing opinion on	Politicians (%)	British public (%)	(Scottish public) (%)
Medical compensation	4	9	(9)
Business compensation	12	30	(32)
Minority schools	18	32	(32)
Death penalty	19	29	(29)
Phone taps/bank inspections	23	30	(33)
Employment quotas	34	51	(49)
Banning racial/religious incitement	40	49	(49)
Banning extreme political organizations	57	62	(63)
AVERAGE	26	37	(37)

Challenges

An entirely different way of assessing the power of argument is to ask a question, record the answer, and then challenge respondents to consider changing their minds. Usually, we challenged respondents irrespective of their initial answer, though occasionally we challenged answers in one direction but not in the other. These challenges always included content of some sort, posing either circumstances or rational arguments that might encourage respondents to change their minds.

The power of these challenges seemed to depend a great deal upon the nature of the question and of the challenge. The numbers who were willing to change their minds ranged from only a few per cent on some questions to well over half on others. Averaging across the eight opinions which we challenged, over one-third of the public (37 per cent) and about one-quarter of politicians (26 per cent) declared their willingness to reconsider their initial opinions.

Opinion was relatively rigid on financial compensation for medical errors, but more flexible on compensation for poor business services. Amongst the public only 9 per cent would reconsider their initial support for medical compensation but 30 per cent their initial support for business compensation. In both cases the challenge was a reminder that medical and other services might have to increase their charges to cover the costs of compensation (Table 7.9). We asked:

1. *Medical compensation*: 'Suppose [an NHS doctor or hospital/a private doctor, or private hospital outside the NHS] makes a serious mistake

in treating a patient. In these circumstances, should the patient get financial compensation, or just be regarded as unfortunate?

IF FOR COMPENSATION: Would you still feel that way if that meant that [taxes/private medical charges] had to be increased substantially to pay for compensation awards?'

For present purposes we shall not distinguish between public and private medicine.

2. *Business compensation*: 'Suppose that [British Rail/British Gas/British Telecom/an Electricity Company] provides a particularly poor service to one of its customers by failing to meet its advertised standards. Should the customer get financial compensation, or just be regarded as unfortunate.

IF FOR COMPENSATION: Would you still feel that way if that meant that [rail fares/gas prices/telephone charges/electricity charges] had to be increased substantially to pay for compensation awards?'

For present purposes we shall not distinguish between these four different industries.

On average around 30 per cent were also willing to reconsider their initial opinions on minority schools, the death penalty, and phone-tapping or inspections of bank accounts, but there were variations according to the nature of their original views or the purposes of surveillance. We asked:

1. *Minority schools*: 'Should [parents who live in Wales/Muslim parents] have the right to have their children educated in publicly funded [Welsh-speaking/Muslim religious] schools if they wish?

IF YES: Would you still feel that way even if it substantially increased the amount of taxes local people had to pay?

IF NO: Would you still feel that way even if, as a result, the continued existence of that [language/religion] was threatened?'

2. *Death penalty*: '[Given that parliament has repeatedly voted against the death penalty/In order to clamp down on rising crime and violence], do you think Britain should reintroduce the death penalty for murder or keep things as they are?

IF FOR DEATH PENALTY: If careful research showed that reintroducing the death penalty *would not* cut the number of murders in Britain would you *still* be in favour of the death penalty?

IF AGAINST DEATH PENALTY: If careful research showed that reintroducing the death penalty *would* cut the number of murders in Britain would you *then* be in favour of the death penalty?'

3. *Surveillance*: 'In order to combat [crime, should the police/terrorism, should the security services/the spread of dangerous and undemocratic ideas, should the security services] ever be allowed to [tap phones/ inspect people's bank accounts]?

IF NO: Would you feel differently about that if you were convinced it would really help to combat [crime/terrorism/the spread of dangerous and undemocratic ideas].

IF YES: If you discovered the [police/security services] had done it to you, would you no longer feel it should be allowed, or would you feel it was just part of the price to be paid by law-abiding citizens for their protection?'[4]

Those members of the public who initially agreed to support minority schools were twice as willing to reconsider their support, when challenged, if the schools in question were Muslim rather than Welsh, which indicates a greater depth of support for Welsh schools. Those who initially supported the death penalty were a little more willing to reconsider when challenged than those who initially opposed it, suggesting that the motivation for *supporting* the death penalty was more utilitarian and less a matter of moral principle than was *opposition* to it. And while very few of those who initially supported surveillance would change their minds if they found themselves under surveillance, almost half of those who initially opposed surveillance would reconsider if they were convinced of its effectiveness— indeed, more than half, if its purpose was to combat terrorism rather than crime or subversive ideas.

Opinion on job quotas, racial incitement, and banning extreme political organizations was even more flexible. About half the public were willing to reconsider their opinions on employment quotas or racial/religious incitement when challenged (Table 7.10). We asked:

1. *Employment quotas*: 'Do you think the law should require [large private companies/the government and civil service] to hire a fixed percentage of [women/blacks and Asians/disabled people], or should [women/blacks and Asians/disabled people] get no special treatment?

IF FOR JOB QUOTAS: Would you feel the same even if this frequently means not hiring the best person for the job?

TABLE 7.10. *The varying effect of challenges*

% willing to consider changing opinion on	Politicians (%)	British public (%)	(Scottish public) (%)
If initially in favour of minority schools			
for Welsh	8	27	(29)
for Muslims	24	48	(45)
Death penalty			
if initially for death penalty	25	31	(33)
if initially against death penalty	13	26	(25)
Phone taps/bank inspections			
if initially for surveillance	7	7	(5)
if initially against surveillance	34	47	(53)
If initially against phone taps/bank inspections to combat			
crime	32	44	(53)
terrorism	56	58	(58)
dangerous ideas	23	44	(49)
If initially for job quotas for			
women	42	68	(81)
blacks and Asians	45	65	(64)
the disabled	31	50	(39)
If initially against job quotas for			
women	33	52	(55)
blacks and Asians	31	37	(44)
the disabled	44	65	(55)
Ban racial/religious incitement			
if initially for ban	45	50	(50)
if initially against ban	34	48	(47)
Ban extreme political organizations/not			
if initially for ban	56	57	(55)
if initially against ban	58	68	(72)

IF AGAINST JOB QUOTAS: Would you feel the same even if it means that [women/blacks and Asians/disabled people] remain economically *very* unequal?'

2. *Racial/religious incitement*: 'Do you think it should be against the law to write or speak in a way that promotes [racial/religious] hatred?

IF YES: If this results in less freedom of speech about important public issues, would you feel differently about it being against the law?

IF NO: If this results in more [racial/religious] prejudice, would you feel differently about it not being against the law?'

Amongst the public, two-thirds of those who initially *approved* employment quotas for women, blacks, and Asians changed their minds when challenged, yet only a third to a half of those who initially *opposed* these job quotas were willing to do so. This pattern was almost exactly reversed on job quotas for the disabled, however, where only half the supporters of quotas would reconsider, while two-thirds of the opponents were willing to do so. Support for employment quotas for women, blacks, and Asians was therefore relatively 'soft', while support for quotas for the disabled was relatively 'hard'. The same was also true amongst politicians, though to a lesser extent. This distinction between 'hard' and 'soft' support may in part be explained by our earlier finding in Chapter 5 that responses to the question on quotas for the disabled primarily reflected attitudes to the micro-principle of economic equality, whereas support for the less-favoured options of quotas for women and ethnic minorities correlated more strongly with the micro-principle of equal rights.

When challenged, half the public were willing to reconsider their attitude to a ban on racial or religious incitement, irrespective of their initial opinion. But amongst politicians, those who initially opposed a ban proved substantially less willing to change their minds. Amongst politicians, therefore, support for a ban on racial/religious incitement was relatively 'soft'.

Finally, 62 per cent of the public and 57 per cent of politicians were willing to reconsider their opinions about banning extreme political organizations. We asked:

Banning extremists: '[Political organizations with extreme views should be banned/We should never ban any political organization whatever its views.] Agree/disagree?

IF AGAINST BAN: Would you still feel that way if the political organization supported violence?

IF IN FAVOUR OF BAN: Would you still feel that way if the political organization did not support violence?'[5]

Amongst the public, but not the politicians, those originally opposed to a ban proved rather more willing to reconsider their opinion when challenged: opposition to a ban on extremists was therefore 'softer' than support for such a ban amongst the public.

INFLUENCES TOWARDS FLEXIBILITY

Averaging across the whole range of these challenges showed that women, the young, and those with low levels of education or little interest in politics had 'softer' opinions than others. Left-wingers were not, in general, any more or any less flexibly minded than right-wingers.

But people, and especially politicians, who placed themselves on the left or right of the ideological spectrum yet expressed an opinion on a particular issue that was more popular in the opposite ideological camp—and hence might be cross-pressured between their attitudes to the particular issue and their (formal or informal, conscious or unconscious) ideological loyalties— were generally more willing to reconsider their initial views when challenged. Politicians who had opinions that were out of line with those held by their ideological comrades were, on average, 16 per cent more willing to reconsider when challenged than politicians whose opinions were in line with those of their ideological comrades. For example, amongst politicians who initially *opposed* the death penalty, 31 per cent of self-confessed right-wingers but only 5 per cent of self-confessed left-wingers were willing to reconsider those original views when challenged. So ideological cross-pressures should be added to youth, female gender, low education, and low interest in politics as influences towards relatively flexible opinions, though these ideological cross-pressures clearly affected politicians rather more than the public (Table 7.11).

CONCLUSION

As we suggested at the beginning of this chapter, most people rarely address questions about civil rights and liberties outside the context of a particular situation. People might, for example, adhere to the principle of free speech, but they are less likely to think about it in abstract terms, more likely to think of it in terms of the right of someone to publish, broadcast, speak about, or teach something that could be seen as contentious. One of the purposes of this study was to see just how tenacious people were about their opinions. Or, to put this objective in a different way, we wished to see how malleable or robust people's opinions were when placed in a context that contradicted, varied, or challenged the way in which they had framed their initial declaration of opinion.

The evidence presented in this chapter gives us some clues about the extent to which answers to questions about civil liberties were shaped by the

TABLE 7.11. *Effect of challenges by ideology*

% willing to consider changing opinion on	Politicians		British public		(Scottish public)	
	Consistent (%)	Not consistent (%)	Consistent (%)	Not consistent (%)	Consistent (%)	Not consistent (%)
Minority schools	12	24	29	37	(22	35)
Death penalty	13	37	22	33	(24	40)
Phone taps/bank inspections	25	46	38	61	(53	52)
Employment quotas	30	50	45	57	(42	48)
Banning racial/religious incitement	33	39	52	49	(51	43)
Banning extreme political organizations	55	67	56	68	(55	68)
AVERAGE	28	44	40	51	(41	48)
Effect of ideological inconsistency	+16		+11		(+7)	

Note: This table is based only on those who described themselves as 'on the left' or 'on the right' in politics. 'Ideologically consistent' is defined as having the opinion which is more popular with those at the same end of the ideological spectrum. For example, those who describe themselves as 'on the left' are 'ideologically consistent' if they have an initial opinion which is more popular on the left than on the right. Thus, for this table, the ideologically consistent initial answers for those 'on the left' are support for minority schools, opposition to the death penalty, opposition to surveillance, support for employment quotas, support for a ban on racial/religious incitement, and opposition to a ban on extremist organizations; and, for those 'on the right', the ideologically consistent answers are the opposite. Obviously this is not the only possible definition of ideological consistency, and other definitions of ideological consistency would be appropriate for other purposes, but it does suggest cross-pressures at least in terms of human interaction, if not always in logic.

context in which they were presented. In the first part, when we discussed a range of ten questions, framed as more or less exclusive and exhaustive alternatives, we looked at the power of questioning more than at the power of argument. With these questions we considered to what extent our respondents were predisposed either to agree or to disagree with the question, regardless of the direction in which it was framed. Our results indicated that the public were more likely than politicians simply to agree with a statement as put to them which, at some level, indicates more deference amongst the governed than amongst those who govern. However, when we analysed this agreeability bias within our public sample, we found that it closely reflected levels of formal education: the more educated were less likely just to go along with a proposition as put to them. And politicians as a whole were no more disagreeable than those members of the public who held university degrees.

We took this a bit further in the second part of the chapter when we took full advantage of our CATI system to analyse how random halves of our samples of the public and politicians responded to questions that presented opposing arguments to each half; questions that did or did not contextualize the proposition being made; and questions that challenged a position they had already taken up.

Our three 'oppositional' questions on the value of decisive government, referendums, and the death penalty were all phrased with arguments that exposed half our respondents to opposing propositions about the value of constitutional checks and balances, parliamentary decision-making, and the need to clamp down on rising crime. Our results suggested that many people wanted government that was both decisive and constitutionally limited—and that was true at all levels of education. But on the other two questions the influence of argument was small and the highly educated reacted against attempts to push them one way or the other. Politicians also reacted against the arguments in our questions. Invoking the authority and prestige of parliament proved either worthless or counter-productive.

We found it easier, however, to manipulate public opinion right across the educational spectrum with those questions that added arguments to our initial propositions about conviction on confession, censoring publication of government documents in the national interest, race and crime, sensational crime, drink and drug consumption, and the power of social workers to remove children from families. Our additional arguments, even in cases where they were obliquely phrased, did have an effect. Both the public and their politicians, both those with high educational qualifications and those with none, all shifted their position when the problems were contextualized in this way.

Finally, we had a series of questions on medical compensation, business compensation, minority schools, the death penalty, surveillance, employment quotas, racial/religious incitement, and banning extremists that systematically challenged whichever position our respondents decided to take. Here too, both the public and politicians proved to be more flexible in their opinions, though the public more so than their politicians: over a third of the public proved willing to change their position on these eight issue areas, but only just over a quarter of the politicians.

However, a simple public-versus-politicians dichotomy did not explain the pattern of malleability completely. Malleability or flexibility—a willingness to shift position and respond to argument—was strongest amongst young people, women, those with limited education, those with low levels of political interest, and those who had initially taken a position that was out of line with their ideological position. In short then, while appeals to authority and prestige could sometimes be counter-productive, more rational arguments could be powerful, particularly when they were rich in substantive content. Active political debate is indeed worthwhile because people are open to rational argument.

But attitudes to civil, political, and social rights are not only shaped by the degree to which individuals have to confront specific situations or face up to arguments which test their commitment to principle. Other factors, particularly their personal experience of discrimination, their contact with state agencies, their experience of social and political participation, and, more generally, the whole pattern of life experiences that varies so systematically across different social backgrounds—across different classes, different religious groups, and different genders—may also have an impact on attitudes to both principle and practice. In the next chapter we look at the influence of the diffuse and cumulated experience associated with different social backgrounds and, in Chapter 10, at the influence of more specific and more personal experiences.

NOTES

1. D. A. de Vaus, *Surveys in Social Research* (London: Allen & Unwin, 1991) ch. 6; Tim May, *Social Research: Issues, Methods and Process* (Buckingham: Open University Press, 1993), 108–9; A. N. Oppenheim, *Questionnaire Design and Attitude Measurement* (New York: Pinter, 1992), 66.
2. Gerry Maher, 'Human Rights and the Criminal Process', in Tom Campbell, David Goldberg, Sheila McLean, and Tom Mullen (eds.), *Human Rights: From Rhetoric to Reality* (Oxford: Basil Blackwell, 1986), 197–222, at 207.

3. On the Orkney child-abuse scandal, see Ch. 2 n. 35.
4. This is a simplified account of the surveillance questions sequence. For the full account see Q75 in Appendix II.
5. This is a slightly simplified version of question sequence and wording. For the full version see Q56 in Appendix II.

8

Social Background

SOCIAL background demarcates both interests and networks of communication. The young and the old naturally have different levels of concern about pension rights, while women and men may react to gender-based job quotas in different ways, precisely because they affect their material interests so differently. And social background can also shape our networks of communication: as Deborah Tannen's research on the conversational styles of women and men has shown, the two sexes have markedly different conversational styles which can impede their communication and their understanding of each other.[1] For both these reasons—the conflict of objective interest and the prevalence of socially structured though often self-imposed barriers to communication—we might expect attitudes towards rights and liberties to vary, sometimes sharply, across different social categories.

Analytic categories are not easily recognizable self-conscious social groups, however. Categories cross-cut each other, nowhere more obviously than with age and gender, and more generally the complexity of cross-cutting social divisions can moderate differences of opinion and encourage a common culture. Ideas and opinions that are not picked up on one network may be accessed through another. Analytically, therefore, we should regard social labels as characteristics of, and indicators of potential influences upon, the individual rather than as a means of compartmenting society into separate groups.

We investigated the influence of age, gender, class, education, income, religion, town size and rurality, parenthood, and occupational sector on attitudes towards rights and liberties. Although we asked respondents for their ethnic or racial self-image, and ethnic differences can be very influential, our subsamples of ethnic or racial minorities are too small, and too diverse, for reliable analysis.[2] There is a common assumption that (old) age and religiosity are likely to encourage relatively conservative values, while advanced education and a comfortable lifestyle may encourage tolerance. As long-standing BBC serials like *The Archers* suggest, 'small-town' values are notoriously conservative. Women, the working class, and the low paid have a particular interest in equality—though they may mean different things by that term. Those employed by the state may naturally be more favourable to state intervention. And parents—almost, but not quite, tautologically—have more paternalist attitudes than those who do not have children. Such common assumptions are worth investigating and quantifying. Focusing only on the limited topic of practical tolerance, Sullivan, Pierson, and Marcus found that, in the USA, tolerance was strongly related to education, especially university education, less related to income, and hardly related at all to class self-image;[3] strongly related to age;[4] strongly related to whether or not people were religious, but not to whether they were Catholics or Protestants;[5] very weakly, if at all, related to gender;[6] and unrelated to the degree of urbanization across most of the range of that variable, except that, at the rural extreme, toleration was lower in communities of less than 2,500 inhabitants.[7] Our own findings are remarkably consistent with these in so far as they go, though our survey investigates a much wider range of principles. In general we found that British attitudes towards the principle of liberty followed patterns broadly similar to those described by Sullivan, Pierson, and Marcus for practical tolerance, but attitudes to the principle of equality— which Sullivan and his colleagues did not research even at the level of practice—followed quite different patterns.[8]

ALTERNATIVE SOCIAL INDICATORS

Our survey provided a wide range of social-background indicators. Class could be measured by whether people supervised others, or felt that they were 'part of the management or part of the workforce' in their present (or last) job. We classified the self-employed with the supervisors in the first case, and with management in the second. Alternatively class could be measured even more subjectively by whether people chose to call themselves 'middle class' or 'working class'. All three measures of class correlated with attitudes towards rights and liberties in broadly similar ways. Since the strength of the correlations with the third measure, self-assigned class, was slightly higher than with the management/workforce measure, and considerably higher than with the supervisor/non-supervisor measure, we shall focus attention on self-assigned class or what is sometimes called 'class self-image'.

Similarly, measures of rurality and town size could be based upon the place where people grew up or the place where they lived at the time of our survey. We shall focus upon the latter, since both measures correlated similarly with attitudes and values, but location at the time of the interview more so than place of upbringing—a point worth pondering in itself.

Religion has many aspects. In our survey we asked whether people had had a religious upbringing and, if so, of what kind; whether they now subscribed to a religion and, if so, what church or faith they claimed as their own; how frequently they attended religious services; and, of Christians only, we asked whether they would describe themselves as 'evangelical'. Opinions on rights and liberties differed between evangelical and non-evangelical Christians, between those who attended religious services frequently and those who did not, between those who adhered to one church rather than another, and between those with a religious upbringing and those without. But the single religious measure that correlated most strongly with such opinions was the simple divide between the religious and the unreligious. So we shall focus upon that division.

Our other social measures were more straightforward. We have measured age on a four-point scale (under 25 years old, 25–35 years old, 35–55 years old, and over 55); education on a three-point scale (no educational qualifications, only school or college qualifications, university or polytechnic qualifications)—though we shall draw some distinctions between different subject areas of education; parenthood by whether or not people had any children; occupational sector by whether their current (or last) job was with a private company or in the public sector; and income by answers to the question: 'What is your own total annual income from all sources, before tax, to the nearest thousand pounds?'

Some social differences between our three samples of politicians, the British public, and the Scots are worth noting because they have implications for attitudes towards rights and liberties. About a third of the public but only 4 per cent of our politicians were aged under 35. Our politicians were, of course, not just local councillors but the leaders of party groups on councils. So our politicians were much older than the public. Our politicians were also 85 per cent male. They were also much more highly educated— four times as likely to have a university degree as a member of the public. Compared to the public, our politicians were about 10 per cent more likely to have children and less likely to live in a big city or work in the private sector. Politicians were also much more likely to describe themselves as 'middle class'. Class self-image was also the social characteristic on which Scots differed most from the British: 60 per cent of politicians, 36 per cent of the British public, but only 26 per cent of Scots declared themselves to be 'middle class'.[9] The familiar stereotype of politicians as being overwhelmingly male, middle aged, and middle class is correct, though the fact that they are so well educated is less frequently included in the stereotype.

SOCIAL BACKGROUND AND PRINCIPLES

For an initial overview of the relationship between values and opinions, on the one hand, and social structure, on the other, we can calculate the correlation coefficients between each of our chosen social measures and our summary measures of liberty and equality. For more insight, we can also look at the correlations between measures of social structure and each of our thirteen micro-principles. Moreover, it is helpful to list these micro-principles in a sequence derived from the factor analysis discussed in Chapter 4. First, there are the six principles most closely associated with the first dimension or macro-principle, liberty, arranged in order of declining association (positive or negative) with that first dimension: authority, traditional values, wealth creation, intolerance, and the right to free speech. Then there are the two micro-principles that sit uneasily between the two macro-dimensions: rights of protest and rebellion, and self-reliance. Finally, there are the five micro-principles associated with the second dimension or macro-principle, equality, arranged in order of decreasing association with it: economic equality, caring, equal rights, protection, and the right to know.

Arranged in this way, the table of correlations shows very clearly that age, religion, and education correlated strongly with liberty and its associated micro-principles, but not with equality. Moreover, they correlated most strongly with precisely those micro-principles that were most closely associated with liberty. The pattern is consistent with reactions to the French Revolution of 1789: the educated, the unreligious, and the young have classic liberal values. They are opposed to authority, antagonistic towards traditional values, in favour of limited government and free speech, and devoted to the principle (at least) of toleration. It is no coincidence that the Revolution of 1789 spawned rationalist and anti-clerical parties across Europe that took the title 'Liberal'.

By contrast, equality and its associated micro-principles correlated most strongly with income, class, and gender—none of which correlated very strongly with liberty. Indeed, in so far as (female) gender correlated with liberty at all, it correlated negatively, mainly because women were so committed to the support of traditional values; while working-class identifiers similarly gave particular support to the micro-principle of wealth creation. Once again, the social measures correlated most strongly of all with precisely those micro-principles that were most strongly associated with equality, notably economic equality in the case of income and class, and equal rights in the case of gender. The first pattern reflects the increasing significance of working-class and socialist parties in politics after the First World War which focused attention on economic equality; the second reflects more recent campaigns for gender and racial equality which, as Elizabeth Meehan notes, 'mark a move away from the principles of universality and anonymity underlying at least some of the intentions of the welfare state . . . by guaranteeing specific forms of equality for groups identifiable by innate characteristics'.[10]

There was little evidence for the myth of small-town values in Britain. Rural residents had a little more respect for authority, a little greater devotion to traditional values, and a little greater antagonism towards protest and rebellion than those who lived in large towns and cities, but the correlations between all of these and town size were small.

Those who worked in the private sector were a little more opposed to economic equality, caring, and equal rights—though also a little more opposed to traditional values—than public-sector workers, but the correlations were all very small.

Parenthood was more strongly related to values and opinions: those with children had noticeably more respect for authority, were noticeably less tolerant yet more caring, and were very much more committed to traditional values.

In the whole of Table 8.1 few, if any, of the directions of these correlations will surprise anyone. But the sizes, and the relative sizes, of the different correlations are a lot more surprising. The power of age and education was expected and, in a land as densely packed as Britain, the insignificance of a distinctive small-town or rural culture was not surprising. But the power of religiosity to structure values, especially amongst politicians where it was the dominant social influence, was greater than we anticipated. Parenthood proved surprisingly powerful, though that may partly have reflected age and religiosity, while occupational sector and gender proved weaker than might have been expected.

This has been a very crude introductory overview that requires a detailed follow-up. Correlation coefficients may underestimate the substantive significance of social characteristics—like advanced education—that apply to only a few people. And our composite measures of micro-principles may compound and confuse as well as summarize efficiently. To take a simple example, our measure of the traditional-values principle was based upon two questions, one, and only one, of which explicitly used religious language. It would be surprising if those two questions were equally closely related to religiosity. So there is a need for some disaggregation and detail.

TABLE 8.1. *Correlations between principles and social background*

	Old (r × 100)	Religious (r × 100)	Education (r × 100)	Income (r × 100)	Working class (r × 100)	Private sector (r × 100)	Have children (r × 100)	Female (r × 100)	Rural residence (r × 100)
POLITICIANS									
Liberty	-44	-54	38	15	·	-17	-13	·	-23
Equality	-10	-19	·	-18	29	-21	·	·	-12
Authority	38	39	-32	·	·	20	·	·	18
Traditional values	40	59	-33	-15	·	13	12	·	21
Wealth creation	32	30	-23	·	·	19	·	·	17
Tolerance	-31	-32	33	12	-13	-12	-13	12	-20
Limited government	-25	-27	16	·	·	-17	·	·	-16
Right to free speech	-13	-12	·	·	·	·	·	·	·
Protest	-21	-26	14	·	17	-24	·	·	-16
Self-reliance	16	23	·	11	-23	21	·	·	15
Economic equality	·	-16	·	-17	27	-20	·	·	·
Caring	·	·	-17	-21	32	-12	·	10	·
Equal rights	-19	-24	·	-10	18	-19	·	11	-17
Protection	·	·	·	·	·	-14	·	·	·
Right to know	-13	-16	·	·	10	-11	·	·	·

BRITISH PUBLIC
(SCOTTISH PUBLIC)

Liberty	−39 (−37)	−44 (−43)	35 (36)	13 (12)	18 ·	·	·	·	−25 (−23)	−10 (−11)	−12	( )
Equality	· ( )	· ( )	· (−13)	−19 (−22)	· (21)	−10	·	·	· ( )	18 (16)	· ( )	( )
Authority	24 (24)	29 (29)	−27 (−29)	· (−10)	·	·	·	·	16 (12)	·	· ( )	(10)
Traditional values	42 (38)	45 (44)	−28 (−28)	−14 (−11)	·	·	· (−14)	·	27 (23)	13 (14)	11	( )
Wealth creation	11 (11)	19 (19)	−27 (−29)	−16 (−14)	10 (13)	·	·	·	· ( )	13 (14)	·	( )
Tolerance	−21 (−19)	−25 (−21)	28 (27)	·	·	· (−10)	·	·	−13 (−15)	· ( )	·	( )
Limited government	−11 (−12)	−19 (−12)	10 ( )	·	·	·	·	·	· ( )	· (−10)	·	( )
Right to free speech	−11 (−10)	−16 (−15)	18 (15)	14	·	·	·	·	· ( )	· ( )	·	( )
Protest	−18 (−13)	−14 (−13)	·	−11	11 (18)	·	·	·	· ( )	· ( )	·	(−10)
Self-reliance	·	· ( )	· (−10)	·	−14	·	·	·	· ( )	· ( )	·	( )
Economic equality	· ( )	· ( )	−11 (−16)	−23 (−19)	20 (23)	·	·	·	· ( )	10 ( )	·	( )
Caring	12 (15)	· (13)	−15 (−28)	−16 (−19)	18 (22)	·	·	·	13 ( )	12 ( )	·	( )
Equal rights	−15 (−13)	−11 (−14)	10 ( )	· (−13)	·	·	·	·	· ( )	16 (16)	·	( )
Protection	· ( )	·	· ( )	· ( )	·	·	·	·	· ( )	· ( )	·	( )
Right to know	−13 ( )	·	10 ( )	· ( )	·	·	·	·	· ( )	· ( )	·	( )

Note: Correlations less than 0.10 have been replaced by full points.

SOCIAL BACKGROUND AND SYMPATHIES

In Chapter 4 we also defined seven types of sympathy and confidence. We found two macro-factors underlying them. The first concerned activists and minorities, militants, and socially disadvantaged groups. Of our eight social variables, these sympathies correlated most strongly with age: the young were particularly sympathetic to activists, militants, and socially disadvantaged groups. And, echoing our analysis of the social correlates of principle, age correlated most strongly with precisely those sympathies that were most closely associated with this first dimension. Religion and education also correlated strongly with sympathies or antipathies towards these groups of citizens.

The other four aspects of sympathy or antipathy were associated with a second dimension which concerned confidence in different institutions. Age correlated strongly with one aspect of that—confidence in the judicial system—but not with other aspects. The religious, however, had relatively high confidence in the political system and civil institutions, while the highly educated had relatively high confidence in the rights industry.

Apart from religion, age, and education, the other social variables generally correlated only weakly with the public's sympathy for citizen groups or confidence in institutions, though women were particularly sympathetic to the socially disadvantaged, the working class were particularly unsympathetic to the judicial system, and parents were particularly unsympathetic towards political activists (Table 8.2).

Age

In the USA, McClosky and Brill found that 'of all the social influences that help to shape the public's attitudes towards civil liberties none, except for education, appears to have a more powerful effect than age'.[11] In Britain, our introductory correlation analysis suggested that the correlation between support for liberty and age slightly exceeded that with education but fell short of the correlation with religion.

Amongst the public, age correlated relatively strongly (at above 0.2) with authority, traditional values, and intolerance but with nothing else. Amongst politicians, age also correlated strongly with these same micro-principles and, in addition, with wealth creation and limited government. All of these were first-dimension (liberty) principles. Correlations with second-dimension (equality) principles never exceeded the 0.2 threshold, though equal rights came close. However, as we shall see, even that apparent exception was misleading.

TABLE 8.2. *Correlations between sympathies and social background*

	Old (r × 100)	Religious (r × 100)	Education (r × 100)	Income (r × 100)	Working class (r × 100)	Private sector (r × 100)	Have children (r × 100)	Female (r × 100)	Rural residence (r × 100)
POLITICIANS									
Activists	−25	−27	15	.	18	−22	.	.	−22
Socially disadvantaged	−31	−31	16	.	12	−22	.	13	−18
Militants	−11	.	.	.	11	−10	.	.	.
Political system	14	20	−11	.	.	.	.	.	.
Civil institutions	16	16	−13	.	10	.	.	.	.
Judicial system	29	32	.	.	−18	15	.	.	11
Rights enforcers	−15	−21	20	.	.	−18	.	.	−14
BRITISH PUBLIC (SCOTTISH PUBLIC)									
Activists	−24 (−20)	−17 (−14)	14 (.)	. (.)	. (.)	. (.)	−16 (−13)	. (.)	. (.)
Socially disadvantaged	−19 (−19)	−16 (−16)	17 (.)	. (.)	. (−10)	. (.)	. (.)	14 (10)	. (.)
Militants	−12 (−15)	. (.)	. (.)	−10 (−15)	. (.)	. (.)	−11 .	. (.)	. (.)
Political system	11 (16)	15 (12)	. (.)	. (.)	. (.)	. (.)	. (.)	. (.)	. (.)
Civil institutions	11 (14)	18 (16)	. (.)	−13 (−11)	. (11)	. (.)	. (.)	. (.)	. (.)
Judicial system	21 (21)	17 (14)	. (.)	. (.)	−13 (−14)	. (.)	12 .	. (.)	12 (.)
Rights enforcers	−10 (.)	. (.)	15 (21)	. (.)	. (.)	. (.)	. (.)	. (.)	. (.)

Note: Correlations less than 0.10 have been replaced by full points.

We divided respondents into four age groups: those under 25, the 25 to 35 year olds, the 35 to 55 year olds, and those aged over 55. Calculating scores for principles on a +/–100 scale, as in Chapter 4, allows us to see how each of these age groups felt about each micro- and macro-principle. Amongst the public average equality scores fell within a narrow 6-point range in all age groups, while liberty scores ranged over 36 points, from minus 3 in the youngest age group down to minus 39 in the oldest. Amongst politicians, average equality scores differed by 10 points between the youngest age group (25–35 year olds, since there were no political leaders under 25 in our sample) and the oldest, but liberty scores differed by 47 points. Age, therefore, had much more influence upon commitment to liberty than on commitment to equality, and much more influence upon politicians than on the public, especially when we take account of politicians' narrower range of ages.

To put it another way, commitment to liberty was 12 points higher amongst old politicians than amongst old people generally, but the commitment of middle-aged politicians was 27 points higher than that of other people of the same age, and amongst young politicians it was 33 points higher than amongst other people of the same age. The large differences between politicians and public of the same age explain why politicians could be more committed to liberty than the public despite their being so much older than the public. But the variation in the effect of elective office is also very clear: youth and elective office had not just additive but 'interactive' (in the statistical sense) effects upon commitment to liberty, the difference between politicians and the public varied sharply with age.

We can pursue the distinction between age effects on first- and second-dimension principles in more detail. Support for authority, traditional values, and intolerance all increased with increasing age. They usually do increase (or decrease) together. Similarly, support for economic equality, caring, and equal rights usually increase (or decrease) together—but, significantly, they do *not* do so with age. Amongst both politicians and the public, increasing age went with declining commitment to economic equality and sharply declining support for equal rights, yet with *increasing* commitment to caring. Perhaps there was an element of self-interest in that, though the effect of age on all second-dimension principles, except equal rights, was weak (Table 8.3).

Age correlated well with most indicators of authority, and respect for authority clearly varied more sharply with age amongst politicians than amongst the public. Attitudes to traditional values also varied more sharply with age amongst politicians. And it is worth noting that age affected attitudes to traditional values whether or not the question was couched in religious language, though perhaps a little more strongly when religious language was

TABLE 8.3. *Principles and sympathies by age* (selected scores on +/-100 scale)

	Politicians			British public (Scottish public)			
	25–35	35–55	>55	<25	25–35	35–55	>55
	(scores)	(scores)	(scores)	(scores)	(scores)	(scores)	(scores)
Liberty	20	1	−27	−3 (−8)	−13 (−16)	−25 (−26)	−39 (−39)
Equality	63	57	53	59 (61)	57 (61)	53 (62)	54 (59)
Authority	−4	15	41	26 (29)	32 (30)	37 (38)	51 (51)
Traditional values	−23	9	47	−2 (6)	16 (23)	39 (41)	62 (62)
Intolerance	−35	−26	−8	−14 (−13)	−8 (−6)	−2 (−2)	4 (4)
Protest	53	33	14	44 (37)	40 (47)	31 (34)	19 (25)
Economic equality	50	47	43	51 (53)	48 (54)	45 (53)	45 (53)
Caring	72	75	79	74 (77)	76 (81)	78 (86)	83 (87)
Equal rights	67	49	36	52 (53)	47 (48)	37 (47)	34 (37)
Activists	13	−4	−21	2 (2)	−6 (−9)	−15 (−14)	−22 (−21)
Socially disadvantaged	57	41	17	−26 (−34)	−27 (−34)	−19 (−32)	−7 (−15)
Judicial system	13	19	39	12 (18)	19 (17)	23 (23)	34 (36)

Note: Although these scores are defined precisely in Chapter 4, it is useful, intuitively, to think of each score on the +/-100 scale as the percentage of statements relevant to a principle with which the respondent completely agrees, minus the percentage with which he or she completely disagrees. While the actual definitions are necessarily more complex, that is a useful approximation, and would be an exact definition if all questions had been in agree/disagree format, and all respondents had had strong views on all questions.

used. Intolerance varied particularly sharply with age, and particularly in response to the proposition that 'we should not tolerate people whose ideas are morally wrong'. Amongst the public, 67 per cent of the old but only 31 per cent of under 25 year olds agreed to that; and amongst politicians, 48 per cent of the old but only 9 per cent of the under 35 year olds agreed.

Concepts of limited government seemed less familiar to the public than to politicians. Amongst the public only 9 per cent of the old and 19 per cent of even the under 25s thought it was more important to 'protect the rights of suspects' than to 'make the streets safe even if we sometimes have to violate suspects' rights'. Amongst politicians, however, 20 per cent of the old but a massive 63 per cent of the young backed the rights of suspects. The age gradient was clear amongst both politicians and the public, though spectacularly so amongst politicians.

The one exception to the general rule that age affected first-dimension (liberty) principles much more than second-dimension (equality) principles appeared to be attitudes to equal rights. However, closer inspection casts some doubt upon that conclusion. Age hardly correlated at all with attitudes towards gender or racial equality but strongly with attitudes towards equality for homosexuals. There must be at least a suspicion that such a pattern had libertarian as well as egalitarian overtones.

The young had more sympathy for activists and the socially disadvantaged groups and less confidence in the judicial system than their elders: compared to older politicians, young politicians gave sympathy/confidence scores that were 34 points more favourable to activists, 40 points more favourable to the socially disadvantaged, and 26 points less favourable to the judicial system. Disaggregating our bundles of sympathy is even more revealing than disaggregating our measures of principle, however. Age correlated strongly with antipathy towards only three of our seven types of activist—'communists', 'gays and lesbians', and 'black activists'. (In each case, the old were far more unfavourable to them than were the young.) Similarly, age correlated far more strongly with antipathy towards immigrants than towards women or the poor. Amongst the public 79 per cent of the old but only 47 per cent of the young agreed that 'immigrants to Britain should try harder to be more like other British people'; and amongst politicians 65 per cent of the old, but only 17 per cent of the young expressed this view about immigrants.

Religion

The aspect of religion that correlated best with principles and sympathies was religiosity, simply measured by whether people would accept or reject a religious designation of any kind.[12] Amongst the public, that correlated relatively strongly and positively with authority, traditional values, and intolerance (at above 0.2). Amongst politicians, it also correlated strongly and positively with self-reliance and wealth creation, and strongly and negatively with limited government, protest, and equal rights. Indeed, amongst politicians it was strongly correlated with eight of our thirteen micro-principles, including five of the six which fell unambiguously into the first dimension (liberty), though with only one of the five which fell unambiguously into the second dimension (equality).

Three other religious indicators—a religious upbringing, frequency of attendance (amongst the religious), and evangelicalism (amongst Christians) —correlated strongly only with traditional values. And our last religious indicator—a sectarian spectrum running from the Established Churches through Protestant Nonconformists to Catholics—failed to correlate strongly with any principle or prejudice. In short, the key influence was not sectarianism, nor religious upbringing, nor frequency of attendance, but the mere existence or non-existence of current religiosity itself. In McClosky and Brill's view: 'because religious "true believers" have embraced a body of received doctrines or dogmas, they have difficulty processing (in Max Weber's phrase) "inconvenient facts"',[13] which makes them relatively intolerant. Lord Percy similarly drew attention to the 'incompatibility of democracy and Christianity'[14] (though his argument applied to most religions), the one founded on rationality, tolerance, and scepticism, the other on revelation, dogma, and faith.

The Religious versus the Unreligious

On equality, the religious differed from the unreligious by only 3 points amongst the public and 12 points amongst politicians; but on liberty they differed by 33 points amongst the public and 43 points amongst politicians (Table 8.4).

As with age and elective office, the effects of religion and elective office on commitment to liberty were interactive: while religiosity reduced commitment to liberty amongst both politicians and the public, this effect of religion was greater amongst politicians.

On commitment to traditional values—measured, in part, by attitudes towards 'following God's will'—the religious differed from the unreligious by 56 points amongst the public and 72 points amongst politicians, but, more significantly, they also differed considerably on all other first-dimension principles, and on protest.[15] Conversely, differences were small or insignificant on all the second-dimension principles except equal rights.

TABLE 8.4. *Principles and sympathies by religion* (selected scores on +/–100 scale)

	Politicians		British public (Scottish public)	
	Religious (scores)	Not religious (scores)	Religious (scores)	Not religious (scores)
Liberty	–22	21	–31 (–31)	2 (1)
Equality	52	64	54 (60)	57 (62)
Authority	35	0	44 (44)	18 (18)
Traditional values	44	–28	48 (49)	–8 (–5)
Tolerance	12	34	–1 (0)	17 (15)
Limited government	7	35	–2 (–1)	15 (10)
Right to speak out	51	60	32 (31)	46 (45)
Protest	17	48	27 (32)	45 (48)
Economic equality	42	52	46 (53)	46 (52)
Caring	77	78	79 (85)	75 (79)
Equal rights	38	61	38 (42)	49 (56)
Activists	–18	7	–17 (–15)	–2 (–3)
Socially disadvantaged	23	53	15 (25)	30 (40)
Judicial system	35	9	27 (27)	13 (15)

Sectarian Differences

Despite the fact that a simple sectarian spectrum failed to correlate strongly with any measure of principle or sympathy, an analysis by church affiliation suggests some clear sectarian effects. Certainly the major division of opinion lay between the religious and the unreligious, and sectarian differences were seldom large amongst the public, though, as usual, somewhat larger amongst politicians. But they were detectable. There were sharp sectarian differences on commitment to the principle of protest, for example. Amongst the public, both Catholics and the unreligious gave it about 18 points more support than Anglicans or Nonconformists. It is more than a linguistic irony that Catholics should support the principle of protest so much more than Protestants, but in Britain they are an anti-establishment church with a history of persecution whose numbers were swelled in the last century by poor, Irish immigrants. Amongst politicians, there was a clear spectrum of support for the principle of protest, ranging from Anglicans through Nonconformists, to Catholics and then the unreligious, with the largest gap between Anglicans and Nonconformists, that is, between the established state church and all others: Protestant Nonconformist politicians gave the principle of protest 16 points more support than Anglicans, and Catholics a further 11 points more than Nonconformists, making a difference of 27 points between Catholics and adherents of the Established Church. Amongst politicians there were also substantial differences between Anglicans and Catholics on micro-principles of authority, wealth creation, limited government, economic equality, and equal rights, and on sympathies towards activists and the socially disadvantaged, with Nonconformists occupying an intermediate position on all of these. In every case, the attitudes of Catholics were more favourable to citizens and less favourable to government than the attitudes of Anglicans.

On many principles and sympathies, it was the unreligious who took one extreme, and adherents of the two Established Churches (the Churches of Scotland and England) who took the other. But on commitment to caring, it was Catholics who took the most egalitarian position; and on commitment to traditional values, it was Protestant Nonconformists who took the most authoritarian position. Thus, one reason why a simple sectarian spectrum failed analytically was that the sectarian groups formed different coalitions on different principles, depending upon whether they were linked to the social and economic interests of the sectarian groups, or with their relationship to the established order, or with the intensity of their religious feelings. The patterns are complex but not, we think, unfamiliar (Table 8.5).

The Scope of Religious Differences

Naturally, indeed almost tautologically, the religious and unreligious differed sharply on any question that used specifically religious language. Amongst the public, those who volunteered or accepted a religious designation gave 6.5 out of ten for the importance of 'following God's will', while those who did not gave only 2.4; amongst politicians this division over 'God's will' was even greater, with marks of 6.3 and 1.1 respectively. Similarly, one indicator of confidence in civil institutions was the rating given for the importance of churches as a protector of rights and liberties. Amongst the public, the religious gave churches a score of 6.1 marks out of ten, while the unreligious gave churches only 4.2, though unreligious politicians were more favourable to churches as socially useful institutions, and gave them 5.0 out of ten. It would be remarkable if the religious and unreligious had not differed from each other on these questions that explicitly asked about God and churches. Indeed it is worth noting that, somewhat surprisingly, large differences in attitudes to God were combined with relatively small differences in attitudes towards religious institutions: religious politicians

TABLE 8.5. *Principles and sympathies by religious sect (selected scores on +/-100 scale)*

	Politicians				British public (Scottish public)			
	C. of E.	Prot.	RC	Not religious	C. of E. (C. of S.)	Prot.	RC	Not religious
	(scores)	(scores)	(scores)	(scores)	(scores)	(scores)	(scores)	(scores)
Liberty	-23	-26	-17	21	-31 (-32)	-35 (-31)	-29 (-30)	2 (1)
Equality	49	55	61	64	54 (59)	52 (58)	58 (67)	57 (62)
Protest	8	24	35	49	25 (30)	23 (22)	40 (47)	45 (48)
Traditional values	42	52	45	-28	46 (48)	61 (50)	49 (52)	-8 (-5)
Caring	74	78	83	78	79 (85)	76 (82)	82 (88)	75 (79)
Equal rights	35	39	50	61	37 (39)	34 (42)	43 (54)	49 (56)
Activists	-22	-13	-3	7	-16 (-17)	-23 (-17)	-15 (-7)	-2 (-3)
Socially disadvantaged	17	26	41	53	12 (22)	14 (23)	21 (37)	30 (40)
Judicial system	37	37	21	9	28 (30)	30 (27)	20 (17)	13 (15)

proved to be only lukewarm towards churches and unreligious politicians were no worse than neutral towards them.

What was far less obvious was that the religious and unreligious should differ *on so much more* than their attitude to religion and religious institutions. Compared to the unreligious, religious politicians gave marks out of ten that were 2.2 higher for 'respect for authority', 1.9 higher for 'traditional ideas of right and wrong', 1.8 higher for 'cutting taxes', 1.7 higher for 'self-reliance', and 2.2 lower for 'guaranteeing equal rights for homosexuals'. Religious politicians were also 20 per cent more willing than their unreligious colleagues to place importance on protecting 'children and young people from wild and immoral ideals', 25 per cent were willing to agree that 'we should not tolerate people whose ideas are morally wrong', 30 per cent more willing to give priority to making 'the streets safe even if we sometimes have to violate suspects' rights', and 25 per cent less likely to say that government had a responsibility for 'evening out differences in wealth between people'.

In the USA, McClosky and Brill found that the religious were very much more authoritarian (or 'conservative') on sexual issues, less so on issues of free speech, and only very slightly more authoritarian on issues of due process, privacy, the death penalty, and, significantly, civil disobedience: 'some of the very religious place a higher value on conscience than they do on legality and conventionality.'[16] No doubt a few very religious people would put conscience above the law anywhere, and more might put conscience above the law in places where the laws were particularly offensive to religious principle, but we certainly did *not* find that true of most religious people in contemporary Britain. When we asked: 'Suppose parliament passed a law you considered unjust, immoral, or cruel. Would you still be morally bound to obey it?', in all three of our samples the religious felt more obliged than the unreligious to obey even an 'unjust, immoral, or cruel' law—by a margin of 12 per cent amongst the British public (17 per cent in Scotland) and 22 per cent amongst politicians. The most frequent attenders at worship, and the minority of Christians who described themselves as 'evangelicals', were a little less deferential to the law than other religious people—indicating a somewhat curvilinear relationship between religiosity and deference perhaps—but, in terms of deference to the law, they were none the less more similar to other religious people than they were to the unreligious.

Religion and Sympathy

The religious and unreligious also differed sharply on sympathy: religious politicians were 25 points less sympathetic towards activists, 30 points less sympathetic towards the socially disadvantaged, and had 24 points more confidence in the judicial system. Sectarian divisions also affected sympathies: compared to their Anglican colleagues, Catholic politicians were 19 points more favourable to activists, 24 points more favourable to the socially disadvantaged, and 16 points less favourable to the judicial system.

When asked to give marks out of ten for how much they liked various groups, religious politicians gave 'gays and lesbians' 1.9 less than did the unreligious, 'feminists' 1.2 less, 'black activists' 1.7 less, and 'communists' 1.2 less; and they gave the police 1.2 more out of ten for their 'fairness and impartiality'. Religious politicians were 37 per cent more likely to agree that 'immigrants to Britain should try harder to be more like other British people', 24 per cent more likely to agree that social workers had too much power, and 28 per cent more likely to agree that 'government regulation of business usually does more harm than good'.

Evangelical Christians

We have already noted that frequency of religious attendance or acceptance of the 'evangelical' label correlated strongly only with traditional values and not with other micro-principles. Self-described evangelicals scored 29 points higher on traditional values than other Christians, but only 10 points lower on tolerance and a mere 2 points higher on respect for authority. We found a particularly high level of evangelicals, and a rather stronger political polarization between evangelicals and non-evangelicals, within the Protestant Nonconformist sects. But even within their small numbers, the evangelicals scored only 10 points more on authority, and 18 less on tolerance, but 39 more on traditional values than the non-evangelicals.

More widely, both frequency of attendance and self-assigned evangelicalism correlated very strongly only with answers to *explicitly religious* questions. Amongst religious politicians, for example, those who attended church at least once a month gave marks out of ten for 'following God's will' that were 3.1 higher than did those who attended less than once a year, and evangelicals gave marks that were 2.1 higher than those given even by other Christian politicians; but in very sharp contrast, frequent and infrequent attenders differed by only 0.5 on marks for the importance of 'traditional ideas of right and wrong', while evangelicals and non-evangelicals differed by only 0.4.

In broad terms these findings are consistent with Stuart Rothenberg and Frank Newport's study of *The Evangelical Voter* in the USA.[17] Rothenberg and Newport employed six different definitions of evangelical voters— belief in a literal bible, an explicitly 'born-again' self-image, an explicitly 'fundamentalist' self-image, familiarity with fundamentalist publications, and religious intensity as measured by frequency of attendance at a place of worship, and by the 'importance' attached to religion. In our terms only the first four of these even approximate our definition in terms of an explicitly 'evangelical' self-image; the fifth we have treated as a separate aspect of religiosity; and the sixth is similar to our question about the importance of 'following God's will', which we have used as an indicator of commitment to traditional values. Consistent with our findings, Rothenberg and Newport found that political attitudes were only weakly related to their first four definitions of evangelicals—which are the only ones that truly get at the distinctive evangelical concept; but political attitudes were more strongly related to religious intensity—and, though evangelicals may be strongly religious, we believe these two religious concepts should not be confused. Indeed, Rothenberg and Newport found that there were 'only limited independent relationships between belief in a literal bible and political attitudes once [they had] controlled for education'.[18] (Such literal belief was less frequent amongst the more educated.) And also consistent with our findings, Rothenberg and Newport found that 'the greatest impact of religion [was] on those political attitudes which have a moral or religious character to them'[19] such as 'school prayer' and 'birth control'. Once other aspects of socio-economic background had been taken into account, religious fundamentalism in the USA had much less impact on other political attitudes and almost none on identification with a particular political party.

Education

The impact of education on principles and sympathies was at least as complex as that of religion. The level of educational attainment clearly affected commitment to principle. But so did the nature of that education—whether it was a training that emphasized knowledge more than debate, or vice versa. Most important of all, the level of educational attainment also affected the coherence, and even the dimensionality, or principle.

The Influence of Education on Principles and Sympathies

Using a three-point scale running from university/polytechnic degrees, through school/college qualifications, down to no educational qualifications at all, we found that education correlated relatively strongly with micro-principles of respect for authority, traditional values, wealth creation, and intolerance—amongst both the public and politicians. The university educated differed from the educationally unqualified by about 36 points on commitment to liberty, though by very little at all on attitudes towards equality (Table 8.6).[20]

TABLE 8.6. *Principles and sympathies by level of educational qualifications*
(selected scores on +/–100 scale)

	Politicians			British public (Scottish public)		
	None (scores)	School (scores)	Univ. (scores)	None (scores)	School (scores)	Univ. (scores)
Liberty	−29	−18	6	−36 (−37)	−20 (−20)	1 (3)
Equality	61	52	56	56 (63)	54 (60)	55 (54)
Authority	41	34	10	49 (51)	36 (34)	12 (17)
Traditional values	48	35	3	53 (55)	31 (32)	7 (13)
Tolerance	3	14	30	−6 (−6)	6 (6)	21 (21)
Protest	20	17	37	29 (35)	30 (35)	40 (34)
Economic equality	51	41	46	50 (57)	44 (51)	43 (44)
Caring	85	77	73	83 (90)	77 (82)	72 (70)
Equal rights	46	38	50	36 (43)	41 (46)	50 (48)
Activists	−16	−17	−2	−19 (−17)	−12 (−11)	−3 (−7)
Socially disadvantaged	24	25	40	10 (24)	20 (29)	33 (33)
Rights Industry	4	8	20	1 (−3)	7 (7)	14 (13)

A closer look at the opinions of those with each of these three levels of education shows that, on most (not all) principles and sympathies, the difference between those with school and university qualifications was greater than between those with school qualifications and with none.[21] However, correlations between principles, sympathies, and education were not entirely due to deviant attitudes amongst the university educated: even school-level qualifications made some difference, and occasionally a large difference.

There was also some evidence of a curvilinear response to education, particularly so amongst politicians, but amongst the public as well. On liberty, university-educated politicians differed twice as much from those with school qualifications as those with school qualifications did from those with none. And on equality, those with school qualifications were the least egalitarian, the university educated slightly more egalitarian, and the unqualified the most egalitarian. In one sense this pattern was weak, because the differences on equality were small, but in another sense this was evidence for a strong version of curvilinearity, since the effect of a lot of education actually *reversed* the effect of a little. It reminds us of the old saying that 'a little learning is a dangerous thing', which so neatly expresses in words the mathematical concept of a curvilinear relationship.

Compared to those with no educational qualifications, university-educated members of the public gave marks out of ten that were 2.0 lower for 'respect for authority', 2.9 lower for 'following God's will', 1.8 lower for the importance of 'traditional ideas of right and wrong', and 2.5 lower for the importance of 'cutting taxes'. Similarly the university educated were 35 per cent less willing to agree that 'if something is morally wrong, then it should be made illegal'; 16 per cent less willing to stress the importance of protecting 'children and young people from wild and immoral ideas'; and 32 per cent less inclined to say that 'we should not tolerate people whose ideas are morally wrong'. Graduates were clearly allergic to moralistic language, whether because they did not attach importance to moral standards, or did not believe in coercion, or feared that standards other than their own might be imposed. They were also 28 per cent less willing to give priority to making 'the streets safe even if we sometimes have to violate the suspects' rights', and 31 per cent more willing to defend freedom of speech, even 'if it means we have to put up with the danger to society from extremist views'.

These are very large differences of opinion, though it should be borne in mind that relatively few members of the British public had university degrees. However, although the university educated might be dismissed as a small subsection of the general public, they were a large and influential section of politicians. Over a third of politicians had university (or polytechnic) degrees and there were large differences of opinion between them and other politicians, just as there were between university-educated members of the public and others. For example, on the proposition that 'we should not tolerate people whose ideas are morally wrong', the difference between the university educated and the unqualified was 32 per cent amongst the public but 27 per cent amongst politicians; and on the option of keeping the streets safe even at the expense of violating suspects' rights, the difference between the university educated and the unqualified was 28 per cent amongst the public but 30 per cent amongst politicians.

Although sympathies were much less correlated with education than with age or religion, education still had some influence. Compared to those with no educational qualifications, university-educated members of the public were 16 points more sympathetic to activists and 23 more towards the socially disadvantaged; they had 13 points more confidence in rights enforcers; they gave 1.5 more marks out of ten for sympathy towards 'gays and lesbians' and 1.3 more for sympathy towards 'black activists'; and they were 35 per cent less likely to agree that 'immigrants to Britain should try harder to be more like other British people'. Last, and not very surprisingly, the university educated were less prejudiced against 'experts'. Amongst politicians, for example, 86 per cent of the unqualified but only 60 per cent of the university educated agreed that they would put their trust 'in the practical experience of ordinary people rather than the theories of experts and intellectuals'. Although the difference was less amongst the public, suspicion of 'experts and intellectuals' was widespread, but rather less widespread amongst the university educated than amongst others.

Education and Elective Office in Combination

Education combined with elective office to affect commitment to liberty very differently from age. Age reduced commitment to liberty while education increased it; and, since politicians were both much older and much better educated than the public, they were therefore more committed to liberty *despite* their age but, in part at least, *because* of their education. At least half of the politicians' greater commitment to the principle of liberty could be attributed to their higher level of education. Consequently 'the difference of principle between politicians and the public, within age categories, was large; while within education categories, it was small. A university education increased commitment to liberty by 35 points amongst politicians and by 37 amongst the public, but elective office increased that commitment by only 7 points amongst the unqualified, and by 5 points amongst the university educated.

These results are consistent with previous research on similar topics. Sullivan and his colleagues note that Robert Jackman's 1972 reanalysis of Stouffer's pioneering, if deeply flawed, 1954 survey of US attitudes to *Communism, Conformism and Civil Liberties* showed that the 'differences between masses and élites [which received so much attention in Stouffer's work] reflected, almost entirely, differences in educational levels'.[22] McClosky and Brill found that education explained most of the differences on civil liberties between their élite and mass-public samples in one survey,[23] though in another 'the differences between the élite sample and the mass public remain impressively large even after the influence of education is, so to speak, neutralized'.[24]

But elective office still had some detectable influence upon attitudes to both the principle and practice of liberty, even after discounting the effects of education. The independent effect of elective office was largest amongst those without qualifications—suggesting that, in this context at least, experience in (local) government substituted for more formal education. And this effect extended to the practice of liberty as well as the principle. Amongst the educationally unqualified, politicians were 29 per cent less willing than the public to agree that 'free speech is just not worth it if it means we have to put up with the danger to society from extremist views'; they were 24 per cent more willing to allow a parade that blocked traffic for a couple of hours; 26 per cent more opposed to the death penalty; and 20 per cent more opposed to random searches in a shopping mall. By contrast, amongst university graduates, the differences between politicians and the public were only 7 per cent, 10 per cent, 9 per cent, and 9 per cent respectively on these same issues.

Technocrats versus the Intelligentsia

Education, like religion, has its sectarian divisions, epitomized by the distinction between technocrats and the intelligentsia, as those words are (or were) defined in *The Concise Oxford Dictionary*. In the 1990 edition, technocrats were defined as 'exponents or advocates of the government or control of society . . . by technical experts' and the intelligentsia as that 'class of intellectuals regarded as possessing culture and political initiative', though older editions defined them as that 'part of the nation that aspires to independent thinking'.[25] It would be natural for those who came from an intellectual background of formulae, 'best practice', and intolerance of ambiguity to take a relatively authoritarian attitude towards political questions. Conversely, it would be natural for those whose intellectual background stressed ambiguity and debate, and persuasive rather than incontestable findings, to show greater commitment to liberty. So we should expect the technocrats to be more authoritarian than the intelligentsia.

We have no direct measures of such elusive concepts as technocrats or intelligentsia, but we did ask graduates what subject they had studied at university, and classified them by broad faculties similar to those used at our own and other universities. Even graduates in the faculties most identified with technocracy were more committed to liberty than those who had only school or college qualifications, and far more so than those who had no formal educational qualifications. But commitment to liberty varied almost (not quite) as much across different faculties as between university graduates and those with only school qualifications. Graduates in the social sciences and in law were the most committed to liberty, followed by those in arts and (natural) sciences. Graduates in the more vocational (and hence technocratic) subjects of medicine, business, engineering—and education—were the least committed to Liberty. This pattern, and even the levels of commitment within faculties, were very similar amongst politicians and the public; indeed, amongst graduates, politicians were only more committed to liberty because they tended to have more arts and social-science degrees and less vocational/technocratic degrees.

TABLE 8.7.   *The intelligentsia versus the technocrats* (scores on +/–100 scale)

	Liberty			Equality		
	Politicians (scores)	British public (scores)	(Scottish public) (scores)	Politicians (scores)	British public (scores)	(Scottish public) (scores)
University degrees in						
Social science	19	19	(17)	62	60	(65)
Law	11	16	(9)	53	58	(57)
Arts	8	6	(6)	62	63	(60)
Science	2	3	(–6)	47	54	(49)
Medicine	–9	–5	(–12)	52	50	(57)
Business	–6	–6	(–5)	57	48	(52)
Engineering	–9	–7	(–9)	45	41	(47)
Education	–10	–8	(–24)	54	60	(61)

Notes: This table is arranged in order of declining commitment to liberty amongst the British public sample.

Because there were so many graduates amongst local political leaders, and because we oversampled graduates in the general public (see Appendix I for details), this table is based upon 460 graduate politicians, 421 graduates in the British public, and 254 graduates in the Scots sample.

Arts and social-science graduates were also the most committed to equality, and engineering graduates again the least committed. But there was evidence that education graduates, who were clearly the least committed to liberty, were amongst the most committed to equality—for reasons that hardly tax the imagination in either case (Table 8.7).

There is a very important difference between religious sects and educational faculties, however: religious sect is largely determined by family background, while educational faculty is far more a matter of personal choice. (Gaining access to a university in the first place may be greatly influenced by family background, but choice of faculty less so.) So we should not assume that different attitudes to liberty and equality amongst graduates were purely the consequence of educational faculty. To some, unfortunately unknown, degree, these principles probably influenced people's choice of faculty in the first place. However, the fact that all faculties of graduate were more committed to liberty than non-graduates suggests that university education did have a significant causal influence. It seems very unlikely that people would avoid going to university, or would fail to gain admission, simply because

TABLE 8.8. *The structure of principle at different levels of educational qualifications* (factor analyses within educational levels)

	Politicians			British public (Scottish public)					
	None (%)	School (%)	Univ. (%)	None (%)		School (%)		Univ. (%)	
Variance explained by one factor	30	37	42	19	(19)	22	(22)	32	(29)
Variance explained by two factors	43	50	54	35	(34)	39	(38)	47	(44)

they were relatively authoritarian. And if we are convinced that university education—in whatever faculty—encourages a commitment to liberty, then it seems reasonable to suppose that education in one faculty rather than another may exert a greater influence. Self-selection may explain a part of the variation in commitment to liberty across different faculties, but only part.

In a similar manner, we also divided those with only college qualifications by subject, and again found those who had trained in social work or social studies to be more committed to liberty and equality than those who had trained in commerce, industry, nursing, or (non-graduate) teaching. Those who had trained in nursing were amongst the less committed to liberty, but amongst the more committed to equality—reminiscent of the pattern associated with graduates in education.

Education and the Structure of Principle

In all kinds of ways education is reputed to affect the structure of opinion— the ways in which people think, as well as the substantive conclusions that they reach. Education clearly had a powerful and direct influence upon people's commitment to rights and liberties, but it also gave greater structure to their opinions in at least two, not entirely unconnected, ways. This becomes clear if we repeat the factor analyses of principles which we presented in Chapter 4, but this time run separate analyses within each of our three educational categories. A pair of factors explained two-fifths of the variation in micro-principles amongst educationally unqualified politicians, but over half amongst university-educated politicians; and only a third amongst educationally unqualified members of the public but almost half amongst university-educated members of the public (Tables 8.8 and 8.9).

TABLE 8.9. *The correlation between commitment to liberty and equality at different levels of educational qualifications*

	Politicians			British public (Scottish public)		
	None (r × 100)	School (r × 100)	Univ. (r × 100)	None (r × 100)	School (r × 100)	Univ. (r × 100)
Correlation between liberty and equality	+19	+32	+45	−16 (−21)	+10 (+6)	+27 (+16)

And education also affected the correlation between commitments to liberty and equality. Overall, that correlation was a strongly positive 0.32 amongst politicians but a negligible 0.02 amongst the British public (and a negative, but also negligible −0.05 amongst the Scottish public). But, although the correlation was negligible amongst the public as a whole, it was negative (−0.16) amongst the educationally unqualified but strongly positive (+0.27) amongst graduates. Indeed, it was almost as strong amongst graduates as amongst politicians. Within the ranks of politicians, the correlation between liberty and equality was positive at all levels of education, but ranged from +0.19 amongst the unqualified up to +0.45 amongst graduate politicians. A very similar pattern occurred when public and politicians were divided according to their expressed interest in politics: a substantial negative correlation between liberty and equality amongst those who expressed no interest in politics, but a strongly positive correlation amongst those who expressed 'a great deal of interest' in politics. So amongst those with the skills and motivation to take an interest in politics, support for liberty and equality went up or down together; and only amongst those without any educational qualifications did support for liberty and equality vary inversely.

Class Self-Image

In contrast to religion, age, or education, class self-image failed to correlate with first-dimension principles (liberty)—amongst either the public or politicians. Instead it correlated relatively strongly (that is at over 0.2) with some, but not all, of the second-dimension (equality) principles.[26] And, just as religion, age, and education correlated best of all with those micro-principles that lay at the heart of the first dimension, so class self-image correlated best of all with those principles that lay at the heart of the second dimension. Amongst the public, only support for economic equality correlated strongly with class self-image, though commitment to caring came close to doing so as well. But amongst politicians, class self-image correlated strongly with caring and self-reliance as well as with economic equality, and also came close to doing so with equal rights.

Middle- and working-class identifiers differed on their commitment to liberty by a mere 3 points amongst the public, and 5 points amongst politicians, though it is significant that it was *working-class* identifiers who proved slightly more authoritarian. On equality, however, class differences were somewhat larger—8 points amongst the public and 15 amongst politicians—and, of course, working-class identifiers were the more egalitarian.

Amongst the public, working-class identifiers were 13 per cent more likely to say that government had a responsibility to ensure that 'everyone who wants a job can have one', and 20 per cent more likely to say government had a responsibility for 'evening out differences in wealth between people'. Amongst politicians, the corresponding class differences were 26 per cent on jobs and 20 per cent on equalizing wealth.

Class differences on all three indicators of caring—the ratings given for the importance of 'providing help for the disabled', 'reducing unemployment', and 'taking care of the needy'—were considerably larger amongst politicians than the public. Since almost everyone gave very high ratings for these priorities, it is instructive to look at the different percentages of middle- and working-class politicians that gave the maximum 'ten out of ten' ratings for each priority: they differed by 19 per cent, 29 per cent, and 22 per cent, on helping the disabled, the unemployed, and the needy. There were also substantial class differences, particularly amongst politicians, on attitudes to gender equality, with working-class identifiers more inclined to stress the importance of 'guaranteeing equality between men and women'.

However, the largest class differences on micro-principles were on attitudes to rights of protest and rebellion, which, as we showed in Chapter 4, cut across both our macro-principles of liberty and equality. Politicians who identified with the working class were 31 points more favourable to these rights than their colleagues who identified themselves with the middle class; and, similarly, working-class identifiers in the general public were 12 points more favourable to rights of protest (20 points more favourable in Scotland) than middle-class identifiers (Table 8.10).

Although class self-image failed to correlate very strongly with any of our composite measures of sympathy, the correlation was stronger amongst politicians. Working-class politicians were 14 points more sympathetic than middle-class politicians to activists, 10 points more sympathetic to the socially disadvantaged, and 12 points less favourable to the judicial system. In more detail, working-class politicians were 16 per cent less willing than middle-class politicians to blame the poor for not trying 'hard enough to get ahead', and they gave 1.1 higher marks out of ten to trade unions as 'important for protecting rights and liberties'. Working-class politicians were also, as might be anticipated, 17 per cent more likely to put their trust 'in the practical experience of ordinary people rather than the theories of experts and intellectuals'.

Less obviously perhaps, while working-class politicians had views about 'environmental campaigners like Greenpeace' or 'animal-rights activists' that were similar to those of the public, middle-class politicians had less sympathy for them. Compared to their working-class colleagues, middle-class

TABLE 8.10. *Principles and sympathies by class self-image*
(selected scores on +/–100 scale)

	Politicians		British public (Scottish public)			
	Middle (scores)	Working (scores)	Middle (scores)		Working (scores)	
Liberty	–10	–15	–23	(–21)	–26	(–27)
Equality	49	64	50	(54)	58	(63)
Authority	27	27	39	(37)	40	(40)
Traditional values	22	32	35	(33)	39	(41)
Intolerance	–21	–13	–5	(–7)	0	(0)
Protest	17	48	23	(20)	35	(40)
Self-reliance	10	–6	18	(11)	10	(8)
Economic equality	42	52	40	(45)	50	(56)
Caring	71	86	73	(77)	82	(87)
Equal rights	38	53	36	(41)	42	(47)
Activists	–17	–3	–17	(–17)	–12	(–12)
Socially disadvantaged	26	36	15	(22)	19	(30)
Judicial system	33	21	30	(32)	21	(22)

politicians gave 0.8 less marks out of ten for their sympathy towards 'environmental campaigners like Greenpeace', and 1.6 less marks out of ten for their sympathy towards 'animal-rights activists'—though that is consistent with their greater opposition to the micro-principle of protest and rebellion, on which middle- and working-class politicians differed by 31 points.

The Public Sector

Amongst the public, employment sector—the division between employment in the public and private sectors—failed to correlate at all strongly with either principles or sympathies. But amongst politicians, the public/private sector divide correlated relatively strongly (above 0.2) with respect for authority, protest, self-reliance, economic equality, and sympathy towards activists and the socially disadvantaged. Its strongest correlations were with protest and self-reliance.

Compared to those employed in the private sector, public-sector politicians were 12 points more committed to liberty, and 11 points more to equality, 15 points less committed to self-reliance and 24 points more to rights of protest and rebellion; they gave 1.2 lower marks out of ten for the importance of 'maintaining strong defence forces', 1.0 lower for 'cutting taxes', and 0.9 lower for the importance of 'self-reliance, having everybody stand on their own two feet'; they were also 14 per cent more willing to back the 'right-to-strike' principle, 16 per cent less likely to feel morally bound to obey an unjust law, 17 per cent more likely to emphasize citizens' rights rather than their duties, 12 per cent more likely to feel 'we have not gone far enough in pushing equal rights in this country', and a massive 25 per cent more likely to say that government has a responsibility for 'evening out differences in wealth between people'.

Public-sector politicians were also more sympathetic to environmental campaigners, black activists, and communists, and less inclined to believe that British judges were fair. They were 15 per cent less likely to accuse the poor of not trying hard enough and 18 per cent less likely to agree that 'government regulation of business usually does more harm than good'. They were 16 points more favourable to activists, 18 points more favourable to the socially disadvantaged, and 10 points more favourable to the rights industry, but 10 points less favourable to the judicial system.

But, by contrast, the differences between ordinary people who worked in the public and private sectors were much smaller, and sometimes non-existent. In Scotland, they sometimes ran slightly in the opposite direction, with the private-sector workers 4 per cent more favourable to government regulation than the public-sector workers—a small difference that could easily be due to random sampling errors and no more, but whose direction strongly supports the conclusion that the public/private sector difference which was so visible amongst the political élite utterly failed to touch the mass public (Table 8.11).

As we did with religion and education, we subdivided the public sector, in this case into six categories: publicly funded education, health or social services, civil servants working for central government (excluding education, health, or social services), local-government employees (again excluding education, health, or social services), and employees of nationalized industries. But there was little variation in attitudes towards liberty or equality across these different groups of public-sector employees, though those employed in health, education, and social services were slightly more committed to equality, and those employed in education were slightly more committed to liberty than others. There is no conflict of evidence with our earlier finding that those with degrees in education were relatively authoritarian: most teachers were graduates in subjects other than education, and graduates as a whole were relatively anti-authoritarian compared to non-graduates.

TABLE 8.11. *Principles and sympathies by employment sector*
(selected scores on +/–100 scale)

	Politicians		British public (Scottish public)			
	Public (scores)	Private (scores)	Public (scores)		Private (scores)	
Liberty	–5	–17	–25	(–28)	–24	(–24)
Equality	61	50	58	(63)	53	(59)
Authority	19	34	38	(41)	40	(38)
Traditional values	19	33	41	(47)	35	(34)
Protest	38	14	33	(34)	29	(35)
Self-reliance	–4	11	10	(8)	14	(9)
Economic equality	51	40	49	(54)	44	(52)
Equal rights	52	37	44	(48)	37	(43)
Activists	–3	–19	–12	(–13)	–15	(–14)
Socially disadvantaged	40	22	21	(28)	15	(27)
Judicial system	23	33	24	(25)	25	(24)
Rights enforcers	17	7	6	(4)	4	(4)

Parenthood

Compared to those who had no children, politicians with children scored 12 points lower on liberty, and members of the public with children 17 points lower. At the same time, parenthood had no effect at all upon commitment to equality.

Having children correlated especially with support for traditional values, and with a few specific indicators of broader principles. Compared to those without children, parents gave 0.8 more marks out of ten for the importance of 'respect for authority', 0.7 more for 'strengthening law and order', 0.7 more for 'following God's will', and 1.3 more for 'preserving traditional ideas of right and wrong'; 1.0 lower marks out of ten for how much they liked 'gays and lesbians', and 1.0 lower for how much they liked 'black activists'. These are quite substantial differences on a ten-point scale. Parents were also more likely to agree that it was 'very important to protect children and young people from wild and immoral ideas'—by a margin of 9 per cent amongst the public and 14 per cent amongst politicians: since that raised agreement from 83 to 94 per cent amongst the public, even a 9 per cent difference was impressive in this instance (Table 8.12).

TABLE 8.12. *Principles and sympathies by parenthood* (selected scores on +/–100 scale)

	Politicians		British public (Scottish public)	
	No child (scores)	Child (scores)	No child (scores)	Child (scores)
Liberty	–2	–14	–12 (–15)	–29 (–29)
Equality	54	55	55 (61)	55 (61)
Authority	20	28	30 (33)	42 (42)
Traditional values	12	29	15 (22)	45 (46)
Tolerance	27	16	9 (9)	0 (0)

But the apparent influence of parenthood very largely reflected the even more powerful influences of age and religiosity. The strong raw correlation between parenthood and opposition to liberty was almost completely eliminated by taking account of age and whether people were religious or not: in a multiple regression the correlation of 0.25 was reduced to a path coefficient of only 0.07 (while the path coefficients of age and religiosity in the same multiple regression remained at 0.30 and 0.38 respectively).

Gender

Amongst both politicians and the public, women scored 7 points higher than men on commitment to equality, but that is a fairly small difference on a +/–100 scale, and gender failed to correlate strongly with any composite measure of principle or prejudice, though it came nearest with equal rights, where women scored 13 points higher than men. Women were also more sympathetic than men to the socially disadvantaged—by 11 points amongst the public, and by 15 points amongst politicians.

Usually patterns that were evident amongst the public were even stronger amongst politicians, but on their commitment to liberty, women scored 6 points *lower* than men amongst the public, yet 8 points *higher* than men amongst politicians. And, while women scored 12 points *higher* than men on support for traditional values amongst the public, they scored 6 points *lower* than men amongst politicians. This same pattern of conflicting gender effects occurred on attitudes to the principle of respect for authority. So, while women in general were biased a little (and only a little) towards traditionalism

TABLE 8.13. *Principles and sympathies by gender* (selected scores on +/−100 scale)

	Politicians		British public (Scottish public)			
	Middle (scores)	Women (scores)	Men (scores)		Women (scores)	
Liberty	−13	−5	−21	(−22)	−27	(−28)
Equality	54	61	51	(57)	58	(63)
Authority	28	19	36	(36)	42	(42)
Traditional values	27	21	31	(32)	43	(45)
Tolerance	16	26	3	(2)	2	(3)
Equal rights	42	55	33	(38)	46	(50)
Socially disadvantaged	28	43	12	(24)	23	(31)

in comparison with men, women politicians were somewhat biased in the other direction. In terms of these principles, women politicians did not represent the attitudes of their own gender in the population at large.

On the other hand, women in the public gave 0.4 more marks out of ten than men for the importance of 'tolerating different beliefs and lifestyles', 0.5 more for 'guaranteeing equality between men and women', 1.2 more for 'guaranteeing equal rights for homosexuals', and 0.9 more for liking for 'gays and lesbians', though they were just 1 per cent less likely than men to agree with the generally unpopular proposition that 'by their nature, men are more suited than women to do senior jobs in business and government'. Amongst politicians these gender differences ran in the same direction as in the public and were usually a little larger than amongst the public. But there was a striking contrast between a gender difference of only 0.4 on the principle of gender equality yet a gender difference of 1.2 on homosexual equality. So, in principle at least (and practice may be very different), gender itself did not seem a matter of much dispute between men and women, though there were clear gender differences on issues of sexuality (Table 8.13).

We looked for evidence of greater gender differences amongst more potentially radical groups—the young and the middle class—but even a breakdown of attitudes towards principle by gender within age cohorts, or within social classes, reveals little evidence of strong gender differences. Amongst the little that does emerge is some evidence that gender differences were greater amongst the old on the traditional value of 'following God's will', and greater amongst the young on 'strengthening law and order' or simple gender prejudice. Amongst both men and women, older cohorts placed more emphasis on 'following God's will', but women aged over 55 did so much more even than men of that age. Amongst under 35 year olds, men gave 3.9 marks out of ten for the importance of 'following God's will' and women 4.4; while amongst the over 55 year olds, men gave it 6.7 and women 8.0. Conversely, the prejudice in favour of men being specially suited for senior jobs, which was held only by a small minority in all ages and both sexes, was particularly unpopular amongst women aged under 35 (and even more so in our smaller sample of women aged under 25). So the gender difference on gender prejudice was only 1 per cent amongst the over 55 year olds, but 7 per cent amongst under 35 year olds, and 13 per cent amongst under 25 year olds. Finally, men aged under 35 (and especially under 25) were particularly unwilling to stress the importance of 'strengthening law and order', while young women had views which were much more similar to older women.

Income

American researchers have always been fascinated by income, either alone, or in combination with education. Typically they have begun by noting that commitment to liberty has been correlated with (high) income; and then sought to 'explain away' that finding by showing that it merely, or at least mainly, reflects the fact that the better-paid in the USA are better educated. They conclude that commitment to the principles and practice of liberty is caused by high education, not by high income.[27] It seemed worth investigating whether income had a similar—and a similarly spurious—effect upon British attitudes. There are some obvious problems with such an analysis. Current income may not be a good indicator of living standards, either because it ignores variations in accumulated wealth, or because it ignores variations in the demands on that income made by children, family, parents, or others. And reported income may not be a good indicator of actual income, either because people fail to add up their various sources of income correctly, or because of confusion between before-tax and after-tax income, or because they tell lies about their income, or because they simply refuse to declare it.

Our measure of income was very simple and crude but it seemed to perform remarkably well. We asked: 'What is your own total annual income from all sources, before tax, to the nearest thousand pounds?' All answers of over £50,000 were recorded as £50,000, which prevents the analysis of income being dominated by a few deviantly high 'outliers'. With income defined in this way, mean and median income differed by less than 1.7, for example.

Although the question did not refer to income only from employment, many respondents probably interpreted it in that way. A sixth of the politicians and a third of the public gave no answer; but the highest rates of non-answers occurred amongst those who were 'looking after the home'. Amongst those in full-time employment, only 7 per cent of politicians and 15 per cent of the British public gave no answer (though Scots were more reticent). For such a sensitive question, put so brutally, those do not seem unduly high rates of non-answers.

Amongst those who did reply, income was strongly related to educational qualifications—over twice as high for graduates as for the unqualified; it rose in middle age and declined thereafter; it was one and a half times as high for men as for women, and for middle-class identifiers as for working-class identifiers; and it averaged about £3,000 a year more for political leaders than for members of the public with similar educational qualifications—rather more if they were school certificates. All of these patterns are plausible and increase our confidence in this simple measure of income (Table 8.14).

Support for liberty correlated far more strongly with education than with income: amongst the public, for example, the correlation was 0.35 with education, but only 0.13 with income. And in a multiple regression predicting liberty, the path coefficient (standardized regression coefficient) of income was reduced from 0.13 to almost zero (0.03) when education was included in the equation. Amongst Scots the coefficient of income was reduced from 0.12 to 0.01, and amongst politicians from 0.15 to 0.02, by the inclusion of education. In other words, income had no influence at all on support for liberty once we took account of education. To that extent our findings for Britain are consistent with earlier findings for the USA.

While the apparent influence of income on support for liberty was spurious and disappeared when we took account of education, its influence upon opposition to equality—especially opposition to the micro-principle of economic equality, though not so much to equal rights—was real and robust, however. Indeed, income's strong influence on opposition to equality overwhelmed and even reversed education's slight influence towards support for equality. Amongst the public, the raw correlation between equality and education was slightly negative, but it became slightly positive once we took account of income. Both the negative and positive correlations were very small, indicating no more than a trace of influence anyway, but they do show that the income that went with higher education acted to counter the influence

268 *Influences*

TABLE 8.14. *Income validation checks*

	Politicians	British public	Scottish public
	Don't know/no answer to income question		
	(%)	(%)	(%)
In full sample	17	28	(33)
Amongst full-time employees	7	15	(22)
	Mean annual income in £ thousands		
	(£000)	(£000)	(£000)
Amongst those with			
no qualifications	13.5	10.3	(8.7)
school qualifications	18.7	14.6	(13.4)
university qualifications	23.4	21.3	(21.7)
Amongst those aged			
<25	n.a.	9.7	(8.2)
25–35	18.7	15.8	(13.0)
35–55	21.9	15.9	(15.6)
>55	17.0	9.6	(9.0)
Amongst			
men	20.4	16.3	(14.3)
women	14.5	11.1	(10.9)
Amongst			
middle-class identifiers	22.3	17.0	(16.2)
working-class identifiers	15.5	11.6	(11.2)

Note: n.a. = not applicable.

of education itself. The correlation between income and opposition to equality was, in fact, particularly strong amongst university graduates, amongst whom it reached 0.25 or more in all three samples. Education did not make people insensitive to worldly wealth: quite the opposite (Table 8.15).

Amongst the public, opposition to equality correlated slightly more strongly (at 0.19) with income than it did even with class or gender. However, path coefficients (standardized regression coefficients) in a multiple regression, predicting equality from income, class, and gender, suggested that, while income had an independent influence of its own (with a path coefficient of −0.11), it was somewhat less than class (0.16) or gender (0.17) separately,

TABLE 8.15. *Correlations between income and commitment to equality within different social groups*

	Politicians (r × 100)	British public (r × 100)	(Scottish public) (r × 100)
In whole sample	−18	−19	(−22)
Amongst those with			
no qualifications	−12	−12	(−14)
school qualifications	−16	−22	(−18)
university qualifications	−25	−26	(−30)
Amongst those with a			
middle-class self-image	−10	−16	(−24)
working-class self-image	−11	−14	(−15)
Amongst			
men	−19	−18	(−27)
women		−10	(.)

and certainly less than class and gender taken together. Within-class and within-gender correlations between income and equality showed that income had more influence upon opinion amongst middle-class identifiers than amongst working-class identifiers, and more amongst men than amongst women.

Small-Town Values

The stereotype of small towns and rural areas depicts them as narrow minded, conservative, illiberal, and intolerant, in contrast to cosmopolitan cities, which cultivate a more liberal and expansive view of the world.[28] McClosky and Brill claim that 'respect for the freedom of others and for their right to think and act as they choose is also furthered by . . . residence in a cosmopolitan environment . . . [which] broadens one's perspective'.[29] It is no accident that the English word 'civilization' has the same Latin origin as 'city'. There may be some truth in the stereotype in sparsely populated countries like Russia, Canada, or the USA, but the evidence is weak in densely populated Britain, and the phrase 'inner cities' hardly conjures up a liberal cosmopolitan image in contemporary Britain. There must be considerable doubt whether any significant portion of the British population lives outside the walls of Civitas Britannica, defined, as it is, by the coverage of national press and television and by easy physical access to a proximate urban centre. Even in the USA, illiberal attitudes are most evident only in the very sparsely populated areas and liberal attitudes most evident in what Americans call the 'suburbs' (more equivalent to 'small towns' in Britain) than in the big cities themselves.[30]

We asked respondents to say whether they lived in a big town or city, a small town, or a rural area, and whether they lived mainly in one or the other when they were growing up. Current location correlated somewhat better than location of upbringing with principles and prejudices, but, even so defined, urbanization failed to correlate strongly with any principle or sympathy amongst the public. On the other hand, amongst politicians, it did correlate strongly (above 0.2) with traditional values, intolerance, and antipathy towards activists; and it came close to doing so on authority, wealth creation, limited government, protest, equal rights, and sympathy for the socially disadvantaged. Amongst politicians, therefore, urbanization came at least close to correlating strongly with five of the six unambiguously first-dimension (liberty) principles, though with only one of the five unambiguously second-dimension (equality) principles.

Support for equality hardly varied at all with urbanization in the public, and it was only 7 points higher amongst politicians who lived in big cities than in rural areas. But support for liberty was 8 points higher in cities than in rural areas amongst the public, and 21 points amongst politicians. Rural residents were also less favourable to protest, by 10 points amongst the public and 21 points amongst politicians.

Compared to those who lived in big cities, politicians living in rural areas were 19 points less favourable to the socially disadvantaged, and 22 points less favourable to activists; they gave 1.2 more marks out of ten for the importance of 'respect for authority', and 1.0 more for 'maintaining strong defence forces', 1.8 more for 'following God's will', 1.1 more for 'preserving traditional ideas of right and wrong', 1.1 more for 'cutting taxes', 1.0 more for 'self-reliance', and 1.8 *less* for 'guaranteeing equal rights for homosexuals'; they gave 1.0 less marks out of ten for how much they liked 'environmental campaigners', 1.6 less for 'gays and lesbians', 1.1 less for 'feminists', 1.2 less for 'black activists', and 1.1 less for 'communists'. They were also 29 per cent more likely to agree that 'immigrants to Britain should try harder to be more like other British people', and 22 per cent more likely to agree that 'government regulation of business usually does more harm than good'. Differences between ordinary members of the public who lived in cities and rural areas reflected these differences between politicians but usually in a severely attenuated form (Table 8.16).

TABLE 8.16. *Principles and sympathies by locality of residence* (selected scores on +/-100 scale)

	Politicians			British public (Scottish public)		
	Big town (scores)	Small town (scores)	Rural area (scores)	Big town (scores)	Small town (scores)	Rural area (scores)
Liberty	−1	−11	−22	−20 (−22)	−26 (−28)	−28 (−26)
Equality	57	58	50	56 (61)	54 (62)	54 (59)
Authority	19	24	36	35 (35)	41 (41)	42 (43)
Traditional values	10	26	39	31 (33)	39 (44)	44 (41)
Intolerance	−26	−18	−11	−5 (−3)	−1 (0)	−1 (−5)
Protest	33	29	12	36 (41)	29 (31)	26 (30)
Economic equality	45	47	41	48 (53)	46 (54)	43 (51)
Caring	76	79	75	78 (83)	79 (85)	79 (84)
Equal rights	51	48	33	43 (47)	38 (46)	38 (41)
Activists	−3	−7	−25	−11 (−12)	−14 (−12)	−17 (−16)
Socially disadvantaged	40	31	21	22 (30)	16 (26)	13 (27)

Psychological Sources of Political Values

Sullivan, Pierson, and Marcus also investigated what they called 'the psychological sources' as well as the 'social sources' of political tolerance.[31] We have some doubts about these 'psychological sources'. As measured by Sullivan and his colleagues they seem too close to the political values and principles that they supposedly influence. Sullivan *et al.* measured tolerance itself by whether respondents would ban members of their Most Disliked Group (MDG)[32] from becoming President of the USA, teaching in school, making public speeches, or holding rallies, and whether members of their MDG should be outlawed or have their phones tapped. Amongst other psychological influences on attitudes to toleration they used a scale of 'dogmatism', based in part on agreement with propositions that included:

[1.] To *compromise* with our political opponents is dangerous because it usually leads to the betrayal of our own side.

[2.] A group which *tolerates* too many differences of opinion among its own members cannot exist for long.

Of course, they found a connection between supporting 'compromise' and 'tolerance' (= opposition to dogmatism), on the one hand, and free speech for their MDG (= tolerance), on the other. But that is almost a tautology. Indeed, perhaps more than a tautology, even an inversion of meaning, since their measure of tolerance did not use the word 'tolerance', while their measure of dogmatism did do so! Their approach would make more sense, however, if we restated it as an attempt to link the *principle of tolerance* (measured by general statements about compromise and tolerance) with the *practice of tolerance* (measured by attitudes to free speech for their MDG). But, in that case, there is little space left for a concept of 'psychological sources' that are clearly distinct from 'abstract principles'. Consequently we made little effort to devise measures of psychology—unless we simply retitle our measures of abstract principles (and sympathies and antipathies) as psychological sources.

However, we did ask two questions that tap a more purely personal dimension of psychology that does seem removed from political principles and prejudices, however abstract.

To measure at least the self-image of *intellectual flexibility* we asked: 'Would you say that once you have made up your mind on an important question, you are not likely to change it easily, or can you often be persuaded to change it if someone has a good argument?' It has to be said that answers to this question did not make much difference to whether people

TABLE 8.17. *Principles and sympathies by self-images of flexibility*
(selected scores on +/−100 scale)

	Politicians		British public (Scottish public)	
	Not flexible (scores)	Flexible (scores)	Not flexible (scores)	Flexible (scores)
Liberty	−12	−12	−30 (−29)	−20 (−22)
Equality	54	56	55 (61)	55 (61)
Authority	27	28	42 (42)	36 (37)
Traditional values	26	28	44 (44)	30 (35)
Intolerance	−16	−19	2 (1)	−6 (−5)

proved willing to change their minds when we challenged them to do so on the issues detailed in the 'challenges' section of Chapter 7; so it measured a self-image, perhaps even an ambition to be flexible, rather than flexibility itself. However, amongst the public, those who had a flexible self-image scored 10 points higher on liberty but no differently on equality from those who did not. Within the three micro-principles on which liberty was based, those with flexible self-images scored only 6 points lower on respect for authority, but 8 points lower on intolerance, and 14 points lower on traditional values. Reasonably enough, therefore, flexibility was most closely associated with a rejection of traditional values (Table 8.17).

To measure a *leadership instinct*, we asked: 'When you work on something, do you like to take charge, or prefer to let others organize the tasks?' Very few political leaders were willing to let others organize their tasks, and differences of principle between those political leaders who preferred to lead and those who preferred to be led were very small. None the less, in our samples at least, the scores on liberty suggest that politicians who preferred *to lead* and members of the public who preferred *to be led* were slightly less committed to liberty than others. And within the three micro-principles on which liberty was based, this effect was more visible—indeed, only visible—on respect for authority, where politicians who preferred *to lead* scored 7 points higher, while members of the public who preferred *to be led* scored 8 points higher. Small though the effects were, they were in opposite directions, and probably not a statistical accident. What we have found is that respect for authority was greater amongst politicians with an instinct to 'take charge', and amongst members of the public who were willing to defer to

TABLE 8.18. *Principles and sympathies by leadership instinct* (selected scores on +/−100 scale)

	Politicians		British public (Scottish public)	
	No leadership instinct (scores)	Yes leadership instinct (scores)	No leadership instinct (scores)	Yes leadership instinct (scores)
Liberty	−9	−12	−30 (−30)	−23 (−24)
Equality	56	55	57 (63)	54 (60)
Authority	21	28	45 (45)	37 (37)
Traditional values	25	27	44 (45)	35 (37)
Intolerance	−19	−17	1 (1)	−4 (−3)

the leadership of others—which seems rational enough. Politicians in general had relatively liberal, anti-authoritarian principles despite their instinct to lead, not because if it (Table 8.18).

SOCIAL BACKGROUND AND PRACTICE

We have found that religion, age, and education correlated strongly with first-dimension (liberty) principles, and class with second-dimension (equality) principles, while gender, urbanization, employment sector, income, and parenthood correlated much less well.

That might reflect no more than varying styles of discourse amongst different social groups—differences in 'politically correct' slogans or terminology. If so, then adherence to abstract principles could vary without having much effect on practice (Table 8.19).

To find out whether social groups differed in practice as well as in principle, we have taken a selection of nineteen specific questions concerning practical scenarios from the more extended list discussed in Chapter 5. The correlations suggest that decisions in practical scenarios were indeed less tied to social background than were principles. None the less, religion, age, and education still correlated relatively well with practical decisions about liberty, and class with practical questions about equality, while gender, urbanization, sector, and parenthood were relatively uncorrelated with practical decisions.

TABLE 8.19. *Correlations between practice and social background*

	Politicians				British public (Scottish public)			
	Age (r × 100)	Relig. (r × 100)	Educ. (r × 100)	Wk-Cl. (r × 100)	Age (r × 100)	Relig. (r × 100)	Educ. (r × 100)	Wk-Cl. (r × 100)
Freedom of expression, association, and protest								
Ban political demonstration	20	19	−13	.	23 (24)	15 (12)	−14 (−16)	. (.)
Ban strikes in essential services	19	24	.	−25	14 (.)	. (.)	. (.)	. (−17)
Ban abuse of Christianity	19	21	−15	12	12 (20)	18 (11)	−16 (−25)	. (.)
Freedom of information								
Ban interviews with terrorists	29	28	−21	.	15 (20)	16 (14)	−19 (−22)	. (.)
Ban intrusions into private lives	19	10	−15	.	16 (.)	. (.)	−10 (−11)	. (.)
Ban publication of confidential government plans	28	25	−14	.	18 (16)	18 (14)	−11 (−15)	. (.)
Freedom of lifestyle								
Abortion morally wrong	.	18	.	.	. (.)	14 (15)	. (−10)	. (.)
IF MORALLY WRONG: Ban abortion	.	16	.	.	. (.)	11 (17)	. (−14)	. (.)
Ban homosexuality	21	18	−17	.	15 (10)	. (15)	−16 (−14)	. (.)
Powers to uphold the law								
Support death penalty	13	19	−17	.	. (.)	13 (10)	−18 (−16)	. (.)
Convict on confession alone	10	.	.	.	. (.)	. (.)	. (.)	. (.)
Support random searches	11	12	.	.	. (.)	. (.)	. (.)	. (.)

TABLE 8.19. *Continued*

	Politicians				British public (Scottish public)			
	Age (r × 100)	Relig. (r × 100)	Educ. (r × 100)	Wk-Cl. (r × 100)	Age (r × 100)	Relig. (r × 100)	Educ. (r × 100)	Wk-Cl. (r × 100)
Powers to defend the state								
Suspend rights in a national emergency	24	20	.	−13	12 (.)	(.)	. (.)	. (.)
Emergency powers justified	17	16	.	.	18 (.)	(.)	. (.)	. (−10)
Allow surveillance	.	.	15	−20	. (.)	(.)	10 (10)	. (.)
Equality								
Ban private medicine	.	−14	.	25	. (.)	. (.)	−10 (−14)	13 (10)
Support job quotas for								
women	.	−12	15	11	.	. (12)	−14 (.)	15 (.)
ethnic minorities	−16	−22	13	.	.	. (.)	. (.)	. (.)
disabled	.	−13	.	13	14 (14)	. (.)	−11 (−14)	11 (.)

Note: In this and subsequent tables in this chapter, to avoid confusion, 'Emergency powers justified' is based on the random three-quarters of the samples who were offered as justifications for emergency powers 'terrorism', 'public disorder', or 'an economic crisis caused by strikes in important industries', but excludes the one-quarter who were offered 'attacks on minority ethnic or racial groups', because of the very different pattern of support for a declaration of emergency in that last circumstance.
Correlations less than 0.10 have been replaced by full points.

Age and Practice

We can illustrate the influence of age upon attitudes towards practice by noting some of the larger differences between the old and the young. Compared to those aged under 35, politicians aged over 55 were 35 per cent less willing to allow a potentially riotous demonstration, 47 per cent more willing to ban interviews with supporters of terrorism, 43 per cent more willing to ban publication of government secrets, 32 per cent more willing to suspend civil rights in a national emergency, and 30 per cent more willing to accept our three (not four—see the note to Table 8.19) excuses for declaring a national emergency; amongst the public the equivalent differences between old and young were 26 per cent, 18 per cent, 23 per cent, 11 per cent, and 16 per cent respectively – less than amongst politicians but all still very substantial age differences.

Amongst young politicians, only 1 per cent would ban homosexuality while, amongst the old, 22 per cent would do so; and within the public, the equivalent figures were 11 per cent and 30 per cent respectively (Table 8.20).

Overall there was little correlation between age and support for surveillance activities by the security services, but that concealed the fact that the old were less favourable than the young towards surveillance against crime and terrorism, yet more favourable than the young to surveillance designed to combat the spread of dangerous ideas.

Decisions on employment quotas revealed an intriguing pattern of correlations with age. Older members of the British public were neither specially favourable nor unfavourable to *gender* and *ethnic* quotas, while older Scots and older politicians were particularly opposed to them. But at the same time, both older politicians and older members of the public (British as well as Scots this time) were particularly favourable towards employment quotas for the *disabled*. There is either a life-cycle or a generational shift in the targets of compassion here—with only cross-sectional data we cannot tell which.

Religion and Practice

Amongst politicians, religion correlated strongly (at over 0.2) with practical decisions about free expression and protest, access to political information, emergency powers, and equality for ethnic groups; and it came close to a strong correlation with practical decisions about lifestyle and the death penalty. Amongst the public, religion never correlated strongly with any of the

TABLE 8.20. *Practice by age* (selected percentages)

	Politicians			British public (Scottish public)			
	25–35 (%)	35–55 (%)	>55 (%)	<25 (%)	25–35 (%)	35–55 (%)	>55 (%)
Freedom of expression, association, and protest							
Ban political demonstration	15	33	50	22 (29)	30 (42)	44 (47)	56 (68)
Ban strikes in essential services	25	27	46	23 (29)	26 (16)	31 (22)	43 (29)
Ban abuse of Christianity	6	15	30	28 (12)	22 (35)	30 (35)	41 (48)
Freedom of information							
Ban interviews with terrorists	4	25	51	37 (39)	40 (44)	46 (55)	58 (68)
Ban intrusions into private lives	30	36	55	48 (51)	41 (48)	52 (47)	66 (58)
Ban publication of confidential government plans	17	34	60	46 (52)	49 (40)	55 (49)	72 (69)
Freedom of lifestyle							
Ban homosexuality	1	7	22	16 (21)	11 (20)	19 (19)	30 (34)
Powers to defend the state							
Suspend rights in a national emergency	58	72	90	68 (71)	72 (70)	79 (76)	83 (76)
Emergency powers justified	41	56	71	45 (64)	60 (56)	69 (60)	76 (72)

Support surveillance to combat							
crime	66	59	54	46 (50)	54 (49)	48 (44)	41 (40)
dangerous ideas	26	36	44	34 (21)	36 (30)	39 (32)	39 (32)
Equality							
Ban private medicine	30	35	29	29 (42)	36 (49)	38 (46)	40 (47)
Support job quotas for							
women	39	19	16	26 (28)	19 (15)	19 (19)	30 (23)
ethnic minorities	27	32	16	16 (24)	23 (23)	12 (19)	13 (14)
disabled	60	84	84	73 (74)	80 (83)	88 (88)	89 (90)
Say it is important to get more							
women MPs	91	81	72	82 (86)	73 (71)	70 (75)	75 (75)
ethnic minority MPs	91	74	65	63 (72)	62 (68)	54 (62)	52 (61)

practical decisions under review, though that partly reflected the unequal division amongst the public between the numbers who would and would not accept a religious designation—the percentage differences on the issues ranged as high as 23 per cent.

Religious politicians were less committed to liberty in practice as well as in principle. Compared to the unreligious, they were 23 per cent less willing to permit a potentially riotous political demonstration, 27 per cent less willing to allow strikes in essential services, and 21 per cent more willing to ban 'abusive attacks on the Christian religion'. It is worth noting that the smallest of these differences on practical questions about free expression, and not the largest, was the one that involved an explicit reference to religion. Religious politicians were 32 per cent more willing to ban media interviews with supporters of IRA or Protestant terrorists in Northern Ireland; 29 per cent more willing to ban newspapers from printing confidential government documents; 13 per cent more willing to ban media intrusions into the private lives of ordinary people or leading politicians; 21 per cent more willing (morally) to condemn abortion and, amongst those who did condemn it morally, 22 per cent more were willing to ban it legally. Only 3 per cent of unreligious politicians would outlaw homosexuality, but 18 per cent of the religious would do so. Religious politicians were 20 per cent more in favour of the death penalty than the unreligious; 19 per cent more willing to accept the suspension of civil rights in some unspecified 'genuine national emergency'; and, amongst those who accepted the need to suspend rights in a national emergency, 19 per cent more willing to accept 'widespread terrorism', 'widespread public disorder', or 'an economic crisis caused by strikes in important industries' as a sufficient justification for declaring an emergency (Table 8.21).

Religious politicians were also less egalitarian in practice as well as in theory. Compared to unreligious politicians, they were 22 per cent more opposed to job quotas for minority ethnic groups and 15 per cent more opposed to a ban on private medicine.

Amongst the public, religious differences were smaller. We found no differences between the religious and the unreligious on the egalitarian issues of ethnic job quotas and private medicine, but there remained religious differences of 19 per cent on political demonstrations, 20 per cent on religious abuse, 20 per cent on interviews with supporters of terrorism, and 23 per cent on publication of government secrets. That reflects the lack of correlation between religion and the principle of equality, as well as the strong (negative) correlation between religion and the principle of liberty amongst the public.

TABLE 8.21. *Practice by religion* (selected percentages)

	Politicians		British public (Scottish public)	
	Religious (%)	Not religious (%)	Religious (%)	Not religious (%)
Freedom of expression, association, and protest				
Ban political demonstration	45	22	46 (53)	27 (37)
Ban strikes in essential services	42	15	34 (23)	25 (26)
Ban abuse of Christianity	27	6	35 (39)	15 (25)
Freedom of information				
Ban interviews with terrorists	45	13	51 (58)	31 (39)
Ban intrusions into private lives	48	35	55 (53)	46 (41)
Ban publication of confidential government plans	53	24	62 (56)	39 (37)
Freedom of lifestyle				
Abortion morally wrong	51	30	50 (57)	32 (37)
IF MORALLY WRONG: Ban abortion	45	23	43 (52)	33 (25)
Ban homosexuality	18	3	22 (27)	13 (10)

TABLE 8.21. *Continued*

	Politicians		British public (Scottish public)	
	Religious (%)	Not religious (%)	Religious (%)	Not religious (%)
Powers to uphold the law				
Support death penalty	31	11	53 (56)	36 (43)
Support random searches	33	20	48 (46)	39 (37)
Powers to defend the state				
Suspend rights in a national emergency	84	65	79 (74)	72 (76)
Emergency powers justified	68	49	68 (64)	65 (55)
Equality				
Support job quotas for				
women	15	26	24 (23)	16 (9)
ethnic minorities	17	39	15 (19)	15 (18)
disabled	81	93	86 (86)	82 (84)
Say it is important to get more				
women MPs	73	88	73 (74)	71 (81)
ethnic minority MPs	65	86	53 (61)	67 (79)

Education and Practice

Unlike religion and age, education correlated equally well with practical decisions amongst the public and politicians. Amongst politicians, university graduates were 17 per cent more willing (than the unqualified) to permit abuse of religion and, amongst the public, 20 per cent more. Similarly, amongst politicians, graduates were 15 per cent more willing to allow potentially riotous political demonstrations and, amongst the public, 23 per cent more.

On banning interviews with supporters of terrorism there was a difference between graduates and the unqualified of 28 per cent amongst politicians, and 32 per cent amongst the public; on banning homosexuality, a difference of 18 per cent amongst politicians and 19 per cent amongst the public; on support for the death penalty, a difference of 18 per cent amongst politicians, but twice as much—35 per cent—amongst the public. Thus the effect of education was usually larger amongst the public than amongst politicians. Only the low numbers of the public with university degrees distorted and depressed the correlation coefficients amongst the public (Table 8.22).

There were some peculiarities about the relationship between education and issues of practice that made it differ somewhat from the relationship between education and principle, however.

Graduates were no more willing to allow strikes in essential services, and significantly less egalitarian especially in their decisions about private medicine—but then, graduates were not particularly egalitarian even in principle.

What is more interesting is the influence of education on the practice—as well as the principle—of liberty. Compared to those without educational qualifications, graduates were notably liberal in their decisions about homosexuality but somewhat less notably so on abortion, though they remained more liberal than non-graduates on that issue also. But there was a most remarkable discrepancy between principle and practice on support for surveillance. Graduates were the *most* willing to let the police or security services tap telephones or inspect people's bank accounts – by a margin of 10 per cent amongst the general public, and 24 per cent amongst politicians, when compared to those without any educational qualifications. In this respect, a university education apparently correlated with authoritarian attitudes in practice. It is a surprising finding about graduates, but our evidence is clear: graduates were much more committed to the principle of liberty, yet much more willing to support state surveillance activities. Yet we should recall from Chapter 5 that, while politicians were more committed than the public to the principle of liberty, they were also more willing to accept such

TABLE 8.22. *Practice by educational qualifications* (selected percentages)

	Politicians			British public (Scottish public)		
	None (%)	School (%)	Univ. (%)	None (%)	School (%)	Univ. (%)
Freedom of expression, association, and protest						
Ban political demonstration	43	47	28	52 (60)	39 (46)	29 (35)
Ban abuse of Christianity	30	25	13	41 (53)	27 (26)	21 (26)
Freedom of information						
Ban interviews with terrorists	53	40	25	58 (68)	43 (48)	26 (34)
Ban intrusions into private lives	61	44	38	59 (58)	52 (48)	42 (39)
Ban publication of confidential government plans	50	53	34	64 (63)	56 (47)	44 (43)
Freedom of lifestyle						
Abortion morally wrong	46	48	44	45 (59)	49 (52)	34 (42)
IF MORALLY WRONG: Ban abortion	50	38	41	48 (59)	49 (44)	34 (38)
Ban homosexuality	25	16	7	28 (30)	17 (21)	9 (10)
Powers to uphold the law						
Support death penalty	33	31	15	59 (61)	47 (51)	24 (29)

Powers to defend the state						
Support surveillance to combat	38	55	62	40 (36)	53 (44)	50 (54)
crime	44	59	62	36 (36)	53 (48)	63 (57)
terrorism	51	66	74	49 (45)	64 (51)	60 (70)
dangerous ideas	21	41	47	37 (28)	40 (32)	29 (29)
Equality						
Ban private medicine	46	28	30	44 (55)	33 (42)	31 (35)
Support job quotas for						
women	12	15	28	33 (18)	17 (23)	22 (11)
ethnic minorities	22	18	33	11 (20)	16 (17)	21 (25)
Say it is important to get more						
women MPs	64	75	85	73 (77)	73 (75)	73 (77)
ethnic minority MPs	70	63	81	52 (60)	56 (65)	67 (72)

surveillance measures. Thus the combination of liberal principles on most issues but greater acceptance of government discretion on surveillance was associated both with high education and with senior positions in political life.

However, the correlation with education becomes at once more complex and more easily interpretable when we distinguish between different scenarios. Random thirds of our respondents were asked to approve surveillance to combat 'crime', 'terrorism', or the 'spread of dangerous and undemocratic ideas'. We might expect that a university education would encourage people to feel, with J. S. Mill, that the best defence against the spread of dangerous ideas is open debate rather than surveillance and other administrative action by the security services. We found in Chapter 5 that politicians were 10 per cent more willing than the public to accept surveillance if the object was to combat crime, but only 2 per cent more if the object was to combat the spread of even *dangerous and undemocratic* ideas. Amongst the British public, we found a similar, but even more pronounced, pattern in the attitudes of graduates: they were 27 per cent more willing than the unqualified to use surveillance against crime, and 11 per cent more willing than the unqualified to use surveillance against terrorism, but actually 8 per cent *less* willing than the unqualified to use surveillance against the spread of dangerous and undemocratic ideas. (And our Scottish sample confirmed the different effects of education on support for surveillance in these three areas.) So on issues of surveillance, graduate members of the public were comparatively liberal with respect to ideas, though comparatively authoritarian with respect to crime and terrorism.

The same could not be said of graduate politicians, however. Amongst politicians, graduates were not only 18 per cent more willing to use surveillance against crime, and 23 per cent more against terrorism, but also 26 per cent more willing to use it against the spread of dangerous ideas. Nor is that simply a spurious consequence of the correlation between graduate status and ideology amongst politicians. It is true that Conservative and right-wing politicians were particularly sympathetic towards surveillance measures; but it is also true that, *even within each ideological or political camp*, graduate politicians were comparatively willing to use surveillance—even when the purpose of that surveillance was to combat the spread of ideas, albeit 'dangerous and undemocratic' ideas. We cannot even explain this finding away by taking cover behind the usual vague references to random sampling errors, since our survey of local political leaders achieved such a high response rate that it was more like a census than a survey. (The response rate was 86 per cent and partisan bias was minimal—see Appendix I.) It seems that higher education, as well as—and in addition to—elective office, encouraged this aspect of what we called in Chapter 3 a 'governing perspective'.

Class and Practice

Unlike religion, age, and education, class did not correlate well with practical issues of liberty—but nor did it correlate well with the *principle* of liberty. In so far as there were any class differences on issues of liberty, they were not consistently in a pro- or anti-libertarian direction. There was little or no class difference on permitting potentially riotous political demonstrations, a ban on homosexuality, the death penalty, conviction on confession alone, or random searches. But the working class were slightly more willing to ban the abuse of Christianity, interviews with supporters of terrorism, press intrusions into private lives, and abortion. On the other hand, they were slightly less willing to ban publication of government secrets, and more clearly less willing to accept a suspension of civil rights in a national emergency.

But by greater or lesser amounts the working class did give more support to issues of equality—as they had to the *principle* of equality. Despite the 'Andy Capp' image of the working class, they were 13 per cent more favourable to gender quotas amongst the British public (though in Scotland the working class were less favourable than the middle class to gender quotas), 3 per cent more favourable to ethnic quotas, and 8 per cent more favourable to disabled quotas in employment. They were also 13 per cent more in favour of a ban on private medicine 'in order to make health services the same for both rich and poor'; and working-class politicians were 24 per cent more favourable than middle-class politicians to a ban on private medicine.

Similarly, permitting strikes in essential services, which we have usually conceptualized as a freedom issue but which has an egalitarian dimension, won 8 per cent more support from the working class amongst the British public (16 per cent more amongst Scots), and 25 per cent more amongst politicians. Only one non-egalitarian issue produced large class differences, and then only amongst politicians. Middle-class members of the public were only slightly more willing to accept surveillance by the security services, but middle-class politicians were 21 per cent more willing to do so than their working-class colleagues. However, the resistance of the working class to surveillance was consistent with their support for strikes in essential services and with their reluctance to accept curtailment of civil rights in a national emergency (Table 8.23).

TABLE 8.23. *Practice by class self-image* (selected percentages)

	Politicians		British public (Scottish public)	
	Middle (%)	Working (%)	Middle (%)	Working (%)
Freedom of expression, association, and protest				
Ban strikes in essential services	45	20	37 (35)	29 (19)
Equality				
Ban private medicine	23	47	29 (38)	42 (50)
Support job quotas for				
women	15	25	15 (24)	28 (19)
ethnic minorities	21	28	13 (15)	16 (21)
disabled	80	90	81 (82)	89 (88)
Say it is important to get more				
women MPs	77	78	73 (74)	75 (76)
ethnic minority MPs	66	76	54 (65)	57 (64)

Urbanization, Employment Sector, Parenthood, Gender, and Practice

We found that *urbanization* correlated with principles amongst politicians but not amongst the public. The same was true for practical decisions. Compared to those who lived in large towns or cities, rural politicians were 23 per cent less willing to accept strikes in essential services, 21 per cent more willing to ban interviews with supporters of terrorism, 19 per cent more willing to ban publication of government secrets, 12 per cent more willing to ban homosexuality, 15 per cent more favourable to the death penalty, 14 per cent more favourable to random searches, 11 per cent more willing to suspend civil rights in an unspecified national emergency, and 13 per cent more willing to accept our three justifications for such an emergency. They were also 10 per cent more opposed to gender quotas, and 15 per cent more opposed to ethnic quotas.

Similarly, *employment sector* correlated with practical decisions only amongst politicians, and not usually very strongly even amongst them. However, private-sector politicians were 15 per cent more willing to ban publication of government secrets, 13 per cent more favourable to the death penalty, and 21 per cent less willing to allow strikes in essential services. They were also 20 per cent more opposed to ethnic job quotas and 15 per cent more opposed to a ban on private medicine.

Parenthood never correlated well with these practical decisions.

Amongst the public, *women* were 11 per cent more in favour of gender quotas for employment, 8 per cent more likely to stress the importance of having more women in parliament, and 12 per cent more willing to change the law to ensure that end. But these were relatively small gender differences and they were not much greater than gender differences on the issues of ethnic quotas (6 per cent) and changes in the law to ensure more 'ethnic and racial minority' MPs (11 per cent). The largest gender difference was on attitudes to surveillance activities by the security services: women were 16 per cent less willing than men to let the security services tap telephones and inspect bank accounts. Women were also more in favour of a ban on press intrusions into private lives. In general, however, differences between men and women were small and did not consistently reflect a gender bias in favour or against libertarian options, though women were always biased towards egalitarian options (Table 8.24).

Amongst politicians—who were overwhelmingly male—gender differences were somewhat greater. Women politicians were 22 per cent less willing to approve surveillance, for example, 14 per cent less willing to accept the suspension of civil rights in a national emergency, 14 per cent more opposed

TABLE 8.24. *Practice by gender* (selected percentages)

	Politicians		British public (Scottish public)	
	Men (%)	Women (%)	Men (%)	Women (%)
Freedom of expression, association, and protest				
Ban political demonstration	43	22	41 (50)	44 (50)
Ban abuse of Christianity	22	22	27 (35)	36 (37)
Freedom of information				
Ban intrusions into private lives	45	43	48 (48)	58 (54)
Freedom of lifestyle				
Abortion morally wrong	47	40	44 (50)	48 (57)
IF MORALLY WRONG: Ban abortion	40	44	43 (54)	42 (46)
Ban homosexuality	16	4	24 (29)	17 (19)
Powers to uphold the law				
Support death penalty	28	14	51 (56)	48 (51)
Powers to defend the state				
Suspend rights in emergency	82	68	81 (73)	74 (76)
Support surveillance	58	36	56 (48)	40 (37)
Equality				
Support job quotas for				
women	19	13	17 (16)	28 (25)
ethnic minorities	24	21	12 (14)	18 (23)
Say it is important to get more				
women MPs	75	87	69 (68)	77 (81)
ethnic minority MPs	68	80	52 (61)	58 (67)
IF YES: Change law to get more				
women MPs	18	22	39 (42)	51 (64)
ethnic minority MPs	18	19	32 (43)	43 (51)

to the death penalty, 12 per cent more opposed to banning homosexuality, and 21 per cent more willing to allow a potentially riotous political demonstration to go ahead.

On several issues—allowing a political demonstration to go ahead, banning press intrusions into private lives, and attitudes to the morality of abortion—women were a little *more* liberal than men amongst politicians, but *less* liberal than men amongst the public. In this, practice reflected principle.

Like women in the public, women politicians were 12 per cent more favourable than men to the need for more women and minority MPs in parliament, but, unlike women in general, women politicians were only very slightly more willing to change the law to achieve that. And, while women in general were a little *more* well disposed than men to job quotas, women politicians were *less* favourable—especially to job quotas for women. A sceptic might say that women who had become political leaders under the existing system had obviously prospered and might therefore be less inclined to see the need for positive action. In fact, as we shall see in Chapter 10, female politicians complained that they had personally suffered discrimination twice as much as women generally (and twice as much as male politicians). So considered opinion rather than complacency seems the more likely explanation of their rejection of quotas, either for jobs or for parliament. No doubt they had thought the issue through and weighed up the practical benefits and disadvantages of quotas, or felt that their own treatment had been so unequal that a move to equal treatment—without positive discrimination or rigid quotas—would be a radical change in itself.

CONCLUSION

We have shown how social-background factors affect not only the principles which people adopt but the extent to which they are prepared to apply these to practical issues. On the question of principle we have shown that religion, age, and education all correlated strongly with the principles we associated with liberty, while class correlated most strongly with those we associated with equality.

Although, when we turned from principle to practice, we found that decisions in specific circumstances were less clearly determined by social-background variables, they still proved to have a similar effect. The decisions that politicians and the public took in practical scenarios were also most strongly correlated with age, religion, education, and class. Religion, age, and education still correlated relatively well with decisions about practical

292 *Influences*

issues to do with liberty, and class with decisions about practical issues to do with equality. However, as on questions of principle, the social-background factors of gender, urbanization, employment sector, and parenthood were relatively uninfluential on practical issues also.

The fact that social background appears to influence principles rather more than practice suggests that the life experiences represented by these broad social categories shape principles but perhaps influence practical decisions mainly through the medium of those principles, and not directly. We shall return to that theme in Chapter 12.

But first, in Chapters 9 and 10, we shall look at the way ideology and partisanship relate to questions about rights and liberties, and assess the influence, if any, of specific personal experiences which appear particularly relevant to civil, political, and social rights—much more specific, immediate, personal, and relevant than may be indicated by such broad categories as class or gender.

NOTES

1. Deborah Tannen, *You Just Don't Understand: Women and Men in Conversation* (New York: Ballantine, 1991).
2. In our British public sample, 96 per cent described themselves as 'white' rather than 'black' or 'Asian'. The 1991 OPCS Population Census gives the figure as 95 per cent—see *1991 Census Monitor for Parliamentary Constituencies* (London: OPCS, 1994). We did, however, find that, in our British public sample, those whose self-image was 'black' or 'Asian' scored 9 points higher on liberty and 11 points higher on equality than those whose self-image was 'white'. But specially targeted samples are necessary for any serious investigation of minority ethnic subcultures. See e.g. Muhammad Anwar, *Race and Politics: Ethnic Minorities and the British Political System* (London: Tavistock, 1986), esp. 62–83.
3. John L. Sullivan, James Pierson, and George E. Marcus, *Political Tolerance and American Democracy* (Chicago: University of Chicago Press, 1982, 1989), 120–5.
4. Ibid. 135.
5. Ibid. 138.
6. Ibid. 130.
7. Ibid. 141.
8. Heath and his colleagues looked briefly at the social patterns of support for the two dimensions defined by their factor analysis of British public opinion—their 'left–right scale' and 'liberal–authoritarian scale'. Our findings differ sharply from theirs both in the content of the scales and in the social patterns of support. For example, we—like Sullivan, Pierson, and Marcus—find that age correlates strongly (and negatively) with liberty, but not with equality. But Heath and his colleagues found that

age correlated with their 'left–right scale' but not significantly with their 'liberal–authoritarian scale'—which we find either implausible or misleading (depending upon scale definition). See Anthony Heath *et al.*, *Understanding Political Change: The British Voter 1964–87* (Oxford: Pergamon Press, 1991), 175.

9. Jack Brand and his colleagues have drawn attention to a 'trend since the mid-1970s . . . for Scottish voters to identify increasingly with the working class despite objectively being in one of the higher social status categories' (Jack Brand, James Mitchell, and Paula Surridge, 'Will Scotland Come to the Aid of the Party?', in Anthony Heath, Roger Jowell, and John Curtice (eds.), *Labour's Last Chance? The 1992 Election and Beyond* (Aldershot: Dartmouth, 1994), 213–28).

10. Elizabeth M. Meehan, *Women's Rights at Work: Campaigns and Policies in Britain and the United States* (Basingstoke: Macmillan, 1985), 4.

11. Herbert McClosky and Alida Brill, *Dimensions of Tolerance: What Americans Believe about Civil Liberties* (New York: Russell Sage Foundation, 1983), 387.

12. McClosky and Brill (ibid. 406) found the same in the USA.

13. Ibid. 411.

14. Lord Percy of Newcastle, *The Heresy of Democracy* (London: Eyre & Spottiswood, 1954), 28.

15. Anthony Heath ('Do People Have Consistent Attitudes?', in Roger Jowell, Sharon Witherspoon, and Lindsay Brook (eds.), *British Social Attitudes: The 1986 Report* (Aldershot: Gower, 1986), 1–16) found the religious differed from the unreligious on only one of his five factors—economic equality, sexual liberty, political liberty, conservation, and defence—namely, sexual liberty. We have found much wider differences.

16. McClosky and Brill, *Dimensions of Tolerance*, 413.

17. Stuart Rothenberg and Frank Newport, *The Evangelical Voter: Religion and Politics in America* (Washington: Free Congress Research and Education Foundation, 1984). Although Newt Gingrich, later Republican Leader in the House of Representatives, was on the Board of Advisors of this Foundation, this research report appears non-partisan.

18. Ibid. 146.

19. Ibid. 148.

20. Anthony Heath ('Do People Have Consistent Attitudes?') found that education affected three of his five factors—sexual liberty, political liberty, and conservation—but not the other two—economic equality and defence. The highly educated were relatively anti-egalitarian on economic equality, however.

21. For a similar pattern in the USA, see McClosky and Brill, *Dimensions of Tolerance*, 84, though less clearly on p. 85.

22. Sullivan, Pierson, and Marcus, *Political Tolerance and American Democracy*, 30; Robert Jackman, 'Political Élites, Mass Publics and Support for Democratic Principles', *Journal of Politics*, 34 (1972), 753–73; and S. Stouffer, *Communism, Conformism and Civil Liberties* (New York: Wiley, 1955). Stouffer's survey was carried out in 1954.

23. McClosky and Brill, *Dimensions of Tolerance*, 249.

24. Ibid. 250–1.

25. The first edition of *The Concise Oxford Dictionary of Current English* was edited by H. W. Fowler and F. G. Fowler, but our quotes are from the 4th edn. (1952) revised by E. McIntosh, and the eighth edition edited by R. E. Allen (Oxford: Oxford University Press, 1990).

26. Anthony Heath and Richard Topf ('Political Culture', in Roger Jowell, Sharon Witherspoon, and Lindsay Brook (eds.), *British Social Attitudes: The 1987 Report* (Aldershot: Gower, 1987), 51–70, at 66) report that 'education would seem to provide the sociological basis both for liberal moral attitudes and for increased political participation. It contrasts with class which provides the basis for attitudes towards the economic order.'

27. See e.g. Seymour Martin Lipset, *Political Man* (London: Heinemann, 1983); Lewis Lipsitz, 'Working Class Authoritarianism: A Re-Evaluation', *American Sociological Review*, 30 (1965), 103–9; Thomas R. Dye and L. Harmon Zeigler, *The Irony of Democracy: An Uncommon Introduction to American Politics* (Belmont, Calif.: Wadsworth, 1970), 133; Jackman 'Political Élites, Mass Publics and Support for Democratic Principles', 753–73; and Sullivan, Pierson and Marcus, *Political Tolerance and American Democracy*, 120–5.

28. See e.g. Sinclair Ross, *As for Me and my House* (Toronto: McClelland & Stewart, 1949); and Alice Munro, *The Beggar Maid: Stories of Flo and Rose* (London: Penguin, 1978).

29. McClosky and Brill, *Dimensions of Tolerance*, 416.

30. Ibid. 84.

31. Sullivan, Pierson, and Marcus, *Political Tolerance and American Democracy*, ch. 5, 'The Social Sources', and ch. 6, 'The Psychological Sources'.

32. For our own definition and use of the MDG concept, see ch. 5.

9

Partisanship and Ideology

IN this chapter we look at the way in which attitudes to civil and political rights relate to partisanship and self-assigned ideology. The causal implications of that relationship may be ambiguous. We recognize that a general left-wing or right-wing, Labour or Conservative, orientation may help people to decide their position on new issues as they arise, yet, at the same time, it is the constellation of existing issues and attitudes that gives meaning to such ideological labels as 'left' and 'right'. Few people in contemporary Britain know about the seating arrangements in the French Revolutionary assemblies of the 1790s (from which such terms derive)—and still less would care if they did. For those who do, the meaning of those terms *in the 1790s* is defined by the attitudes and behaviour of the deputies who sat on different sides of the chamber at that time. In a similar way, for most people, the *contemporary* meaning of such terms as 'left', 'right', and 'centre' is defined by the attitudes and behaviour of those who accept such labels now—or who have these labels thrust upon them.

Of course, there are other approaches to the definition of ideology. We could define ideology in the terms used by our favourite political theorists or, less controversially, by a representative selection of political theorists. Another alternative approach would be to base our definition purely upon a statistical analysis of political attitudes—without taking account of which respondents accepted ideological labels. We could, for example, revert to the factor analyses presented in Chapter 4 and simply label the first dimension 'liberal/authoritarian' and the second dimension 'left/right', defining—on our own authority as analysts—the egalitarian dimension as being *the* 'left/right' dimension. Or, again, we could be even more restrictive and define 'left/right' purely in terms of economic egalitarianism, as distinct from gender, ethnic, or religious egalitarianism. Other studies follow these three alternative approaches. In essence each of these approaches is an assertion that the analyst, and the analyst alone, has the ultimate right to define what 'left/right' means.

That is a valid approach for certain purposes, but it is not our approach here. We are not seeking the 'best' theoretical definition of ideology. And we claim no right of definition. Our objective is purely empirical: to understand

how the British public and their political leaders use ideological labels—
whether or not that differs from the way in which they are used either by
political theorists or by factor analysts.

We note, for example, that the slogans of those who claim to be on the
'left' have often linked equality with liberty—and not just in the familiar
context of the French Revolution.[1] The British Labour Party's official badge,
displayed outside its London headquarters—and therefore still frequently
seen on television despite the efforts of image consultants to publicize the
Party's modern red-rose logo—consists of a crossed pen and spade with one
word written right across the centre of the badge in large, clear letters. That
single word is *not* 'Equality', but 'Liberty'. However symbolic that may be,
of course, it may not tell us much about the attitudes of the great mass of
left-wing people or of Labour supporters.

On the other side of the political spectrum, Brian Girvin identifies 'three
broad varieties' of 'contemporary conservatism':

[1.] *liberal conservatism* . . . strongly pro-capitalist, asserting the strongest possible
relationship between the market economy, individual liberty, and the rule of
law
[2.] *Christian Democracy* . . . [with] an emphasis on a Christian moral order . . .
[and thus] an enhanced role for the state in regulating personal behaviour
[3.] *authoritarian conservatism* . . . believing that a strong state is necessary to
protect conservative values . . . nationalism and populism are much more influential amongst authoritarian conservatives.[2]

Conservatives of any and every variety have always been opposed to equality. Girvin's first 'variety of contemporary conservatism' links opposition to
equality with support for liberty; but the other two varieties clearly link
opposition to equality with opposition to liberty, by emphasizing either our
micro-principle of traditional values or our micro-principle of respect for
authority. Desmond King describes the 'new right' as a potentially incoherent combination of liberals bent on 'a restatement of liberal values, authoritarians concerned to re-establish state power, moralists wishing to restore
religious and pre-1960s values, and conservatives who fear the reduction of
inequality'[3] in which 'the contradiction between liberalism and conservatism
concerning the role of the state is striking . . . [because] liberalism implies
limited government, [while] conservatism requires a strong state to maintain
social order and authority'.[4] King's description of the new right's solution to
this dilemma—'a strong government . . . with a reduced state'[5]—unambiguously links opposition to equality with opposition to every form of liberty
except consumer choice.

But what we seek to do here is not to rely upon symbolism or anecdotal evidence, nor to fudge the difference between parties and ideologies, but simply to find out the differences in attitudes between those who call themselves 'left', 'right', or 'centre', and between those who claim to be supporters of different parties. In essence, that means using our survey to show what those who apply these labels to themselves mean by these terms—whether or not their meanings are in accord with our own expectations, or those of anyone else. It is an empirical definition of the meaning of ideology and partisanship in contemporary Britain that lets self-confessed party and ideological identifiers speak for themselves—not the only important definition by any means, but not an unimportant definition either.

Yet, while some attitudes may give meaning to ideological or party labels, others are very clearly influenced by party loyalty or ideological orientation. Opinions on issues may incline people towards or against particular parties, but, at the same time, opinion on any specific issue, and especially on a new issue, may be influenced by pre-existing party loyalty. Trends in voting intentions during the approach to the EC Referendum of 1975 and (in Scotland and Wales) to the Devolution Referendums of 1979 show very clearly the power of pre-existing partisanship to influence attitudes on specific issues of the day.[6] Causal influence clearly does operate in both directions between attitudes, on the one hand, and partisanship or ideological orientation, on the other. We suggest that the dominant direction of that influence is likely to be *from fundamental principles* to partisanship or ideological orientation; but then from partisanship or ideological orientation *to positions on transient or specific issues of practice*. But, whether that is so or not, and however clear or ambiguous the causal relationship between attitudes and partisanship or ideological orientation, we shall at least be able to show just what it means, *in terms of principle*, to be on the left or the right or in the centre, or to be a partisan of one party or another.

SELF-IMAGES OF PARTISANSHIP AND IDEOLOGY

We shall use two indicators of partisan self-images. First, *party preference* in a hypothetical general election held 'tomorrow'; and second, a more psychological and detailed measure of *party support* based upon the following series of questions:

Generally speaking, do you think of yourself as a *supporter* of any one political party?

IF A SUPPORTER: Which? And how strongly do you support that party: very strongly, or not very strongly?

IF NOT A SUPPORTER: Do you think of yourself as a little closer to one political party than to the others?

IF YES: Which?

This combination of questions allows us to classify respondents into those who were:

1. strong supporters (literally, 'very strong')
2. supporters (but 'not very strong' ones)
3. leaners (i.e. closer to one party than to others, but would not describe themselves as a 'supporter' of it)
4. non-party people (not even 'closer' to one party than to others).

As an indicator of ideological self-images, we asked:

In politics, would you say that you are generally on the left, in the centre, or on the right?

IF CENTRE: Do you lean a little more towards the left or the right? Which?

IF LEFT OR RIGHT: Strongly or not very strongly?

These questions allow us to place all but a few respondents on a scale that runs as follows:

1. strongly left
2. left (but not very strongly)
3. centre left
4. centre (with no leaning to left or right)
5. centre right
6. right (but not very strongly)
7. strongly right.

Such a simple measure of ideological self-image is open to some obvious, but irrelevant criticisms. We recognize that it cannot provide a fully adequate index of political attitudes. Its terms may mean different things to different people, and nothing at all to many. It is one-dimensional, and cannot represent the multidimensional structure of attitudes we found in Chapter 4, for example. But that is not our purpose in using it. We asked about left, right, and centre because these are the most familiar ideological labels used by the public, and it is our empirical object to find out what, if anything, these terms mean to the people who use them.

Acceptance of Ideological and Partisan Labels

Our first concern must be about the extent to which people are comfortable with these concepts. Despite the scepticism that has sometimes been expressed by political scientists, we found that both the public and their politicians accepted these labels quite easily.[7] Only 2 per cent of politicians and 7 per cent of the public (both in Britain as a whole, and also in Scotland) were either unable or unwilling to answer our questions about ideology—rather low levels of 'don't know/won't say' compared to the answers given to many other questions in our survey. Although we shall exclude such people, our analyses of ideology therefore include almost everyone.

Under 1 per cent were either unable or unwilling to answer our questions about whether or not they thought themselves a 'supporter' of any party. Reasonably enough, we have counted them as not being party supporters (Table 9.1).

Amongst politicians only 6 per cent were non-party people (remember that our politicians included leaders of Independent groups, as well as party groups, on local councils), and the vast majority, as we might expect, described themselves as 'very strong' party supporters. Amongst the public, however, a quarter were non-party people and the remainder were spread much more evenly across the categories of strong supporters, mere supporters, and leaners. Only a minority of each party's adherents were strong supporters, and that was especially true for the Liberal Democrats.

There was a similar discrepancy between the ideology of politicians and the public. Amongst politicians, the most frequent ideological categories were 'strongly left' and 'strongly right'. By contrast, the most frequent ideological categories amongst the public were 'centre right' and 'centre left'. Both distributions were bi-modal, but the peaks were much closer together amongst the public than amongst politicians (Table 9.2).

In addition, politicians were, on average, more left wing than the public. That is surprising, because here—as throughout this book—we have weighted our sample of politicians to have the same pattern of party voting preferences (though not the same pattern of party support, however) as the public. So, *despite identical patterns of voting preferences*, the politicians were none the less more ideologically left wing than the public.

The Relationship between Ideology and Partisanship

We can discover why politicians as a whole were more left wing than the public if we assign numerical values to ideological positions in the following way:

TABLE 9.1. *Party support*

	Politicians (%)	British public (%)	(Scottish public) (%)
Non-party people	6	24	(26)
Conservatives			
strong supporters	34	12	(4)
supporters	3	13	(7)
leaners	2	10	(7)
Labour			
strong supporters	32	13	(11)
supporters	1	8	(11)
leaners	1	8	(12)
Liberal Democrats			
strong supporters	17	3	(2)
supporters	1	3	(2)
leaners	1	6	(3)
SNP (Scottish National Party)			
strong supporters	2	1	(8)
supporters	0	0	(3)
leaners	0	1	(5)

Notes: Percentages in this table have been calculated after excluding those who supported or leaned to a party but refused to say which one, or chose the Welsh Nationalist Party (Plaid Cymru), the Green Party, or another party. Collectively that excluded only 3% of the Politicians and British public samples, and only 1% of the Scots sample. We have treated the Scottish Nationalists differently from the Welsh only because we have a special Scottish sample—in which they had substantial support.

Comparing this table with Table 10.15, note that the total number of people who were not party 'supporters' includes both the 'non-party people' and the 'leaners'.

TABLE 9.2. *Ideological self-images*

	Politicians (%)	British public (%)	(Scottish public) (%)
Very strongly left	24	10	(12)
Left (but not very strongly)	13	13	(15)
Centre left	16	18	(22)
Centre (with no leaning)	9	15	(15)
Centre right	12	21	(21)
Right (but not very strongly)	12	14	(11)
Very strongly right	15	9	(4)

TABLE 9.3. *Right-wing ideological self-images by voting preferences*
(scores on +/−15 scale)

	Politicians (scores)	British public (scores)	(Scottish public) (scores)
All respondents	−1.6	0.2	(−1.6)
Voting preference			
Conservative	9.2	6.8	(6.0)
Labour	−11.2	−6.4	(−5.5)
Liberal Democrat	−5.6	−0.8	(+0.9)
SNP	−6.7	n.a.	(−3.2)

Notes: Plus and minus 10 mean 'right' and 'left'; plus and minus 15 mean 'strongly' so.
Figures for SNP partisans in the public are drawn from the Scottish sample only.
n.a. = not applicable.

    −15 strongly left
    −10 left
     −5 centre left
      0 centre
      5 centre right
     10 right
     15 strongly right

This allows us to calculate an average ideological position within any sample or subsample.

Overall, politicians averaged out at minus 2 compared to the public at zero. So, on average, politicians were a little left of centre, while the public were exactly in the centre. Although Conservative politicians were 2.4 points further to the right than their own voters, Labour politicians were 4.8 points further to the left than theirs; Liberal Democrat politicians were also 4.8 further to the left than their voters, and SNP politicians 3.5 further to the left than theirs.

The ideological differences between party politicians and their own voters were perhaps most striking in the case of the Liberal Democrats. While Liberal Democrat politicians placed themselves firmly on the centre left, their voters placed themselves in the centre—and, in Scotland, slightly to the right of centre, probably because the SNP had taken so much of the left-of-centre third-party vote there (Tables 9.3 and 9.4).[8]

Ideology was also related to the *strength* of partisanship. Amongst both the public and politicians, strong Conservatives placed themselves further to

Influences

TABLE 9.4. *Right-wing ideological self-images by party support*
(scores on +/−15 scale)

	Politicians (scores)	British public (scores)	(Scottish public) (scores)
Non-party people	0.4	0.1	(−0.1)
Conservatives			
very strong supporters	10.0	9.8	(9.4)
supporters	7.1	6.6	(7.1)
leaners	4.9	5.3	(4.6)
Labour			
very strong supporters	−11.7	−8.5	(−8.5)
supporters	−10.4	−7.1	(−5.7)
leaners	−8.4	−5.1	(−5.9)
Liberal Democrats			
very strong supporters	−6.1	−1.6	(1.0)
supporters	−4.1	−2.1	(−0.7)
leaners	−1.6	−1.1	(−0.5)
SNP (Scottish National Party)			
very strong supporters	−6.5	n.a.	(−3.7)
supporters	none	n.a.	(−5.0)
leaners	none	n.a.	(−1.7)

Notes: Plus and minus 10 mean 'right' and 'left'; plus and minus 15 mean 'strongly' so.
Figures for SNP partisans in the public are drawn from the Scottish sample only.
n.a. = not applicable.

the right than weak Conservative supporters or leaners; and strong Labour people placed themselves further to the left than weak Labour supporters or leaners. None the less, the ideological difference between Conservative and Labour leaners was far larger than the ideological difference between leaners and strong supporters in either party; so the major ideological divide was between these parties, not within them.

SNP supporters were substantially to the left of SNP leaners. And although there was no relationship between strength of party support and ideology amongst Liberal Democrats in the public (either in Britain as a whole or in Scotland, where strong Liberal Democrats were slightly to the right of other Liberal Democrats), amongst Liberal Democrat politicians the stronger their partisanship the more left-wing they were.

Interestingly, both the small number of non-party politicians and the much larger number of non-party people in the public placed themselves exactly in the ideological centre.

CORRELATIONS WITH PRINCIPLES

Both ideological self-images and partisanship reflected commitments to principles of liberty and equality. To some extent we can assess those relationships by calculating correlation coefficients, and we shall begin by doing just that. However, we shall then have to go beyond correlation coefficients to see how principles were related to both the strength and direction of partisanship and how smoothly principles varied across the full range of the ideological spectrum.

Principles and Ideological Self-Images

Few, if any, associate the 'right' with equality, but Ted Honderich claims that the 'right' has also been the enemy of liberty: 'the New Right has been no friend to civil liberties, but a resolute adversary . . . nor have Conservatives of whatever species been friends to civil liberties . . . Conservatism's support of certain economic freedoms distinguishes it. Its opposition to social *and civil* freedoms is a further great distinction of it.'[9]

Ideology correlated strongly with a wide range of principles and prejudices—more strongly than any of the social variables we looked at in Chapter 8—though, like social variables such as religion, age, education, or class, ideology correlated with principles much more strongly amongst politicians than amongst the public. But, while religion, age, and education correlated much better with first-dimension (liberty) principles than with second-dimension (equality) principles, and class correlated much better with second-dimension principles than with first, ideology correlated well with both first- and second-dimension principles and, indeed, with those few micro-principles that seemed to span both first and second dimensions—protest and self-reliance. Amongst the public the correlation was 0.39 with equality but also 0.29 with liberty; and amongst politicians, 0.68 with equality but also 0.56 with liberty.

In their attack on 'The Fallacy of Democratic Élitism', Paul Sniderman and his colleagues produce Canadian and US evidence to justify their claim that party and ideological (as defined by ideological self-images) 'differences among élites in support for civil liberties eclipse, both in size and political significance, the differences between élites and citizens'.[10] McClosky and Brill concluded that, 'whether one measures ideology by membership of

TABLE 9.5. *Correlations between right-wing ideological self-images and principles*

	Politicians (r × 100)	British public (r × 100)	(Scottish public) (r × 100)
Liberty	−56	−29	(−26)
Equality	−68	−39	(−39)
Authority	61	33	(32)
Traditional values	45	19	(17)
Wealth creation	58	16	(16)
Tolerance	−35	−17	(−14)
Limited government	−54	−26	(−18)
Right to speak out	−20	−11	(−10)
Protest	−58	−36	(−34)
Self-reliance	65	31	(33)
Economic equality	−64	−37	(−26)
Caring	−34	−22	(−15)
Equal rights	−64	−30	(−24)
Protection	−26	.	(−11)
Right to know	−30	.	(.)

Note: Correlations less than 0.10 have been replaced by full point.

criterion groups [such as political parties], by self-designation, or by a carefully validated scale, the results are the same':[11] a very strong correlation, even stronger amongst the élite, between ideology and support for civil liberties. Our survey shows that is clearly true in Britain as well (Table 9.5).

More importantly, our findings highlight something which is only implicit in the US and Canadian studies whose primary focus was on civil liberties: left/right ideology, as defined by those people who themselves accepted such labels, should *not* be identified with only one of the two dimensions of opinion that we uncovered in Chapter 4, but with both. In terms of the way the British use their language, nothing could be more misleading than to label the equality dimension 'left/right', and to invent some other name for the liberty dimension. Left/right ideology, as defined by the opinions of those who claimed those labels for themselves, was about liberty almost as much as it was about equality. That finding might not surprise the French politicians of 1789, nor those who designed the British Labour Party's badge, but it is at odds with current usage amongst political analysts. Heath and his colleagues, for example, distinguish between a 'left/right' and a 'liberal/authoritarian' dimension of opinion,[12] while we have shown that the British

TABLE 9.6. *Correlations between right-wing ideological self-images and sympathies*

	Politicians (r × 100)	British public (r × 100)	(Scottish public) (r × 100)
Activists	−64	−38	(−36)
Socially disadvantaged	−63	−35	(−31)
Militants	−23	−21	(−14)
Political system	21	15	(15)
Civil institutions	.	.	(.)
Judicial system	52	30	(27)
Rights enforcers	−49	.	(.)

Note: Correlations less than 0.10 have been replaced by full points for clarity.

public and their politicians use the terms left and right just as much to denote differences on support for liberty as on support for equality.

Amongst politicians, ideology correlated very strongly, at around 0.6, with principles of self-reliance, economic equality, equal rights, respect for authority, protest, wealth creation, and limited government. Even amongst the public it correlated at around 0.3 with all of these except for wealth creation. On the other hand, it correlated less well with tolerance, the right to speak out and the right to know.

Ideology also correlated better than any social variable with our measures of sympathies. Amongst politicians, it correlated at over 0.6 with antipathy towards activists and the socially disadvantaged, and at over 0.5 with confidence in the judicial system. Amongst the public, it correlated at over 0.35 with antipathy towards activists and the socially disadvantaged, and at close to 0.3 with confidence in the judicial system (Table 9.6).

Combinations of Principle and Ideological Self-Images

We can look at the relationship between principle and ideology from the opposite perspective by calculating the average ideological position claimed by those who had different levels of commitment to particular principles. This is particularly useful for looking at the ideological self-images of those with particular *combinations* of commitment to principles. In particular, we can divide people according to whether they had above- or below-average scores on commitment to liberty and equality, and then look at the ideological self-images of those with each of the four possible combinations of principle.

Those with below-average commitment to both liberty and equality put themselves, on average, on the centre right if they were ordinary members of the public, and simply on the right if they were politicians. Those with above average commitment to both liberty and equality put themselves on the centre left if they were ordinary members of the public and simply on the left if they were politicians.

Those who combined average commitment to one principle with below-average commitment to the other put themselves in the centre. There was a consistent difference between the two possible combinations of conflicting principles, however: those who were above average on equality but below average on liberty put themselves very slightly to the left of centre; while those who were below average on equality but above average on liberty put themselves very slightly to the right of centre. None the less, both groups with conflicting principles put themselves nearer to the centre than to either the centre left or the centre right (Table 9.7).

Principles and Party

Partisanship is inherently more multidimensional than left/right ideology. However, we can still calculate correlations between party preference and principles. We shall use multivariate statistical methods for that purpose in Chapter 12, but simpler approaches are possible. One such simple but re-vealing way to examine the correlation between party preference and prin-ciple is to begin by placing the parties on a numerical scale, roughly reflecting the ideology of their supporters or voters. Amongst the public we found the average ideology scores of those with different voting preferences were approximately minus 6 for Labour, minus 3 for SNP, minus 1 for Liberal Democrats, and plus 7 for Conservatives. On ideology at least, Liberal Demo-crats were approximately halfway between Labour and Conservative voters, while SNP voters were closer to Labour than to the Conservatives. So sim-plifying slightly, and imposing symmetry between Labour and Conservative preferences, we defined a partisan scale as follows:

> −6 Labour vote preference
> −3 SNP vote preference
> 0 Liberal Democrat vote preference
> +6 Conservative vote preference.[13]

Using this scale of partisanship instead of ideology we recomputed all the correlations with principles. Of course, they were similar to the correlations between principles and ideology itself. But people have a clear idea of their

TABLE 9.7. *Right-wing ideological self-images by combinations of commitment to the principles of liberty and equality (scores on +/-15 scale)*

		Politicians		British public (Scottish public)	
		Commitment to equality		Commitment to equality	
		HIGH (scores)	LOW (scores)	HIGH (scores)	LOW (scores)
Commitment to liberty	HIGH	-10.5 Left	2.4 Centre	-6.0 (-5.7) Centre left (Centre left)	2.4 (0.2) Centre (Centre)
	LOW	-1.4 Centre	7.7 Right	-0.2 (-1.7) Centre (Centre)	4.3 (2.1) Centre right (Centre)

Notes: Ideology scores have been assigned the nearest label from the +/-15 ideology scale.

High and low on equality and liberty are defined as above and below the point mid-way between the average scores in the British public and politicians' samples. Since both politicians and the public had an average score of 55 on equality, the cut point was 55 for equality; on liberty, politicians averaged -12, and the public -25, so the cut point was -18.5. See Chapter 4 for further details of average scores on principles.

party preference. If their concept of left and right were much less clear than their concept of Labour, Liberal Democrat, and Conservative preference, then we should expect that the correlations with this party preference scale would be higher than with the ideology scale simply because people would place themselves more accurately upon it. In fact, we found quite the opposite: the correlation between principle and *ideology* nearly always proved slightly higher than the correlation between principle and *party*.

The Effect of Education

The sheer size of these correlations suggests that self-proclaimed ideology is meaningful to most people and is not merely the preserve of the politically active or the highly educated. None the less we might expect correlations with ideology to be higher amongst the well educated partly because they might have given more considered answers to questions about rights and liberties, and partly also because they might have a clearer, more homogeneous, and more self-conscious understanding of ideological labels such as 'left' and 'right'.

And indeed that is so. We found that correlations between ideology and principles did vary with levels of education. They were lower than average—though by no means negligible—amongst those without educational qualifications, and particularly high amongst the university educated. Both education and deep involvement with politics—as a leading local politician—increased the correlation between ideology and principle. Surprisingly perhaps, neither proved a complete substitute for the other: higher education increased the correlation between ideology and principle amongst politicians just as it did amongst the public; and conversely, deep involvement in practical politics increased the correlation amongst university graduates as well as amongst the less well educated.

However, it does seem clear that education increased the correlation with ideology more amongst the public than amongst politicians (where it was already high), and more with principles of liberty than with principles of equality (which correlated fairly strongly with ideology even amongst the educationally unqualified). Ironically, left/right ideology only came near to being exclusively correlated with equality (and not with liberty) amongst members of the public who had no educational qualifications at all. And, even amongst them, there was a clear, if small, correlation between being on the left and support for the principle of liberty.

Principles correlated *slightly less with ideology* than with voting preferences amongst educationally unqualified members of the public; and *slightly*

TABLE 9.8.   *Correlations between right-wing ideological self-images and principles,*
at different levels of educational qualifications

	Politicians (r × 100)	British public (r × 100)	(Scottish public) (r × 100)
Correlations with liberty amongst those with			
no qualifications	−43	−12	(−16)
school qualifications	−51	−31	(−32)
university qualifications	−67	−51	(−47)
Effect of education on correlations with liberty	24	39	(31)
Correlations with equality amongst those with			
no qualifications	−62	−35	(−25)
school qualifications	−67	−39	(−31)
university qualifications	−71	−59	(−51)
Effect of education on correlations with equality	9	24	(26)

Note: Size of effect = correlation amongst graduates minus correlation amongst unqualified.

more with ideology than with voting preferences amongst those who had school or university qualifications; but these differences were only slight. Irrespective of whether we used partisan or ideological self-images, the correlation between principles and self-images was much higher amongst the well educated. That suggests the effect of higher education was more to clarify the principles of civil and social rights than to clarify the meaning of ideology (Table 9.8).[14] (That view is consistent with our findings in Chapter 8, where repeated factor analyses within different educational groups showed that higher education did indeed clarify principles by tying micro-principles more closely to the two macro-principles of liberty and equality.)

Education also affected the degree of correlation between ideology (or vote preference) and sympathies. Once again, correlations were higher, often much higher, amongst university graduates than amongst the unqualified. Taking the four aspects of sympathy that correlated best with right-wing ideology—antipathy towards activists or the socially disadvantaged, lack of confidence in rights enforcers, and confidence in the judicial system—the average correlation with ideology was 0.19 amongst unqualified members of the public, just under 0.50 amongst both educationally unqualified politicians and university-educated members of the public, and 0.65 amongst university-educated politicians, a pattern of figures remarkably similar to the pattern of correlations between ideology and principle.

HOW PRINCIPLES VARIED: NON-LINEAR RELATIONSHIPS

Correlation coefficients give us a very rough idea of how well opinions on civil and political rights fit with ideology and partisanship, but they are no help in answering some of the more detailed questions that might be asked about those relationships.

Principles and the Full Ideological Spectrum

As we have defined it, ideological self-image is a uni-dimensional scale, but one with seven positions ranging from strongly left to strongly right. We would like to know how different those seven positions really are. Do values and opinions vary uniformly and continuously as we traverse the scale from strongly left to strongly right? Or are there some critical points on the scale where opinions change particularly sharply? Is there perhaps just a left, right, and centre? Or are there significant differences of opinion between, for example, the centre left and the left, or between the right and the strongly right? Correlation analysis only tells us that opinions vary as we traverse the scale; it does not tell us *where* on the scale they vary most. Nor does it exclude the possibility that opinions might vary in a strongly curvilinear fashion: for example, are those who describe themselves as *strongly* left or right more authoritarian than those who place themselves in the centre? It is often alleged that extremism and intolerance go together, and if strong ideological self-images were the same thing as extremism, then we might expect such a curvilinear pattern (Table 9.9).

All these questions can be answered by calculating scores for each principle at each point on the ideological spectrum. These show:

1. There is no evidence of curvilinear patterns of opinion that would contrast the ideological centre with a coalition of both ideological extremes. Alan Marsh, following Rokeach, suggested that, while support for equality would rise steadily from the extreme right to the extreme left of the spectrum, support for liberty would peak in the moderate left and moderate right and decline on both extremes.[15] It is an old and plausible idea—surely 'extremists are bound to be illiberal, almost by definition'—but it is not consistent with our findings on

TABLE 9.9. *Principles by ideological self-image* (scores on +/−100 scale)

	Liberty		Equality	
	Politicians (scores)	British public (Scottish public) (scores)	Politicians (scores)	British public (Scottish public) (scores)
Strongly left	14	−6 (−11)	76	70 (72)
Left	5	−12 (−16)	69	61 (64)
Centre left	−9	−23 (−24)	64	61 (64)
Centre	−23	−27 (−25)	52	56 (58)
Centre right	−31	−31 (−31)	45	52 (58)
Right	−29	−28 (−31)	33	44 (50)
Strongly right	−36	−38 (−42)	29	37 (48)

ideological self-images. We have found that support for liberty also rises steadily from extreme right to extreme left (except for a slight drop in the centre right). On our two macro-principles, *and on every one of our thirteen micro-principles*, the opinions of those in the centre were intermediate between those of the left and the right.

2. On liberty, there was some evidence of opinion 'compression' or consensus on the right—by which we mean that the difference between the opinions of the centre right and the strongly right was much less than the difference between the opinions of the centre left and the strongly left; while on equality there was compression or consensus on the left.

3. Differences of opinion across the ideological spectrum were large. With principles scaled to run from a minimum of minus 100 to plus 100, politicians at extremes of the ideological spectrum differed by 50 points on liberty and 47 points on equality; while members of the public at extremes of the ideological spectrum differed by 32 points on liberty and 33 points on equality. It is significant that the extremes of left and right differed as much on liberty as on equality. Though that could be the result of more sensitive measures of liberty than of equality, other evidence suggests that is not so.

4. Differences on some micro-principles were even larger than on our macro-principles of liberty and equality. Amongst politicians, the ideological extremes differed by 80 points on attitudes to protest, by over 60 on the first-dimension principles of respect for authority, traditional values, and limited government; and by 71 points on the second-

dimension principle of equal rights, though only by 47 points on economic equality. Amongst the public, the ideological extremes differed by 61 on protest, by 43 on respect for authority, and by 46 on equal rights. Even within the range of our second-dimension principles it is noteworthy that differences were larger on equal rights than on economic equality, which reinforces our finding that left and right differed by at least as much, and probably by more, on liberty than on equality.

Principles, Party, and the Strength of Partisanship

Even ignoring lesser parties, there were three possible party preferences in England (four in Scotland), and ten varieties of party support in England (thirteen in Scotland), which could hardly be arranged along a one-dimensional scale without some distortion.

Amongst the public, Conservatives were somewhat less committed to liberty than those who preferred other parties but, as one might expect, very much less committed to equality. By contrast, differences between those who preferred other parties were slight, though those with Labour preferences were—by a narrow margin—the most committed to both liberty and equality.

Amongst politicians also, Conservatives were clearly out on a limb compared to the other parties. They showed far less commitment to either liberty or equality than politicians from any other party. While SNP politicians were noticeably less committed to liberty than Labour or Liberal Democrat politicians, they were much closer to them on this principle than to Conservative politicians. Labour politicians were clearly the most egalitarian, as we might expect.

When we compared each party's politicians with its ordinary voters on the principle of liberty, we found that not only were Conservative politicians very close to their own voters in terms of a low commitment to liberty, but also closer than other politicians to the public. SNP politicians were 14 points more committed to liberty than their voters, Labour politicians 23 points more than theirs, and Liberal Democrats 28 points more than theirs. These discrepancies between Labour and Liberal Democrat politicians, on the one hand, and their own voters, on the other, accounted for almost all of the overall difference on liberty between politicians and the public in Britain as a whole. On liberty, politicians from left-wing parties were peculiarly unrepresentative of their voters—and, no doubt, proud of it.

Politicians were just a little more polarized than their voters on equality, however, and there was a symmetry between Labour and Conservative: Labour

TABLE 9.10. *Principles by voting preference* (scores on +/−100 scale)

	Liberty		Equality	
	Politicians	British public (Scottish public)	Politicians	British public (Scottish public)
	(scores)	(scores)	(scores)	(scores)
Conservative	−33	−31 (−33)	34	44 (50)
Labour	4	−19 (−25)	73	63 (66)
Liberal Democrat	5	−23 (−23)	63	58 (60)
SNP	−9	n.a. (−23)	66	n.a. (64)

Notes: Figures for SNP partisans in the public are drawn from the Scottish sample only.
n.a. = not applicable.

politicians were 10 points more committed to equality than their voters, while Conservative politicians were 10 points more opposed to equality than their voters (Table 9.10).

We can carry out a more detailed analysis of attitudes to principle in terms of the strength of party support. Since we have already noted that, except for determinedly non-party politicians, politicians were nearly all 'very strong' supporters, rather than supporters or leaners, we must restrict this analysis to the public.

Differences of principle between strong Labour and Conservative supporters were nearly always smaller than between those who described themselves as strongly left or right, and sometimes much smaller. On liberty, strong Labour and Conservative supporters differed by 19 points while strong left and right identifiers differed by 32 points. On equality, strong Labour and Conservative supporters differed by 27 points while strong left and right identifiers differed by 33 points. Partisanship was therefore linked rather more to equality than to liberty, while ideology was linked equally to both.

Strong Labour supporters differed slightly in terms of principle from weak Labour supporters or leaners; and strong Conservative supporters differed slightly in terms of principle from weak Conservative supporters or leaners. But the difference of principle between Labour and Conservative leaners was greater than the difference between leaners and strong supporters in either party. On principle, as on ideological self-images, the main division lay between the Labour and Conservative parties, not between strong and weak supporters of the same party (Table 9.11).[16]

None the less, on liberty, Labour and Conservative leaners differed by

TABLE 9.11. *Principles by party support* (scores on +/-100 scale)

	Liberty		Equality	
	British public (scores)	(Scottish public) (scores)	British public (scores)	(Scottish public) (scores)
Non-party people	-23	(-25)	57	(59)
Conservatives				
very strong supporters	-36	(-41)	40	(49)
supporters	-31	(-33)	42	(48)
leaners	-30	(-26)	48	(50)
Labour				
very strong supporters	-17	(-24)	67	(73)
supporters	-20	(-23)	62	(62)
leaners	-20	(-23)	62	(64)
Liberal Democrats				
very strong supporters	-23	(-26)	59	(64)
supporters	-24	(-23)	58	(58)
leaners	-15	(-24)	58	(61)
SNP (Scottish National Party)				
very strong supporters	n.a.	(-28)	n.a.	(65)
supporters	n.a.	(-19)	n.a.	(63)
leaners	n.a.	(-22)	n.a.	(63)

Notes: Figures for SNP partisans in the public are drawn from the Scottish sample only.
n.a. = not applicable.

only 10 points while strong Labour and Conservative supporters differed by 19 points; and on equality, Labour and Conservative leaners differed by 14 points, but strong partisans by 27 points. On the other hand, Labour and Conservative politicians differed by 37 points on liberty and 39 points on equality; so even strong partisans in the public had less polarized principles than their parties' politicians.

The principles of Liberal Democrats and non-party people were closely similar to those of Labour and, taking both the British and Scots samples together, there was no systematic difference between the principles of strong Liberal Democrat supporters, weak supporters, and leaners. (Sampling variability is high, of course, for Liberal Democrats, because there are so few of them, and any apparent patterns should, therefore, be treated with caution.)

IDEOLOGY, PARTISANSHIP, AND PRACTICE

Ideology and partisanship correlated strongly with attitudes to practical issues of liberty and equality, especially on issues where the parties' policies were clear. Perhaps the best example concerns public attitudes towards some of the mechanisms for protecting rights and freedoms that we discussed in Chapter 6. In that chapter we highlighted three Charter 88 mechanisms: a Bill of Rights, a Freedom of Information Act, and an elected House of Lords; and contrasted them with four Conservative Party mechanisms: the sale of council houses, privatization of industry, NHS reforms, and elected school boards. The ratings given to each of these mechanisms as a means of defending citizens' rights and liberties correlated, more or less strongly, with both our left–right ideology scale and our Labour–SNP– Liberal Democrat–Conservative party-preference scale. However, these correlations, which ranged from less than 0.10 right up to 0.81, were much higher amongst politicians than amongst the public; and they were much lower for the Charter 88 mechanisms (which were less clearly tied to party policy) than for the Conservative Party mechanisms, especially amongst the public. Indeed the correlations for those Conservative Party mechanisms were slightly higher with party than with ideology amongst politicians, though slightly higher with ideology than with party amongst the public (Table 9.12).

On other practical issues, the size of the correlations with ideology and party was much lower than for the Conservative Party mechanisms, and more like the correlations between party, ideology, and the Charter 88 mechanisms. Although, under a right-wing government, the highest correlations were between right-wing ideology and banning publication of confidential

TABLE 9.12. *Correlations between mechanisms of liberty, right-wing ideological self-images, and right-wing voting preferences*

| | Right-wing ideological self-image | | Right-wing voting preference | |
	Politicians (r × 100)	British public (Scottish public) (r × 100)	Politicians (r × 100)	British public (Scottish public) (r × 100)
Charter 88 mechanisms				
Bill of Rights	−37	. (.)	−33	. (10)
Freedom of Information Act	−49	−15 (−18)	−47	−14 (−13)
elected House of Lords	−54	−18 (.)	−54	−14 (.)
Conservative Party mechanisms				
council-house sales	58	29 (29)	60	17 (20)
privatization of industry	72	43 (40)	76	43 (32)
NHS reforms	76	47 (38)	81	44 (37)
elected school boards	54	32 (33)	62	27 (26)

Note: Correlations less than 0.10 have been replaced by full points.

government documents—which is explicable in terms of the government's and its supporters' self-interest—the correlations were almost as high with support for the death penalty and opposition to a ban on private medicine, neither of which involved formal differences of official party policy, but both of which had clear ideological and party links (Table 9.13).

CONCLUSION

Our concern in this chapter has been to provide an empirical definition of the meaning of ideology in Britain, to understand whether both the public and their politicians were content to use ideological and partisan labels, and, if they were, to consider how their partisan and ideological self-images correlated with their attitudes to the fundamental principles of liberty and equality that underscored support for civil, political, and social rights.

We defined ideological position in terms of people's image of themselves as being on the 'left', or on the 'right', or in the 'centre'. Our working hypothesis at the beginning of the chapter was that people's commitment to fundamental principles of liberty and equality enables them to adopt both a general partisan loyalty and a general ideological position which may then combine with their original principles to shape their stand on specific issues.

We were not surprised to find that politicians were consistently stronger party supporters than their voters. But we were more surprised—given how we weighted the politicians to have exactly the same voting preferences as the public—that politicians were more ideologically left wing than the public, even after that weighting. In turn, that reflected a particularly strong commitment to liberty amongst Labour and Liberal Democrat politicians.

Our findings on the relationship between ideology and principle are significant, not only because ideology correlated more strongly with principle than any of the social variables discussed in Chapter 8, but also because the correlation between ideology and principle was nearly always stronger than that between principle and party, indicating that self-proclaimed ideology does have a clear meaning to most people in Britain.

Moreover, we found that left/right ideological self-images correlated well with both liberty and equality—amongst the public as well as amongst politicians. In British politics, the left is distinguished from the right as much by its strong commitment to liberty as by its strong commitment to equality.

We turn in the next chapter to look at questions that are perhaps considered a little less often in analyses like ours, but are none the less significant in

TABLE 9.13. *Correlations between attitudes to practical issues, right-wing ideological self-images, and right-wing voting preferences*

	Right-wing ideological self-image		Right-wing voting preference	
	Politicians (r × 100)	British public (Scottish public) (r × 100)	Politicians (r × 100)	British public (Scottish public) (r × 100)
Issues of liberty				
Ban potentially disorderly political demonstration	27	20 (10)	30	16 (.)
Ban publication of confidential government documents	49	26 (24)	49	22 (21)
Support death penalty	45	19 (17)	43	11 (.)
Suspend civil rights in an emergency	42	16 (15)	38	17 (13)
Issues of equality				
Ban private medicine	−46	−24 (−17)	−51	−25 (−19)
Support job quotas for women	−35	−11 (.)	−38	. (+12)
ethnic and racial minorities	−45	−17 (−12)	−43	−19 (−15)
the disabled	−32	(−10)	−31	−15 (.)

Note: Correlations less than 0.10 have been replaced by full points.

understanding how people's attitudes to rights and liberties may be formed, reshaped, or substantially changed. We consider how a range of people's specific and personal experiences—of discrimination, of contact with government and the police, and of participation in their communities or engagement with national politics—affected their attitudes towards both the principles and practice of rights.

NOTES

1. In 1793, for example, the Scots John Morton, James Anderson, and Malcolm Craig were charged with sedition for being members of a 'Club for Equality and Freedom'; while John Elder and William Stewart were charged with sedition for possessing a medallion inscribed with 'A nation is the source of all sovereignty' on one side, and 'Liberty and Equality' on the other. See Peter Berresford Ellis and Seumas Mac a'Ghobhainn, *The Scottish Insurrection of 1820* (London: Pluto Press, 1989), 61. For a much more recent emphasis on the linkage between liberty and equality, see Roy Hattersley, *Choose Freedom: The Future for Democratic Socialism* (London: Michael Joseph, 1987); a shorter and more recent version of his argument appears as Roy Hattersley, 'Though Equality to Liberty', in William L. Miller (ed.), *Alternatives to Freedom: Arguments and Opinions* (London: Longman, 1995), 133–50.
2. Brian Girvin, 'Varieties of Conservatism', in Brian Girvin (ed.), *The Transformation of Contemporary Conservatism* (London: Sage, 1988), 1–12, at 9–10.
3. Desmond S. King, *The New Right: Politics, Markets and Citizenship* (London: Macmillan, 1987), 16–17.
4. Ibid. 23.
5. Ibid. 24.
6. The effect of party loyalty on voting choice in the 1979 Scotland Act Referendum and, to a much lesser extent, on attitudes towards devolution, is shown in a sequence of 16 surveys reported in William L. Miller, *The End of British Politics? Scots and English Political Behaviour in the Seventies* (Oxford: Oxford University Press, 1981), 251.
7. An extreme example of such scepticism is David Butler and Donald Stokes, *Political Change in Britain: The Evolution of Political Choice* (London: Macmillan, 1974), 323–37, at 329, where they suggest that only 25% of the public 'ever thought of themselves personally as being to the left, centre or right in politics'. In retrospect that finding seems an artefact of the way they put the question.
8. On the SNP capture of former Liberal Party areas and voters, see Miller, *The End of British Politics*, 205–6.
9. Ted Honderich, *Conservatism* (London: Hamish Hamilton, 1990; Penguin, 1991), 123 of the Penguin edition.
10. Paul M. Sniderman, Joseph F. Fletcher, Peter H. Russell, Philip E. Tetlock, and Brian J. Gaines, 'The Fallacy of Democratic Élitism: Élite Competition and Commitment to Civil Liberties' *British Journal of Political Science*, 21 (1991), 349–70, at

349. They go on to suggest on p. 368 that in a two-party system the distribution of opinion on civil liberties might be bi-modal amongst the highly partisan élite, though uni-modal amongst the less partisan public. Britain is not a very polarized two-party system, however. It has a well-supported centre, in terms of both party and ideology. Perhaps that explains why we found that liberty and equality were uni-modal amongst both public and politicians. Though the variances were higher amongst politicians, the distributions remained clearly uni-modal.

11. Herbert McClosky and Alida Brill, *Dimensions of Tolerance: What Americans Believe about Civil Liberties* (New York: Russell Sage Foundation, 1983), 291, and 290–6 generally.

12. Anthony Heath *et al.*, *Understanding Political Change: The British Voter 1964–87* (Oxford: Pergamon, 1991), 174–5.

13. Of course, any other set of numbers would be equivalent, for calculating correlations, provided the Liberal Democrats were placed halfway between Labour and Conservative, and the SNP halfway between Labour and the Liberal Democrats.

14. Butler and Stokes, *Political Change in Britain*, suggest on p. 334 that 60% of the British public have 'no recognition' and a further 20% only 'minimal recognition' of the ideological meaning of the terms left and right. That is totally inconsistent with our findings. However, we have sought to uncover the meaning the public gives to these terms, not set them a test to see whether they conformed to our understanding of them.

15. Alan Marsh, *Protest and Political Consciousness* (London: Sage, 1977), 170–1, quoting M. Rokeach, *The Nature of Human Values* (New York: Free Press, 1973). No doubt their response to our findings would be that our extremes were insufficiently extreme for their hypothesized pattern to become visible. If so, that pattern could apply only to a very few people with very extreme ideologies.

16. We explore within-party variations in principles and ideology further in Chapter 12.

10

Personal Experience

IN this chapter we move from the broad questions of social background, partisanship, and ideology to look at people's more personal and specific experience of being a *victim* of discrimination, a *consumer* of state services, or a *participant* in social and political life. Although the causes of these experiences may be interesting in themselves, we are more interested here in their consequences—in the impact that these kinds of experiences may have on people's attitudes to civil, political, and social rights.

EXPERIENCE AS A VICTIM OF DISCRIMINATION

We began by asking our respondents directly whether they had ever suffered discrimination: 'Have you personally ever felt discriminated against, in some important matter, on grounds of your sex, race, ethnic background, religion, age, disability, or political beliefs?' To those who said they had personal experience of discrimination we put two further questions: 'Was that mainly because of sex, race, ethnic background, religion, age, disability, or political beliefs? And was that mainly by an employer, the police, a local or national government official, or someone else?'

Needless to say, we can report only what our respondents told us. Our findings concern perceived experience of discrimination not experience itself. Whether the reality exceeds or falls short of the level of complaints we cannot say. Many may not complain of real discrimination. And variations in the propensity to complain across social groups may greatly affect our findings. However, it seems to us that it is the perception of personal discrimination—rather than some 'objective' reality—that is most likely to affect commitment to our general principles of liberty and equality (Table 10.1).

Women, young people, and (our very small subsample of) ethnic minorities were particularly likely to complain about personal discrimination. Education and political experience also had this effect. Complaints about personal experience of discrimination were much higher amongst university graduates than other members of the public; and considerably higher amongst political leaders. In both cases, it is possible that their greater exposure to

TABLE 10.1. *Personal experience of discrimination*

	Politicians (%)	British public (%)	(Scottish public) (%)
All respondents	41	28	(27)

debates about discrimination made it easier for graduates and politicians to identify and complain about their experiences. Indeed, it is significant that complaints about discrimination rose steadily with people's level of interest in politics.

The interaction of gender with either political leadership or education produced very high levels of complaints: 65 per cent of female politicians, and 56 per cent of female graduates in the British public, complained of discrimination. Amongst the public, women were only 10 per cent more likely than men to complain about discrimination, but amongst politicians women were 28 per cent more likely to do so. And within the public, women with no educational qualifications were only 3 per cent more likely to complain of discrimination than similarly unqualified men, but graduate women were 22 per cent more likely to do so than graduate men (Tables 10.2 and 10.3).

Grounds for Discrimination

Amongst the public, the main grounds for the alleged discrimination were gender (37 per cent), followed by age (21 per cent)—except in Scotland, where slightly more complained of religious discrimination (17 per cent) than age discrimination (16 per cent). Combining complaints about racial and ethnic discrimination, words which may indicate fine distinctions to political theorists but perhaps not to the public, showed 13 per cent in Britain and slightly less in Scotland complaining of discrimination on these grounds—putting racial/ethnic discrimination in third place in Britain as a whole, though fourth in Scotland (Table 10.4).

Interestingly, the grounds on which politicians claimed personal experience of discrimination were rather different from those of the public at large. While amongst those members of the public who complained of discrimination only 7 per cent said it was because of their political beliefs, 52 per cent of those politicians who complained of discrimination said it was political discrimination. Conversely, while 37 per cent of the public who complained of discrimination said it was sex discrimination, only 19 per cent of politicians

TABLE 10.2. *Experience of discrimination by social background*

	Politicians (%)	British public (%)	(Scottish public) (%)
Age			
<25	n.a.	39	(35)
25–35	55	36	(34)
35–55	48	29	(27)
>55	33	19	(19)
Educational qualifications			
none	33	19	(19)
school	45	33	(31)
university	40	44	(38)
Gender			
men	37	23	(25)
women	65	33	(30)
Racial self-image			
black or Asian	66	52	(60)
white	41	28	(27)
Interest in politics			
none	31	23	(21)
some	33	25	(24)
a lot	34	34	(32)
a great deal	44	37	(41)

TABLE 10.3. *Experience of discrimination by education and gender in combination*

	Politicians		British public (Scottish public)	
	Men (%)	Women (%)	Men (%)	Women (%)
Educational qualifications				
none	31	48	17 (22)	20 (17)
school	41	70	25 (25)	39 (37)
university	35	64	34 (31)	56 (47)

TABLE 10.4. *Grounds of discrimination*

	Politicians (%)	British public (%)	(Scottish public) (%)
Gender	19	37	(37)
Age	8	21	(16)
Race or ethnicity	6	13	(10)
Religion	5	8	(17)
Politics	52	7	(9)
Disability	2	4	(4)
Other	8	10	(7)

Note: Figures are percentages of those who alleged discrimination.

who complained of discrimination said it was sex discrimination. Relatively few politicians complained of anything else: less than 8 per cent in each case said the discrimination they had suffered had been on grounds of age, race, or religion. No doubt these infrequent causes of discrimination were strongly felt by the small minority of politicians who experienced them personally, of course.

But what types of discrimination did different groups of citizens complain of most? Amongst those members of the general public who complained of any form of discrimination, the young and old—but not the middle aged— were particularly likely to complain of age discrimination; and old people were also particularly likely to complain of discrimination on grounds of disability. The highly educated complained most frequently about sex discrimination and proved particularly unlikely to complain about religious discrimination. Unsurprisingly, women were eight times more likely than men to complain of sex discrimination; and those whose racial self-image was 'black' or 'Asian' were six times more likely than those whose racial self-image was 'white' to complain of racial or ethnic discrimination (Table 10.5).

Amongst politicians who complained of discrimination, age had little effect upon allegations of discrimination, but the other patterns reflected those in the British public. In particular, 70 per cent of women politicians but only 4 per cent of men complained of sex discrimination, and 32 per cent of black or Asian politicians but only 6 per cent of whites complained of racial or ethnic discrimination.

Over half the politicians of all ages, and close to half at all levels of education, complained of political discrimination. While 63 per cent of male politicians compared to only 14 per cent of female politicians complained of

TABLE 10.5. *Grounds of discrimination named by social background, British public only*

	Age				Educational qualifications			Gender		Racial self-image	
	<25 (%)	25–35 (%)	35–55 (%)	>55 (%)	None (%)	School (%)	Univ. (%)	Men (%)	Women (%)	Black and Asian (%)	White (%)
Experienced discrimination on grounds of											
age	28	14	20	29							
disability	1	2	5	7							
gender					27	39	45	7	56		
religion					14	7	4				
race/ethnicity										62	10

Notes: Figures are percentages of those who alleged discrimination.

For emphasis, only those entries most relevant to the particular social background categories are shown.

326 *Influences*

political discrimination, the discrepancy can be explained, in part, by the fact that we asked people to identify the single main reason for the discrimination they had suffered. The high level of complaints about sex discrimination from female politicians, and the high level of complaints about racial discrimination from black and Asian politicians, left less scope for complaints by these groups about other forms of discrimination.

The Culprits

Although politicians and the public differed sharply on the alleged causes of discrimination, they were more agreed on the culprits: by far the greatest number of complaints were about employers—47 per cent in the case of politicians, 57 per cent in the case of the British public, and as high as 62 per cent in Scotland. Discrimination in the workplace, and especially by *employers* rather than by employees, was by far the most significant cause of complaints. A long way behind employers, just under a third of each group said the discrimination they had suffered had been at the hands of unspecified 'other people'.

In terms of political culture it is very significant that so few members of the public blamed the police or government officials for their experience of discrimination. Amongst those who complained, only 8 per cent of the public (though 20 per cent of politicians) blamed government officials, and only 6 per cent of the public and a mere 2 per cent of politicians blamed the police. By comparison, although it was not explicitly based on personal experience, a recent survey of public opinion in the former Soviet Union, found that well over 80 per cent of respondents did *not* expect fair treatment by government officials.[1] Once again, however, we must remember that the small numbers who did complain about discrimination by the police or other government officials in Britain no doubt felt very strongly about it (Table 10.6).

The Consequences of Discrimination

But fascinating though these social patterns of discrimination may be, our main concern here is with the political consequences of perceived discrimination. Complaints of discrimination correlated with greater commitment to both liberty and equality. As one might expect, those who complained of discrimination showed more opposition to authority, greater tolerance, and greater sympathy for the socially disadvantaged and for activists, though not for militants. They had less confidence in the judicial system, though, surprisingly, not much more confidence in rights-enforcement agencies

TABLE 10.6. *Sources of discrimination*

	Politicians (%)	British public (%)	(Scottish public) (%)
Employers	47	57	(62)
Other people	30	28	(30)
Government officials	20	8	(5)
Police	2	6	(3)

Note: Figures are percentages of those who alleged discrimination.

TABLE 10.7. *Correlations between principles, sympathies, and experience of discrimination*

	Politicians (r × 100)	British public (r × 100)	(Scottish public) (r × 100)
Commitment to			
liberty	19	18	(16)
equality	17	.	(12)
Sympathies for			
activists	21	17	(17)
socially disadvantaged	21	16	(18)
militants	13	.	(.)
judicial system	−20	−17	(−17)
rights enforcers	.	.	(.)

Note: Correlations less than 0.10 have been replaced by full points.

such as the Equal Opportunities Commission or the Commission for Racial Equality.

Amongst the public, those who complained of discrimination scored 12 points higher on commitment to liberty but only 3 points higher on commitment to equality. They were 12 points more sympathetic to activists, 13 points more sympathetic to the socially disadvantaged, and 12 points less sympathetic to the judicial system (Table 10.7).

However, it was the *nature* of the alleged discrimination rather than the experience of discrimination *per se* that generated the most striking differences of principle or sympathy amongst different groups of citizens. As the vast majority of the public who complained of discrimination alleged that this had been on grounds of gender, age, race/ethnicity, and religion, we shall restrict our analysis to these four categories in order to avoid basing our conclusions on excessively small subsamples.

Compared to those who did not complain of discrimination, those who said they had suffered gender or racial/ethnic discrimination scored 16 points higher on liberty, though only between 6 and 9 points higher on equality; they also proved between 17 and 20 points more favourable to activists, and between 19 and 24 points more favourable to the socially disadvantaged, but between 10 and 23 points less favourable to the judicial system.

By contrast, however, those who alleged age discrimination were fairly close, on all these scales, to those who had suffered no discrimination at all. And those who complained of discrimination on grounds of religion were actually *less* committed to liberty or equality than those who said they had suffered no discrimination at all (Table 10.8).

We were not surprised to find that those who complained of different kinds of discrimination differed socially from each other—and from those who did not complain of any kind of discrimination. Those who complained of gender discrimination were 93 per cent female, while 32 per cent of those who complained of racial or ethnic discrimination said they were black or Asian. Those who complained of age discrimination were twice as likely to be under 25 years old as those who did not complain at all. Those who complained of religious discrimination were more likely to accept a religious designation (96 per cent compared to 83 per cent amongst the uncomplaining), less likely to identify with the Established Churches of England or Scotland (only 12 per cent compared to 60 per cent of the uncomplaining), and more likely to be Protestant Nonconformists (29 per cent compared to 8 per cent), Catholic (38 per cent compared to 13 per cent), Jewish or Muslim (12 per cent compared to less than 1 per cent of the uncomplaining).

Since these social groups differed to a greater or lesser extent on principles and sympathies, we might suspect that social bias alone could account for some of the differences in attitudes between those who complained of discrimination and those who did not. To test this we can remove the effect of social bias by weighting the social composition of those who did not complain of discrimination to make it the same as for those who did.

Let us start with the example of those who complained of gender discrimination first of all. First, we weighted the gender composition of those who did not complain of any kind of discrimination to make it the same as amongst those who complained of gender discrimination—that is, 93 per cent female—and recalculated the mean scores on each principle and prejudice for this

TABLE 10.8. *Principles and sympathies by experience of discrimination, public only (scores on +/−100 scale)*

| | British public (Scottish public) | | | | |
| | Commitment to | | Sympathies for | | |
	Liberty (scores)	Equality (scores)	Activists (scores)	Socially disadvantaged (scores)	Judicial system (scores)
Personally experienced discrimination?					
no	−28 (−28)	54 (59)	−17 (−16)	14 (24)	28 (28)
yes	−16 (−18)	57 (64)	−5 (−4)	27 (38)	16 (16)
Experience discrimination on grounds of					
gender	−12 (−9)	63 (67)	3 (−2)	38 (49)	18 (9)
race or ethnicity	−12 (−13)	60 (63)	0 (−4)	33 (27)	5 (12)
age	−22 (−18)	51 (60)	−15 (−7)	14 (36)	23 (7)
religion	−31 (−31)	49 (64)	−32 (−15)	19 (30)	23 (14)

weighted sample. Because it is so female, commitment to liberty in this weighted sample of non-complainers sinks from minus 28 to minus 31, which therefore actually *increases* our estimate of the effect, on attitudes to liberty, of experiencing gender discrimination from 16 points to 19.

This same technique can be used to remove the effects of biased social profiles from estimates of the effect of racial/ethnic, age, and religious discrimination. However, it makes little difference to estimates of the effects of any kind of discrimination: the estimated effect on attitudes towards liberty of experiencing gender discrimination rises, as we have seen, from 16 to 19 points; the estimated effect of racial/ethnic discrimination slips from 16 to 14 points; while the estimated effect of age discrimination slips from a trivial 6 to just 3 points; and the estimated effect of religious discrimination is reduced to zero. Similarly the estimated effect on confidence in the judicial system of gender discrimination remains at 10 points, while that of racial/ethnic discrimination slips from 23 to 18 points; and that of age or religious discrimination becomes even more trivial than before.

In short, these careful controls for social bias merely strengthen and confirm our original finding that it was only personal experience of gender or racial/ethnic discrimination that was reflected in greater commitment to liberty or less confidence in the judicial system. Personal experience of discrimination could have a powerful effect upon basic principles and prejudices, but the effect depended critically upon the basis for that discrimination and on its source (Table 10.9).

People's principles and sympathies were clearly affected by the sources of the discrimination they experienced. In particular we noticed that the few people who complained of police discrimination gave 22 points more support to liberty than those who did not complain at all; they were 23 points more sympathetic to activists; and, most striking of all, they had a massive 41 points less confidence in the judicial system.

Although the experience of discrimination by the police or government agencies did have a large impact on people's principles and sympathies, experience of discrimination was seldom blamed on government or its agents. Although, as we shall see in the next section people had a great deal of contact with state officials, much of it was entirely satisfactory to them.

EXPERIENCE AS A CONSUMER OF GOVERNMENT SERVICES

In order to investigate the effects of interaction with agents of government we looked at personal experience of using government services in education,

TABLE 10.9. *Effect of experience of discrimination on commitment to principles, after controls for social profiles of complainers, British public only (scores on +/-100 scale)*

	Commitment to		Activists (scores)	Sympathies for	
	Liberty (scores)	Equality (scores)		Socially disadvantaged (scores)	Judicial system (scores)
Amongst those who have experienced					
no discrimination	-28	54	-17	14	28
gender discrimination	-12	63	3	38	18
no discrimination, weighted to gender profile of above	-31	57	-16	17	28
racial or ethnic discrimination	-12	60	0	33	5
no discrimination, weighted to racial profile of above	-26	57	-14	17	23
age discrimination	-22	51	-15	14	23
no discrimination, weighted to age profile of above	-25	54	-15	15	26
religious discrimination	-31	49	-32	19	23
no discrimination, weighted to sectarian profile of above	-31	56	-18	13	27

health, and social welfare, and at personal experience of dealing with the
police, councillors, MPs, and civil servants in local and national government
offices.

We asked whether our respondents, or anyone in their households, had
benefited from government-provided services by receiving unemployment
benefit, income support, or NHS hospital treatment in the past few years.
About a third said someone in their household had received unemployment
benefit or income support, and three-quarters that someone in their household had used NHS hospital services. We also asked whether people had
opted out of government-provided services by using either private schools or
private medicine. More politicians, but fewer Scots, tended to opt out of
state education and health care, and recourse to private schooling or private
medicine was strongly related to class amongst both politicians and the
public.

We asked our respondents about their personal experience of contacting
government officials, both elected and non-elected, in particular whether
they had 'personally ever contacted' an elected local councillor, council
offices, their MP, or an office of a central-government department such as
the DHSS, DoT, or DoE about some problem. We also asked about any
contact they had had with the police—either as a result of being stopped and
interviewed or as a result of being a victim of crime.

We were not at all surprised to find that a large majority of politicians said
they had contacted both elected and non-elected officials, nor that a majority
of the public had never made such contacts, but we were interested to find
a much higher level of contacts in our sample of the public than that uncovered by Parry, Moyser, and Day in their study of British political participation in 1984, though their questions used a different time-frame and some of
their figures are implausibly low by any standard (Table 10.10).[2]

Just under half the public and just over half the politicians claimed to have
been victims of crime—which frequently involved subsequent contacts with
the police. And many more politicians, 66 per cent compared to 42 per cent
of the public, said they had been stopped and questioned by the police, either
about traffic violations or about other matters. Amongst both politicians and
the public, the young were much more likely than the old to report that they
had been stopped by the police (amongst the public, 17 per cent more) and,
running counter to common cultural misperceptions, somewhat more likely
to report having been victims of crime (amongst the public, 6 per cent more).
These questions, like our questions about discrimination, were phrased in
terms of 'have you ever . . .'; and since experience is necessarily cumulative,
any individual necessarily acquires more experiences, of whatever kind, as

TABLE 10.10. *The extent of personal contact with agents of government*

	Politicians (%)	British public (%)	(Scottish public) (%)
Had received unemployment benefit, etc.	20	34	(37)
Household had NHS hospital treatment	74	73	(73)
Used private schools	15	7	(3)
Used private medicine	25	18	(9)
Been stopped by police	66	42	(36)
Been crime victim	56	48	(43)
Contacted			
councillor	70	35	(35)
council offices	92	44	(40)
MP	91	25	(22)
(central) government offices	82	46	(45)

they grow older. But memories also fade, and different generations have different experiences. In any case, we were primarily concerned with the impact of consciously remembered experience upon attitudes towards principles.

Satisfaction

We asked those who had been stopped by the police, whether they had been treated 'courteously or rudely'; and those who had contacted councillors, council officials, MPs, and civil servants, or who had contacted the police after being a victim of crime, whether they had found these contacts 'helpful or unhelpful'. Only a small minority of those politicians (14 per cent) or the public (19 per cent) who had been stopped by the police had found them rude. But, though a similar proportion of politicians (19 per cent) who had initiated contacts with the police in the wake of a crime had found them unhelpful, the public's experience was more negative: a third of them complained that, in these circumstances, the police had been unhelpful.

This discrepancy between the experience of politicians and the public grew larger when we asked about contacting councillors and council officials, but reduced in the context of contacting MPs and central-government civil servants. Naturally enough, our leading local-government politicians very seldom found those in *local government* unhelpful, and they had an

TABLE 10.11. *Dissatisfaction with agents of government*

	Politicians (%)	British public (%)	(Scottish public) (%)
NHS hospital			
If used: dissatisfied	6	11	(8)
If satisfied: because of staff	81	82	(83)
If dissatisfied: because of resources	63	56	(75)
If stopped by police: police rude	14	19	(23)
If crime victim: police unhelpful	19	32	(28)
If contacted			
councillor unhelpful	8	29	(35)
council offices unhelpful	5	34	(37)
MP unhelpful	18	26	(22)
government offices unhelpful	28	31	(28)

Note: Figures are percentages of those who had a view one way or the other—that is, they exclude 'don't knows', 'neither helpful nor unhelpful', etc.

easier time than the public when approaching the police, but they experienced a similar degree of unhelpfulness as the public when contacting the offices of *central government.*

Only about one-tenth of the public, and less amongst politicians, were dissatisfied with their experience of NHS hospital treatment. We asked why people were satisfied or dissatisfied with it and, in particular, whether that was because of the staff or the resources available. Of those who had a view, over 80 per cent attributed their *satisfaction* to the staff, while around 60 per cent (75 per cent in Scotland) attributed their *dissatisfaction* to lack of resources. Rightly or wrongly, NHS staff seem to have won the credit and escaped the blame (Table 10.11).

The Consequences of Dissatisfaction

By themselves, contact with councillors, council offices, MPs, or government departments, or the simple fact of using NHS hospital treatment, were largely uncorrelated with principles and sympathies. However, recourse to private education and health care was correlated with opposition to the principle of equality, and the experience of being stopped and questioned by the police was correlated with support for the principle of liberty.

We might expect that those who were consciously dissatisfied with their personal experience of government and its agents would have a greater commitment to liberty and less confidence in established authority. And indeed, satisfaction or dissatisfaction with these contacts mattered more than mere contact. Although dissatisfaction with treatment in an NHS hospital failed to correlate with principles or sympathies, adverse experience of the police, government offices, MPs, councillors, or council offices correlated quite strongly with a lack of confidence in the judicial and political systems. The strongest correlations were between adverse experience of the police and lack of confidence in the judicial system. But although these experiences seem to have generated direct reactions against the judicial and political systems, they had much less impact upon principles, though adverse experience with the police and, to a lesser extent, with central-government officials did correlate with greater commitment to liberty (Tables 10.12 and 10.13).

Since commitment to liberty correlated both with the fact of being stopped by the police and, if stopped, with the police being rude, we might expect that the two effects would cumulate. In fact, police behaviour mattered far more than the mere fact of being stopped. Compared to those members of the public who were not stopped by the police, those who were stopped but treated courteously scored only 9 points higher on our scale of liberty, but those who were stopped and treated rudely scored 24 points higher. And the distinction between the effects of simply being stopped and the effects of police behaviour was even more clear in terms of confidence in the judicial system: those members of the public who were stopped but courteously treated actually had 3 points *more* confidence in the judicial system than those who were not stopped at all, while those who were treated rudely had 30 points *less*.

As we might reasonably expect, police behaviour in these circumstances had no effect at all on the second dimension of principle, commitment to equality (Table 10.14).

EXPERIENCE AS A PARTICIPANT IN POLITICS

Those who advocate increased social and political participation have often argued that, amongst its many other virtues, participation would encourage and strengthen liberal and democratic values: 'the major function of participation in the theory of participatory democracy is . . . an educative one, educative in the widest sense, including both the psychological aspect and the gaining of practice in democratic skills and procedures';[3] 'civic activity

TABLE 10.12. *Correlations between age, principles, sympathies, and extent of contact with government agents*

	Age (old) (r × 100)	Commitment to		Confidence in	
		Liberty (r × 100)	Equality (r × 100)	Political system (r × 100)	Judical system (r × 100)
POLITICIANS					
used private schools	.	−12	−29	.	18
used private medicine	.	−14	−33	.	21
stopped by police	−17	18	.	.	−14
crime victim	−17	20	.	.	−13
BRITISH PUBLIC (SCOTTISH PUBLIC)					
used private schools	. (.)	. (.)	−12 (−14)	. (.)	. (.)
used private medicine	. (.)	. (.)	−17 (.)	. (.)	. (.)
stopped by police	−13 (−11)	20 (19)	−11 (−10)	. (.)	. (.)
crime victim	. (−11)	10 (16)	. (.)	. (.)	−11 (−10)

Note: Correlations less than 0.10 have been replaced by full points.

TABLE 10.13. *Correlations between age, principles, sympathies, and dissatisfaction with government agents*

	Age (old)	Commitment to		Confidence in	
	(r × 100)	Liberty (r × 100)	Equality (r × 100)	Political system (r × 100)	Judicial system (r × 100)
POLITICIANS					
If stopped: police rude	.	.	.	.	−21
If crime victim: police unhelpful	−11	19	11	−17	−34
If contacted					
councillor unhelpful	.	.	.	−13	−11
council offices unhelpful	.	.	.	−12	−13
MP unhelpful	−11	23	16	−23	−24
government office unhelpful	−15	19	.	−17	−21
BRITISH PUBLIC (SCOTTISH PUBLIC)					
If stopped: police rude	−19 (−26)	19 (15)	. (12)	−15 (−17)	−38 (−37)
If crime victim: police unhelpful	−15 (−13)	. (.)	11 (.)	−15 (.)	−23 (−27)
If contacted					
councillor unhelpful	−10 (.)	. (.)	. (.)	−15 (−28)	−15 (−26)
council offices unhelpful	−16 (−16)	. (.)	. (.)	−18 (−21)	−16 (−23)
MP unhelpful	−19 (.)	. (.)	. (.)	−14 (−20)	−14 (−21)
government office unhelpful	−14 (.)	14 (.)	. (.)	. (−10)	−22 (−25)

Note: Correlations less than 0.10 have been replaced by full points.

TABLE 10.14.   *Effect of police behaviour on commitment to principles and sympathies* (scores on +/–100 scale)

	Politicians			British public (Scottish public)		
	Commitment to		Confidence in Judicial System (scores)	Commitment to		Confidence in Judicial System (scores)
	Liberty (scores)	Equality (scores)		Liberty (scores)	Equality (scores)	
If not stopped by police	−21	58	35	−30 (−29)	57 (62)	26 (27)
If stopped and treated						
courteously	−8	52	28	−21 (−21)	51 (56)	29 (28)
rudely	−4	60	6	−6 (−10)	56 (62)	−4 (−2)

educates individuals how to think publicly as citizens . . . politics becomes its own university, citizenship its own training ground, and participation its own tutor.'[4] So we looked to see whether those who participated most had distinctive principles or sympathies.

Psychological Involvement with Politics

Participation can be social or political; and it can be public and active, or more private, personal, and psychological. It may seem to distort and devalue the meaning of 'participation' if we include mere psychological involvement with politics. Advocates of participatory democracy would not accept psychological involvement as 'participation'. They mean something much more active than that. Indeed, even electoral participation is not enough to satisfy them: 'some advocates of participatory democracy are not enthusiastic about direct legislation [referendums, etc.] as the right path to human development . . . [because] voting demands only the most minimal commitment . . . [and] is conducted in secret and therefore irresponsibly.'[5]

Mere psychological involvement with politics is certainly a very weak form of participation, yet it may be a necessary foundation for more active involvement and it is quite possible that a keen interest in political news and current affairs, or a purely psychological identification with political parties, might, by itself, affect political attitudes. McClosky and Brill claim that 'respect for the freedom of others and for their right to think and act as they choose is also furthered by greater exposure to the media, residence in a cosmopolitan environment, and by membership in educated and sophisticated

TABLE 10.15. *Extent of psychological involvement with politics*

	Politicians (%)	British public (%)	(Scottish public) (%)
Watch current affairs on TV	75	69	(73)
Attention to politics			
none	3	29	(28)
some	3	32	(34)
quite a lot	22	28	(27)
a great deal	71	12	(11)
Party supporter			
not	10	47	(52)
supporter	5	24	(23)
strong supporter	85	29	(25)

subcultures'—none of which imply active physical involvement; 'whatever broadens one's perspective tends to generate empathy and promote tolerance by making one aware of the extraordinary variety of standards and forms of social organization under which different people have lived'.[6]

We used three measures of psychological involvement—whether people:

1. regularly watched 'current-affairs programmes like *Panorama* or *World in Action*' on television
2. paid 'a great deal of attention, quite a lot, some, or not much' attention to politics from day to day
3. described themselves as a 'supporter' of any political party (and, if so, how strongly).

Three-quarters of politicians and only slightly less of the public regularly watched current-affairs programmes on television, but that proved no real indicator of the depth of their interest in politics, since 71 per cent of politicians but only 12 per cent of the public said they paid 'a great deal' of attention to politics, while 29 per cent of the public but a mere 3 per cent of politicians said they paid 'none at all'. We suspect that this reflects a common perception amongst the public that 'politics' is about parties and government, rather than issues of current affairs, though it is also possible that people may watch television programmes in which they have little interest just because they find it relaxing or perhaps have nothing better to do with their time (Table 10.15).[7]

TABLE 10.16.   *Correlations between social background, principles, and psychological involvement with politics*

	Politicians			British public (Scottish public)		
	TV	Interest	Strength of party support	TV	Interest	Strength of party support
	(r × 100)	(r × 100)	(r × 100)	(r × 100)	(r × 100)	(r × 100)
Age (old)	.	−16	−20	10 (15)	12 (18)	12 (11)
Education (high)	.	16	13	. (.)	17 (11)	. (.)
Female	.	.	.	. (.)	−15 (−19)	. (.)
Liberty	.	18	17	. (.)	. (10)	. (.)
Equality	17	17	.	11 (.)	. (.)	. (12)

Note: Correlations less than 0.10 have been replaced by full points.

Only 29 per cent of the public, but 85 per cent of politicians, declared that they were 'strong' party supporters. Indeed 47 per cent of the public denied that they 'supported' a party to any degree at all. We should recall that some of our politicians led groups of Independent councillors, and might well deny that their activities and interests were 'political', which may explain why even 3 per cent of them denied any interest in politics and 10 per cent denied being party supporters.

Amongst the public, men paid more attention than women to politics. Both men and women may see 'politics', in the sense of parties and governments, as a very masculine arena.[8] Amongst both politicians and the public, psychological involvement with politics also correlated with high levels of education. But the most intriguing social pattern concerned age: psychological involvement correlated with older members of the public, yet with younger politicians. Amongst the public, both strong partisanship and an interest in politics *increased* with age, though they *decreased* with age amongst politicians. Amongst politicians, a strong sense of party identification declined sharply with age from 97 per cent amongst the young to 77 per cent amongst the old, while amongst the public it increased with age from 23 per cent amongst the young to 33 per cent amongst the old. Age clearly affected the partisanship of people and politicians in very different ways (Tables 10.16 and 10.17).

Neither interest in politics, nor addiction to TV current-affairs programmes, nor strength of partisanship correlated much with principles amongst the

TABLE 10.17. *Party support by age*

	Politicians			British public (Scottish public)			
	25–35 (%)	35–55 (%)	>55 (%)	<25 (%)	25–35 (%)	35–55 (%)	>55 (%)
Party supporter							
not	0	6	15	63 (63)	54 (59)	45 (49)	40 (45)
supporter	3	3	8	15 (19)	20 (19)	27 (23)	27 (29)
strong supporter	97	91	77	23 (18)	25 (22)	28 (28)	33 (27)

TABLE 10.18. *Correlation between commitments to liberty and equality, at different levels to interest in politics*

	Politicians (r × 100)	British public (r × 100)	(Scottish public) (r × 100)
Interest in politics			
none	−22	−19	(−21)
some	+18	−1	(−9)
quite a lot	+22	+11	(0)
a great deal	+34	+27	(+15)

public, however, though they correlated weakly with liberty and equality amongst politicians. However, interest in politics did affect the structure of people's attitude to principle—in much the same way as did education.[9] For example, the correlation between support for liberty and equality was fairly strongly negative amongst the least interested (as amongst the least educated) but fairly strongly positive amongst the most interested (as amongst the most educated)—and the pattern was sufficiently strong for this to be more than a simple reflection of the effect of education (Table 10.18).

As we saw in Chapter 9, the *direction* of partisanship did correlate strongly with principles, but its *strength* did not: mere psychological involvement with a party, irrespective of which party, had little connection with fundamental attitudes towards liberty or equality. Of course, strength of partisanship intensified the correlation that already existed between principle and the direction of partisanship: the attitudes to principles of very strong Labour supporters did differ from those of weak Labour supporters or casual Labour voters, and the principles of very strong Conservative supporters did differ from those of weak Conservative supporters or mere casual Conservative voters, but these differences ran in opposite directions, and therefore cancelled out in aggregate. Very strong party supporters were more polarized in terms of principles but not more liberal or egalitarian than those who identified less with parties.

So, while mere psychological involvement had some interesting 'second-order' effects upon attitudes to principle, it did not affect the levels of support for different principles. Perhaps more active involvement might have more net impact. We shall see.

Active Participation in Society and Politics

We used twelve measures of active participation. We asked people whether, in the last few years, they had taken an *active* part in:

- a sports club
- an arts organization, for example, a choir or a film club
- a school board, parent–teacher association, or other school organization
- a church or religious organization
- a charity organization, like Oxfam, Barnardos, Sue Ryder, or Famine Relief
- the affairs of a trade union or a professional association
- a business organization, for example, a Chamber of Commerce, or a Round Table
- an election campaign
- any other political campaign
- working with others in your community to solve some community problem.

We also asked whether they had

- signed a petition
- taken part in a demonstration, picket, march, or protest meeting.

These twelve measures of active involvement in society and politics[10] proved particularly revealing. As we noted at the start of Chapter 3, some theories of political participation suggest that any kind of political—or even purely social participation—will bring people so much into contact with the varied interests and opinions of others that it will make them more tolerant, broad minded, and liberal. Following that line of argument, we could combine our twelve measures of participation into a composite measure of civil and political activism, but we found that that obscured more than it illuminated; it did not, for example, produce clearer patterns of correlation with either social background or principles.

More usefully, we can divide our measures into four groups representing different kinds of active participation: first, active participation in what appear, on the surface, to be purely social organizations such as sports clubs or arts organizations; second, active participation in socio-political organizations whose primary function is social, but which very frequently try to influence political debate—such as, for example, churches and trade unions; third, active participation in electoral politics; and, fourth, active participation in various kinds of non-electoral politics (Table 10.19).

There were, of course, huge differences between politicians and the public in the extent of their overtly *political* activity of all kinds—whether electoral or non-electoral. But much less obviously, politicians were also much more active than the public in *socio-political* organizations, and even in what seemed *purely social* organizations. Even in sports clubs, politicians were a little more active than the public, which is truly remarkable when we consider that politicians were so much older than the public. And there were huge differences between politicians and the public on activity connected with socio-political organizations such as schools, charities, trade unions, and business organizations.

At the same time, politicians were less than total activists, even in political matters: slightly less than half said they had been on a protest march or attended a protest meeting 'in recent years', and only 62 per cent said they had been active in a political campaign other than an election campaign, though 95 per cent declared an active involvement in community action groups—appropriately enough for politicians engaged in local government.

Purely Social Organizations

Active participation in sports organizations was more frequent amongst the young, the highly educated, and males. Active participation in arts organizations was less socially structured, and only correlated with education. Neither of these activities correlated with commitment to equality, though both correlated weakly with commitment to liberty. Whatever effects such activity had, it must have been largely social; it certainly did not extend very far or very deeply into political culture (Table 10.20).

Socio-Political Organizations

Active participation in school-related organizations correlated only with education amongst the public, and with nothing at all amongst politicians. Amongst the public, women were slightly more active than men in charities, though such activity failed to correlate with principles; men, and the highly educated, were more active in trade-union or professional associations, though

TABLE 10.19. *Four types of active participation*

	Politicians (%)	British public (%)	(Scottish public) (%)
Took 'active' part in social organizations			
sports club	34	31	(31)
arts organization	26	12	(10)
Took 'active' part in socio-political organizations			
school organization	72	15	(10)
religious organization	32	18	(20)
charity organization	60	32	(27)
trade union or professional association	43	14	(13)
business organization	31	7	(5)
Took 'active' part in electoral politics			
election campaign	95	7	(7)
Took 'active' part in non-electoral politics			
other political campaign	62	3	(3)
community action group	95	25	(23)
signing a petition	80	70	(66)
demonstration, picket, march, or protest meeting	49	13	(15)

TABLE 10.20. *Correlations between social background, principles, and active participation in purely social organizations*

	Politicians		British public (Scottish public)	
	Sport (r × 100)	Arts (r × 100)	Sport (r × 100)	Arts (r × 100)
Age (old)	.	.	−19 (−16)	. (.)
Educational qualifications (high)	.	13	18 (18)	15 (13)
Women	.	.	−15 (−15)	. (.)
Liberty	.	.	11 (11)	12 (.)
Equality	.	.	. (.)	. (.)

Note: Correlations less than 0.10 have been replaced by full points.

such activity only correlated very weakly with liberty; men, and the middle class, were more active in business organizations, though such activity was only correlated very weakly with opposition to equality. So active participation in these socio-political organizations had little effect upon the principles or sympathies of the public.

However, amongst politicians, active involvement in trade-union or business organizations, though not in charities, was correlated much more strongly with principles and sympathies. Politicians who were active in trade unions were unusually committed to both liberty and equality, sympathetic to activists and the socially disadvantaged, and unsympathetic towards the judicial system. And, to a lesser extent, politicians active in business organizations had the opposite attitudes.

Active participation in religious organizations correlated with age, identifying with the middle class, and especially with being religious—though it should be remembered that most people who accepted a religious designation were *not active* in church or religious organizations (76 per cent of the religious in Scotland, 79 per cent in Britain, and 58 per cent of religious politicians did *not* participate actively in church or religious organizations), and a few who did not accept a religious designation were none the less willing to take an active party in a church organization. Religious activity was uncorrelated with commitment to equality, but it did correlate quite strongly with a lack of commitment to our macro-principle of liberty. However, it correlated even more strongly with the micro-principle of commitment to traditional values. Although actively religious politicians were somewhat more committed than others to the micro-principle of respect for authority and less committed to the micro-principle of tolerance, the negative correlation between actively religious politicians and liberty was due mainly to their commitment to the micro-principle of traditional values. And amongst the public, the negative correlation between being actively religious and liberty was due almost entirely to commitment to the micro-principle of traditional values (Tables 10.21 and 10.22).

Indeed, our measure of commitment to traditional values itself was based upon answers to two questions, one of which was the priority given to 'preserving traditional ideas of right and wrong', while the other was the priority given to 'following God's will'. If we disaggregate the micro-principle of traditional values, and look separately at the correlations between 'following God's will', 'preserving traditional ideas of right and wrong', and church activity, we find that, while a very modest correlation between church activity and 'traditional ideas of right and wrong' remains, most of the correlation is due to the use of the explicitly religious language about 'God's will'. So even the link between church activity and traditional values is more apparent than real. The high raw correlation between church activity and opposition to liberty is therefore misleading.

Electoral Politics

Very few politicians—mainly elderly, and only 5 per cent in total—denied being active in electoral campaigns. Conversely, almost equally few members of the public, only 7 per cent, claimed such involvement. Those who were active in electoral campaigns were slightly more committed to liberty, but the correlation was very weak (Table 10.23).

Non-Electoral Politics

In sharp contrast to all these findings of fairly weak or even non-existent correlations, we found consistently large correlations between principles and most forms of active participation in non-electoral politics. The exception was 'working with others in your community to solve some community problem', which failed to correlate with anything except education.

Signing petitions, taking an active part in demonstrations and protests, and (amongst politicians only) active participation in non-electoral campaigns were much more frequent amongst the young, the unreligious, and the highly educated. In view of the churches' historic use of processions as a peaceful method of witness to their faith, it is ironic perhaps that the religious were so much less likely than others to have been on a march or demonstration, or to have attended a protest meeting. On the other hand, it is easy to imagine

TABLE 10.21. *Correlations between social backgrounds, principles, sympathies, and active participation in socio-political organizations*

	Politicians					British public (Scottish public)				
	School (r × 100)	Charity (r × 100)	TU/Prof. (r × 100)	Business (r × 100)	Church (r × 100)	School (r × 100)	Charity (r × 100)	TU/Prof. (r × 100)	Business (r × 100)	Church (r × 100)
Religious	.	.	−11	.	36	.	.	. ()	. ()	17 (21)
Age (old)	.	.	−13	.	11	.	. (10)	. ()	. ()	11 (10)
Educational qualifications										
(high)	.	.	.	.	.	18 (21)	. (12)	14 (20)	. (12)	. (13)
Women	.	.	.	−11	.	. ()	11 (10)	−16 (−15)	−11 . ()	. (12)
Working class	.	.	13	.	.	. ()	. ()	. ()	−11 . ()	−11 (−10)
Liberty	.	.	22	−13	−30	. ()	. ()	11 (11)	. ()	−20 (−17)
Equality	.	.	24	−12	−11	. ()	. ()	. ()	−11 (−11)	. ()
Activists	.	.	29	−13	−15	. ()	. ()	10 (14)	. ()	. ()
Socially disadvantaged	.	.	30	−17	−13	. ()	. ()	. ()	. ()	. ()
Judicial system	.	.	−23	11	21	. ()	. ()	−11 . ()	. ()	. ()

Note: Correlations less than 0.10 have been replaced by full points.

TABLE 10.22. *Correlations between religious activity and alternative indicators of commitment to traditional values*

	Politicians (r × 100)	British public (r × 100)	(Scottish public) (r × 100)
Liberty	−30	−20	(−17)
Authority	14	.	(.)
Tolerance	−16	.	(.)
Traditional values	39	29	(28)
'Right and wrong'	16	10	(.)
'Following God's will'	45	35	(32)

Note: Correlations less than 0.10 have been replaced by full points.

TABLE 10.23. *Correlations between social background, principles, and active participation in electoral campaigns*

	Politicians (r × 100)	British public (r × 100)	(Scottish public) (r × 100)
Age (old)	−16	.	(.)
Liberty	12	.	(10)
Equality	.	.	(.)

Note: Correlations less than 0.10 have been replaced by full points.

why the old should not go on marches and demonstrations; and, although old age should be no barrier to signing a petition, it quite probably was a barrier to being in those places where signatures might be sought. And, since education encourages most kinds of political and social activity, it is not surprising that it correlated with non-electoral political activity.

Amongst the public, commitment to liberty correlated strongly with active participation in non-electoral campaigning, with signing petitions, and especially with taking part in demonstrations, pickets, marches, or protest meetings. Commitment to equality also correlated with taking part in demonstrations. Amongst politicians, liberty and equality both correlated strongly with active participation in all forms of non-electoral politics except community action (Table 10.24).

Those who had been active in demonstrations and protests scored low on

TABLE 10.24. *Correlations between social background, principles, sympathies, and active participation in non-electoral politics*

	Politicians				British public (Scottish public)			
	Community action group (r × 100)	Petition (r × 100)	Non-electoral campaign (r × 100)	Demonstration (r × 100)	Community action group (r × 100)	Petition (r × 100)	Non-electoral campaign (r × 100)	Demonstration (r × 100)
Religious	.	−18	−20	−28	. (.)	. (−10)	. (−13)	−20 (.)
Age (old)	.	−20	−26	−30	. (13)	−15 (−10)	. (.)	−18 (−13)
Educational qualifications (high)	.	10	18	11	14 (10)	18 (27)	. (.)	18 (14)
Women	.	.	.	.	. (.)	. (.)	. (.)	. (.)
Working class	.	.	.	14	. (.)	. (.)	. (.)	. (.)
Liberty	.	25	34	45	. (.)	18 (24)	18 (16)	31 (22)
Equality	.	34	18	45	. (.)	. (.)	. (.)	18 (16)
Activists	.	34	27	50	. (.)	13 (13)	10 (11)	25 (24)
Socially disadvantaged	.	29	28	48	. (.)	10 (21)	12 (.)	20 (22)
Judicial system	.	−24	−26	−42	. (.)	. (.)	−13 (−13)	−24 (−21)
Rights enforcers	.	21	19	34	. (.)	. (.)	. (.)	. (10)

Notes: Demonstration = Demonstration, picket, march, or protest meeting.
Correlations less than 0.10 have been replaced by full points.

our micro-principles of respect for authority, traditional values, or wealth creation, and high on tolerance, limited government, and (naturally enough) rights of protest and rebellion. Perhaps it is worth emphasizing here that the micro-principle of rights of protest and rebellion was *not* included in the computation of either of our macro-principles, liberty and equality; so our findings about macro-principles involved no spurious circularity caused merely by question wording.

Amongst the public, the correlations with protest action were generally strongest with micro-principles associated with liberty, especially respect for authority. The greatest correlation with any micro-principle associated with equality was with equal rights, rather less with economic equality, and hardly any at all with caring. Protest activity also correlated strongly with sympathy for activists and the socially disadvantaged but not with sympathy for militants; and with a lack of confidence in the judicial system but not with attitudes towards the political system, civil institutions, or even towards rights enforcers.

Amongst politicians, correlations with protest activity were very strong indeed: protest activity correlated at 0.50 with sympathy for activists, and 0.48 with sympathy for the socially disadvantaged, 0.42 with a lack of confidence in the judicial system, 0.49 with rejection of authority, and 0.47 with support for limited government. And amongst politicians, unlike the public, active involvement in protests and demonstrations correlated as well with support for economic equality and equal rights as it did with opposition to authority and traditional values.

Effect on Mean Scores for Liberty and Equality

Correlations may fail to detect a real and interesting link between principles and active involvement when only a very few people are active (or only a very few are not active) in a particular way. That applies especially to public involvement in business organizations (7 per cent), election campaigns (7 per cent), and 'other political campaigns' (only 3 per cent); and to politicians' involvement in election campaigns (95 per cent) and community action groups (95 per cent). So, as a double check on our conclusions, we have calculated the mean scores on our +/−100 scales for liberty and equality amongst those who did and did not participate in each of the twelve kinds of activity, and computed the differences between the scores of the active and the inactive (Table 10.25).

This approach confirms the weakness of the link between principle and active participation in social organizations, charities, and community action groups; the somewhat stronger link with active participation in trade-union

TABLE 10.25. *Effect of active participation on commitment to principles* (scores on +/-100 scale)

	Difference between active and inactive on liberty score			Difference between active and inactive on equality score		
	Politicians (scores)	British public (scores)	(Scottish public) (scores)	Politicians (scores)	British public (scores)	(Scottish public) (scores)
Social organization						
sports	-3	+7	(+6)	0	-3	(-4)
arts	+4	+11	(+6)	0	0	(-2)
school	0	+4	(+7)	+4	0	(-2)
Socio-political organization						
religious	-22	-15	(-12)	-6	-1	(-1)
charity	-3	+1	(+2)	0	+2	(-1)
trade union/professional	+15	+9	(+9)	+12	+4	(+5)
business	-10	+2	(+3)	-7	-10	(-10)
Electoral politics						
election campaign	+19	+6	(+11)	+8	0	(+6)
Non-electoral politics						
'other' political campaign	+23	+31	(+25)	+10	+10	(+7)
community action group	-5	+5	(+3)	+3	0	(+2)
signing a petition	+21	+12	(+14)	+22	+4	(+2)
demonstration, protest, etc.	+31	+27	(+18)	+23	+12	(+9)

Note: Figures are the score amongst those who were actively involved minus the score amongst those who were not actively involved.

or professional organizations, and churches or religious organizations; and the particularly strong links with all forms of non-electoral political activity except community action. But it suggests a stronger link than the correlation analysis revealed between principles and both electoral and non-electoral campaigning. The very few members of the public who were actively involved in non-electoral political campaigns scored 31 points higher on liberty than the vast majority who were not; and the very few politicians who were *not* actively involved in electoral campaigns scored 19 points less on liberty than the vast majority who were. Indeed, this second approach confirms our finding that active involvement was generally linked more to liberty than to equality.

We can also use this approach to untangle the connection between religion and being active in church organizations by comparing the scores of those who were active in church organizations with the scores of those who accepted a religious designation but were not active in church organizations as well as with those who were unreligious. Those who were active in religious organizations scored 40 points less on liberty than the unreligious, but only 8 points less than religious people who took no active part in church organizations. And even that difference reflected the micro-principle of traditional values which was partly based on religious language about 'God's will'. On the other micro-principles associated with liberty, those active in church organizations scored only 24 points more on authority and 19 points less on tolerance than the unreligious, and they were scarcely any different from religious people who took no part in church organizations (indeed, in Scotland, the actively religious were very slightly more tolerant and less respectful of authority than the inactively religious). So participation in church organizations, by itself, had no effect upon our measures of principle other than on those that explicitly used religious language (Table 10.26).

Causal Implications

The causal implications of these correlations between principles and active involvement are open to dispute, however. Using cross-sectional data such as ours, it is impossible to be certain whether taking part in demonstrations and protests stimulates anti-authoritarian feelings, or results from them. No doubt there is a bit of both. But what is clear, is that there is a strong link between principles and active involvement in demonstrations, marches, or protest meetings, while there is *not* such a strong link between principles and other kinds of activity. In particular, our evidence shows that active involvement in social organizations connected with sports, arts, school, or church organizations, charities, and community action groups does *not* greatly affect

TABLE 10.26. *Difference between actively religious and others, on commitment to liberty* (scores +/–100 scale)

	Difference between actively religious and inactively religious			Difference between actively religious and unreligious		
	Politicians (scores)	British public (scores)	(Scottish public) (scores)	Politicians (scores)	British public (scores)	(Scottish public) (scores)
Liberty	-8	-8	(-5)	-48	-40	(-36)
Authority	-1	-2	(-3)	+33	+24	(+23)
Tolerance	-3	-2	(+2)	-24	-19	(-14)
Traditional values	+21	+26	(+22)	+85	+77	(+70)

Notes: Figures in the columns on the left are the score amongst those who were actively involved in church organizations minus the score amongst those who were religious but were not actively involved in church organizations.

Figures in the columns on the right are the score amongst those who were actively involved in church organizations minus the score amongst the unreligious.

TABLE 10.27. *Extent of press readership*

	Politicians (%)	British public (%)	(Scottish public) (%)
Tabloids			
Tory	11	28	(14)
Labour	6	15	(39)
Broadsheets			
Tory	24	8	(2)
Independent	30	6	(3)
Scottish	8	2	(21)
None	11	34	(18)
Other	12	7	(3)

the principles and prejudices of those who take part in them. Whether or not *political action* does significantly influence political values rather than merely reflecting them, these forms of *social action* certainly do not do so.

EXPERIENCE OF THE PRESS

We have distinguished three types of experience—as a victim of discrimination, as the consumer of state services, and as a participant in social and political life. It is not perhaps obvious whether we should regard the readers of the British press as active participants in political life or just willing victims of media manipulation. But, however we regard them, readers of the intellectual, left-wing *Guardian* and the anti-intellectual, right-wing *Sun* clearly experienced somewhat different kinds of political information and stimulation in their daily diet of news and current affairs (Table 10.27).[11]

We can divide our samples into those who read

1. Tory tabloids (*Sun, Daily Mail, Daily Star, Daily Express*)
2. Labour tabloids (*Daily Mirror, Daily Record*)
3. Tory broadsheets (*Daily Telegraph, The Times*)
4. independent broadsheets (*Guardian, Independent*)
5. Scottish regional papers (*Herald, Scotsman, Courier and Advertiser, Press and Journal*)
6. other papers
7. none.

Amongst politicians, the majority read a broadsheet, and slightly more read an independent broadsheet than a Tory one. Although only a small proportion of politicians read tabloids, almost twice as many who did do so read Tory tabloids rather than Labour tabloids. Amongst the public in Britain as a whole, the majority read either a Tory tabloid or nothing, and slightly more read nothing than read a Tory tabloid. Scotland, for once, was dramatically different: two and a half times as many Scots read a Labour tabloid as a Tory one; one and a half times as many read a Scottish regional paper as read a Tory tabloid; very few read an English broadsheet; and only half as many read nothing at all as in England and Wales.

Amongst the public, the young read tabloids much less (21 per cent less) than the old, with the result that they read fewer papers at all. University graduates also read far less (44 per cent less) tabloids than the unqualified, but they substituted broadsheets—especially independent broadsheets—for tabloids, and ended up reading just as many papers as the average overall. The middle class read more broadsheets than the working class, and many fewer Labour tabloids, though almost as many Tory tabloids. Much more surprisingly, the religious read more tabloids and fewer independent broadsheets, than the unreligious.

In Scotland, the dominance of Labour tabloids amongst tabloid readers, and of Scottish regional papers amongst broadsheet readers, combined to produce very strong class and education patterns. Compared to the unqualified, university-educated Scots were 42 per cent less likely to read a Labour tabloid and 33 per cent more likely to read a Scottish regional broadsheet (Table 10.28).

In terms of the principles and prejudices of their readers, the press could not be arranged along a single spectrum, since the division into broadsheets and tabloids cross-cut the division between Tory papers and non-Tory papers, and these two divisions affected different principles in different ways. Three different spectra of principle emerged (Table 10.29).

Spectrum 1 (liberty). On liberty, and its associated micro-principles of authority, traditional values, tolerance, wealth creation, and free speech, there was a spectrum of opinion that ran from the relatively pro-liberty readers of independent broadsheets at one extreme, to the relatively anti-liberty tabloid readers at the other. There was little difference between readers of Tory and Labour tabloids amongst the public, though, amongst politicians, the Tory tabloid readers were clearly at the extreme. Readers of Tory broadsheets had intermediate views but were usually closer to tabloid readers than to readers of independent broadsheets.

TABLE 10.28. *Correlations between social background and press readership*

	Religious (r × 100)		Old (r × 100)		Educational qualifications (r × 100)		Working class (r × 100)	
POLITICIANS								
Tory tabloids	12		14		−14		.	
Labour tabloids	.		.		−20		25	
Tory broadsheets	12		13		.		−24	
independent broadsheets	−27		−20		27		.	
BRITISH PUBLIC (SCOTTISH PUBLIC)								
Tory tabloids	.	(.)	.	(.)	−15	(.)	.	(.)
Labour tabloids	.	(12)	.	(.)	−15	(−19)	15	(24)
Tory broadsheets	.	(.)	.	(.)	14	(10)	−21	(−12)
independent broadsheets	−17	(.)	.	(.)	26	(10)	−12	(.)
Scottish regional	.	(.)	.	(10)	.	(20)	.	(−19)

Note: Correlations less than 0.10 have been replaced by full points.

TABLE 10.29. *Principles by press readership, public only* (scores on +/−100 scale)

	Spectrum 1 liberty (score)	Spectrum 2 economic equality (score)	Spectrum 3 equal rights (score)
BRITISH PUBLIC	13 Ind	56 L tab	67 Ind
	−24 T brd	52 Ind	42 L tab
	−30 L tab	44 T tab	34 T brd
	−33 T tab	30 T brd	33 T tab
(SCOTTISH PUBLIC)	(−21) S reg	(46) S reg	(42) S reg

Note: T = Tory, L = Labour, brd = broadsheet, tab = tabloid; S = Scottish, reg = regional.

Spectrum 2 (economic equality). On the micro-principles of economic equality and caring, the spectrum of opinion ran from the *economically egalitarian* readers of Labour tabloids at one extreme, to the relatively anti-egalitarian readers of Tory broadsheets at the other. Tory tabloid readers were roughly halfway between the two extremes.

Spectrum 3 (equal rights). On the micro-principles of equal rights, protest, and self-reliance, the spectrum of opinion ran from the *socially-egalitarian* readers of independent broadsheets at one extreme to the relatively anti-egalitarian readers of the Tory press at the other. Labour tabloid readers had intermediate opinions. Although our macro-principle of equality was based upon micro-principles of economic equality, caring, and equal rights, opinion on equality also followed this third spectrum because the extremism of independent broadsheet readers on equal rights was so much greater than that of Labour tabloid readers on economic equality or caring.

Readers of independent broadsheets were also by far the most favourable to activists, the socially disadvantaged, and rights enforcers; and had the least confidence in the judicial system. Readers of Tory papers, of one kind or another, were at the opposite extreme.

In Scotland, despite their low readership—and our correspondingly small sample of their readers—it was again the independent broadsheet readers who took the most left-wing position on the first spectrum. Once again Tory tabloid readers took the most extreme right-wing position on the first spectrum, while Tory broadsheet readers did so on the second. Readers of the Scottish regional broadsheets nearly always took an intermediate position.

Of course, reading newspapers, *unlike* being discriminated against or being stopped by the police, but *like* participation in demonstrations, is a relatively voluntary experience. So those with an unusually strong commitment to liberty may have chosen to read the *Guardian* rather than the *Sun*—though anyone who got their news and views from the *Guardian* rather than the *Sun* was more likely to be have their commitment to liberty confirmed and strengthened. There is no real question about the direction of causation here: it is very unlikely that it runs only in one direction or the other, and very likely that it runs in both. Our findings show the striking differences of principle between those who read different newspapers; but, while it is unlikely that the papers themselves bore no responsibility for these differences, the extent of their influence cannot be estimated from a cross-sectional survey.

OVERALL PERCEPTIONS

To sum up people's experience as victim, consumer, and participant and to gauge their opinions about the environment of rights and liberties in contemporary Britain, we asked them to place their perceptions of Britain on both historical and cross-national comparative scales. We asked:

[1.] On balance, British governments have been [reducing/increasing] the rights
and liberties of British citizens in recent years. Agree/disagree?

[2.] On the whole, the rights and liberties enjoyed by British citizens are [less/
greater] than those enjoyed by people who live in [America/West European
countries like France and Germany/Scandinavian countries like Norway,
Denmark or Sweden]. Agree/disagree?

The public were divided right down the middle about the extent of citizens' rights and liberties in contemporary Britain when compared with the
past, and politicians were decidedly pessimistic. But their views about trends
were heavily influenced by partisanship—only Conservatives took a favourable view of the trends—and views may have reflected attitudes to 'recent
British governments' more than a genuinely independent evaluation of trends
in rights and liberties. If not, our findings on this point are grim.

Views about other countries were less influenced by partisanship: within
every party, people rated rights and liberties in Scandinavia higher than in
Western Europe, and higher in Western Europe than in America. And they
put rights and liberties in Britain well above those in America, well behind
those in Scandinavia, and much the same as those in Western Europe. A
general commitment to a notion of 'positive' rather than 'negative' rights
and liberties—freedoms that result from the state intervening to promote the
welfare of citizens, rather than ones that result from individuals being protected against interference by the state or other persons—seems to be implied by the fact that Britons placed their rights and liberties so far above
those in America, where negative freedoms are constitutionally entrenched
in the Bill of Rights, and so far behind those in Scandinavia, where 'the
political culture has traditionally placed a high value on the principles of
social equality'.[12] Perhaps it is an indication of our increasing links with
Europe that both politicians and the public tended to see the rights and
liberties of British citizens roughly on a par with those enjoyed by people
in major countries of Western Europe, such as France and Germany.

One other noticeable pattern occurred in the answers to the different variants of these two questions. It is significant, in part, because it reverses the
findings of McClosky and Brill in their study of public attitudes to civil
liberties in the USA. We are inclined to think it indicates a subtle difference
between British and American culture rather than a simple conflict of evidence. McClosky and Brill found that American élites had more favourable
perceptions than their public of the amount of freedom enjoyed by people in
the USA.[13] We found the opposite in Britain: British politicians were slightly

TABLE 10.30. *Comparative perceptions of rights and liberties in contemporary Britain*

	Politicians (%)	British public (%)	(Scottish public) (%)
Less than in the past	61	52	(62)
Less than elsewhere	53	48	(52)
less than in USA	42	40	(43)
less than in West Europe	51	45	(50)
less than in Scandinavia	66	62	(66)

but consistently less optimistic than their public about rights and liberties in Britain when compared either to other places or to the past (Table 10.30).

CONCLUSION

In this chapter we have investigated both the social origins, and the subsequent impact on attitudes to political principles, of people's personal experience of civic life. We approached this question from as broad a perspective as possible, looking at a variety of possible ways in which citizens can interact with the state and its agents. We intentionally looked not only at how people's active and conscious decisions to participate affected their principles, but also at the way that government, broadly defined, impacted on the lives of citizens and shaped their views of civil rights and freedoms. So this chapter was not just about political activists and their views of rights. It was also about the way in which experiences of watching television, reading newspapers, experiencing discrimination, contacting a government official, or receiving health care or welfare shaped attitudes on rights.

Although many citizens might not be affected by a particular form of interaction with the state, our triple focus—on victims of discrimination, on consumers of state services, and on participants in varied aspects of social and political life—meant that the personal experience of most citizens in Britain was addressed in some way in this chapter.

Our results show that these three broad dimensions of civic life have varying impacts on our attitudes to rights and liberties. Just over a quarter of the British public, and even more of their local politicians, reported personal experience of discrimination. In both cases the grounds of the discrimination varied: for the public it was primarily for reasons of gender and age, for politicians it was most often because of their political beliefs. And in both cases, these experiences of discrimination had been primarily at the hands of their employers. Moreover, gender, age, and education all had an impact: discrimination was felt most frequently by women, by young people, and by those with higher levels of education.

Experience of discrimination generally raised people's commitment to liberty and equality, although this did depend both on the source and the nature of that discrimination. Regrettably, but not perhaps surprisingly, experience of discrimination did not strengthen people's confidence in rights enforcers—organizations like the Equal Opportunities Commission or the Commission for Racial Equality—which were set up to root out discrimination in British society.

When we looked at people's experiences as consumers of government services we were careful not just to look at those occasions where people had initiated contact with an elected or administrative official of central or local government, but the more likely points of contact (as our survey confirmed) when people were taken into an NHS hospital, were stopped by the police, or were impelled to contact the police because they had fallen victim to a crime. It was interesting to note that most people found their contact with state officials to be helpful, though politicians systematically found officials to be more helpful to them than the public: the status or experience of being a leader in local government made it easier to elicit a helpful response from both elected and administrative officials—at least from those officials who were involved in local government.

Just as the source and nature of discrimination proved important in the results of our first section, here we found that both the point and nature of the contact had a significant impact on people's attitudes to principles of rights. Generally, contact, whether with NHS hospitals or government agencies, was largely uncorrelated with principles or sympathies, though we did find that those who chose to opt out of state education or health care were (unsurprisingly) more opposed to the principle of equality. What was more interesting in this section, however, was the way in which adverse experiences with the police not only correlated with support for liberty, but significantly reduced confidence in the judicial system.

We found the public were quite deeply involved in politics at the mainly spectator level of watching current-affairs programmes, reading the press, and even signing petitions; but, not surprisingly, much less engaged than politicians in partisan activism. Neither interest in politics, strength of partisanship, nor addiction to TV current-affairs programmes correlated much with principles amongst the public, though these factors correlated weakly with liberty and equality amongst the politicians, and we found striking differences of principle amongst the readers of different newspapers.

More active involvement in party or community politics was largely the preserve of politicians. However, those few members of the public who were actively involved in non-electoral political campaigns were also much more committed to liberty than those who were not. Conversely, the small minority of politicians who were *not* involved in such campaigns proved less committed to liberty than those who were.

Our results also confirmed the lack of a strong link between principle and active participation in community social organizations, a somewhat stronger link between principle and active participation in trades unions, professional or religious organizations, a stronger link still with most forms of non-electoral politics, and a very strong link between principles and participation in protest meetings, marches, or demonstrations. It takes such radical political action, rather than routine activity in the social affairs of the community, to have a major effect on principles.

Towards the end of this chapter we noted how both politicians and the public agreed that the rights and liberties enjoyed by British citizens were not as good as those enjoyed by Scandinavians, but significantly better than the rights and liberties of American citizens. Many Americans might agree with that. The seductively easy assumption that the political culture of a people simply reflects the continuity of its history, constitution, and institutions is often a half-truth and sometimes a complete falsehood. People can ignore their own history, or even react against it. And they can draw political conclusions and derive fundamental political principles from the history, the experience, and the myths of other countries. Ideas do not respect frontiers.

In the next chapter, we address the question of whether British political culture is British, and we do so in two ways: first, by looking within Britain to see how far the attitudes of Scots vary from those of people in England and Wales; and then by shifting our focus across the Atlantic and examining how public attitudes to civil and political rights here in Britain compare with those of Canadian citizens. Beyond our immediate concern about the boundaries of British political culture is the more general question of how closely political culture reflects the details of a people's history and institutions.

NOTES

1. William L. Miller, Stephen White, Paul Heywood, and Matthew Wyman, 'Parties and Democratic Values in Russia and East-Central Europe: December 1993', a paper to the panel chaired by Renata Siemienska on The Emerging Party Systems in Central-Eastern Europe, XVI World Congress of IPSA, Berlin, 1994, p. 6.
2. In their 1984 survey of political participation in Britain, Parry, Moyser, and Day found that only 21% of the British public had contacted a local councillor, 17% their town hall or a local-government official, 10% an MP, and only 7% a department of central government or a civil servant 'in the last five years'. See Geraint Parry, George Moyser, and Neil Day, *Political Participation and Democracy in Britain* (Cambridge: Cambridge University Press, 1992), 43–5. Our own question asked whether people had 'ever' contacted such officials. But even within a five-year period it is very unlikely that only 7% had contact with a central-government office about tax, social security, car licensing, or the myriad of other affairs that link citizens to government in contemporary Britain. It is also possible that there was some genuine trend towards increasing contacts between British citizens and their government as Nie and his colleagues found in the USA. Cf. Sidney Verba and Norman Nie, *Participation in America: Political Democracy and Social Equality* (New York: Harper & Row, 1972), 31; and N. Nie, S. Verba, H. Brady, K. Schlozman, and J. Lunn, 'Participation in America: Continuity and Change', paper presented at the Midwest Political Science Association Annual Meeting, Chicago, Illinois, 1988; cited by Parry, Moyser, and Day, *Political Participation and Democracy in Britain*, 44.
3. Carol Pateman, *Participation and Democratic Theory* (Cambridge: Cambridge University Press, 1970), 42.
4. Benjamin R. Barber, *Strong Democracy: Participatory Politics for a New Age* (Berkeley and Los Angeles: University of California Press, 1984), 152.
5. David Butler and Austin Ranney (eds.), *Referendums: A Comparative Study of Practice and Theory* (Washington: American Enterprise Institute, 1978), 33. For a review of the current practice of participatory democracy, see also the sequel: David Butler and Austin Ranney (eds.), *Referendums around the World: The Growing Use of Direct Democracy* (London: Macmillan, 1994).
6. Herbert McClosky and Alida Brill, *Dimensions of Tolerance: What Americans Believe about Civil Liberties* (New York: Russell Sage Foundation, 1983), 416.
7. See Patrick Barwise and Andrew Eurenberg, *Television and its Audience* (London: Sage, 1988), 19. For a more sophisticated analysis of the ways in which television viewing is structured, see Roger Silverstone, *Television and Everyday Life* (London: Routledge, 1994).
8. See Vicki Randall, *Women and Politics* (London: Macmillan, 1982), 38–41, and Joni Lovenduski, *Women and European Politics* (Brighton: Wheatsheaf, 1986), 129–30, who both comment on women's greater tendency to be interested in 'issue-oriented' rather than party politics.
9. Joseph F. Fletcher ('Participation and Attitudes towards Civil Liberties: Is there an "Educative" Effect?', *International Political Science Review*, 11 (1990), 439–59)

concluded that 'the effect of participation is neither so robust nor so general as the formulations of the participatory democrats would have us believe' (p. 453), but he found the correlations between attitudes to principle and practice were higher amongst the more involved. On both points our findings are consistent with his, though they differ in detail.

10. Cf. Parry, Moyser, and Day, *Political Participation and Democracy in Britain*. However, although their study was also based on a broad interpretation of the term 'political participation', it touches only slightly on the *consequences* of participation for those individuals who actually participate, primarily self-reports on whether respondents felt that active participation had increased their knowledge or made them more favourable towards 'the way politics works'; see esp. ch. 13, pp. 286–98.

11. For a recent analysis of what people get out of reading different papers, see William L. Miller, *Media and Voters: The Audience, Content, and Influence of Press and Television at the 1987 General Election* (Oxford: Oxford University Press, 1991), ch. 6.

12. Berte Siim, 'Welfare State, Gender Politics and Equality Policies: Women's Citizenship in the Scandinavian Welfare States', in Elizabeth Meehan and Selma Sevenhuijsen (eds.), *Equality Politics and Gender* (London: Sage, 1991), 175–192, at 177.

13. McClosky and Brill, *Dimensions of Tolerance*, 78.

11

The Institutional Setting

IN this chapter we look, both within Britain and beyond, for evidence that political culture reflects variations in the institutional and historical setting. In particular, we compare the political culture of Scotland with that of Britain as a whole; and we compare the political culture of Britain with that of its former dominion, Canada. Our aim is to consider whether, in fundamental respects, there is a common political culture that pervades these countries. We shall test the proposition that attitudes towards civil, political, and social rights reflect the limited—but not trivial—variations in the historical and institutional context between such closely connected, yet different, countries as Scotland, England, and Canada.

Historically and institutionally, Scotland, England, and Canada have a lot in common despite important differences. Up until 1982, when the Canadian Constitution was finally patriated,[1] the same parliament—at Westminster—had ultimate control over each country's constitutional destiny. And ironically, the parliament that agreed to patriate the Canadian Constitution in 1982, having first entrenched within it the 1982 Canadian Charter of Rights and Freedoms, was the same parliament (even the same MPs, elected in 1979) that not only refused to confirm the provisions of the 1979 Scotland Act setting up a devolved parliament in Edinburgh, but also refused to introduce a Bill of Rights for Britain.

CULTURE AND CONSTITUTION

No doubt, political culture at some level does reflect the historical and institutional setting to some degree. However we wish to test the proposition that political culture does not entirely depend upon the *details* of national history and institutions; that, there are common perspectives on rights that pervade the whole of Britain and, despite recent constitutional changes, still link it with Canada.

Constitutions do not always determine political behaviour. As Stephen Sedley notes, the behaviour of Stalin's government in the 1930s did not reflect the spirit of the constitution he himself had devised for the Soviet

Union. And, only slightly more controversially, Sedley claims that American politics have repeatedly failed to live up to the US Constitution.[2] But conversely, while political *practice* may fail to live up to the spirit of the constitution within that constitution's own jurisdiction, the *spirit* of that constitution may spread far beyond its legal jurisdiction. Political culture need not always recognize state boundaries.

Many people in Britain would agree with Lord Hailsham that 'the theory of limited government must be built into our [i.e. the British] constitution as it is into the American'.[3] His nationality was British but, in very important respects, his political culture was self-consciously American. And while the liberal principles of the US Constitution may be popular in Europe, European ideals of social justice are popular in the USA—despite the US Constitution.[4] Paul, Miller, and Paul note that 'ever since the constitutional revolution of the 1930s, constitutional law and theory [in the USA] have been dominated by questions of civil rights ... [but] these were *not* the issues that most deeply concerned the Framers of the Constitution'.[5]

It is worth pointing out here that analyses of 'civil rights' in the USA are often constructed around T. H. Marshall's framework of civil, political, and social rights. Recent texts chronicle the struggles of American blacks, first to end social discrimination (civil rights), then to gain effective voting rights (political rights), and then to reduce economic inequality between blacks and whites (social and economic rights)—often in a lengthy chapter typically entitled 'Civil Rights'.[6] Indeed, the concept of rights in the USA has gone far beyond social and economic rights for racial minorities. James Davis has used a cross-national social attitudes survey to support his view that the British and US publics have near identical views on police powers and civil liberties but divergent views on government responsibility for social and economic welfare or for encouraging more equality.[7] But others such as Dye and Zeigler quote US survey data to show that

as the federal government has expanded its role in economic and social life, Americans have come to expect 'rights' that, whatever their moral justification, are *not* found anywhere in the US Constitution. Majorities believe that they have a 'right' to be protected from serious crime, to obtain effective teaching in school, to have consumer products certified as safe, to enjoy a steadily improving standard of living, to have an adequate retirement income adjusted annually for inflation, to be guaranteed a job, to have access to higher education, and to be guaranteed medical care.[8]

It is, in fact, no accident that we began this book with an opening chapter on the *UN* Declaration and the *European* Convention on Human Rights. Whatever their content, their mere existence asserts the claim that political culture should be international, transnational, and indeed supranational in its fundamentals.

We can pursue this question of the effective boundaries of our common political culture by means of both an internal and a transatlantic comparison. We shall begin by examining the evidence for two political cultures within Britain itself. In one sense, British political culture must be overwhelmingly English political culture. Reflecting the proportions in the electorate, 84 per cent of our British public sample lived in England, 6 per cent in Wales, and 10 per cent in Scotland. That population imbalance explains why Richard Rose chose the title *Politics in England* for his celebrated text on *British* government.[9] Although our British sample provides an exact guide to political culture in Britain, it also provides a closely approximate guide to political culture in England simply because it is so overwhelmingly English. We added a special Scottish sample (because there are not enough Scots in the British sample for separate analysis) and routinely compared findings from our British and Scottish samples in order to investigate the proposition that 'Scotland is a distinct society'.[10] We did so partly to investigate the general proposition that history and institutions mould political culture, but also because the question of a distinctive Scottish political culture—whether answered in the affirmative or not—is an important question about the alleged complexity and heterogeneity of British political culture.

Perhaps the institutional and other contextual differences between Scotland and England, though real, are too small and too much overlaid by a common British heritage for them to generate large differences in political culture, however. If so, the greater contextual and constitutional differences between Britain and Canada, especially since 1982, should provide more scope for institutions, context—and constitutions—to influence culture differently and we therefore go on to compare political culture in Britain and Canada. Our survey of opinion in Britain was inspired by a previous opinion survey in Canada,[11] which was, in turn, prompted by the passage of the Canadian Charter through the *British* parliament in 1982. And the inspiration we drew from that Canadian study means that the two surveys enjoy considerable similarities in sample design, methodology, and question wording which permit fairly detailed comparison.

IS SCOTLAND A 'DISTINCT SOCIETY'?

Scottish history—at least in popular myth—is essentially an anti-English history of many defeats and a few glorious victories.[12] The distinctive characteristics of the main social and political institutions in Scotland were, under the 1707 Treaty of Union with England, to be preserved 'in all time coming', and, although that bargain has been broken in some respects, new institutions—especially those related to the mass media, education, and political parties—have arisen to emphasize the continuing difference between the Scottish and English social and political context.

The law, the courts, local and national government administration are all significantly different in Scotland as against England and Wales; and it is precisely on criminal, civil-rights, and constitutional law, rather than on commercial law, that the two legal systems differ most. According to Hurwitt and Thornton: 'The rights of citizens in Scotland are quite different from those in England and Wales, especially those which concern police powers and the criminal law'[13]—though their list of differences significant to the ordinary citizen (rather than the lawyer) was short. In Scotland, unlike England and Wales, conviction on uncorroborated confession was not possible, prosecution was the responsibility of the Procurator-fiscal not the police,[14] cases had to come to trial within 110 days or be abandoned, and public demonstrations were authorized (or banned) by elected local governments not the police—which suggests a generally narrower range of functions for the police in Scotland than elsewhere.

But constitutional law is also different in Scotland. Lord Jenkins, amongst others, has noted that parliamentary sovereignty is accepted under English law but disputed (some would say rejected) under Scots law.[15] The 1689 Bill of Rights was and remains an English Bill passed by an English parliament before the Union of 1707; it is not a British Bill, and most certainly not a Scottish Bill. The Established Church in Scotland is Calvinist and totally different from the Established Church in England. (The Episcopalian Church in Scotland, which is part of the Anglican communion, even has a revolutionary, anti-state history which proved to be of some importance to the church in America during and immediately after the Revolution.) Indeed the whole religious balance is different.

So is the media balance: the popular press in Scotland is dominated by Labour tabloids in contrast to England, where it is dominated by Tory tabloids; and the broadsheet press in Scotland is dominated by geographically differentiated city papers based on Glasgow, Edinburgh, Aberdeen, and Dundee—on the North American model—in contrast to the ideologically differentiated broadsheets which dominate the English market.

Freedom of information is also affected by the legal differences. Injunctions are regularly taken out to suppress publication of facts in England by people who either do not know, or do not care, that these injunctions stop at the Scottish border. So the Scottish press regularly carries material banned in London. During our survey the *Scotsman* took advantage of this to name Paddy Ashdown and give details of allegations about a former affair at a time when the London press held back. As its rival the London-based *Guardian* reported shortly afterwards, a little ruefully: 'It was left to the *Scotsman* newspaper to name Mr Ashdown . . . [whose] lawyers had failed to include newspapers north of the border when sending out the injunction.'[16] The *Guardian* was wrong in one crucial respect, however. Sending (English) High Court injunctions to Edinburgh would have had no effect anyway; Ashdown's lawyers would have needed an 'interdict' (similar to an English 'injunction') from the (Scottish) Court of Session.

Conversely, the most shockingly open attack on the BBC's freedom to publish occurred in Scotland, when Metropolitan police from London were sent across the border to assist in raiding BBC studios in Glasgow and seizing a whole six-part current-affairs series, entitled *The Secret Society*, made for the network by BBC-Scotland TV.[17]

As we were revising this manuscript for publication, the Court of Session in Edinburgh banned a television interview with Prime Minister John Major which was scheduled to appear on the BBC's flagship current-affairs programme *Panorama*, because it was to be screened just three days before the Scottish local-government elections in April 1995 (though a full month before the local-government elections in England and Wales). BBC executives in London announced that they would take an appeal to the House of Lords in London, to override the Scottish court, apparently overlooking the fact that appeals can only go to London with the approval of the Court of Session itself—an approval which it declined to give. The BBC had to withdraw the interview not only from its Scottish transmitters, but also from those in northern England and Northern Ireland whose signals could be received in Scotland. It was a small victory for those Scots who had been appalled by the *Secret Society* affair, though George MacDonald Fraser's fictional hero would have savoured it.

Apart from legal differences, the simple facts of geography mean that most Scots live over 400 miles away from the Westminster/Whitehall/Buckingham Palace triangle. Inevitably they view it 'from outside', in the same way that the English tend to view government from Brussels.

Beyond all that, there are party political differences which have sharpened over the last few decades. In the 1992 general election, the Conservative Party won less than 26 per cent of the Scottish vote and only eleven of the seventy-two parliamentary seats, yet once again imposed its Secretary of State on Scotland—and its own distinctively Scottish policies, for which it had no electoral mandate either in Scotland or in Britain as a whole. It is a situation frequently described by Scottish politicians—only half in jest—as 'colonial'. So Scots could be expected to resent government from London even more than those who live in provincial parts of England.

Scotland has a proud record of contributions to international culture. It can also claim a vibrant and distinctive local and national culture in social and artistic affairs. And James Kellas is clearly right to claim that there is a *Scottish Political System*.[18] But there is less agreement and more ambiguity about whether there is any distinctively and specifically Scottish *political culture*.[19] It is widely alleged that Scotland's isolation, its population stability (more noted for emigration than immigration), its religious and cultural background, and its status as a quasi-subject nation give Scots a greater sense of community, a greater respect for equality, and a stronger attachment to public services—the Scottish 'egalitarian myth', as David McCrone calls it, which is 'not dependent on "facts" because it represents a set of . . . self-evident values, a social ethos, a celebration of sacred beliefs'.[20] But elsewhere the same author says:

it is an irony that . . . Scottish political behaviour has never in post-war politics been so divergent from its southern counterpart, a situation seemingly *achieved with little help from 'Scottish national culture'*. Here it seems, is a political manifestation which is *not* tied to a specific cultural divergence . . . this expression of political difference . . . has developed without the encumbrance of a heavy cultural baggage. (emphasis added)[21]

Altogether there was good reason to expect that, if social, historical, and institutional environments do have a great impact upon political culture, then it should show up in the contrast between our British and Scottish samples— even if there were always great doubts about the likely results of such a comparison. It would be a fair test of the thesis.

Political Culture in Scotland: The Evidence

Scotland, like other countries, is not a nation of lawyers, historians, constitutional experts, journalists, or sociologists. So, despite all the very plausible reasons why Scots should be different, our comprehensive comparisons have suggested far more similarity than difference between those who live in Scotland and those who live in the rest of Britain. Indeed, as we warned at the outset, our Scottish sample has done more to confirm our findings about the British public than to support the somewhat romantic notion that Scottish political culture was fundamentally distinct from that in other parts of Britain.

Certainly Scottish political opinion was very different from the English on, for example, party preferences—but those were differences of opinion within the same political culture, not proof of a fundamental difference of culture. National identity was clearly different in one sense: when asked to choose a national self-image, about a third in Scotland, England, and Wales described themselves as 'British', while over half in each country opted for the more local label—'Scottish' (in Scotland), 'English' (in England), or 'Welsh' (in Wales).[22] Those identities were different in detail but fundamentally similar in character. Two thieves obviously have separate identities, but not necessarily different characters: they may fight to the death over the division of their booty but, in doing so, they may express a fundamental unity of culture combined with a sharp difference in material interest. Introductory texts on British politics and government are quite right to draw attention to the fact that the Scots, English, and Welsh feel that they have separate identities and, to a far lesser degree, separate interests; but these texts are wrong to suggest that this implies a fundamental difference of political culture. It does not.

Clearly there really was a *slight* difference in more fundamental attitudes to principle between those who lived in Scotland and those who lived in the rest of Britain.[23] In terms of macro-principles, people who lived in Scotland scored exactly on the British average for their commitment to liberty, but 6 points higher on support for equality. In terms of micro-principles, the Scots scored 7 points higher on economic equality, though only 5 points higher on caring or equal rights. And a look in detail at the indicators of economic equality shows that the largest difference occurred on attitudes towards 'government responsibility for evening out differences in wealth between people'. On that, the Scots were 12 per cent more egalitarian than the British as a whole, whereas they were only 2 per cent more egalitarian on 'government responsibility for providing equal opportunities for everyone' (Table 11.1).

In terms of sympathies and antipathies also, the differences between Scots and others were clearly limited and small. The only substantial difference was that Scots were 10 points more favourable to the socially disadvantaged— which matches their slightly greater egalitarianism—though scarcely different from the rest of Britain in their antipathy towards activists and militants— which matches their similarity to the rest of Britain on the macro-principle of liberty. In addition, perhaps reflecting a slight sense of national oppression, Scots were 10 per cent more likely than others to agree that British governments had been reducing citizens' rights in recent years (Table 11.2).

Even on matters of practice, the differences between Scots and the rest of

TABLE 11.1. *The pattern of principle in Scotland* (scores on +/−100 scale)

	British public (scores)	Scottish public (scores)	Difference in Scotland (scores)
Liberty	−25	−25	0
Equality	55	61	+6
Respect for authority	39	39	0
Respect for traditional values	37	39	+2
Wealth creation	53	58	+5
Tolerance	3	2	−1
Limited government	1	1	0
Right to speak out	35	34	−1
Right to protest and rebel	31	35	+4
Self-reliance	13	9	−4
Economic equality	46	53	+7
Caring	79	84	+5
Equal rights	40	45	+5
Protection	53	52	−1
Right to know	87	90	+3

Note: Since a tenth of the British public lived in Scotland, Scottish/English differences would be fractionally greater than Scottish/British differences, but not enough to change any of the figures in the third column by more than one point.

TABLE 11.2. *The pattern of sympathy in Scotland* (scores on +/−100 scale)

	British public (scores)	Scottish public (scores)	Difference in Scotland (scores)
Sympathy for			
socially disadvantaged	18	28	+10
activists	−14	−13	+1
militants	−65	−65	0
Confidence in			
rights enforcers	5	4	−1
judicial system	24	25	+1
civil institutions	13	16	+3
political system	1	3	+2

Britain were small. There was almost no difference between Scots and others on the issue of 'conviction on confession', despite the differences in the legal environment. (To simplify a complex issue, conviction on uncorroborated confession was legal in England at the time of our survey but not in Scotland.)

Compared to the British as a whole, people living in Scotland were 8 per cent more likely to identify themselves as being 'on the left' (including the 'centre left') rather than the right. They were 9 per cent more willing to allow strikes by workers in essential services, and 10 per cent more willing to ban private medicine. Incidentally, they were also 9 per cent less likely to have used private medicine. So in practice, Scots were slightly more left wing than people who lived elsewhere in Britain.

They were generally a few per cent less willing to back parliament in a confrontation with local government, British courts, European courts, or the will of the people as expressed in a referendum. But the largest of these differences—which occurred on the referendum issue and was probably influenced by nationalist campaigns for a referendum on Scottish devolution or independence—was only 9 per cent. As we saw in Chapter 6, even on the issue of more self-government for the different parts of Britain, Scots were distinguished most by their low level of 'don't knows' on all questions about self-government, and by their specially favourable attitude towards more self-government *for English regions* (Scots were 13 per cent more in favour than other Britons of devolution for regions within England), rather than by a particularly favourable attitude towards more self-government for Scotland itself. So in practice, Scots were more anti-Westminster than others, but only a little.

Scots also had slightly different views on matters of religion and morals. They were 8 per cent more inclined to describe abortion on demand as immoral, and 8 per cent more inclined to make it illegal. They were no more inclined to complain of discrimination but, amongst those Scots who did complain, they were 9 per cent more likely to say it was on grounds of religion. Consistent with that sensitivity to problems of religious divisions, Scots were slightly more willing to ban religious processions, publication of religious abuse, or television interviews with apologists for either the IRA or Protestant terrorists from Northern Ireland. They were 12 per cent less willing to support religious education in state schools, and 10 per cent more inclined to insist that any such religious education must treat all the major religions equally. By any measure, Scots were slightly *more* religious than the rest of Britain but, in practice, they were at once a little more morally conservative and, at the same time, more aware of the dangers that religious divisions posed for public tranquillity. But, as on everything else, these differences between Scotland and the rest of Britain were limited in scope and small in size.

However, it would be a very serious mistake to interpret these findings as evidence that Scots had attitudes to issues and principles that were consistent with the English law and constitution. It was not a peculiarly English culture that dominated the public mind on either side of the border. On the contrary, our evidence was that *neither* the Scots *nor* the English had principles which were consistent with the British constitution. Instead, they reflected a commitment to common Western values whose egalitarian aspects were more consistent with European or Scandinavian constitutions, and whose libertarian and populist aspects were more consistent with the US Constitution.

There are, of course, huge differences in political culture within Britain, but they are differences between the culture of the old and the young, the educated and the uneducated, the religious and the unreligious, but there is not a huge difference in political culture between those who live in Scotland and those who live in England and Wales.

BRITAIN AND CANADA: DIVERGING CONSTITUTIONAL TRADITIONS

Despite Canada's geographical proximity to the USA, its political and constitutional traditions have placed it close to Britain. As we indicated at the start of this chapter, Canada and Britain have been linked by the political, economic, and cultural dynamics of colonialism and by the umbilical nature of the post-colonial ties that followed the era of empire. Initially manifest in terms of trade and defence, these links have persisted in the mirrored forms of parliamentary democracy and in the sharing of a constitutional monarch; in parallel efforts, during the era of post-war reconstruction, to develop the infrastructure of a welfare state and, until recently, in the protracted nature of constitutional ties, that made it impossible for Canadians to amend their own constitution without reference to the British parliament.

However, much of this changed in 1982, when the Canadian Constitution was patriated from Britain and entrenched with a Charter of Rights and Freedoms. After intense debate in Canada, and some tense debate in Britain,[24] the British parliament passed the 1982 Canada Act, giving force of law in Canada to the Charter of Rights and Freedoms. This Charter was a superior instrument to the 1960 Canadian Bill of Rights, which had been used to a limited extent by the courts.[25] Indeed, its constitutional status meant that the Charter guaranteed that Canadian citizens could enjoy certain fundamental freedoms (of conscience, religion, thought, expression, assembly, and association), democratic rights (related to elections), mobility rights (immigration and emigration), rights of 'due process' (against arbitrary imprisonment, for example), the equal protection and equal benefit of laws (without discrimination on the basis of race, national and ethnic origin, colour, religion, sex, age, or mental or physical disability, and with provision for remedial programmes to counteract the effects of historic discrimination), and equality for the French and English languages in all institutions of the government of Canada. Although the rights and freedoms entrenched in the Charter were subject to 'such reasonable limits prescribed by law as can be demonstrably justified in a free and democratic society' (section 1) and by the provisions for a five-year, renewable legislative override on certain sections (section 33), it is clear that since 1982 Canadians have had access to the kind of constitutional instrument which some reformers would like to see introduced in Britain.[26]

Although, at first glance, the entrenchment of the Charter in the Canadian Constitution seemed to mark a 'radical break in Canadian political culture in which communitarian ideals of collective bonds and social order were replaced by a liberal emphasis on individual rights and freedoms',[27] a closer examination of public attitudes to civil and political liberties in Canada demonstrates that Canadians have not become entirely 'rights oriented' in the sense that is commonly associated with the USA and that many of the conservative and communitarian values that have long distinguished Canadian political culture from that of its immediate neighbour remain intact. As Seymour Martin Lipset notes, 'the Canadian Charter of Rights and Freedoms is not the American Bill of Rights. It preserves the principle of parliamentary supremacy and places less emphasis on individual, as distinct from group, rights than does the American document.' And Canada, claims Lipset 'remains more respectful of authority, more willing to use the state, and more supportive of the group basis of rights than its neighbour'.[28]

However, even though Canada may not have completely replaced its founding traditions of peace, order, and good government with a radically new rights-based contract between citizens and the state, its political environment can be distinguished in many respects from that of contemporary Britain. Canada is a confederation, with centrifugal tendencies that have become increasingly marked in recent years. Britain, by contrast, retains a unitary system of government that has become increasingly centralized over the past decade. Canada has a constitutionally entrenched Charter of Rights, which Britain does not. In Britain, traditions of an unwritten constitution (many would say no constitution at all) and monarchical sovereignty cloak the reality of a sovereign parliament, in practice a sovereign government, unchecked by the British courts. And, despite the significant gains made by two regionally based federal parties in the 1993 Canadian general election,[29] Canada has a long tradition of national catch-all parties which, despite having some clear philosophical differences, are more easily interpreted as brokerage organizations than the ideologically driven British parties.[30]

Whatever the virtues or deficiencies of the Canadian Charter, and however conservative or communitarian Canadians may be by nature, the long and intense debate over the Charter must surely have made them more aware of the concepts and mechanisms of a constitutional regime. By contrast, Britain is almost unique amongst modern democracies in having no constitution—all the excuses about it having lots of 'constitutional law' notwithstanding. And, in further contrast, the decade of the 1980s was a period in which—it was alleged—civil liberties in Britain were reduced rather than extended,[31] a period in which they became even more dependent upon the good sense—or the whims—of those in government.[32] According to Ewing and Gearty, a process that was already going on in the 1970s (with, for example, the 1974 Prevention of Terrorism Act) became 'more pronounced' under Thatcher: 'All our traditional liberties have been affected, partly by new statutory initiatives and partly by the Government and other public officials relentlessly pushing back the frontiers of the Common Law, the traditional guardian of the people.' The Thatcher government, they alleged, was more concerned with free markets than free citizens. And indeed legislation in the 1980s extended the powers of the police, the power to intercept communications, and the power to impose public order at the expense of freedom of assembly.

On the other hand, the case for civil liberties may be advanced more persuasively by the actions of its enemies than by the rhetoric of its friends. Margaret Thatcher's successive electoral victories were not built upon a growth of popular support for Thatcherism, however defined.[33] In Britain Charter 88 was launched as a public petition in 1988 and transformed into an organization and pressure group in 1989. It had considerable success in placing the need for a written constitution and a Bill of Rights on the agenda of opposition politicians, if not on the agenda of the government. Margaret Thatcher's successor, John Major, sought to define his own image by launching a rival 'Citizens' Charter' in 1991, which sought to divert attention away from traditional civil-rights issues and questions of social justice by focusing attention on the more limited theme of consumer standards for public services.[34]

Outside Scotland and Wales, constitutional reform did not appear to be an issue of overt concern for the wider public and even within those nations public attention was mainly limited to the question of devolution to elected Scottish and Welsh Assemblies (with considerably less powers than Canadian provincial legislatures). None the less, the notion of wide-ranging constitutional reform became familiar to Britain's 'chattering classes' and 'political classes' during the 1980s.

The European project also provided a kind of creeping constitutional development within Britain. As members of the Council of Europe and the European Communities (now the European Union), British people gradually became used to the idea that somebody, somewhere might routinely overrule the British parliament without causing a constitutional or political crisis. The European Convention on Human Rights was signed in 1950, ratified by Britain in 1951, and came into force in 1953. With all its limitations and deficiencies, the associated European Court of Human Rights in Strasbourg acts like a Supreme Court for Britain every time it overrules the laws of the British parliament. Cases may go before the European Court of Human Rights only if the state concerned has accepted the compulsory jurisdiction of the Court (or expressly consented to the particular case), which Britain has done since 1966. Cases can only be brought by member states or by the Court's secretariat, the European Commission of Human Rights—though since 1983 individual complainants have had the right to be represented in proceedings of the Court. This sequence of dates shows how the constitutional regime has gradually been strengthened over the years—from 1951 to 1953 to 1966 to 1983.

Technically the European Court of Human Rights is separate from the European Union, but all member states of the EU (as well as some non-EU states) have ratified the European Convention on Human Rights and the EU's own international court, the European Court of Justice in Luxembourg has stated that human rights as set out in the Convention form part of the common legal traditions of EU members and it has begun to take these into account. In terms of their effect upon the political culture of Britain it is more misleading than otherwise to distinguish between these two European courts.

The European Court (and its associated Commission) of Human Rights has received more complaints about Britain than about any other state.[35] It is not at all obvious whether that indicates that the British state is the most repressive, or the British people the most assertive. Either way, it has contributed towards public awareness in Britain of '*the* European Court', or 'going to Strasbourg' with a grievance. According to Hurwitt and Thornton, the European Court's rulings have forced Britain to make important changes in regard to laws concerning privacy, immigration, inhuman and degrading treatment of suspects and prisoners, and the rights of mental patients, parents, and workers.

The European Convention has never been incorporated into British law, so cases cannot be taken before British courts. Some advocates of civil rights have argued that incorporation of the Convention would automatically have the effect of providing a written constitution and a Bill of (Citizens') Rights for Britain.[36] But others argue that 'it is the judicial response to the [Canadian] Bill of Rights and not the [Canadian] Charter which may be a more appropriate yardstick for likely behaviour in Britain'.[37] Ewing and Gearty dismissed the Canadian Bill of Rights as a 'rather sterile measure in the hands of Canadian judges' until the political debate over the Charter gave it a significance it had not originally enjoyed. Similarly in Britain, they say, it would take a wide-ranging political debate to change the culture of British courts as well as the law they administer. Psychologically and politically, that might require the enactment of a British Bill of Rights rather than the quiet legal incorporation of the European Convention into British law.

None the less, despite all the good reasons for caution, Britain's membership of the EU and her submission to the Council of Europe's European Court of Human Rights may well have damaged the concept of parliamentary sovereignty beyond repair. Britain may have entered these arrangements as a sovereign state, but their regular, routine, overruling of Britain's parliament makes its lack of sovereignty visible and, what is more important, 'normal'. So it remains an empirical question whether Canadians, with their recently entrenched Charter and exposure to the proximate example of the rights-based culture of the USA, do in fact have a greater sense of constitutionality than the British, with our long history of unconstitutional (or 'non-constitutional') government.

The Surveys

We base our comparison of British and Canadian political culture on two surveys: the 1987 Canadian Charter Study Survey and our own 1991–2 British Rights Survey. Since our British survey was inspired by the Canadian example, there is a common core of over forty relevant questions (in addition to standard background questions) which allow detailed comparison. To avoid basing an international comparison upon transient opinion, over-influenced by the peculiar events of a particular time, interviewing for both the Canadian and British surveys was spread over a period of several months.

The Canadian survey comprised a representative sample of the electorate and a sample of relevant élites, both interviewed first by phone and then by means of a follow-up mail-back questionnaire. Our British survey was similar except that it did not use a mail-back questionnaire. For the electorates that gives a maximum, in Canada, of 2,084 respondents to the telephone part of the interview but only 1,250 respondents to the mail-back part. For this analysis we have excluded respondents who displayed significant mismatches between phone and mail parts of the interview. So our findings for the Canadian electorate are based upon a maximum of 1,952 replies to questions in the telephone part of the interview and 1,103 replies to questions in the mail-back part. As throughout this book, our findings for the British electorate are based upon a maximum of 2,060 respondents in our sample of the British public.

The Canadian mail-back questions differ from telephone questions in two ways. First, answers are available for only half the sample. Second, and more important, the mail-back questionnaire inevitably had to offer explicit 'don't know/can't say/can't choose' options, whereas the telephone interviews (on both sides of the Atlantic) recorded 'don't know, etc.' answers but did not explicitly prompt for them. Consequently, the mail-back questionnaire produced much higher levels of 'don't know, etc.' answers. However, this is a difference between questions within the Canadian survey rather than between the British and Canadian surveys. To facilitate comparison we have eliminated all 'don't knows' and calculated percentages 'of those with a view'. That is not a perfect solution to the problem, but it is one that, at least, allows us to compare Britons and Canadians who have articulated clear opinions.

Relevant élites were also defined rather differently in the two countries, but, for comparative purposes, we have selected fairly comparable élites. In Canada, the élite sample consisted of politicians, lawyers, civil-servants in justice ministries, and police officers. In Britain, we focused on a more specific policy-making élite. Our élite sample consisted only of politicians; so we have restricted our analysis of Canadian élites to politicians also. The sample of Canadian politicians was drawn from lists of past and present (elected) members of the federal and provincial legislatures. It comprised 513 respondents to the phone part of the interview, and, excluding mismatches with the postal returns, our analysis of Canadian politicians is based upon a maximum of 493 answers to phone questions and 286 answers to mail-back questions. In Britain we interviewed 1,244 senior local-government politicians. By international standards, British local governments are large in population, resources, and responsibilities, and, while leaders of party groups on these councils are obviously different from back-bench members of a Canadian Provincial Legislature, they could claim at least comparable political status.

Cultural Similarities

Both surveys attempted to measure value priorities by asking how much importance people attached to various value statements about freedom, authority, equality, and more materialistic objectives. Six of these (with minor differences) were common to both surveys:

[1.] preserving traditional ideas of right and wrong

[2.] respect for authority (Britain)

   to strengthen respect and obedience for authority (Canada)

[3.] following God's will

[4.] protecting ethnic and racial minorities (Britain)

   to make a special effort to protect ethnic and racial minorities (Canada)

[5.] guaranteeing equality between men and women (Britain)

   to guarantee equality between men and women in all aspects of life (Canada)

[6.] cutting taxes (Britain)

   to reduce taxes for the average citizen (Canada).

The wordings are close or identical, though the Canadian question on ethnic minorities refers to a 'special effort' which may imply more 'affirmative action'.

Unfortunately for strictly comparative purposes, the answers in Britain were measured by 'marks out of ten for how important to you' (i.e. an eleven-point scale) and in Canada by a three-point scale—'very important, somewhat important, and not important'. So a direct comparison of absolute importance is not possible. However, the relative importance of the different priorities can be compared by scoring 'not important' as zero, 'somewhat' as 5, and 'very' as 10, computing average scores in Britain and Canada, and then ranking priorities by their average score. The results are remarkably similar in Britain and Canada.

In both countries, and amongst both the public and politicians, gender equality came top of the list of priorities, while following God's will came

TABLE 11.3. *Value priorities in Britain and Canada*

	Britain		Canada	
	Politicians (marks/10)	Public (marks/10)	Politicians (marks/10)	Public (marks/10)
Gender equality	8.0	8.3	9.0	8.4
Authority	7.4	8.2	6.7	7.7
Traditional ideas	7.5	8.0	7.6	7.7
Ethnic protection	8.0	7.3	7.8	6.5
Tax cuts	4.5	6.5	6.4	7.6
God's will	5.0	5.7	6.0	6.4

Notes: Ranked by value priorities in the British public; entries are the average score on marks out of 10.

In Canada, 10 was assigned to 'very important', 5 to 'somewhat important', and zero to 'not important'.

at or near the bottom. Respect for authority, and for traditional ideas of right and wrong, came near to the top; tax cuts near to the bottom; and protection for ethnic and racial minorities near the middle. In Britain, politicians give less weight than the public to every value priority except protection for ethnic and racial minorities; in Canada, politicians give less weight than the public to everything except protection for ethnic and racial minorities and gender equality (Table 11.3).

We asked about the abstract principles of liberty and equality:

[1.] Free speech is just not worth it if it means we have to put up with the danger to society from extremist views. (Britain)

Free speech is just not worth it if it means we have to put up with danger to society from radical and extremist views. (Canada)

[2.] We [have gone too far/have not gone far enough] in pushing equal rights in this country. (Britain)

We have gone too far in pushing equal rights in this country. (Canada)

Again the wordings were closely comparable. In the equal-rights question a random half of the British sample were given the question in the Canadian format, the other half in the negative format. It made little difference to the

TABLE 11.4. *Abstract principles of liberty and equality in Britain and Canada*

	Britain		Canada	
	Politicians (%)	Public (%)	Politicians (%)	Public (%)
Free speech	89	64	89	64
Equal rights	75	73	84	69

Note: Entries are percentages of those with an opinion, i.e. of those who either agree or disagree; they show the percentages who supported free speech or equal rights, measured as follows: free speech: % disagree with proposition in text; equal rights: % disagree with Canadian version of proposition in text, or agree with opposite version.

balance of the answers (especially amongst the public) between the pro- and anti-rights sides, and we shall treat disagreement with the second version as equivalent to agreement with the first. Again there was little difference between Canada and Britain on free speech or on equal rights, though considerable differences between the public and their politicians within each country (Table 11.4).

Finally we come to individualism. We asked:

[1.] Ideally society should be like:
  • a unified body pursuing a common goal;
  • a collection of people independently pursuing their own goals.

[2.] In Britain today, too much emphasis is placed on individual interests at the expense of the community's interest. (Britain)

In our society today, too much emphasis is placed on
  • individual freedom at the expense of the community's interest;
  • conformity and obedience to the community. (Canada)

The first question was worded identically in both countries; the second was worded similarly, but as an agree/disagree in Britain though as a choice in Canada. Again, opinion in Britain and Canada was very similar, though politicians in Britain were somewhat more favourable than the public to the idea of a common goal for society (Table 11.5).

Britons and Canadians also had similar attitudes towards state responsibilities for welfare. We asked:

Influences

TABLE 11.5. *Individualism in Britain and Canada*

	Britain		Canada	
	Politicians (%)	Public (%)	Politicians (%)	Public (%)
Individual goals	35	44	41	38
Individual interests	35	33	34	34

Note: Entries are percentages of those with an opinion; percentages show support for self-reliance rather than collectivism; see text for question wordings.

Here are a number of things which many people feel are very desirable goals but, at the same time, many people feel that it is *not* the responsibility of the government to provide them. Do *you* think each of the following should, or should not, be the *government's* responsibility:

- a decent standard of living for everyone?
- that everyone who wants a job can have one? (Britain)

In the matter of jobs and standard of living the government should:

- see to it that everyone has a job and a decent standard of living
- let each person get ahead on his own. (Canada)

About 10 per cent more of the British public than the Canadian said it was the government's responsibility to provide jobs and decent living standards for all, though differences between British and Canadian politicians were smaller.

British and Canadian views about the targeting of family allowances and old age pensions were also very similar. Politicians, especially in Canada, were more reluctant than the public to target these benefits, but overall national differences were slight (Table 11.6). We asked:

State benefits like family allowances should only be paid to those who really need them. (Britain)

Social insurance programs like old age pensions and family allowances should be based on family income, so people who don't need this type of assistance don't get it. (Canada)

Cultural similarities between Britain and Canada extended beyond basic values to more practical aspects of civil rights. In both countries we asked a complex question about random searches in a shopping mall, designed to

TABLE 11.6. *Attitudes to welfare in Britain and Canada*

	Britain		Canada	
	Politicians (%)	Public (%)	Politicians (%)	Public (%)
Government has a responsibility for				
jobs and living standards	n.a.	n.a.	70	67
jobs	67	78	n.a.	n.a.
living standards	84	77	n.a.	n.a.
Apply means test	55	64	49	69

Note: n.a. = not applicable.

show how support for such searches was influenced by purpose (to stop drug use, or to stop theft), by agents (security guards, the police, or store owners), and by targets (shoppers or employees). The British version of this question randomly and independently varied all three of these. It read:

In the case where there is concern about [illegal drug use/shoplifting] in a shopping centre, do you think that a [security guard/police officer/shop owner] should have the right to make random searches of the bags carried by [shoppers/people who work in that shopping centre]?

The Canadian version omitted one of these twelve possible variants, namely a store owner searching shoppers for drugs.

Overall, Canadians were only marginally less willing than the British to support random searches; in both countries, people were more willing to support searches of employees than of customers; and in both countries, politicians gave much less support than the public to random searching. There were some national differences, however: Canadians were more willing to accept searches for theft than for drugs, while the British took the opposite view; and Canadians did not distinguish between police and store owners, while the British did (Table 11.7).

On telephone tapping also, the patterns of British and Canadian opinion were similar. We asked:

In order to combat [crime, should the police/terrorism, should the security services/the spread of dangerous and undemocratic ideas, should the security services] ever be allowed to [tap phones/inspect people's bank accounts]? (Britain)

TABLE 11.7. *Support for random searches in Britain and Canada*

	Britain		Canada	
	Politicians (%)	Public (%)	Politicians (%)	Public (%)
Support searches (all variants)	30	46	25	42
for drugs	32	48	22	40
for theft	28	43	28	44
by guards	30	43	22	45
by police	40	54	24	43
by owners	19	40	29	38
of shoppers	27	43	22	37
of employees	32	48	28	46

Some people feel that Canada's security services should be able to tap the telephones of people who [hold ideas that may lead to the overthrow of our democratic system/ are agents of a foreign government/are suspected of terrorism/are suspected of being spies]. Do you think the security service should be able to wire-tap them or not? (Canada)

Despite differences in question formats, we can at least compare support for wire-taps aimed at terrorism and at the spread of undemocratic ideas. Support varied sharply with the target of the taps—but it did not vary much between Britain and Canada. In both countries there was very much more support for using wire-taps to combat terrorism than to combat the spread of undemocratic ideas. And in both countries, politicians were slightly more willing to accept wire-taps than the public—an unusual reversal of politicians' generally more liberal stance, but one that was common to both Britain and Canada (Table 11.8).

Although capital punishment had not been used in either Britain or Canada for some time, the death penalty remained a crucial issue in debates about civil rights. It was an issue on which politicians differed sharply from the public. We asked:

[Given that parliament has repeatedly voted against the death penalty/In order to clamp down on rising crime and violence], do you think Britain should reintroduce the death penalty for murder, or keep things as they are? (Britain)

TABLE 11.8. *Support for wire taps in Britain and Canada*

	Britain		Canada	
	Politicians (%)	Public (%)	Politicians (%)	Public (%)
Accept wire taps to combat				
terrorism	73	67	76	67
undemocratic ideas	43	42	43	35

TABLE 11.9. *Support for the death penalty in Britain and Canada*

	Britain		Canada	
	Politicians (%)	Public (%)	Politicians (%)	Public (%)
Support death penalty	26	50	35	55
with crime prompt	24	50	n.a.	n.a.
with parliament prompt	28	50	n.a.	n.a.

Note: n.a. = not applicable.

Are there some crimes for which the death penalty is justified or is the death penalty never justified or are you not sure? (Canada)

Excluding the 23 per cent of Canadians who took the easy option of accepting the proffered 'not sure', just about half the public in both countries supported the death penalty. Amongst politicians, support for the death penalty was much less—only a quarter in Britain, and one-third in Canada. Attempts to push the British towards or against the death penalty by invoking references to rising crime or parliament's opposition failed completely. Allowing for the differences of question wording, the evidence here is that Canadians and Britons had very similar attitudes, which helps to explain the heated debates in both countries when either Canadian or British citizens end up on death row in the USA (Table 11.9).

Cultural Differences

On many indicators, Canadians appeared less tolerant than the British. We considered the principle of tolerance first of all by asking respondents to agree or disagree with the following statements:

Influences

TABLE 11.10. *The abstract principle of tolerance in Britain and Canada*

	Britain		Canada	
	Politicians (%)	Public (%)	Politicians (%)	Public (%)
Tolerance	65	47	49	34

Note: Entries are percentage who disagree with proposition in text.

We should not tolerate people whose ideas are morally wrong. (Britain)

We shouldn't be tolerant of ideas that are wrong morally. (Canada)

Politicians were once again significantly more liberal than the public in both countries, but the British as a whole also appeared significantly more tolerant than the Canadians. The questions were similar, though the reference to tolerating 'people' in the British survey differed from that of tolerating 'ideas' in the earlier Canadian survey. The British wording of this question was designed to be a little more logically rational than in the original Canadian version, but that seems unlikely to account for all of the difference in the response. Another possibility is that the word 'morally' has slightly different meanings in different language cultures—more sexually oriented in some, more broadly interpreted in others. But there remains the simple explanation that the citizens of *The Peaceable Kingdom*[38] were indeed less tolerant than the British (Table 11.10).

We went on to see how far people would sympathize with, or tolerate, different groups in society. We found that Canadians tended, more than the British, to blame the disadvantaged for their own problems. We looked at this issue from both a social and an economic perspective, using two agree/ disagree questions. First we asked about women and men at work:

By their nature, men are more suited than women to do senior jobs in business and government. (Britain)

Women don't get along with each other on the job as well as men do. (Canada)

We then tacked the question of economic disadvantage more directly by asking: 'The poor are poor because [they don't try hard enough to get ahead/

TABLE 11.11. *Blame the socially disadvantaged in Britain and Canada*

	Britain		Canada	
	Politicians (%)	Public (%)	Politicians (%)	Public (%)
Blame poor	14	22	19	39
Blame women	8	16	18	28

Notes: Blame poor = don't try; blame women = not as good as men in workplace.

Both British and Canadian figures for blaming the poor have been calculated by dividing percentage who blame poor by percentage blaming either rich or poor—a total that came to much less than 100% in both countries. In Britain, this calculation was based upon random half samples asked different questions; in Canada by simply excluding neutral answers. See text for further details of questions.

the wealthy and powerful keep them poor].' In Britain a random half of the sample was asked each form of this question. In Canada all respondents in the mail-back survey were asked to choose between these two options.

Despite the differences of question format, the evidence suggests that both women and the poor were blamed for the disadvantages they experienced much more in Canada than in Britain. Clearly the second question fails to cover the range of popular explanations for poverty. In Canada, where both options were offered to all respondents, 29 per cent of the public and 37 per cent of politicians checked the 'neither of the above' code. Amongst the British public, 16 per cent agreed that the poor were to blame and 58 per cent that the rich were to blame—which suggests that at least 26 per cent thought neither was true; and amongst British politicians the same calculation suggests that 39 per cent thought neither was true. There was a strong element of cross-national similarity here, despite the different question format, which may indicate a common appreciation about the systemic causes of poverty in both Britain and Canada (Table 11.11).

Questions about AIDS also showed the Canadians to be less tolerant. We asked:

Should [people who cook for restaurants or schools/surgeons and dentists] be required to take a test to prove that they have not been infected with the virus which causes AIDS? (Britain)

Should people who cook for restaurants or schools be required to take a test to verify that they have not been exposed to AIDS? (Canada)

TABLE 11.12. *Support for compulsory AIDS tests in Britain and Canada*

	Britain		Canada	
	Politicians (%)	Public (%)	Politicians (%)	Public (%)
Support compulsory AIDS tests for cooks	47	60	58	74

We can only compare answers to the question about cooks. The questions were very similar, and the answers showed that the British were substantially less inclined than Canadians to inflict AIDS tests on cooks, though that may have reflected growing public awareness about the transmission of HIV in the interval between the two surveys. And, although comparative data is not available, a large majority of Britons would inflict AIDS tests on surgeons and dentists (Table 11.12).

Following Sullivan, Pierson, and Marcus,[39] we sought to measure social and political tolerance towards groups that people disliked, in particular towards the 'most disliked group', or 'MDG', chosen from a list. Sullivan and his colleagues argue that we cannot tolerate a group we like: defending the liberties of a group we like is close to being an expression of self-interest—or at least of approval—rather than tolerance. We can only be said to tolerate a group if we dislike it, and the more we dislike it, the greater the tolerance we show when we defend its liberties. As we have argued before, there is an obvious logical flaw in this method of measuring tolerance, since everyone is likely to be intolerant of some groups or actions. The MDG chosen from a restricted list is not the same as the group—chosen from an infinitely long unrestricted list—that inspires the greatest intolerance. None the less, provided we recognize the limitations of this approach, and bear in mind the content of the list, it can be a useful measure of willingness to tolerate groups we dislike. In the Canadian survey, selection of the MDG was explicit; in the British survey it was calculated automatically and unobtrusively, by computer, from a set of likeability ratings for different groups. We asked:

[1.] I am going to read you a list of groups which some people like but others dislike. Please give a mark out of ten to show how much you like each group. (Britain; from this our computer calculated the MDG)

I am going to read you a list of groups and then ask you which of the groups you like the least. (Canada; this identifies the MDG)

[2.] Now I'm going to ask you whether you agree or disagree with some statements about one of the groups you dislike.

- I would be *un*happy if a [MDG] moved in next door to me.
- I would be *un*happy if a child of mine became emotionally involved with a [MDG].
- [MDG]s should *not* be allowed to make public speeches in my locality.
- [MDG]s should *not* be allowed to teach in publicly funded schools.

(Britain; despite the ambiguous wording at the start the group named was always the MDG)

Now I am going to read you a statement about MDG. I would like you to tell me whether you strongly agree, agree, are uncertain, disagree or strongly disagree with the following statement. [(Null)/the statement I am going to read raises a very serious issue—an issue on which there are strong arguments on either side. So I would like to ask you to stop and take a moment to think carefully before answering.] The statement is: MDG should be allowed to hold public rallies in our cities. (Canada)

In Britain the most frequently chosen MDGs were Northern Irish terrorists on both sides of the sectarian/nationalist divide, plus the extreme right-wing British National Front. In Canada the most frequently chosen MDGs were the Ku Klux Klan/racists, communists, and fascists. Clearly there were some points of similarity as well as difference here. In Britain politicians proved to be even more antagonistic than the public towards the National Front; while in Canada, politicians were similarly more antagonistic, even than the public, towards fascists. However, British and Canadian attitudes towards communists were poles apart. At least in 1987, before the fall of the Soviet Union, the Canadian public were still much more antagonistic than their politicians towards communists—even though it was the Canadian government that had blacklisted left-wing activists as recently as the 1970s. Canada, of course, also had a particularly large and well-organized community of virulently anti-communist Ukrainian émigrés who had neither forgotten nor forgiven the man-made famines inflicted on Ukraine under Stalin.[40] Very few British people chose communists as their least liked group, however.

But the approach of Sullivan and his colleagues was designed to allow tolerance to be compared internationally, even if the objects of dislike varied

from country to country. Judged by their attitudes towards permitting speeches
or rallies by their MDG, Canadian politicians were only very slightly less
tolerant than British politicians, but the Canadian public were massively less
tolerant than the British. British and Canadian politicians differed by only 4
per cent in their willingness to ban speeches and rallies by their MDG, but
the British and Canadian publics differed by 23 per cent (Table 11.13).

Demonstrations and strikes have long been recognized as 'free speech in
action'. Both surveys asked questions on these topics. While the survey
questions were not as similar as we might wish, the topic is too important
to be neglected. We asked:

[1.] If there is a real possibility that a [political demonstration/football match]
may lead to public disorder or even a riot, should it be banned in advance or
should the authorities make special arrangements to deal with trouble but
allow it to go ahead. (Britain)

Should a town or city be able to limit public demonstrations that city officials
think might turn violent against persons or property. (Canada)

[2.] Should [all workers, even those in essential services like the Ambulance
Service or the Fire Brigade/workers who do not work in essential public
serves]

• have the right to join a trade union if they wish?
• and have the right to strike? (Britain)

Should workers have the right to stay out on strike indefinitely, even if the
government believes continuation of the strike will cause hardship to the
public? (Canada)

Despite the differences in wording it is impossible to avoid the conclusion
that the British were more tolerant of demonstrations and strikes. Three-
fifths of the British would let a potentially disorderly political demonstration
go ahead (and even more would allow a potentially disorderly football match),
while only a very few Canadians felt city officials should not be able to limit
potentially disorderly demonstrations. Even accepting the obvious point that
some might want city officials to 'be able to' yet not actually exercise that
power, the discrepancy between the British and Canadian responses was
huge. Similarly two-thirds of the British supported the right of the Ambulance Service, Fire Brigade, and other essential services to strike, but only
15 per cent of Canadians would permit indefinite strikes that caused hardship. Strikes by essential public-service workers cause immediate hardship;

TABLE 11.13. Attitudes to MDGs in Britain and Canada

	Britain		Canada	
	Politicians (%)	Public (%)	Politicians (%)	Public (%)
Most disliked group (MDG)				
IRA sympathizers	18	25		
Protestant terrorist sympathizers	19	19		
National Front supporters	30	16		
black activists	6	10		
Militant Tendency supporters	10	9		
muslim activists	6	8		
gays and lesbians	4	6		
communists	3	3		
animal-rights activists	3	2		
feminists	1	1		
Greenpeace	0	0		
Most disliked group (MDG)				
Ku Klux Klan/racists			43	43
communists			13	25
fascists			39	16
pro-abortionists			2	7
anti-abortionists			0	5
atheists			1	3
socialists			1	2
Ban rally/speeches of MDG	29	44	33	67

Influences

TABLE 11.14. *Support for practice of right to protest or strike in*
Britain and Canada

	Britain		Canada	
	Politicians (%)	Public (%)	Politicians (%)	Public (%)
Allow				
potentially disorderly demonstration	60	57	23	14
strikes in essential services/strikes that cause public hardship	65	68	14	15

indeed the two-thirds support for strikes by essential workers in Britain contrasted with much higher British support for strikes by non-essential workers. Even more clearly on strikes than on demonstrations, therefore, the discrepancy between Canadian and British responses was too large to be explained away by differences of wording (Table 11.14).

Although it has been argued that Canada is over-governed,[41] Canadians not only proved to have more respect than the British for politicians and experts, but were better disposed than the British to the idea of government regulating the private sector. We asked:

[1.] Most politicians can be trusted to do what they think is best for the country.

[2.] I'll put my trust in the practical experience of ordinary people rather than the theories of experts and intellectuals. (Britain)

In the long run, I'll put my trust in the simple down-to-earth thinking of ordinary people rather than the theories of experts and intellectuals. (Canada)

[3.] Government regulation of business usually does more harm than good. (Britain)

Government regulation of business:
  • usually does more harm than good, or
  • is necessary to keep industry from becoming too powerful. (Canada)

The first two questions were very comparable, though the Canadian format of the third may have encouraged a pro-regulation response.

TABLE 11.15. *Perceptions of government in Britain and Canada*

	Britain		Canada	
	Politicians (%)	Public (%)	Politicians (%)	Public (%)
Politicians can be trusted	58	33	90	63
Experts can be trusted	26	33	38	41
Government regulation does good/is necessary	50	34	63	58

On our evidence the British were much more suspicious of politicians than the Canadians: amongst the public, only half as many trusted politicians in Britain as in Canada. Naturally, in both countries, politicians themselves trusted other politicians much more, but huge British/Canadian differences remained. Moreover, other questions showed that Britons were not universally or mindlessly suspicious: they trusted most ordinary people they met in everyday life, they just did not trust politicians. Canadians were also more willing to trust experts and intellectuals, reflected perhaps in the greater extent to which experts and intellectuals were drawn into the development of public policy in Canada.[42] And Canadians were also more favourable to government regulation than the British: a pattern that also occurs in comparisons between Canada and the USA, and is, as Nemetz, Stanbury, and Thompson have noted, 'a pervasive (Canadian) social phenomenon, born of historical tradition, which entails a greater acceptance of the legitimacy and authority of the government to attend to social concerns'[43]—but it is more remarkable in a comparison with Britain than with the USA (Table 11.15).

Questions of due process featured in both surveys. At the time of the British survey, recent bad publicity had damaged the image of the British police, and English and Welsh courts had been criticized for convicting people on uncorroborated confessions (which were accepted by courts in England and Wales, though not in Scotland) or on false evidence manufactured by the police. We asked three relevant questions:

[1.] Do you think the police need to be subject to strong external control in order to protect civil liberties? (Substituting RCMP for 'police' in Canada)

[2.] In dealing with mugging and other serious street crime, which is more important:

TABLE 11.16. *Support for due process in Britain and Canada*

	Britain		Canada	
	Politicians (%)	Public (%)	Politicians (%)	Public (%)
Police need external control	79	78	74	64
Protect rights of suspects	32	14	20	9
Right to silence	56	43	61	37

- to protect the rights of suspects?
- to stop such crimes and make the streets safe even if we sometimes have to violate the suspects' rights?

[3.] A person charged with a crime should have the right to refuse to answer questions in court without it being held against them. (Britain)

A person suspected of a serious crime:

- should have to answer questions from the police
- should be able to remain silent. (Canada)

The need for external control of the police was recognized by a substantially higher percentage in Britain than Canada. Alas for civil liberties, however, there was little support for the unspecified 'rights of suspects' anywhere, though politicians gave them more support than the public, and the British more than the Canadians. However, in both countries, roughly two-fifths of the public and three-fifths of politicians backed the right to silence (Table 11.16).

Constitutional Cultures

The Canadian survey showed that the Charter was not only well recognized in Canada but exceedingly popular with the general public: 84 per cent had heard of it and 93 per cent of them approved. At the same time, almost every politician had heard of it and 88 per cent approved. Obviously there can be no precise equivalent to this question in Britain, but we got as near to it as we could. In Britain we asked people to give 'marks out of ten' to seventeen different institutions, actual or proposed, to indicate how much they felt citizens' rights and liberties were (or would be) protected by each one. The list included three proposed reforms:

- a Bill of Rights, passed by parliament, and enforced by the courts
- a Freedom of Information Act, giving more legal access to government information
- a reformed House of Lords, whose members were elected

along with fourteen existing institutions that included the traditional intermediate institutions of civil society (the press, trade unions, and churches), plus judicial or quasi-judicial bodies (British courts, European courts, and bodies like the Equal Opportunities Commission or the Commission for Racial Equality), plus elected bodies (back-bench MPs in parliament, and local-government councils), plus the Conservative government's own proclaimed means of defending and extending rights through the sale of council houses to sitting tenants, privatization of nationalized industries, the introduction of elected school boards, and 'recent changes in the way the NHS is organised' —this last comprising Hospital Trusts, General Practitioner (GP) Budgets, and an internal market within the NHS.

Top of both the British public's and politicians' lists came a Freedom of Information Act, followed by a Bill of Rights. Next on the British public's list were the quasi-judicial Commissions for Equal Opportunities and Racial Equality, and an elected House of Lords (equivalent to the proposal for Senate reform in Canada that was built into the 1992 Charlottetown Accord but rejected later that year when the Referendum destroyed the entire Accord[44]). Then came British and European courts—with the Conservatives' sale of council houses just squeezing in between the courts. They were followed by television and the quality press, trade unions, and churches, MPs and local-government councils (well down the list!), the three remaining Conservative government reforms, and, at the bottom, the tabloid press. The British politicians' list was similar to that of the public except that our local-government politicians had much less favourable views than the public about the forced sale of (local-government-owned) council houses, and more favourable views than the public of back-bench MPs and more especially of local-government councils.

The important point for our present discussion is that elements of a written constitution—a Freedom of Information Act and a Bill of Rights—scored better than all these other plausible proposals or traditional mechanisms for defending rights and liberties. The British seemed to value the written constitution which they did not have just as highly as Canadians valued the Charter that they did have. Interestingly, however, in Britain, unlike Canada, a Bill of Rights was (slightly) more popular with politicians than the public (Table 11.17).

TABLE 11.17. *Support for a written constitution in Britain and Canada*

	Britain		Canada	
	Politicians (marks/10)	Public (marks/10)	Politicians (%)	Public (%)
% heard of the Canadian Charter	n.a.	n.a.	100	84
% (of above) who approve Charter	n.a.	n.a.	88	93
Freedom of Information Act	8.2	7.7	n.a.	n.a.
Bill of Rights	7.6	6.7	n.a.	n.a.
EOC/CRE	6.5	6.7	n.a.	n.a.
Elected House of Lords	6.6	6.6	n.a.	n.a.
British courts	6.5	6.5	n.a.	n.a.
Sale of council houses to tenants	5.8	6.4	n.a.	n.a.
European courts	6.6	6.3	n.a.	n.a.
Broadsheets (*Guardian/Daily Telegraph*)	6.7	6.3	n.a.	n.a.
Television	6.5	6.3	n.a.	n.a.
Trade unions	6.5	6.0	n.a.	n.a.
Churches	5.9	5.8	n.a.	n.a.
Back-bench MPs	6.6	5.7	n.a.	n.a.
Local-government councils	6.9	5.6	n.a.	n.a.
Elected school boards	5.6	5.5	n.a.	n.a.
Privatization of nationalized industries	4.1	4.4	n.a.	n.a.
Recent changes in the NHS	4.2	4.3	n.a.	n.a.
Tabloid press (*Sun/Daily Mirror*)	3.6	3.9	n.a.	n.a.

Notes: British entries in order of declining support amongst the British public.
    n.a. = not applicable.

But support for a Bill of Rights or a Freedom of Information Act in Britain might reflect a superficial response to an attractive slogan. Perhaps the British are in favour of the principle (or slogan) of limited government but not in favour of actual limitations in particular circumstances. There is no point in supporting a written constitution if we do not accept the right of a court to overrule parliament; and no point in accepting limitations on government that can be capriciously swept aside whenever government finds them irksome.

In fact, we were able to make more precise comparisons between Britain and Canada on the *practice* of constitutionality than on the *principle*. We asked:

[1.] Suppose parliament passed a law you considered unjust, immoral, or cruel. Would you still be morally bound to obey it? (Britain and Canada)

- Yes, it's our duty to obey any law adopted under proper constitutional procedure;
- No, because we have a higher duty to our own conscience and to what we think is right and wrong. (explicit options in Canada only)

[2.] Suppose we had a constitutional Bill of Rights, as some other countries do. If parliament passed a law but the courts said it was unconstitutional, who should have the final say, parliament or the courts? (Britain)

Suppose someone in Britain objects to a law passed by parliament and takes the case to the European Court of Human Rights. Who should have the final say, the European court or the British parliament? (Britain)

When the legislature passes a law [(null)/for example, to control unions/for example, to assist poor people] but the courts say it is unconstitutional on the grounds that it conflicts with the Charter of Rights, who should have the final say, the legislature or the courts? (Canada)

[3.] 'If there is a genuine national emergency, is it all right to suspend some of our usual civil rights?

IF YES: Who should have the power to declare an emergency: parliament or the government alone? (Britain)

If the cabinet says there is a national emergency and a majority in parliament agrees, is it all right to suspend the usual civil rights? (Canada)

Although politicians felt more moral pressure than the public to obey an unjust law in both countries, the British as a whole were slightly more submissive than the Canadians, though not by much. Attitudes towards legal enforcement of rights against the will of parliament were more complex. Two-thirds of the Canadian public but only one-third of Canadian politicians would back the courts. In Britain, public attitudes towards British courts were less favourable: less than half the public, though still one-third of politicians, would back British courts. But public attitudes in Britain towards the European court were more favourable: over half the public and even greater numbers of British politicians would back the European court against

TABLE 11.18. *Acceptance of parliamentary sovereignty in Britain and Canada*

	Britain		Canada	
	Politicians (%)	Public (%)	Politicians (%)	Public (%)
Obey unjust law	66	51	55	45
(Domestic) courts to have final say	36	48	42	69
European court to have final say	59	55	n.a.	n.a.
All right to suspend civil rights	80	78	69	67

the British parliament. Taking account of the European dimension therefore, the British public remained somewhat less favourable to courts than the Canadian public; but British politicians were actually more favourable than Canadian politicians to courts overruling parliament. As we have shown elsewhere, part of the explanation for our findings about British attitudes to both British and European courts is that they reflect strongly partisan responses,[45] but the levels of support remain, whatever the causes or influences upon them.

At least some parts of most constitutions, including the European Convention and the Canadian Charter, can be suspended in periods of emergency. It may be some reflection of the impact of the Canadian Charter on constitutional attitudes that only 67 per cent of Canadians compared with 78 per cent of the British would accept a suspension of civil rights during emergencies, though that is only an 11 per cent difference—hardly evidence of a radically different culture. Canadian opinion may reflect memories of the massive arrests and suspension of habeus corpus in Quebec when Trudeau declared a state of emergency in October 1970, following terrorist attacks on government ministers by the Front de Libération du Québec,[46] though that had an almost exact parallel in the reintroduction of internment (detention without trial) in Northern Ireland at much the same time (Table 11.18).

Both surveys asked about the government's responsibility to provide equal opportunities:

Here are a number of things which many people feel are very desirable goals but, at the same time, many people feel that it is not the responsibility of the government to provide them. Do *you* think each of the following should, or should not, be the *government*'s responsibility (the list of possible government responsibilities included eleven items in all):

TABLE 11.19. *Support for equal employment rights in Britain and Canada*

	Britain		Canada	
	Politicians (%)	Public (%)	Politicians (%)	Public (%)
Government responsibility for equal opportunities	92	91	42	65
Quotas for women in				
government employment	19	24	65	54
large private companies	18	22	45	32

• equal opportunities for everyone? (Britain)

While equal opportunity to succeed is important for all Canadians, it's not really the government's job to guarantee it. (Canada)

Given that the principle of equal opportunity is so clearly encoded in the Canadian Charter, we were surprised to find that the general principle of government responsibility for equality of opportunity was backed by almost all the British, but by only two-thirds of the Canadian public and a mere two-fifths of Canadian politicians. The explanation may lie in the different question wording, which emphasized the opportunity to succeed in the Canadian case but not in the British. Or it could lie in the fact that in Britain the term 'equal opportunities' has broader overtones than in Canada because, in the past, it has been linked to class and income inequalities as well as, since the 1970s, to the additional concerns of race, gender, and disability. But it may have reflected Canadian awareness that an affirmative answer to this question implied support for coercive legislation.

We went on to ask more specifically about the legal regulation of equal employment opportunities (Table 11.19):

Do you think the law should require [large private companies/the government and civil service] to hire a fixed percentage of [women/blacks and Asians/disabled people], or should [women/blacks and Asians/disabled people] get no special treatment? (Britain)

Do you think large companies should have quotas to ensure a fixed percentage of women are hired, or should women get no special treatment? (Canada)

Do you think the government in Ottawa should make sure that a certain proportion of the top jobs in government go to [French Canadians/women]? (Canada)

Paradoxically, Canadians backed legal enforcement of equal opportunities for women in the job market very much more strongly than the British. The explanation for this paradox may lie, as we have already hinted, in Canadians' greater familiarity with affirmative action programmes to remedy past discrimination, programmes which were fully legalized in Section 15(2) of the Canadian Charter. Since the 1986 Employment Equity Act in Canada, when the terminology for affirmative action was formally changed, it has become compulsory for federally regulated companies to devise plans to enhance the representation of women and minority groups within their workforce, to set targets, and to report regularly to the Minister for Employment and Immigration on the degree to which these targets have been achieved.[47] In Britain, by contrast, although targets are legal, they are not mandatory and there is no requirement to report progress towards achieving them.[48]

We could make cross-national comparisons of attitudes only to quotas for women. Canadians, especially politicians but also the public, and especially in regard to government employment but also in regard to large private companies, were very much more favourable than the British to gender-based quotas. And in further contrast with Canada, politicians in Britain were even less favourable than their public towards gender quotas. These responses were interesting, not only because the use of fixed, gender-based, quotas is not legal in either Canada or Britain, but because the 1984 Royal Commission on Equality in Employment in Canada (which preceded the 1986 Employment Equity Act) reported that many Canadians were resistant to the imposition of quotas to promote more equitable employment opportunities for women and minority groups.[49]

The Correlation between Principles and Practice

Quite apart from similarities or differences in the *levels of support* for civil rights in Britain and Canada, there is the question of whether attitudes are more *coherent and structured* in one country than the other. We might expect politicians in both countries to have more structured attitudes than their corresponding publics, since they are political thinkers by profession if not by academic training. But overall, it is not obvious which country should have the more tightly structured set of attitudes.

TABLE 11.20. *Correlations between principles and practice in Britain and Canada*

	Britain		Canada	
	Politicians (%)	Public (%)	Politicians (%)	Public (%)
% of correlations exceeding 0.2	36	4	32	4
% of correlations exceeding 0.1	not calc.	29	not calc.	26

On the one hand, we might expect Canada's explicit constitutional framework to encourage Canadians to link principles to practice much more clearly and explicitly than in Britain. On the other, we might expect that stronger ideological traditions in Britain would help to structure attitudes more coherently along party lines.

To find out, we begin by calculating correlation coefficients linking abstract principles, values, or sympathies (most of the comparable variables on trust, self-reliance, tolerance, liberty, and equality), with attitudes to the practical implementation of rights (most of the comparable variables on support for parliament, the courts, a constitution, the death penalty, censorship, abortion, and employment quotas, etc.). We can construct twenty-four measures of practice in Canada and twenty-six in Britain, together with nineteen measures of principles, values, and sympathies in both countries. There is a close but not always perfect match between the variables used in Canada and Britain. That gives 456 pairwise correlations for Canada and 494 for Britain, each correlation linking an abstract value with a specific implementation of rights. If we take an arbitrary threshold of 0.20 as indicating a substantial correlation (correlations much less than this are statistically significant but not substantively impressive), then the proportion of correlations that exceed this threshold gives a rough guide to the overall fit between support for abstract values and practical policies in the two countries (Table 11.20).

For politicians in Britain and Canada about a third of the correlations exceed this threshold but, for the public, less than 4 per cent. Obviously principles and practice fit together very much more closely amongst politicians than amongst the public. It would be very surprising if that were not so. But our purpose here is to focus on the comparison between Britain and Canada, not to compare publics and politicians: amongst politicians, 36 per cent of correlations exceeded the threshold in Britain and 32 per cent in

Canada. British politicians thus seem to have at least as coherent and the-
oretically structured an approach to questions of civil rights as Canadian
politicians, and perhaps even a little more so.

Amongst the publics, only 4 per cent of correlations exceeded the threshold of 0.20 in both Britain and Canada. If we drop the threshold to 0.10 to
assist the comparison, then, once again, a slightly higher percentage of correlations (29 per cent) exceed the threshold in Britain than in Canada (26 per
cent). Of course we recognize that the precise size of correlation coefficients
depends in part upon the details of question wording. Our British/Canadian
comparison is necessarily fairly rough and ready. But, none the less, our
evidence suggests that, despite their written constitution and Charter of Rights
and Freedoms with all the political debate that surrounded them, neither
politicians nor the public in Canada seem to link the theory and practice of
civil rights any more closely than in Britain.

As an example of the large amount of data underlying that conclusion, let
us take two of our simplest and yet most important abstract values—respect
for authority (see Table 11.3) and support for equal rights (see Table 11.4)—
and show how these relate to practical decisions about the implementation
of rights in Britain and Canada. We have grouped various practical decisions
about rights into those which seem (*a priori*) likely to depend upon attitudes
to authority, and those which seem likely to depend upon attitudes to equal
rights. We have included support for a written constitution, courts overruling parliament, and the right to hold damaging strikes in both groups. We
take correlations between abstract respect for authority and each practical
issue in the first group; and between abstract support for equal rights and
each practical issue in the second group. All the correlations were in the
intuitively expected directions. What is interesting is not their direction but
their size and, in particular, the relative size of the correlations in Britain and
Canada.

Respect for authority and support for equal rights correlated about
equally well with practical decisions in both countries. In both they correlated much better amongst politicians than amongst the public, and better
with some practical decisions than others, but the cross-national similarities
were clear.

There were a few cross-national differences, however. Respect for authority correlated much better in Britain than Canada with attitudes towards
suspects' rights, or towards the death penalty—especially amongst the public; with attitudes towards letting a court overrule parliament; with attitudes
towards a Freedom of Information Act—especially amongst politicians. By
contrast, the only noteworthy examples of a stronger correlation with respect

Table 11.21. *Correlations between practice and the micro-principle of respect for authority in Britain and Canada*

	Britain		Canada	
	Politicians (r × 100)	Public (r × 100)	Politicians (r × 100)	Public (r × 100)
Correlations between respect for authority and				
rating for Bill/Charter of Rights	−11	·	·	·
rating for Freedom of Information Act	−24	·	n.a.	n.a.
courts/Euro-Court may overrule parliament	−33	−17	·	·
allow damaging strikes	−29	−11	−26	−10
all right to suspend rights in emergency	32	·	30	19
should obey unjust law	34	17	32	17
allow disorderly demonstration	−34	−26	−26	−20
let MDG make speeches/hold rally	−20	−16	−15	−14
support AIDS test for cooks	35	24	29	21
support external control of police	−27	−10	−33	·
allow wire taps	·	10	16	11
allow random searches	19	15	25	16
suspects' rights important	−40	−28	−29	−11
support right to silence	−29	−14	−21	−14
support death penalty	33	26	24	·

Note: Correlations less than 0.10 have been replaced by full points.

for authority in Canada than in Britain was the public's (but not politicians') attitudes towards suspending rights in an emergency, and politicians' (but not the public's) attitudes towards wire-taps. Clearly, this evidence cannot support the proposition that Canadians link abstract respect for authority with the practice of rights any more coherently than the British. Quite the reverse (Table 11.21).

There were more cross-national differences in correlations with abstract support for equal rights. Support for 'means-testing'—that is, restricting social welfare benefits to those in proven need—correlated strongly (and negatively) with support for equal rights only amongst British politicians, where it raised the spectre of historic political campaigns of the 1930s. Similarly, it was only amongst British politicians that support for equal rights correlated strongly with a willingness to allow damaging strikes. There was, therefore, a clearer class dimension to the practical implementation of equal rights in Britain. In addition, support for equal rights only correlated strongly with a willingness to let courts overrule parliament amongst British

Influences

TABLE 11.22. *Correlations between practice and the micro-principle of equal rights in Britain and Canada*

| | Britain | | Canada | |
	Politicians (r × 100)	Public (r × 100)	Politicians (r × 100)	Public (r × 100)
Correlations between support for equal rights and				
rating for Bill/Charter of Rights	26	.	35	20
rating for Freedom of Information Act	36	.	n.a.	n.a.
courts/Euro-court may overrule parliament	41	15	14	.
allow damaging strikes	37	15	13	12
government responsible for equal opportunities	25	14	32	14
quotas for women/minorities	25	10	n.a.	n.a.
quotas for women/French in government jobs	n.a.	n.a.	34	.
quotas for women in private companies	n.a.	n.a.	25	.
means-tested benefits	−27	.	.	.
government responsible for jobs/living standards	n.a.	n.a.	28	.
government responsible for jobs	28	10	n.a.	n.a.
government responsible for living standards	30	.	n.a.	n.a.

Note: Correlations less than 0.10 have been replaced by full points.

n.a. = not applicable.

politicians—and then only with respect to the European court, not domestic British courts.

On the other hand, there was a much larger correlation amongst the Canadian public than amongst the British, between support for equal rights and a support for a Charter/Bill of Rights or a Freedom of Information Act.

Abstract support for equal rights therefore correlated particularly well with actual operational mechanisms—different in the two countries—for the protection of rights. But, overall, we cannot say that abstract commitment to equal rights was more closely linked to practical decisions in Canada than in Britain (Table 11.22).

The Influence of Socio-Political Background

Finally, we can ask how far British and Canadian attitudes towards civil rights reflected social and political background. Were they socially and ideologically determined to the same degree? We have taken six measures of socio-political background:

1. educational qualifications (none/school/university)
2. age (under 25/25–35/35–55/over 55)

3. gender
4. religiosity (attend weekly/monthly/less/not religious)
5. self-assigned ideology (left/centre/right)
6. party choice (see below).

These variables include the most powerful socio-political predictors of attitudes to civil rights which we have uncovered in earlier chapters. We can correlate each of these background measures with all of our measures of principles, values, sympathies, and attitudes to practice.

In the case of the last background measure, party choice, we focus on the three main parties in each country at the time of the surveys by restricting the analysis to those whose party preference (Britain), last federal vote (Canadian public), or party label (Canadian politicians) was Conservative, Liberal, or Labour in Britain; and Progressive Conservative, Liberal, or New Democrat (NDP) in Canada, and use a multiple regression with two party dummies (a third would be logically redundant) to predict each civil-rights attitude. We use the multiple correlations from these party-based regressions for comparison with bivariate correlations between other background variables and attitudes to rights (Table 11.23).

Of our socio-political predictors of attitudes toward *practice*, ideology (left/right) and party preference tied for top spot in both countries. In Britain they were followed, a long way behind, by education, age, and religiosity; and in Canada, by religiosity, then education, and age. Ideology and party preference were also the best predictors of *abstract principles*, values, and sympathies in each country. And ideology and party preference were more predictive amongst politicians than amongst the public in both countries. Conversely, religiosity was more predictive amongst the public than the politicians in both countries, but especially so in Canada. But taking education, age, gender, and religiosity together, Canadian opinion on rights seemed, surprisingly, to be as socially structured as that of the British—if not more so.

Even more surprisingly, given the history of brokerage rather than ideologically driven parties in Canada, both partisanship and ideology correlated with attitudes to rights just about as well in Canada as in Britain—rather better with abstract principles in Canada, but rather better with practice in Britain. The most that could be said is that the correlations with partisanship varied more between Britain and Canada than the correlations with ideological self-images. On the principles and practice of rights at least, party, therefore, made as much difference in Canada as in Britain, though in a slightly different way.

Influences

TABLE 11.23. *Correlations between socio-political background and principles, sympathies, or attitudes to practice in Britain and Canada*

	Britain		Canada	
	Politicians (%)	Public (%)	Politicians (%)	Public (%)
Correlations between practice and				
education	12	31	n.a.	29
age	19	27	n.a.	29
gender	0	12	n.a.	13
religiosity	12	19	0	38
ideology (left–centre–right)	77	65	67	63
party preference	77	69	75	50
Correlations between principles or sympathies and				
education	32	47	n.a.	63
age	37	53	n.a.	58
gender	0	16	n.a.	11
religiosity	32	37	21	53
ideology (left–centre–right)	74	63	68	68
party preference	74	47	79	58

Notes: Entries are percentages of correlations that exceed the thresholds (0.2 for politicians, 0.1 for the public).

In the Canadian survey, the education, age, and gender of Canadian politicians was suppressed to preserve their anonymity. It was recorded, but is not available for analysis.

n.a. = not available.

A COMMON CULTURE?

We have now reviewed a wide range of Canadian and British attitudes to civil and political rights. What consistent features, if any, emerge from this transatlantic comparison? In his British/US comparison, James Davis found similarities on liberty but differences on equality.[50] That is *not* what we have found in our British/Canadian comparison. Against a general background of remarkable similarity, which, perhaps surprisingly, extended to important aspects of equality, we have found a few important transatlantic differences—which are perhaps even more surprising—on aspects of liberty.

The British were significantly more tolerant of those they thought wrong, they were less inclined to blame women and especially the poor for their own problems, and less likely to demand AIDS tests for cooks. The British were more willing to allow their 'most disliked group' to hold rallies or make speeches, and very much more willing to permit potentially disorderly demonstrations and damaging strikes. Conversely, Canadians were more likely to trust politicians and experts, and accept the necessity for government regulation. The British were more likely to see the need for external control of the police and more likely to support the rights of suspects, though the two nations hardly differed on the 'right to silence'. In these respects, Canada seemed the more conservative society and Britain the more liberal.

In other respects, Canadians did seem more attached to legally enforced individual rights. Canadians were less willing to accept the suspension of their legally established civil rights during an emergency, and more willing to let their (domestic) courts overrule parliament. And, despite being much *less* willing to accept the principle that government had a responsibility to ensure equal opportunities, Canadians were also very much *more* willing to support job quotas for women, especially within government employment. Thus Canadians were more favourable to legally backed rights and less favourable to the sovereignty of parliament—in keeping with their written constitution and Charter of Rights.

But the similarities between Britain and Canada were far more striking than these differences. The evidence indicates a common culture despite minor differences. Despite the geographical distance between them, despite the difference in geographical proximity to the USA, and despite the fact that Canada had a Charter of Rights and Britain had not—despite all this, people and politicians in Britain did not differ that much or that consistently from those in Canada. In particular they had common patterns of value priorities, common attitudes to the principles of free speech and equal rights, and even common attitudes towards self-reliance and government responsibility for social welfare. Interestingly, a recent analysis concludes that 'when it comes to the economic components of the political cultures [of Canada and the USA] similarities are more striking than differences'.[51] If the British have libertarian principles that are more consistent with the US Constitution than with their own constitutional tradition, it is also true that, contrary to popular misconceptions, even citizens of the USA have egalitarian principles that are more consistent with European constitutions than with their own.[52]

Britons and Canadians have common attitudes towards 'means-tested' welfare, and, though rather more Britons hold government responsible for jobs and living standards, it was only around 10 per cent more. They have similar attitudes to random searches, wire-taps, and, perhaps surprisingly, the death penalty.

What is perhaps most interesting about our comparison is that it suggests that debates about the Canadian Charter have not educated Canadians to the point where they link the principles and practice of rights more closely than the British. Canada made a fairly significant departure from British legal tradition in 1982 when the Charter of Rights and Freedoms was entrenched in its newly patriated constitution. But neither this historical process, nor the debates and well-publicized Supreme Court judgments that flowed from it, seem to have encouraged either its citizens or its politicians to become either more adept than the British at connecting abstract principles with practical decisions or more rigid and formal about the way these should be recognized and enforced.

Conversely—and perhaps even more surprisingly—Canadian attitudes to civil rights were just as tightly organized by party and ideology as they were in Britain. Canadian parties have been characterized as being 'brokerage' parties, that fish for new bases of support at each election, 'constantly competing for the same policy space . . . with appeals to narrow interests and proposals that amount to little more than short-term tinkering'.[53] So it is particularly surprising to find that party voters and politicians differ on civil-rights issues as much in Canada as in Britain, though that was perhaps implicit in Sniderman and his colleagues' finding, based on the Canadian survey, that the 'differences among élites in support for civil liberties eclipse, both in size and political significance, the differences between élites and citizens'.[54] They were, of course, referring to ideological and party differences amongst the Canadian élites.

CONCLUSION

The general finding that emerges from these comparisons with Scottish and Canadian opinion is that in fundamental respects British political culture is not particularly British—and it is certainly not English. Its reach is far wider than that. Of course, we cannot infer some worldwide culture of civil rights from the limited comparisons presented in this chapter. When questions somewhat similar to those used in the British and Canadian surveys were put to the public and politicians in Russia, Ukraine, Hungary, Slovakia, and the Czech Republic, they produced rather different answers.[55] Some differences in history and institutions clearly do leave their imprint on the political culture. But we can conclude that political culture is not bound by (and does not bind) constitutional niceties. Culture and institutions may be linked, but not as closely as we might assume. Indeed our results prove that any assumption that the culture of a people can be inferred, with any accuracy, from its institutions of government is false.

NOTES

1. Until the patriation of the Canadian Constitution in 1982, the Westminster parliament retained the power to amend it. For a highly readable account of the patriation process, see Peter H. Russell, *Constitutional Odyssey: Can Canadians be a Sovereign People?* (Toronto: University of Toronto Press, 1992; 1993), 107–26.
2. Stephen Sedley, 'Charter 88: Rights and Wrongs', in Geoff Andrews (ed.), *Citizenship* (London: Lawrence & Wishart, 1991), 219–27, at 220.
3. Lord Hailsham, *The Dilemma of Democracy: Diagnosis and Prescription* (London: Collins, 1978), 221.
4. For a fascinating collection of papers illustrating this point, see Vivien Hart and Shannon C. Stimson (eds.), *Writing a National Identity: Political, Economic and Cultural Perspectives on the Written Constitution* (Manchester: Manchester University Press, 1993).
5. Ellen Frankel Paul, Fred D. Miller Jr., and Jeffrey Paul, *Reassessing Civil Rights* (Oxford: Blackwell, 1991), 196.
6. See e.g. 'Chapter 12: The Politics of Civil Rights', in Thomas R. Dye and L. Harmon Zeigler, *American Politics in the Media Age* (Belmont, Calif.: Wadsworth, 1983), 410–48. See also Vivien Hart, 'The Right to a Fair Wage: American Experience and the European Social Charter', in Hart and Stimson (eds.), *Writing a National Identity*, 106–24, at 107.
7. James A. Davis, 'British and American Attitudes: Similarities and Contrasts', in Roger Jowell, Sharon Witherspoon, and Lindsay Brook (eds.), *British Social Attitudes: The 1986 Report* (Aldershot: Gower, 1986), 89–114.
8. Dye and Zeigler, *American Politics in the Media Age*, 382; the evidence for these claims is given on pp. 382–5.
9. Richard Rose claims that 'England will never be overlooked by any British government. Politicians who wish to advance in Parliament must accept English norms if they wish to prosper. It is thus correct to speak of *British Government in conjunction with English Society*' (emphasis added) (Richard Rose, *Politics in England Today* (London: Faber & Faber, 1974), 36.
10. The question of whether Scotland is a distinct society is particularly interesting in the light of our comparisons between Britain and Canada. We have borrowed the phrase 'a distinct society' from recent constitutional debates in Canada over the nature and status of Quebec. Although this question has always been an issue in Canada, the idea of Quebec being formally recognized as a distinct society emerged as a constitutional concept in 1987, when it was written into a proposed constitutional amendment (the Meech Lake Accord) as 'the minimal basis upon which Quebec's formal adhesion to the constitution might be secured': see Kenneth McRoberts, 'Quebec: Province, Nation or "Distinct Society"?', in Michael Whittington and Glen Williams (eds.), *Canadian Politics in the 1990s* (Scarborough: Nelson, 1990), 98–117, at 116.

The phrase itself was first coined, in 1980, when the Continuing Committee of Ministers on the Constitution recommended that a patriated constitution should recognize 'Canada's distinct French-speaking society, centred in though not confined to Quebec': see Roy Romanow, John Whyte, and Howard Leeson, *Canada . . . Notwithstanding: The Making of the Constitution* (Toronto: Carswell/Methuen, 1984), 85.

11. See esp. Paul M. Sniderman, Joseph F. Fletcher, Peter H. Russell, and Philip E. Tetlock, *The Clash of Rights: Liberty, Equality and Legitimacy in Pluralist Democracy* (New Haven: Yale University Press, 1996).

12. Succinctly but evocatively put by George MacDonald Fraser in the penultimate chapter of *The Sheikh and the Dustbin* (Glasgow: Fontana, 1989), 'Ye Mind Jie Dee, Fletcher?', at pp. 173–5 especially.

13. Malcolm Hurwitt and Peter Thornton, *Civil Liberty: The Liberty/NCCL Guide* (4th edn., London: Penguin, 1989), 323.

14. Though the law has since been changed on this point to bring England and Wales more into line with Scotland. At the time of writing, the UK Lord Chancellor is a Scottish lawyer, Lord MacKay of Clashfern.

15. Lord Jenkins of Hillhead, 'The Case for a People's Bill of Rights', in William L. Miller (ed.), *Alternatives to Freedom: Arguments and Opinions* (London: Longman, 1995), 21–32, at 22.

16. John Mullen, Alan Travis, and Richard Norton, 'Nudge-Nudge, Wink-Wink Game after a Muzzling Injunction in the High Court', Guardian, 6 Feb. 1992, p. 2.

17. K. D. Ewing and C. A. Gearty, *Freedom under Thatcher: Civil Liberties in Modern Britain* (Oxford: Oxford University Press, 1990), 147–52.

18. James G. Kellas, *The Scottish Political System* (4th edn., Cambridge: Cambridge University Press, 1989).

19. David McCrone, 'Scottish Culture', ch. 7 in David McCrone, *Understanding Scotland: The Sociology of a Stateless Nation* (London: Routledge, 1992), 174–96.

20. Ibid. 120.

21. Ibid. 195–6.

22. Richard Rose, *Understanding the United Kingdom: The Territorial Dimension in Government* (London: Longman, 1982), 14. The group most likely to choose the 'British' label were Protestants in Northern Ireland. A forced choice between national identities may be a false choice, however: many people may wish to choose 'both British and Scottish', for example. See Jack Brand, James Mitchell, and Paula Surridge, 'Will Scotland Come to the Aid of the Party?', in Anthony Heath, Roger Jowell, and John Curtice (eds.), *Labour's Last Chance? The 1992 Election and Beyond* (Aldershot: Dartmouth, 1994), 213–28, at 220.

23. Throughout this book we use the term 'Scots' interchangeably with 'those who lived in Scotland'. This is appropriate because we are primarily concerned with the effect of the institutional context (and not, for example, of race or ethnicity) on political culture. For the record, the 1991 Census shows that 89% of Scottish residents were born in Scotland: see OPCS, *1991 Census Monitor for Parliamentary Constituencies in Scotland* (Edinburgh: General Register House; London: OPCS, 1994), 30. The SNP defines 'Scots' to include 'everyone resident in Scotland on the day of independence'. So, in the Scottish case, residence also coincides with much more than mere residence.

24. On both sides of the Atlantic, this debate concerned the right of the federal government of Canada to seek patriation of the Canadian Constitution without the consent of all the provinces. The British Parliament's Select Committee on patriation (chaired by Sir Anthony Kershaw) recommended that, because the Canadian government's request for the entrenchment of a Charter of Rights and Freedoms in the Constitution affected the federal structure of Canada, it should be 'conveyed with at least that degree of Provincial concurrence (expressed by governments, legislatures or referendum majorities) as that required for a post-patriation amendment': see House of Commons, *British North America Acts: The Role of Parliament* (London: Her Majesty's Stationery Office, 1981). Pierre Trudeau, then Prime Minister of Canada, likened the Kershaw Report to the science fiction movie, *The Empire Strikes Back*, and Jean Chrétien, his Minister of Justice, issued a paper rebutting the Kershaw recommendations: (Canada, Department of Justice, *The Role of the United Kingdom in the Amendment of the Canadian Constitution* (Ottawa: Publications Canada, 1981)). For a full discussion of these points, see Russell, *Constitutional Odyssey*, pp. 117–18.
25. *E. C. S. Wade and A. W. Bradley's Constitutional and Administrative Law*, co-authored by A. W. Bradley, T. St J. N. Bates, and C. M. G. Himsworth (London: Longman, 1987), 587.
26. Lord Jenkins of Hillhead, 'The Case for a People's Bill of Rights'.
27. Christine Sypnowich, 'Rights, Community and the Charter', *British Journal of Canadian Studies*, 6 (1991), 39–59, at 39.
28. Seymour Martin Lipset, *Continental Divide: The Values and Institutions of the United States and Canada* (New York: Routledge, 1990), 3. For an influential analysis of the differences in Canadian and American political culture, see Gad Horowitz, 'Conservatism, Liberalism and Socialism in Canada: An Interpretation', *Canadian Journal of Economics and Political Science*, 32 (1966), repr. in Hugh G. Thorburn (ed.), *Party Politics in Canada* (5th edn., Scarborough: Prentice Hall, 1985), 41–59.
29. Annis May Timpson, 'Canada's Electoral Earthquake', *The World Today*, 50 (1994), 6–7.
30. Hugh G. Thorburn, 'Interpretations of the Canadian Party System', in Thorburn (ed.), *Party Politics in Canada*, 20–40; Janine Brodie and Jane Jenson, *Crisis, Challenge and Change: Party and Class in Canada Revisited* (Ottawa: Carleton University Press, 1988), 3–7; Harold D. Clarke, Jane Jenson, Lawrence LeDuc, and John H. Pammett, *Absent Mandate: The Politics of Discontent in Canada* (Toronto: Gage, 1984), 10–16.
31. Lord Jenkins of Hillhead, 'The Case for a People's Bill of Rights', 28.
32. See e.g. K. D. Ewing and C. A. Gearty, *Freedom under Thatcher: Civil Liberties in Modern Britain* (Oxford: Oxford University Press, 1990).
33. Anthony Heath, John Curtice, Roger Jowell, Geoff Evans, Julia Field, and Sharon Witherspoon, *Understanding Political Change* (Oxford: Pergamon Press, 1991), ch. 11, 'The Great Moving Right Show'.
34. G. Bruce Doern, 'The UK Citizen's Charter: Origins and Implementation in Three Agencies', *Policy and Politics*, 21 (1993), 17–20.
35. Hurwitt and Thornton, *Civil Liberty*, 108.

412   *Influences*

36. See, e.g. Lord Jenkins of Hillhead, 'The Case for a People's Bill of Rights', 28.
37. Ewing and Gearty, *Freedom under Thatcher*, 266.
38. William Kilbourn, *Canada: A Guide to the Peaceable Kingdom* (New York: St Martin's Press, 1970).
39. John L. Sullivan, James Pierson, and George E. Marcus, *Political Tolerance and American Democracy* (Chicago: University of Chicago Press, 1982, 1989).
40. A visit to the famine exhibition at the museum in Kiev makes the Canadian connection very clear. The *World Almanac* (New York: Newspaper Enterprise Corporation, 1984) lists the current ethnic mix in Alberta as including 3 per cent Ukrainians, 6% in Manitoba, and 5% in Saskatchewan. Ukrainians constitute a significant ethnic minority all the way from the Great Lakes to the Rockies.
41. Henry S. Ferns, *The Disease of Government* (London: MauriceTemple Smith, 1978).
42. An excellent, relatively recent, example of this is the extensive (72-volume) research study commissioned by academics and experts for the Royal Commission on the Economic Union and Development Prospects of Canada, which was published as a series by the University of Toronto Press in 1985. But on the more general relationship between academia and the state in Canada, see Doug Owram, *The Government Generation: Canadian Intellectuals and the State 1900–1945* (Toronto: University of Toronto Press, 1986).
43. Peter N. Nemetz, W. T. Stanbury, and Fred Thompson, 'Social Regulation in Canada: An Overview and Comparison with the American Model', *Policy Studies Journal*, 14 (1986) 588–602, at 595.
44. David Elton, 'The Charlottetown Accord Senate: Effective or Emasculated?', in Kenneth McRoberts and Patrick Monahan (eds.), *The Charlottetown Accord and the Future of Canada* (Toronto: University of Toronto Press, 1993), 37–57, at 53. This proposed reform became obsolete, however, in October 1992, when the constitutional accord was rejected in a national referendum. See Annis May Timpson, 'Rejection Slip for Unused Accord', *Times Higher Education Supplement*, 6 Nov. 1992, p. 17.
45. William L. Miller, Annis May Timpson, and Michael Lessnoff, 'Public Opposition to Parliamentary Sovereignty', in William L. Miller (ed.), *Alternatives to Freedom: Arguments and Opinions* (London: Longman, 1995), 31–46, at 43.
46. Stephen Clarkson and Christina McCall, *Trudeau and our Times*, Vol. 1: *The Magnificent Obsession* (Toronto: McClelland & Stewart, 1990), 206.
47. Annis May Timpson, 'The Politics of Employment Inequality in Canada: Gender and the Public Sector', in Julia Evetts (ed.), *Women and Careers: Themes and Issues in Advanced Industrial Societies* (London: Longman, 1994), 44–57.
48. Linda Clarke, *Discrimination* (London: Institute of Public Management, 1994).
49. *Report of the Commission on Equality in Employment* (Ottawa: Minister of Supply and Services), 7. For a discussion of this report and the legislation that followed from it, see Annis May Timpson, 'Between the Royal Commissions: Women's Employment Opportunities in Canada 1966–86', *London Journal of Canadian Studies*, 4 (1987), 68–81, at 75–9.
50. Davis, 'British and American Attitudes'.
51. H. D. Clarke and M. C. Stewart, 'Political Culture and Political Economy: Canada

and the United States in Comparative Perspective', paper presented at the Canadian Politics in Comparative Perspective Conference, Center for Advanced Study in the Behavioral Sciences, Stanford, May 1993.

52. Dye and Zeigler, *American Politics in the Media Age*, 382–5.
53. Clarke, Jensen, LeDuc, and Pammett, *Absent Mandate*, 10.
54. Paul M. Sniderman, Joseph F. Fletcher, Peter H. Russell, Philip E. Tetlock, and Brian J. Gaines, 'The Fallacy of Democratic Élitism: Élite Competition and Commitment to Civil Liberties', *British Journal of Political Science*, 21 (1991), 349–70.
55. William L. Miller, Stephen White, and Paul Heywood, *Values and Political Change in Post-Communist Europe* (London: Macmillan, forthcoming); see also William L. Miller, Stephen White, Paul Heywood, and Matthew Wyman, 'Democratic, Market and Nationalist Values in Russia and East Europe: December 1993', paper presented at the Political Studies Association Annual Conference, Swansea, 1994; and William L. Miller, Stephen White, and Paul Heywood, 'The Locus of Democratic Values', paper presented at the ESRC Conference on Mass Response to the Transformation of Post-Communist Societies, St Antony's College, Oxford, 1995.

PART FIVE
Conclusion

12

An Overview Model

IN earlier chapters we have reviewed a wide variety of potential influences upon attitudes to civil and political rights. But so far we have looked at them separately and in sequence; now we shall look at them in parallel and in combination. Quite properly we have distinguished between the views of men and women, between those who describe themselves as working class and middle class, between those who have high educational qualifications and those who have none, and between those who complain of personal discrimination and those who do not. Comparisons between genders or between classes remain valid and important, whatever the reasons that lie behind them.

DESIGNING AN OVERVIEW MODEL

But, since these social characteristics are themselves interrelated, it is possible that women have distinctive views only because they have suffered more personal discrimination than men, or that the middle class have distinctive views only because they are, on the whole, better educated. Less obviously, the opposite may also be true: the middle class might have even more distinctive views if the influence of their occupational class characteristics had not been offset by the countervailing influence of their relatively high levels of education. So in this chapter we shall bring together different aspects of social background, and link those various aspects of social background with experience, principles, prejudices, partisanship, ideology, argument, and practical decisions. Inevitably a great deal of simplification will be necessary if the results are to be comprehensible, and we shall also have to impose a clear theoretical structure before attempting any analysis. Such constraints are irksome and many details and qualifications discussed in earlier chapters will now be obscured or lost altogether, but, in compensation, we hope to construct a relatively simple yet powerful description of the patterns, sources, and consequences of public attitudes towards civil, political, and social rights. The view out of an aircraft window as it takes off and climbs into the sky is neither better nor worse than the view from the ground, but it is certainly different. In this chapter we hope to gain in comprehensibility and understanding what we lose in subtlety and detail. Despite a switch to multivariate analysis, we aim not at greater complexity but at greater simplicity.

Causal Hierarchy

As a first step we shall assume a nested causal hierarchy with five levels or shells:

1. social background
2. personal experience
3. principles and prejudices
4. party preference
5. ideological self-images, mechanisms, and issues of practice.

This hierarchy postulates: first, that social background (factors such as class, age, sex, and religion which we analysed in Chapter 8) affects experience (such as discrimination, or contact with the police and other officials which we analysed in Chapter 10); secondly, that background and experience combine to influence principles and sympathies. We see principles and sympathies as closely linked to each other but not with a clear causal hierarchy between them: each affects the other to an unknown degree. Hence we have placed them at the same level. Thirdly, this hierarchy postulates that all of these combine to influence party preference.

Few will dispute our claim that social background is causally prior to party preference. A few atypical individuals—perhaps including Prime Minister John Major—may have self-consciously adopted a party preference as a means of social advancement, but party preference is not likely to affect educational performance and religious adherence greatly, nor age and gender at all. We have few misgivings about our assumption that social background influences principles, prejudices, and party preference but is not, itself, influenced by them.

The relationship between principles, prejudices, and party preferences is more problematic. We accept that, at least for those with a strong sense of party identification, party preference is likely to influence opinion upon the issues and policies of the day. So we shall assume that party preference, along with social background, experience, principles, and prejudices, does influence attitudes towards practical issues of civil and political rights, and towards alternative mechanisms for implementing and supporting rights. But we shall not assume that party preference is capable of determining basic value orientations—towards liberty and equality, for example. Thus in our causal hierarchy, we have placed party preference *after* principles and prejudices but *before* mechanisms and practice.

The simplest and most naïve theory of ideological self-images (left, centre, right, etc.) would interpret them purely as an expression of principle, a convenient way of summarizing attitudes towards liberty, equality, or other more specific principles. The words 'left' and 'right' have no intrinsic meaning —other than their literal, but now completely irrelevant, spatial meaning which referred originally to the seating arrangements in the French Revolutionary Assembly of 1789. Indeed, the words like 'left' and 'right' could gain political meaning—even in 1789—only through their common association with other things. But what other things? While we see ideological self-images as an expression of principle, we accept that they may also reflect sympathies, experience, and social identification. Some political scientists have argued that ideological self-images are merely expressions of party preference: that Labour voters claim to be on the left, Conservatives on the right, and Liberal Democrats in the centre, and there is nothing more to be said. That extreme view is wrong. Party supporters do make such ideological claims, but many people have weak or non-existent party preferences yet do have an ideological self-image. Moreover, ideological self-images vary, and vary systematically, *within* each party—which obviously cannot be explained in terms of party itself. Ideological self-images may reflect party identification, but they certainly reflect more than that.

Yet, whatever ideological self-images express or reflect, they have no intrinsic meaning of their own and we do not see them, in themselves, as a causal influence upon attitudes to mechanisms or issues of practice. So the final shell of our causal hierarchy postulates that attitudes to mechanisms and practical decisions are influenced not by ideological self-images but primarily by principles, though also perhaps by sympathies and, more or less indirectly, by experience and social background.

In addition, we postulate that attitudes to issues of practice are influenced by explicit arguments and challenges. The power of argument stands somewhat outside the five-level causal hierarchy, since we see it as an influence upon attitudes to practice but in no way dependent upon any of the variables that occur earlier in the hierarchy.

In relation to mechanisms and practice, party can be viewed as an implicit argument. Policies such as regional devolution, the building of council houses, or their sale to sitting tenants have all been advanced as mechanisms for protecting or extending citizens' liberties. They may have a special appeal to people from different backgrounds or with different principles. In logic, both the Labour and Conservative parties could—and have—supported each of these policies at one time or another, though with somewhat different rhetorics. Devolution was advocated by the Conservative Party and opposed by Labour in the late 1960s and early 1970s, but has been advocated by Labour and attacked by the Conservatives since then. Similarly, the Conservative Party came back to power in the 1950s with the claim (justified by later achievements) that it could build far more council houses than the Labour Party. Later it attacked discounted rents for council tenants. Then in the 1980s it offered discounted property sales to those same tenants, while the Labour Party opposed them. Now both parties support discounted sales to sitting tenants as a policy that enhances the liberties of sitting tenants.

On all these issues there have been no consistent party positions in the long term. If there were a necessary logic linking party to these policies, it escaped the notice of the party leaders. But, by the early 1990s, a decade of party warfare had linked Labour to devolution, and council sales to the Conservative Party, so strongly that it would be natural for people to divide along party lines on these issues, purely out of loyalty to their preferred party or out of antagonism towards the party enemy. Consequently we view party preference as a potential influence upon attitudes to mechanisms and issues of practice, but we would expect that influence to be very variable, and apply only where forceful and sustained party campaigning had tied an issue very clearly to party.

Thus Fig. 12.1 shows, in an extremely simplified form, our schematic model of attitudes towards civil and political rights.

Selecting a Subset of Variables for Analysis

Despite our attempt to keep this model as simple as possible, some of the blocks in the causal diagram in Fig. 12.1 must be translated into complexes of several variables. Our chapter on the influence of social background investigated age, religion, education, class, private/public sector employment, urban/rural location, parenthood, gender, and income. From the bivariate correlations reported there, seven of these seem to have at least a moderately strong influence on principles—age, religion, education, class, gender, income, and parenthood. Multivariate analysis shows, however, that we can ignore the last of these. Those with children were more authoritarian, but not more authoritarian than their age and religiosity would predict. The apparent effect of income on liberty largely reflected that of education; and its apparent effect upon equality, though partly genuine, also reflected the effects of class and gender to a considerable degree. Moreover, the high percentage of

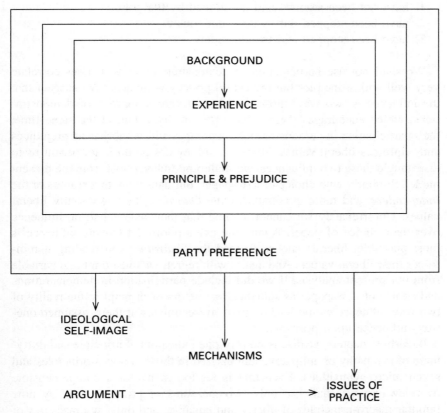

FIG. 12.1. *Schematic model of attitudes towards civil and political rights*

respondents who did not (and often, quite properly, could not) answer the income question means that we could only include income at the cost of restricting our analysis to just over two-thirds of the total public. So we shall retain just the first five social background variables in our subsequent analyses.

In our chapter on personal experience, we found that complaints of personal discrimination, interactions with the police, participating in demonstrations or protests, and reading different kinds of newspaper correlated with principles and sympathies. For present purposes we shall retain an indicator of whether or not people complained of discrimination and construct an indicator of interaction with the police with three equally spaced numerical values representing:

1. have not been stopped and questioned by the police
2. have been stopped but treated courteously
3. have been stopped and treated rudely.

We shall not use participation in demonstrations here. It does correlate very well with principles but the causal priority is unclear. We suspect that the influence is two way: those with liberal values approve of demonstrations, which encourages them to take part in them; but, at the same time, their participation in demonstrations encourages anti-authoritarian prejudices and reinforces liberal values. Since our survey design does not permit us to disentangle these two influences, we shall omit this variable from the present model. Similarly with choice of newspaper: our data show that readers of the *Independent*, and more especially of the *Guardian*, have unusually liberal values. Unfortunately we cannot assume that their values had no influence over their choice of paper. Again, the assumption of two-way influence is most plausible: liberals choose to read the *Guardian*, and reading it reinforces their liberal values. And again, with regret, we must omit this variable from our present analysis. If we did include participation in demonstrations and choice of newspaper as statistical predictors of principles, the reality of two-way influence would lead to gross overestimates of their (assumed one-way) influence upon principle.

In earlier chapters we discussed fifty-one indicators of principle and thirty-three of sympathy or antipathy, summarized in thirteen micro-principles and seven micro-sympathies. Even that is far too many for a comprehensible overview. So we shall use only two measures of principle—the by now familiar macro-principles of liberty and equality; and only two measures of sympathy—for social and political claimants (defined as the average of sympathy for the socially disadvantaged, activists, and militants), and for the judicial/political system (defined as the average of confidence in the judicial system and the political system).

As measures of party preference, we shall use single-party preferences for the Conservative Party, the Liberal Democrats, Labour, and the SNP. In each case we contrast those with a voting preference for that party against everyone else, but, since we shall use all four variables as a set, we are effectively drawing a contrast between those with each of these preferences and those with none. For ideological self-image, we shall use the seven-point left–right scale defined in Chapter 9.

Finally, we model added arguments by means of 'dummy variables' which take the value one when the argument is used and zero otherwise. Alternative arguments can be modelled similarly. Challenges require a somewhat different approach. To model challenges, we shall replicate the data-set, so that each interviewee is included once with his or her original answer, and again with his or her answer after each successive challenge. It will be easier to understand our modelling of challenges if we postpone a more detailed explanation until we have a concrete example to discuss.

Path Coefficients

As a standard procedure for measuring influences, we shall calculate 'path coefficients', also known as 'standardized regression coefficients' or 'beta-weights'. It is important to note the advantages and disadvantages of using path coefficients.

Suppose we are using age bands (on a scale from 1 to 4) and equality scores (on a scale from minus 100 to plus 100) to predict ideological self-image. 'Unstandardized' regression coefficients for age and equality would tell us the change in ideological self-image consequent upon a change of one age band and one unit on the equality score: that is a change of approximately fifteen years in the case of age, and a change of a mere 0.5 per cent in the number of egalitarian propositions supported. (Our equality score roughly equals the percentage of egalitarian propositions the interviewee accepts minus the percentage he or she rejects.) Such 'unstandardized' coefficients are almost impossible to interpret because years of age are incommensurable with agreement to egalitarian propositions. Such coefficients would, for example, fail to help us answer the question: 'does age or principle have more influence upon ideological self-image?'

But 'standardized' regression coefficients (known as 'path coefficients' because they measure the relative importance of different causal paths in a causal model) can make even such disparate variables as age and principle commensurable, because they measure the effect upon ideological self-image of a one standard deviation shift in age or principle. Thus they relate the change in the dependent variable (ideological self-image in this example) to the amount of variation in age and in principle that actually occurs within the data-set. They show the effect upon ideological self-image of being relatively young or relatively egalitarian—when relative means 'relative to the amount of variation in age and egalitarianism that actually occurs within the data-set'. A high path coefficient for age, close to plus or minus one, would show that age almost completely determines ideological self-image. Conversely, a low path coefficient, close to zero, would show *either* that ideological self-image is unaffected by age differences, *or* that age varies very little within the sample, *or* some combination of the two. What all of these three possibilities have in common is the assurance that age is not an important determinant of ideological self-image within this sample—although it might well be more important in another sample in which age varied more. Similarly, if the path coefficient for equality exceeds that for age, then it shows that, *within this sample at least*, variations in commitment to equality have more effect upon ideological self-image than do variations in age.

The advantage of using path coefficients is that we can now compare the effects of age and egalitarianism in a meaningful way. We can even compare the influence of an argument with the influence of a principle or of a social category. For example, we can ask: which of these three—the power of argument, commitment to principle, or gender—has the most influence upon support for job quotas? Path coefficients make that question meaningful and provide the answer. But the disadvantage with path coefficients is that both the comparison and the meaning depend critically upon the particular sample or, more precisely, on the particular population that the sample represents. Path coefficients could be misleading if used to compare samples representing fundamentally different populations where age, for example, varied much more within one than within another.

A Combined Sample of the British Public, the Scottish Public, and Politicians

In this study, we have been concerned with three samples, representing three different populations—the British public, the Scottish public, and senior local-government politicians. In terms of the amount of socio-political variation within them, there are only a few differences between these samples. Age and gender vary less amongst senior politicians, because they are so notoriously male and middle aged. Conversely, voting preferences for the SNP vary more within the Scottish sample, because so very few in the Britain-wide samples prefer the SNP. Apart from these differences, however, the standard deviations of all relevant variables in the samples of Scots and of politicians lie between 0.8 and 1.2 times the corresponding standard deviations in the British public sample. So while, in general, we cannot compare path coefficients across different samples, we could compare path coefficients across the three samples used in this study provided we remembered that path coefficients measuring the effect of age and gender in the politicians' sample would be somewhat reduced by the fact (real enough) that age and gender vary less amongst politicians than amongst the public, and that path coefficients measuring the effect of an SNP preference in the British samples would be very considerably reduced by the fact that so few in Britain (compared to so many in Scotland) have an SNP preference. This second caveat is so intuitively obvious as to be unnecessary, though the constraint on age and gender effects amongst politicians is a little less obvious.

But in this final summary chapter we shall break with precedent. In earlier chapters we analysed our three samples separately. Broadly speaking, those earlier chapters showed that the patterns in our Scottish sample are remarkably similar to the patterns in our sample of the British public as a whole, while the patterns within our sample of politicians are also similar in nature, but greater in strength. So instead of continuing to compare patterns within each of our three samples, we propose to combine all three in order to reach findings that apply (approximately) to the British in general. In our analyses we shall look out for differences between the British public, the Scottish public, and British politicians but pay attention to them only when the differences are substantial.

There are many ways in which such a combined analysis might be done. We have reweighted the three samples to make them count equally, and in our regression analyses we have added 'dummy variables' to distinguish Scots and politicians from the British public. Inevitably, these choices affect the results, as would any alternative strategies. The key features of our chosen strategy are first, the decision to accord equal weight to each of the three samples; and, second, the decision to treat the differences between them as additive rather than interactive. Both need a few words of explanation.

Equal weight. It might be argued that our approach gives too much weight to the Scots, who, after all, constitute only around one-tenth of the British population. That would matter more if the Scots were very different from the British as a whole, but previous chapters have shown that they are not. Reducing the Scots to one-tenth of the public would certainly depict Scottish differences as being trivial when viewed in a British context, simply because there are proportionately so few Scots. However, we wish to make the stronger—and much more surprising—case that Scottish differences would not be of great importance even if Scots were *not* such a small minority. As for the relative weighting of politicians and people, it would be absurd to reduce the politicians' sample to the actual proportion of politicians in the population. Any strictly proportionate analysis based on path coefficients would appear to show that differences between politicians and people were unimportant because there were so few politicians. In one sense that would be correct, but, as with the Scots, we want to see whether the differences between people and politicians would be important if the analysis were not distorted by such unequal proportions of people and politicians. The important contrast is between conceptual rather than proportionate categories.

Of course, it would be possible to combine the three samples, weight them strictly to the proportions of Scots and politicians in the population, and then base the analysis on *un*standardized regression coefficients; but we have already explained why standardized coefficients are necessary if we are to compare the competing influences of principles, arguments, party loyalties, experience, and social background in a comprehensible way. In fact, there are no problems and great advantages in our strategy of treating the three samples equally provided we bear that equality of treatment in mind when interpreting the results.

Additive versus interactive differences. By simply including 'dummy variables' representing the Scots and politicians as additional predictors in all our regressions, we highlight additive differences while suppressing or ignoring interactive differences. For example, when predicting commitment to liberty from education, this strategy will detect any tendency amongst Scots or politicians to be more (or less) committed to liberty than their level of education would predict. But it will not reveal any tendency for levels of education to have more (or less) effect upon commitment to liberty amongst Scots or politicians. In practice it will 'average out' any variations in the effect of education *within* the three different samples and highlight the variations *across or between* the three different samples. Since previous chapters have shown that influences tend to be equally effective amongst Britons and Scots, but somewhat more effective amongst politicians, this averaging-out will overestimate effects within the public slightly, and underestimate effects amongst politicians a little more. So our estimates will represent slightly 'computer-enhanced' versions of the pattern of opinion within the public, and slightly 'fuzzy' versions of the pattern of opinion amongst politicians. But, as a simple summary of the pattern of opinion 'within Britain', that has much to recommend it. Remember that our objective in this chapter is comprehensiveness combined with simplicity not with complexity.

However, despite our strong feeling that the simplest and best statement of our findings consists of an analysis based upon the combined sample of Britons, Scots, and politicians, we recognize that others may not agree. So our tables will also show findings based upon our sample of the British public alone. Apart from their inability to highlight infrequent differences between Scots and others, and more frequent differences between politicians and the public, findings based on the British public sample usually confirm those based upon the combined sample.

A MODEL OF PRINCIPLES, PARTY, AND IDEOLOGY

We can now begin to quantify the model set out in Fig. 12.1, starting with the pathways of influence from social background to experience, and then working progressively through the model.

Experience

We begin by calculating the path coefficients from social background to complaints about discrimination and rude police officers. *Amongst the British public* the highly educated complained of discrimination more than others, producing a path coefficient of 15 from education to discrimination. So did the young and women, though their path coefficients were slightly smaller. Religion and class had little effect once these other influences were taken into account. It is unlikely that the educated in fact experienced more discrimination than others. Quite the reverse: the educated do relatively well for themselves—in Britain as in most other societies. But they certainly complained more than others about discrimination. *In our combined sample* youth, gender, and education had about the same effect on the propensity to complain about discrimination, though, for the special reasons that we discussed in Chapter 10, the mere fact of being a politician had much more effect upon propensity to do so than any social factor.

The young also complained more about being stopped and questioned by rude police officers, while women complained very much less, producing a path coefficient of minus 30 from (female) gender. Nothing else had much effect (Table 12.1).

Principle and Prejudice

Adverse personal experiences appeared to increase commitment to liberty until we took account of simultaneous direct influences from religion, age, and class. Once these social predictors were included in the equation, it was clear that specific adverse experiences added little to the direct effects of social background on commitment to liberty. For liberty, the path coefficients were minus 37 from religion, minus 23 from age, and plus 23 from education. No other aspect of social background, nor the specific experience of discrimination or rude police officers, had much effect once these three aspects of social background were taken into account. Over and above the effects of their social characteristics, however, politicians were more committed to liberty, with a path coefficient of 14.

TABLE 12.1. *Effect of social background on adverse experiences*

| | Combined sample (British public only) | | | |
	Experienced discrimination		Experienced rude police	
Multiple correlation (×100)	26	(24)	40	(39)
Path coefficients (×100) from				
religious	.	(.)	.	(.)
age (old)	−11	(−11)	−13	(−13)
education (high)	11	(15)	.	(.)
gender (female)	13	(12)	−30	(−32)
class (working)	.	(.)	.	(.)
Scottish sample	.	n.a.	.	n.a.
politicians' sample	19	n.a.	.	n.a.

Notes: Figures outside parentheses are for the combined sample of Britons, Scots, and politicians weighted to count equally. Figures inside parentheses are based upon the sample of the British public alone.

Path coefficients less than 0.10 have been replaced by full points. We have not shown any indicators of 'statistical significance'. They test the probability that, despite the existence of a relationship in a sample, there is no relationship (zero path coefficient) in the population that it purports to represent. They usually mislead. As conventionally calculated, they require unclustered random samples, which are seldom found in survey research. So they are usually too lax. However, since our CATI samples of the British and Scottish public are random unclustered samples, they would, unusually, be appropriate. Since our sample of politicians includes over 85% of our target population, the usual criteria for statistical significance do not apply (they are too stringent). It is extremely unlikely that any problems with our analysis are attributable to random sampling error and it would be misleading to focus upon that. There are problems of biased non-contacts and refusals which we have tried to offset by weighting. There is the problem of whether even a complete population of political leaders in local government can be regarded as representative of 'politicians'. There is the problem, revealed in earlier chapters, that details of question wordings can affect not only the level of responses but their correlations with answers to other questions. And there is the further problem that real but small effects might confuse our findings by detracting from their simplicity. Given the size of our samples, path coefficients smaller than 0.10 are statistically significant by the usual criteria (so all the figures we report and some that we do not are 'statistically significant' by the usual criteria), but they are not substantively significant. We do not wish to draw attention to very weak influences even if there is statistical evidence that they are probably non-zero influences.

n.a. = not applicable.

TABLE 12.2. *Effect of social background and experience on principles*

	Combined sample (British public only)			
	Liberty		Equality	
Multiple correlation (×100)	63	(59)	33	(28)
Path coefficients (×100) from				
felt discrimination	.	(.)	.	(.)
rude police	.	(.)	.	(.)
religious	−37	(−33)	−11	(.)
age (old)	−23	(−25)	.	(.)
education (high)	23	(20)	.	(.)
gender (female)	.	(.)	14	(16)
class (working)	.	(.)	22	(18)
Scottish sample	.	n.a.	.	n.a.
politicians' sample	14	n.a.	11	n.a.

Notes: Path coefficients less than 0.10 have been replaced by full points.
n.a. = not applicable.

Very different aspects of social background affected commitment to equality. Class with a coefficient of 22, and gender with a coefficient of 14 proved the only major influences. The working class and women were, of course, the more committed to equality. Over and above those effects, the religious were slightly less committed to equality and politicians slightly more. Overall, commitment to equality proved very much less socially-predictable than commitment to liberty. Judged by their path coefficients, the influences of religion, age, and education on liberty were each independently as great as the influence of class on equality and much greater than the influence of gender on equality.

Because of its ambiguous causal status we excluded indicators of newspaper readership from our multiple regressions predicting principles and prejudices. Had we included them, however, the statistical calculations would have implied that reading independent broadsheets (the *Independent* and *Guardian*) had at least as much effect as education on commitment to liberty and at least as much effect as class or gender on equality (Table 12.2).

The old and the religious were substantially more unsympathetic to social and political claimants and more confident of the judicial/political system. Conversely, the working class and those who complained of discrimination were more sympathetic to claimants and less sympathetic towards the

TABLE 12.3. *Effect of social background and experience on sympathies*

	Combined sample (British public only)			
	Social and political claimants		Judicial/political system	
Multiple correlation (×100)	37	(34)	40	(33)
Path coefficients (×100) from				
felt discrimination	12	(.)	−12	(−15)
rude police	.	(.)	−11	(.)
religious	−15	(−14)	17	(15)
age (old)	−20	(−19)	17	(15)
education (high)	.	(.)	.	(.)
gender (female)	10	(13)	.	(.)
class (working)	16	(11)	−12	(−13)
Scottish sample	.	n.a.	.	n.a.
politicians' sample	13	n.a.	13	n.a.

Notes: Path coefficients less than 0.10 have been replaced by full points.
n.a. = not applicable.

judicial/political system. And beyond all those effects, politicians were uniquely more prejudiced in favour of *both* claimants *and* the judicial/political system—which is consistent with their unique combination of support not only for citizens' liberties but also for government's prerogatives as well (Table 12.3).

Party Preference

Whether our predictions of party preferences were based solely upon principles, or upon principles supplemented by sympathies, experience, and social background, Conservative preference was the easiest to predict and Liberal Democrat preference the most difficult. Commitment to equality proved a far more powerful influence than commitment to liberty upon Conservative and Labour preferences, though it had relatively little effect upon Liberal Democrat or SNP preferences.

Taking account of prejudices and social background confirmed commitment to equality as the strongest influence upon Conservative and Labour preferences, followed by sympathies for social and political claimants and identification with class. Unsurprisingly, SNP support was particularly strong in the Scots sample. Less obviously, SNP strength in the Scots sample was balanced by Conservative and Liberal Democrat weakness but was not accompanied by any substantial Scottish bias towards Labour. Labour's remarkable success in Scottish elections rests partly upon stronger working-class identification but mostly upon Conservative weakness and divided opposition to Labour, rather than unusual Labour strength.

SNP preference proved more predictable than Liberal Democrat preference, but not because it was greatly influenced by principles of liberty or equality, for it was not. The greatest influence on SNP preferences was a lack of confidence in the judicial/political system, followed, a long way behind, by sympathy for social and political claimants. In our terms, therefore, support for the SNP was more a vote of sympathy and prejudice than of principle; support for Labour and the Conservatives was primarily dependent upon attitudes to equality, though influenced to a lesser extent by support for liberty; while support for the Liberal Democrats was influenced by attitudes to both liberty and equality, though both influences were weak (Table 12.4).

Given the nature of these findings, and at the risk of losing yet more detail, we can usefully construct a single summary measure of party preference which we shall call the 'vote-preference scale' with values as follows:

   −10 for Labour preference
   −5 for SNP preference
   0 for Liberal Democrat preference, or no preference
   +10 for Conservative preference.[1]

This essentially measures Conservative versus Labour preferences and treats all other preferences as intermediate, though with SNP preferences treated as closer to Labour than Conservative (as justified in Chapter 9). We make no claims for this scale other than that it is a useful crude summary of one aspect of voting preferences. Judged by the path coefficients, the pattern of principle underlying this vote-preference scale was very similar to that underlying support for the Conservatives alone. That was because the pattern underlying Labour support was approximately inverse to that underlying Conservative support, while the patterns of principle underlying Liberal Democrat and SNP support were comparatively (and absolutely) weak.

Ideological Self-Images

Using only commitments to principle as predictors, right-wing ideological self-images proved even more predictable than party preferences; and, once

TABLE 12.4. *Effect of social background, experience, principles, and sympathies on voting preferences*

	Vote-preference scale	Conservative preference	Labour preference	Liberal Democrat preference	SNP preference
			Combined sample (British public only, except for SNP: Scots only)		
Multiple correlation (×100):	54 (40)	57 (43)	39 (34)	17 (10)	36 (.)
Path coefficients (×100) from					
liberty	−19 (−15)	−23 (−15)	14 (15)	10 (.)	. (.)
equality	−43 (−36)	−44 (−39)	35 (30)	. (10)	. (.)
Scottish sample	−16 n.a.	−16 n.a.	. n.a.	−11 n.a.	34 n.a.
politicians' sample	. n.a.	. n.a.	. n.a.	. n.a.	. n.a.
Multiple correlation (×100):	61 (49)	63 (51)	47 (44)	22 (14)	40 (27)
Path coefficients (×100) from					
liberty	−12 (.)	−15 (.)	10 (.)	11 (.)	. (.)
equality	−30 (−28)	−32 (−30)	24 (20)	10 (12)	. (.)
claimants	−19 (−19)	−18 (−16)	15 (19)	. (.)	. (10)
judicial/political system	12 (12)	15 (14)	. (.)	. (.)	−12 (−17)
class (working)	−18 (−17)	−14 (−15)	19 (16)	−10 (.)	. (.)
Scottish sample	−14 n.a.	−14 n.a.	. n.a.	−10 n.a.	33 n.a.
politicians' sample	. n.a.	. n.a.	. n.a.	. n.a.	. n.a.

Notes: Path coefficients less than 0.10 have been replaced by full points.

Complaints of discrimination, or being stopped by rude police, religiosity, age, education, and gender were also included as predictors in the second regressions but none of their path coefficients ever reached 0.10.

n.a. = not applicable.

TABLE 12.5. *Dynamic preferences in the 1986–7 election campaign, by ideological self-image*

	Left (%)	Centre left (%)	Centre (%)	Centre right (%)	Right (%)
Party preferences over five interviews					
Consistently Conservative	2	5	29	38	62
Flip-flop Conservative/ Liberal Democrat	5	8	19	28	14
Flip-flop Labour/Liberal Democrat	17	32	14	11	2
Consistently Labour	63	33	8	7	8

again, commitment to equality had more influence than commitment to liberty though both the path coefficients were large: minus 33 from liberty and minus 45 from equality.

It has been argued that ideological self-image in Britain (and Europe generally) is little more than a reflection of party preference.[2] There certainly is a close connection between the two, both statically and dynamically. The 1987 General Election Campaign Study showed the dynamic connection particularly well. It followed a panel of voters through five interviews over the year leading up to the election and into the week following it, asking respondents about their past, present, and future voting intentions and about their sense of party identification (Table 12.5).

Throughout that panel, 63 per cent of voters who placed themselves 'on the left', and 62 per cent of those who placed themselves 'on the right', were consistently Labour (if on the left) or Conservative (if on the right). Amongst those who placed themselves 'in the centre but leaning to the left', 33 per cent remained consistently Labour and a further 32 per cent flip-flopped between Labour and the Liberal Democrats. Similarly, amongst those who placed themselves 'in the centre but leaning to the right', 38 per cent remained consistently Conservative while a further 28 per cent flip-flopped between the Conservatives and the Liberal Democrats. Those who placed themselves firmly 'in the centre' divided between loyalty to all three parties and every kind of inconsistency over time (Table 12.6).[3]

But ideological self-images may none the less reflect more than party preference. First, we tested that in a way that gave maximum scope to party

TABLE 12.6. *Effect of principles and voting preferences on right–wing ideological self-images*

	Combined sample	(British public only)
Multiple correlation (×100)	60	(48)
Path coefficients (×100) from		
liberty	−33	(−27)
equality	−45	(−38)
Multiple correlation (×100)	73	(67)
Path coefficients (×100) from		
liberty	−22	(−19)
equality	−23	(−20)
Conservative preference	31	(30)
Labour preference	−26	(−28)
Liberal Democratic preference	.	(.)
SNP preference	.	(.)
Multiple correlation (×100)	73	(66)
Path coefficients (×100) from		
liberty	−23	(−19)
equality	−23	(−20)
vote-preference scale	50	(50)

Notes: Path coefficients less than 0.10 have been replaced by full points.

In all the regressions in this table on the combined sample, indicators for the Scottish and politicians' samples were also included as predictors, but their path coefficients never reached 0.10.

preference by including in our multiple regressions four separate dummy variables for Conservative, Labour, Liberal Democrat, and SNP preferences. Conservative and Labour preferences had the greatest influence upon ideological self-image, but there remained substantial direct and independent influences from principle. Moreover, once party had been taken into account, the influence of liberty approximated that of equality: commitment to liberty retained a path coefficient of minus 22, and equality minus 23. So not only is it wrong to suggest that ideological self-images merely reflect partisanship; it is also wrong to suggest that the only principles they reflect are egalitarian. Ideological self-images reflect libertarian principles to much the same extent as egalitarian. In recent years, right-wing political theorists have attempted to hijack the term 'libertarian' for their own purposes.[4] They may have claimed the word but they have not stolen the concept. Amongst the

British public and politicians, liberty—like equality—is a principle of those who place themselves on the left, not the right.

Once again, because the patterns involving Labour and the Conservatives are nearly inverse, while the patterns involving other parties are extremely weak, we can simplify our findings by using our single 'vote-preference scale' instead of separate indicators of preference for each party. That shows party preference had twice as much influence upon ideological self-images as commitment either to liberty or to equality separately, but all three had a strong influence.

Of course, even if there had been no direct and independent effect of principle over and above the effect of party preference, we would still have emphasized the importance of principle because we have argued that principle has a strong influence upon choice of party in the first place. Thus the evidence against a direct effect of principle on ideological self-image, over and above that of party, would have meant only that principle exercised its influence indirectly, through the medium of party. That indirect influence is indeed strong, but we have now shown that there is also a strong direct influence in addition. Adding sympathies, experience, and background into the regression equation as further predictors suggested that prejudice against social and political claimants tilted ideological self-images towards the right, but nothing else had any substantial independent effect.

A second test confirms our conclusion that ideological self-images reflect more than party preferences. Some people had no party preferences yet they had ideological self images. And within each party, different people had different self-images. Moreover, these differences were not random: in particular, they related to principle. Principles inclined some Conservatives to describe themselves as more right wing than others, and some Labour politicians and voters to describe themselves as more left wing than others. And principles had an even greater influence upon the ideological self-images of those who preferred neither the Conservatives nor Labour—that large number of Liberal Democrats, Scottish Nationalists, and people without a party preference.

There was a striking asymmetry in these predictions, however. The best predictor of ideological self-image amongst Conservatives was commitment to equality with a path coefficient of minus 23; while amongst Labour voters it was commitment to liberty with a path coefficient of minus 32. Clearly what united Labour voters was their commitment to equality and what divided them was their varying degree of commitment to liberty; while what divided Conservatives most was their differing views about equality.

Taking all those without a Conservative or Labour preference together, including those without any party preference, liberty and equality had about the same effect upon ideological self-images with path coefficients of minus 30 and 31 respectively. Ideological self-images of Liberal Democrats were somewhat more influenced by commitment to liberty, while those of SNP voters more by equality (Table 12.7).

The path coefficients from the Scots sample show no important differences except that Scottish Liberal Democrats had somewhat more right-wing (or less left-wing) self-images than Liberal Democrats generally—a finding that is certainly consistent with the geographic pattern of their support in Scotland, where it is based more upon remote rural areas and less on urban or suburban areas than in England. Path coefficients from the politicians' sample were larger, more frequent, and more interesting. They show that Conservative politicians had more right-wing self-images than Conservative voters with the same attitudes to liberty and equality (path coefficient plus 13); and Labour politicians correspondingly more left-wing self-images than Labour voters with similar principles (path coefficient minus 16). Liberal Democrat and SNP politicians, like Labour, also had more left-wing self-images than their principles alone would warrant. We already know that the principles of party politicians differed from those of their voters, but our multiple regressions have already taken that into account. The path coefficients for politicians show the difference in ideological self-images between party politicians and those of their voters who shared their principles to exactly the same degree.

Taking account of prejudices, experience, and social background as well as principles naturally reduced, but did not eliminate, the effects of principle on ideological self-image within parties. Commitment to equality tied with class identification as the main influence upon the ideological self-images of Conservatives, followed closely by prejudice against claimants. Nothing else had much influence. Commitment to liberty was by far the strongest influence on ideological self-images amongst labour, but old age, sympathy for claimants, and prejudice against the judicial/political system, commitment to equality, and being a Labour politician rather than a Labour voter, all made for somewhat more left-wing self-images.

Amongst Liberal Democrats, only commitment to liberty and equality, and being in the Scottish or politicians' samples had any substantial influence: all the other predictors proved unimportant. Amongst the SNP, sympathy for claimants, (working-)class identification, and (old) age, in addition to attitudes towards liberty and equality, all contributed towards rather more left-wing self-images.

TABLE 12.7. *Effect of principles on right-wing ideological self-images, within parties*

	Combined sample (British public only, except for SNP: Scots public only)				
	Conservative	Labour	Liberal Democrat	SNP	Neither Conservative nor Labour
Multiple correlation (×100)	32 (22)	49 (35)	55 (40)	44 (41)	49 (45)
Path coefficients (×100) from					
liberty	−10 (.)	−32 (−30)	−32 (−35)	−26 (−24)	−30 (−33)
equality	−23 (−22)	−18 (−16)	−22 (−24)	−35 (−35)	−31 (−32)
Scottish sample	. n.a.	n.a.	12 n.a.	. n.a.	n.a.
politicians' sample	13 n.a.	−16 n.a.	−19 n.a.	−10 n.a.	−16 n.a.

Notes: Path coefficients less than 0.10 have been replaced by full points.

'Neither Conservative nor Labour' includes Liberal Democrats, SNP, PC, other parties, and 'no preference'/'don't know', etc.

n.a. = not applicable.

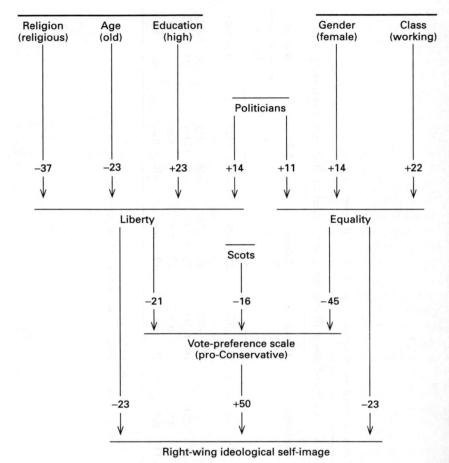

Fɪɢ. 12.2.   *Influences in principles, party preferences, and ideological self-images*

A Diagrammatic Representation

We can depict our findings up to this point in a relatively simple diagram,
showing the important paths of influence and their path coefficients—which
assess their relative importance. There is no need to include our measures of
personal experience because they failed to exert a strong independent influence upon principle or anything else; and by using our party-preference scale
rather than indicators of preference for each party separately, we can greatly
simplify the diagram without greatly distorting the findings. Fig. 12.2 brings
together all the important findings of preceding tables.

MODELS OF PRACTICE

Our general model postulates that attitudes towards specific mechanisms for protecting citizens' rights or towards the practice of rights are influenced most immediately by principles, prejudices, and arguments, but also perhaps by party preferences, personal experiences, and social background. We would expect the relative weight of these different influences to vary according to particular circumstances. Some arguments may prove more powerful than others. Some policies may be more closely tied to party propaganda than others. Some policies may appeal to material interests sufficiently to override principles. We cannot possibly attempt to show how arguments, principles, prejudices, partisanship, and interests combine to influence attitudes towards every individual item of policy, and it would be pointless to try assessing their influence towards such a meaningless concept as the 'average policy'. Even a comprehensive review of their influence on all the specific policies touched upon in our survey is beyond our scope. But we can look in detail at a range of examples which span the broad subject areas of policy covered in our survey and which also illustrate the different ways in which influences may combine. If the result is a collage rather than a conclusion, so be it. Any more simple conclusion would be simply wrong. The collage should at least give a more correct impression of the way different factors influence policy attitudes in contemporary Britain.

For each issue of practice, our standard analytic procedure has been to carry out a sequence of regression analyses predicting attitudes towards that issue from:

1. sample membership i.e. the British public versus the Scottish public versus politicians
2. *plus* commitment to liberty and equality
3. *plus* arguments, if any
4. *plus* party preferences
5. *plus* sympathies, personal experience, and social background.

Thus at the first step we used only sample membership as predictors to show the difference between Scots, politicians, and the British public, while at the fifth step we used all possible influences as predictors. It would be tedious to present all the results of this five-step procedure in each case, especially because we expect that personal experience and social background will usually prove to have little or no direct influence on practical decisions over and above their indirect influence through commitment to principle. Indeed, even party preferences will usually prove to have little or no effect upon practical decisions once commitment to principle has been taken into account. And because principle and prejudice are so interrelated conceptually as well as statistically, it will not usually prove very illuminating to divide the predictive load between, for example, commitment to equality and sympathy for social and political claimants. So, while we shall routinely present the results of the third-stage regressions—based upon sample membership, principles, and arguments—we shall only present fourth- or fifth-stage regressions when they show substantial additional influences from partisanship or social background. If we do not draw attention to them, it means that we have inspected them and have found no important additional influences beyond sample membership, principle, and argument.

Support for Alternative Mechanisms of Liberty: The Influence of Principle and Partisanship

In Chapter 6 we looked at a wide variety of mechanisms for protecting citizens' rights and liberties. Amongst them were four which we designated 'Conservative Party mechanisms' because they were put forward by the Conservative Party, over the decade prior to our survey, as its contribution towards extending and reinforcing citizens' rights. These were: council-house sales, privatization of industry, NHS reforms including a pseudo-market of health providers and purchasers, and elected school boards to which some local-government powers were to be transferred. All four were manifestations of Conservative Party commitment to devolving power 'from government to the citizen'. By contrast, we also looked at three mechanisms we designated 'Charter 88 mechanisms' because they were advocated by Charter 88 amongst others, mainly on the left and centre left of British politics. These were: a Bill of Rights, a Freedom of Information Act, and an elected House of Lords. All three of these aimed at improving and democratizing the operation of government rather than reducing its scope.

We might expect that support for these different mechanisms would be influenced by principles, and also perhaps by background and experience. But we should also expect that party preference would have an especially large role in influencing attitudes towards the Conservative Party mechanisms simply because they were so strongly advocated by that party—and only by that party. Charter 88 mechanisms, on the other hand, were advocated by politicians across several parties and by others who had an interest in good government but were not party representatives. Thus we should expect that support for them would be less influenced by party preferences.

Respondents were asked to give each mechanism a 'mark out of ten' for how important they thought it was for protecting rights and liberties. To simplify the analysis we have averaged the four 'marks out of ten' given to the Conservative Party mechanisms and the three given to Charter 88 mechanisms to produce two summary measures.

Surprisingly, despite the very constitutional flavour of the Charter 88 proposals, it was commitment to equality with a path coefficient of 41 that increased support for them, while commitment to liberty had little or no effect. But, as expected, the introduction of party preferences had almost no effect upon our analysis of Charter 88 reforms: support for them reflected principle, not partisanship. There was a very slight tendency for Liberal Democrats to support Charter 88 proposals more than their principles would warrant, but it was very slight, and was only evident when politicians were included in the analysis. Politicians as a whole were also more favourable to these Charter 88 reforms than were the general public (Table 12.8).

Commitment to equality reduced support for Conservative Party mechanisms, but commitment to liberty even more so—with path coefficients of minus 28 and minus 40 respectively. As expected, support for Conservative Party mechanisms, unlike support for Charter 88 mechanisms, reflected partisanship as well as principle—with path coefficients of 28 from Conservative preference, minus 23 from Labour preference, and minus 12 from SNP preference. Simplifying the analysis by substituting our vote-preference scale for the four separate indicators of party preference gave party a path coefficient of 44. Once account was taken of party preference, commitment to equality had no effect upon support for the Conservative Party mechanisms, and, while commitment to liberty remained important with a path coefficient of minus 31, its influence was exceeded by that of party preference.

Further analysis showed that experience and background had no effect upon support for either kind of mechanism, though confidence in the judicial/political system increased support for *both* the Conservative Party mechanisms and the Charter 88 mechanisms.

Looking at each of the seven mechanisms separately revealed some differences between the patterns of support for mechanisms within each of the two categories. Amongst Charter 88 mechanisms, support for a Freedom of Information Act or for an elected House of Lords was strongly influenced by commitment to equality but by nothing else. By contrast, support for a Bill of Rights was less strongly influenced by commitment to equality. On the surface it appeared to be particularly popular with politicians, but that influence disappeared once we took into account fairly strong influences from

TABLE 12.8. *Effect of principles and voting preferences on practical decisions about mechanisms*

	Combined sample (British public only)			
	Conservative Party mechanisms		Charter 88 mechanisms	
Multiple correlation (×100)	51	(37)	43	(31)
Path coefficients (×100) from				
liberty	−40	(−33)	.	(.)
equality	−28	(−17)	41	(31)
Scottish sample	.	n.a.	.	n.a.
politicians' sample	.	n.a.	11	n.a.
Multiple correlation (×100)	63	(49)	45	(31)
Path coefficients (×100) from				
liberty	−29	(−27)	.	(.)
equality	.	(.)	37	(31)
Conservative preference	28	(28)	.	(.)
Labour preference	−23	(−12)	.	(.)
Liberal Democrat preference	.	(.)	10	(.)
SNP preference	−12	(.)	.	(.)
Scottish sample	.	n.a.	.	n.a.
politicians' sample	.	n.a.	11	n.a.
Multiple correlation (×100)	63	(49)	44	(31)
Path coefficients (×100) from				
liberty	−31	(−28)	.	(.)
equality	.	(.)	37	(31)
vote-preference scale	44	(34)	.	(.)
Scottish sample	.	n.a.	.	n.a.
politicians' sample	.	n.a.	11	n.a.

Notes: Path coefficients less than 0.10 have been replaced by full points.

Conservative mechanisms were proposed only by the Conservative Party (council-house sales, privatization, NHS trusts, school boards).

Charter 88 mechanisms were proposed by Charter 88 and others (Bill of Rights, Freedom of Information Act, elected House of Lords).

n.a. = not applicable.

TABLE 12.9. *Effect of principles and voting preferences on practical decisions about two mechanisms advocated by the Conservative Party*

	Combined sample (British public only)			
	Council-house sales		NHS reforms	
Multiple correlation (×100)	47	(31)	61	(47)
Path coefficients (×100) from				
liberty	−32	(−25)	−25	(−20)
equality	−1	(+6)	−13	(−11)
vote-preference scale	25	(15)	43	(35)
Scottish sample	11	n.a.	.	n.a.
politicians' sample	.	n.a.	.	n.a.

Notes: Path coefficients less than 0.10 have been replaced by full points, except for the coefficient for equality, where we note that it is almost zero or even positive when predicting support for council-house sales, but significantly negative when predicting support for NHS reforms.

n.a. = not applicable.

prejudice *in favour* of the judicial/political system. Logically, of course, support for a Bill of Rights should depend upon a degree of confidence in the judicial system at least, and that appears to be the case.

Support for all four of the Conservative Party mechanisms was strongly affected by commitment to liberty, prejudice in favour of the judicial/political system, and party preference. But there were some very clear differences. Partisanship had much more influence upon attitudes to NHS reforms than upon attitudes to council-house sales. And once partisanship had been taken into account, commitment to equality reduced support for NHS reorganization but not for council-house sales. Indeed, amongst the public, commitment to equality then *increased* support for council-house sales. Clearly, there were detectable nuances of opinion that matched the specific attractions of particular mechanisms and policies (Table 12.9).

Support for Electoral Mechanisms: The Influence of Principle, Partisanship, Argument, and the Governing Perspective

At least by implication, three of our survey questions raised issues concerning voting and elections—the core mechanisms of democracy. We asked whether people supported 'greater powers of self-government' for Scotland

and the English regions, and whether they supported the use of referendums. Voting is an essentially egalitarian mechanism, and commitment to equality raised support for all three, while commitment to liberty also raised support for devolution.

Although the Conservative Party strongly opposed all three reforms, party preferences had only a weak influence amongst the public, but much more amongst politicians; so that, in our combined sample, the path coefficients from party preference ranged as high as minus 25. Our combined sample also showed that, while SNP voters were unusually strong supporters of devolution for Scotland, Scots as a whole were not—simply because the idea had such strong support in England and Wales as well as in Scotland. In addition our combined sample showed that politicians were more favourable than others to the idea of devolution for the English regions. As we noted in Chapter 6, Scots were also more favourable to English regional devolution until we took account of their party preferences, but not once party had been taken into account.

More strikingly, politicians differed massively from the public on support for referendums—with a path coefficient of minus 28. For the referendum question we used two alternative introductions, one designed to increase support for referendums by arguing that they 'let the people decide', the other designed to reduce support for referendums by arguing that 'important issues are too complex' to be decided in referendums. The alternative versions, posed to random half samples, were:

[Important political issues are too complex to be decided by everyone voting in a referendum, and it should be left to parliament to decide/It would be better to let the people decide important political issues by everyone voting in a referendum, rather than leaving them to parliament as at present.] Agree/disagree?

Amongst the British public, the influence of these alternative arguments was substantial, with a path coefficient of 14, but in our combined sample it was not. That was because politicians reacted *against* overt attempts to push them towards or against a referendum. Indeed, in a regression restricted solely to politicians, the path coefficient for the use of our pro-referendum argument was *minus* 15, equal in size but opposite in direction to the effect of the same argument amongst the public. In the combined sample, therefore, a positive response to argument amongst the British public (and amongst the Scots) was offset by this reaction against argument amongst politicians (Table 12.10).

TABLE 12.10. *Effect of principles and arguments on practical decisions about democratic mechanisms*

	Combined sample (British public only)					
	Devolution for Scotland		Devolution for English regions		Referendums	
Multiple correlation (×100)	38	(28)	39	(24)	37	(22)
Path coefficients (×100) from						
liberty	18	(11)	19	(.)	.	(.)
equality	31	(25)	30	(23)	15	(17)
pro-referendum intro.	n.a.	n.a.	n.a.	n.a.	.	(13)
Scottish sample	.	n.a.	.	n.a.	.	n.a.
politicians' sample	.	n.a.	10	n.a.	−29	n.a.
Multiple correlation (×100)	46	(31)	43	(26)	41	(26)
Path coefficients (×100) from						
liberty	11	(10)	13	(.)	.	(.)
equality	19	(19)	20	(17)	.	(14)
pro-referendum intro.	n.a.	n.a.	n.a.	n.a.	.	(14)
Conservative preference	−19	(.)	−18	(−10)	−14	(.)
Labour preference	.	(.)	.	(.)	.	(.)
Liberal Democrat preference	.	(.)	.	(.)	.	(.)
SNP preference	15	(.)	.	(.)	.	(.)
Scottish sample	.	n.a.	.	n.a.	.	n.a.
politicians' sample	.	n.a.	10	n.a.	−28	n.a.
Multiple correlation (×100)	43	(30)	43	(26)	38	(24)
Path coefficients (×100) from						
liberty	13	(.)	15	(.)	.	(.)
equality	21	(20)	21	(18)	10	(14)
pro-referendum intro.	n.a.	n.a.	n.a.	n.a.	.	(13)
vote-preference scale	−25	(−13)	−21	(−13)	−10	(.)
Scottish sample	.	n.a.	.	n.a.	.	n.a.
politicians' sample	.	n.a.	11	n.a.	−28	n.a.

Notes: Path coefficients less than 0.10 have been replaced by full points.
n.a. = not applicable.

Issues of Free Expression and the Right to Protest: The Influence of Principle and Partisanship

As examples, let us take three issues related to free expression and protest —whether to allow a potentially riotous political demonstration or football match to go ahead, and whether workers should have the right to strike. We included the right to strike as one indicator of the micro-principle we called protest but that was not used in the construction of either of our macro-principles, liberty and equality. So there is no spurious circularity in using these macro-principles to predict support for the right to strike.[5] The question about a potential riot used political demonstrations and football matches as alternative wordings; so each was applied to only half of our sample but even half samples are adequate for this analysis. The question about the right to strike specifically excluded 'essential workers' when put to half the sample and included them when put to the other half. Here we use the full sample, without distinction (Table 12.11).

Principles had a large influence upon attitudes towards two of these practical decisions—the right to strike and political demonstrations—but much less effect upon attitudes towards allowing potentially riotous football matches to go ahead. Commitment to liberty had a large effect upon willingness to allow a potentially riotous political demonstration to go ahead; and commitment to equality had a similarly large effect upon support for workers' rights to strike; but neither had much effect upon attitudes towards permitting a potentially riotous football match to go ahead. It seems that our respondents could see the relevance of political principle to the first two decisions more clearly than to the third: political demonstrations and the right to strike really were issues of free expression and/or protest, and attitudes towards them did depend upon political principles to a degree that attitudes towards a football riot did not. We would agree with our respondents on that.

Party preferences had little or no influence upon attitudes to demonstrations and football matches, but a large influence upon attitudes towards the right to strike, with a path coefficient of minus 25, somewhat greater than the path coefficient from equality. The Labour Party grew out of the trade unions, and even in the 1980s Conservative Party rhetoric focused more upon unions and strikes than upon public disorder, not least because the Labour Party's history and continuing close association with the unions meant that it could not avoid defending trade unions and the right to strike while its instincts as a potential party of government meant that it could not defend public disorder.[6] Even so, the joint effect of liberty and equality principles upon attitudes towards strikes was as great as that of partisanship in our combined sample, and greater amongst the public. Sympathy for

TABLE 12.11. *Effect of principles and voting preferences on practical decisions about free expression*

	Combined sample (British public only)					
	Allow political demonstration		Allow football match		Support right to strike	
Multiple correlation (×100)	33	(33)	19	(14)	37	(32)
Path coefficients (×100) from						
liberty	30	(31)	15	(.)	17	(16)
equality	10	(12)	.	(11)	31	(28)
Multiple correlation (×100)	35	(36)	20	(19)	44	(38)
Path coefficients (×100) from						
liberty	28	(30)	14	(.)	11	(12)
equality	.	(.)	.	(10)	19	(20)
Conservative preference	−11	(−10)	.	(−12)	−18	(−14)
Labour preference	.	(.)	.	(.)	12	(10)
Liberal Democrat preference	.	(.)	.	(−14)	.	(.)
SNP preference	.	(.)	.	(.)	.	(.)
Scottish sample	−11	n.a.	.	n.a.	.	n.a.
politicians' sample	.	n.a.	.	n.a.	.	n.a.
Multiple correlation (×100)	34	(34)	19	(15)	42	(37)
Path coefficients (×100) from						
liberty	28	(30)	14	(.)	12	(13)
equality	.	(10)	.	(.)	20	(21)
vote-preference scale	.	(.)	.	(.)	−25	(−20)

Note: Path coefficients less than 0.10 have been replaced by full points.

Indicators of being in the Scottish or politicians' samples were included in all these regressions, but only reached 0.10 in the single entry shown.

n.a. = not applicable.

social and political claimants increased support for allowing a political demonstration to go ahead, but experience and background had no direct influence on any of these decisions except for a slight tendency for the old to oppose political demonstrations.

Issues of Freedom of Information: The Influence of Principle and Argument

As examples of these issues, let us take support for bans on publishing confidential government documents and sensational crime reports. With each of

TABLE 12.12. *Effect of principles and arguments on practical decisions about freedom of information*

	Combined sample (British public only)			
	Ban publication of confidential government plans		Ban publication of sensational crime stories	
Multiple correlation (×100)	41	(32)	31	(27)
Path coefficients (×100) from				
liberty	−34	(−29)	−30	(−26)
equality	−19	(−12)	.	(.)
Scottish sample	.	n.a.	.	n.a.
politicians' sample	.	n.a.	.	n.a.
Multiple correlation (×100)	43	(34)	36	(32)
Path coefficients (×100) from				
liberty	−34	(−29)	−30	(−27)
equality	−19	(−12)	.	(.)
add 'national interest'	11	(10)	n.a.	n.a.
add 'unfair to accused'	n.a.	n.a.	20	(19)
add 'encourage crime'	n.a.	n.a.	.	(16)
Scottish sample	.	n.a.	.	n.a.
politicians' sample	.	n.a.	.	n.a.

Notes: Path coefficients less than 0.10 have been replaced by full points.
n.a. = not applicable.

these questions we employed added arguments. For half the sample we added 'because publication might damage our national interests' to the question about confidential government documents. For one-third we added 'because it may encourage others to commit more crimes' to the question about banning sensational crime reports; and for another third 'because, later on, it may prevent an accused person getting a fair trial'.

Commitment to liberty greatly reduced support for either ban while commitment to equality also reduced support for a ban on publishing confidential government documents (Table 12.12).

Arguments were also influential. Judged by the path coefficients, the addition of a phrase about the 'national interest' increased support for a ban on publication of government documents, but its effect was much less than that of principle. Arguments in favour of suppressing publication of sensational crime stories were more influential. Amongst the public the path coefficients were minus 27 from liberty, but plus 16 for the argument about encouraging copy-cat crime and 19 for the fair-trial argument. In our combined sample, however, only the fair-trial argument appeared to have a substantial effect, because politicians were unmoved by the copy-cat argument. None the less, the fair-trial argument still had two-thirds the effect of principle, and it was twice as effective as the national-interest argument against publishing government secrets.

Prejudice, party preference, experience, and background had no effect upon these practical decisions about freedom of information, except for a slight tendency for women to be more inclined to ban sensational crime reports, and a slight tendency for partisanship to influence the views of politicians.

An Issue of Lifestyle: The Influence of Principle, Argument, and the Governing Perspective

We asked half our sample whether 'people should be allowed to take whatever drugs they like' and, for half of them, we added 'provided they do not harm or behave offensively to other people'. Commitment to liberty greatly increased permissive attitudes towards drugs, as also did the proviso about not harming others: the path coefficients were 28 and 20 respectively amongst the public and much the same in our combined sample. But over and above the effects of principle and argument, politicians were more opposed to freedom of drug use—with a path coefficient of minus 15. This was a striking and significant exception to the usually greater level of permissive liberalism amongst politicians.

There was a very slight tendency for sympathy for social and political claimants to encourage more permissive attitudes to drugs, but, apart from that, neither prejudice, party preference, experience, nor background had any influence (Table 12.13).

Issues of Law Enforcement: Principle Outweighed by Argument

We chose two examples of the practice of law enforcement: first, support for conviction on confession alone; and, second, support for the death penalty. Each question involved arguments and, as we shall see in the next section, the second involved a challenge.

We asked whether people supported conviction on confession alone. For one-third of our sample we added the phrase 'because people sometimes confess to things they haven't done', and for another third the phrase 'because people are sometimes put under so much pressure they confess things they have not done', as arguments against conviction on confession alone.

TABLE 12.13. *Effect of principles and argument on practical decisions about lifestyle: willingness to permit unrestricted use of drugs*

	Combined sample	(British public only)
Multiple correlation (×100)	33	(33)
Path coefficients (×100) from		
liberty	25	(28)
equality	.	(.)
add 'provided no harm to others'	21	(20)
Scottish sample	.	n.a.
politicians' sample	−15	n.a.

Notes: Path coefficients less than 0.10 have been replaced by full points.
n.a. = not applicable.

This was clearly a difficult question for public and politicians alike. Commitments to liberty and equality both reduced support for conviction on confession, but not by as much as arguments against it. The path coefficients were minus 14 from liberty and minus 11 from equality, but minus 17 from the 'false-confession' argument and minus 20 from the 'pressure-to-confess' argument. On this issue, explicit arguments clearly mattered more than principle.

But exactly the opposite was true for our explicit arguments about the death penalty. For half the sample we introduced our question 'do you think Britain should reintroduce the death penalty for murder, or keep things as they are?' with the phrase 'given that parliament has repeatedly voted against the death penalty'; for the other half we introduced the same question with the phrase 'in order to clamp down on rising crime and violence'. On this question, principle had a strong effect, and argument—or at least these arguments—had none at all. Commitment to both liberty and equality reduced support for the death penalty with path coefficients of minus 29 and minus 20 respectively. Opposition to the death penalty primarily reflected principles of liberty and authority but also, to a lesser extent, principles of equality.

It must come as no surprise to find that people with a high commitment to liberty were more opposed to the death penalty than authoritarians. Perhaps it is less obvious why egalitarians should also be more opposed to it. However, the macabre statistics on executions in the USA—the only developed democracy that uses the death penalty extensively—provide one clue:

except in times of revolution, it tends to be the poor, the uneducated, and ethnic minorities who most frequently feel the full vengeance of the law.

Dye and Zeigler point out that there are three main arguments against the death penalty in the USA. The first is that it is a 'cruel and unusual' punishment and, as such, explicitly banned by the 8th Amendment to the Constitution (part of the 1789 Bill of Rights). This first argument has obvious links to the liberty/authority dimension of principle. The second argument is that 'the death penalty is imposed in arbitrary fashion; there are no clear, consistent criteria for deciding who should be executed and who should be spared'. That argument has links to the concepts of both liberty (which opposes arbitrary government) and equality (which implies the same penalty for the same crime). The third argument against the death penalty is based entirely on the principle of equality:

it is used in a discriminatory fashion in violation of the 'equal-protection' clause of the 14th Amendment. Although blacks make up only 12 per cent of the population of the nation, over half of those ever executed have been black. Moreover, among both blacks and whites it has generally been the less educated and less affluent who have been executed . . . The principal advocate on the Supreme Court for abolishing the death penalty has been [the black] Justice Thurgood Marshall, who has argued that it is the ultimate form of racial discrimination.[7]

British people may not be familiar with the precise statistics of US executions, but the news media probably ensure that they are familiar with the general pattern. Nor is there any reason to believe that the pattern is peculiarly American. It is several decades since anyone has been executed in Britain, but recent celebrated miscarriages of justice in Britain have involved defendants who were relatively poor, uneducated, and from the (Irish) ethnic minority. The arguments set out so clearly by Dye and Zeigler apply with equal force in Britain.

But, whatever the explanation, our survey proves beyond dispute that British egalitarians tended more than others to oppose the death penalty— even when we discounted the influence of their concurrent attitudes towards liberty and authority by using multiple regression (Table 12.14).

Over and above the effects of principle and argument, politicians were far more opposed to the death penalty than the public, with a path coefficient of minus 17. Once principles and arguments had been taken into account, prejudice, party preference, experience, and background had no effect except for very slight tendencies for the old to oppose conviction on confession (accumulated memories of miscarriages of justice perhaps?) and for the highly educated and those who sympathized with social and political claimants to

TABLE 12.14. *Effect of principles and arguments on practical decisions about law enforcement*

| | Combined sample (British public only) | | | |
	Convict on confession		Support death penalty	
Multiple correlation (×100)	26	(24)	44	(32)
Path coefficients (×100) from				
liberty	−14	(−12)	−29	(−28)
equality	−11	(.)	−20	(−16)
add 'sometimes confess wrongly'	−17	(−18)	n.a.	n.a.
add 'pressure to confess'	−20	(−22)	n.a.	n.a.
add 'parliament has voted against it'	n.a.	n.a.	.	(.)
push against death penalty	n.a.	n.a.	−12	(−13)
push towards death penalty	n.a.	n.a.	11	(11)
Scottish sample	.	n.a.	.	n.a.
politicians' sample	.	n.a.	−17	n.a.

Notes: Path coefficients less than 0.10 have been replaced by full points.
n.a. = not applicable.

oppose the death penalty. Perhaps the most striking thing about these additional findings is that partisanship did *not* affect attitudes to the death penalty once the strong effect of principle had been taken into account—an important and somewhat surprising null finding.

Challenging Attitudes towards the Death Penalty

Whatever answer people initially gave to our question about the death penalty we immediately challenged them to change their minds. If they initially supported the death penalty, we continued: 'If careful research showed that reintroducing the death penalty *would not* cut the number of murders in Britain, would you *still* be in favour of the death penalty?' Let us call this the 'anti-death push'. Conversely, if they initially opposed the death penalty we asked: 'If careful research showed that reintroducing the death penalty *would* cut the number of murders in Britain, would you *then* be in favour of the death penalty?' Let us call this the 'pro-death push'.

In order to quantify the effect of these challenges in a way that is comparable to the way in which we have measured the effects of added arguments we proceeded as follows:

1. Replicate the data set twice, producing three copies in all. Then take account of the 'anti-death push' in the first copy, and the 'pro-death push' in the second copy, as follows.

2a. *Anti-death push.* Assume that this would not change the opinions of those who were already opposed to the death penalty (and who were never faced with this challenge). But for all those initially in favour of the death penalty who no longer supported it when challenged, count them as now opposed to it.

2b. *Pro-death push.* Assume this would not change the opinions of those who were already in favour. But for all those initially opposed to it who no longer opposed it when challenged, count them as now in favour.

3. Combine the three versions of the data-set to make a single data-set with three times as many interviews as in the original, and in which one-third have been unexposed to any challenge, one-third exposed to the 'anti-death push', and one-third exposed to the 'pro-death push'. This new, enlarged data-set can now be analysed as if a pro-death argument had been added to one-third of the sample and an anti-death argument had been added to another third.

Following this procedure produces path coefficients of about plus or minus 12 for the 'pro- and anti-death pushes'. Thus, while arguments that invoked the majesty of parliament against the need to clamp down on crime had no effect upon attitudes to the death penalty, challenges based upon hypothetical evidence about its ability to reduce the murder rate do seem to have had a modest effect. Even so, the effect of challenges on attitudes towards the death penalty was nowhere near as great as the effect of our arguments against conviction on confession.

Issues of Equality: The Influence of Principle, Argument, and Partisanship

We asked whether it was 'important to have more [women/ethnic or racial minority] MPs in parliament?' and, if so, 'should the *law* be changed to ensure more [women/ethnic or racial minority] MPs?' Answers to the first question were strongly influenced by commitment to equality—the path coefficient was 35, but only a little by liberty, and certainly by nothing else. Slight though its influence was, however, let us note that commitment to liberty *increased* support for more women or minority MPs.

A much more complex and conflicting pattern of influences lay behind answers to the second question, about changing the law to ensure more women or minority MPs. On this aspect of the issue, commitment to equality continued to exert a substantial influence in favour of changing the law, but commitment to liberty now *reduced* support for change. Despite the rhetoric of right-wing politicians that so often claims the principles of liberty and equality necessarily conflict, our study has repeatedly shown that they seldom conflict and that they usually exert their influence in the same direction as each other. That was true even for the *objective* of more women and minority MPs, but it was not true for the *mechanism* of using the law to achieve it. Conservatives were peculiarly opposed to changing the law for this purpose, with a path coefficient of minus 17, and politicians as a whole were even more opposed, with a path coefficient of minus 27.

Taking account of prejudice, experience, and background revealed even more complexities. Judged by the path coefficients for liberty and equality, the negative influence of commitment to liberty on support for legal change now exceeded the positive influence of commitment to equality. Support for changing the law, amongst those who favoured more women and minority MPs, was also influenced positively by self-identification with the working class and by sympathy for social and political claimants, but negatively by age and education.

We also asked whether 'the law should require [large private companies/ the government and civil service] to hire a fixed percentage of [women/blacks and Asians/disabled people], or should [women/blacks and Asians/disabled people] get no special treatment?' Only commitment to equality exerted a strong influence upon support for job quotas. As with the death-penalty issue, we challenged everyone to change their minds on job quotas. Anyone who initially supported job quotas was asked: 'Would you feel the same even if this *frequently* means not hiring the best person for the job?'; while those who initially opposed job quotas were asked: 'Would you feel the same even if it means that [women/blacks and Asians/disabled people] remain economically *very* unequal?' The influence of these challenges can be quantified using the same approach as we used to quantify the influence of challenges to opinion about the death penalty.

Challenges proved more influential on the issue of job quotas than on the death penalty, with path coefficients of minus 17 and plus 24. Indeed that made challenges more influential than anything else on this issue. Job quotas is thus the second issue—the first was conviction by confession—on which we have now shown that opinion was so soft, so malleable, that the influence of argument outweighed the influence of principle, regardless of whether the respondent had originally been for or against quotas.

Finally, we asked whether private medicine should be banned 'in order to make health services the same for both rich and poor . . . even though the ban would reduce the freedom of individuals to do what they want?' That was a very political question, and party preference influenced answers to it. But over and above the purely partisan response, commitment to the principle of equality also increased support for a ban on private medicine, with a path coefficient of 17. As Table 12.15 shows, commitment to liberty did not have a substantial influence upon attitudes to a ban on private medicine, but what influence it did have was negative.

This same pattern—of a positive influence from equality combined with a negative influence from liberty—was most visible on attitudes towards parliamentary quotas, slightly less visible on attitudes towards banning private medicine, and only just detectable on job quotas—all of which involve the use of legal coercion to achieve greater equality. On the issue of whether it was important to have more women and minority MPs, which in itself did not involve coercion, the influence of liberty was positive. None of these influences from liberty was large. After all, these four issues were primarily issues of equality. But the *difference* between the influence of liberty on these different issues was more substantial: a difference of 23, for example, between the effect of commitment to liberty on attitudes to the goal of more women and minority MPs and the mechanism of using the law to achieve it.

A FINAL COMPARISON OF INFLUENCES ON ISSUES OF PRACTICE

We have assessed the influence upon various practical issues of:

- two general principles—liberty and equality
- four party preferences—for the Conservatives, Labour, the Liberal Democrats, and the SNP contrasted with no preference
- the effect of living in Scotland
- the effect of being a politician, and
- the effect of being exposed to various arguments and challenges.

But how great is the influence of 'principle' compared to the influence of 'party preference' and 'argument'? There is no way of reaching an answer that does not take account of the different practical issues, but it is possible to assess the overall influence of 'principle' rather than of two separate principles, the overall influence of 'party preference' rather than of four or

TABLE 12.15. *Effect of principles and arguments on practical decisions about equality*

	Combined sample (British public only)							
	More women or minorities in parliament		Legal quotas for parliament		Legal quotas for jobs		Ban private medicine	
Multiple correlation (×100)	39	(30)	39	(28)	40	(41)	37	(29)
Path coefficients (×100) from								
liberty	+12	(+8)	−11	(−11)	0	(−2)	−3	(−7)
equality	35	(28)	15	(20)	15	(13)	17	(16)
push against job quota	n.a.	n.a.	n.a.	n.a.	−17	(−19)	n.a.	n.a.
push towards job quota	n.a.	n.a.	n.a.	n.a.	24	(25)	n.a.	n.a.
CON preference	.	(.)	−17	(−15)	.	(.)	−15	(−14)
LAB preference	.	(.)	.	(.)	.	(.)	12	(.)
LIB-DEM preference	.	(.)	.	(.)	.	(.)	.	(.)
SNP preference	.	(.)	.	(.)	.	(.)	.	(.)
Scottish sample	.	n.a.	.	n.a.	.	n.a.	.	n.a.
politicians' sample	.	n.a.	−27	n.a.	.	n.a.	.	n.a.
Multiple correlation (×100)	40	(30)	38	(28)	39	(41)	36	(28)
Path coefficients (×100) from								
liberty	+13	(+8)	−10	(−12)	0	(−3)	−4	(−7)
equality	35	(29)	16	(21)	15	(13)	16	(15)
push against job quota	n.a.	n.a.	n.a.	n.a.	−16	(−18)	n.a.	n.a.
push towards job quota	n.a.	n.a.	n.a.	n.a.	23	(25)	n.a.	n.a.
vote-preference scale	.	(.)	−10	(−10)	.	(.)	−25	(−19)
Scottish sample	.	n.a.	.	n.a.	.	n.a.	.	n.a.
politicians' sample	.	n.a.	−28	n.a.	.	n.a.	.	n.a.

Notes: Path coefficients less than 0.10 have been replaced by full points, except for path coefficients from liberty which are numerically small but whose signs are important, and have been emphasized.

n.a. = not applicable.

five different preferences, and the overall influence of 'argument' rather than of the several arguments that we sometimes used on the same issue.

To illustrate our method of carrying out this assessment, let us focus upon the patterns of support for a ban on the publication of sensational crime reports, as revealed in a regression based upon commitments to liberty and equality, party preferences for the Conservative Party, Labour, the Liberal Democrats, and the Scottish National Party, and also upon the arguments that such reports might prejudice a fair trial or encourage more crime. We have already reported the path coefficients, but the full details of that regression are as set out on the left of Table 12.16.

Now, let us construct measures of principle, party preference, and argument as follows:

principle $= -5.545901 \times$ liberty $+ 0.602806 \times$ equality
party preference $= -0.399357 \times$ Con. Pref. $- 0.500496 \times$ Lab. Pref. $- 0.397892 \times$ Lib. Dem. Pref. $- 1.088567 \times$ SNP Pref.
argument $= 2.497778 \times$ 'prejudice trial' $+ 1.116369 \times$ 'encourage crime'.

Each of these consists of a part of the original regression equation. They can also be regarded as 'scales' of principle, preference, or argument, but scales that best predict support for a ban on publishing sensational crime stories. If we use these measures of principle, party preference, and argument in a new regression, we find, necessarily, that their *unstandardized* regression coefficients are always exactly equal to one. What is interesting, however, is the size of their *standardized* regression coefficients, or path coefficients. These tell us by how much support for a ban on publishing sensational crime stories changes when each of our 'scales' of principle, party preference, and argument change by one standard deviation while other factors remain constant. These are shown on the right of the Table 12.16.

Why use such scales of principle, party preference, or argument? They clearly must change from issue to issue, depending upon which aspects of principle, preference, or argument best predict attitudes to the issue in question. That, however, is their virtue, not their vice. We showed in Chapter 4 that, amongst the public, commitments to liberty and equality were uncorrelated— that is, they cannot be combined into an intrinsically meaningful scale. And earlier regressions in this chapter have shown that, while they sometimes act in the same direction—for example, on support for the death penalty—on other occasions they act in opposite directions—for example, on support for gender quotas in parliament. These differences are statistically clear and intuitively reasonable. It would be absurd to suggest that two such different

TABLE 12.16. *Multiple regression equations*

multiple correlation	36 B	36 beta × 100	multiple correlation	36 B	36 beta × 100
Liberty	-5.545901	-30	Principle	1.000000	29
Equality	0.602806	2	Party preference	1.000000	4
Conservative vote preference	-0.399357	-3			
Labour vote preference	-0.500496	-4			
Liberal Democrat vote preference	-0.397892	-2			
SNP vote preference	-1.088567	-5			
Argument: prejudice trial	2.497778	20	Argument	1.000000	17
Argument: encourage crime	1.116369	9			
Scottish sample	0.245939	2	Scottish sample	0.245939	2
Politicians' sample	-0.619389	-5	Politicians' sample	-0.619389	-5
Constant	-3.014762		Constant	-3.014762	

Note: B = unstandardized regression coefficients; beta = standardized regression coefficients or 'path coefficients'; the constant term is always zero when the equation is written in standardized form.

principles should always combine in the same way. Hence the virtue, even the necessity, in constructing custom-built scales of principle that reflect the way principles combine on specific issues.

Perhaps this is even easier to appreciate when we consider party preferences. On some issues there is a Conservative versus Labour polarization—for example, on support for the Conservative Party mechanisms or the right to strike; on others a Liberal Democrat versus Conservative polarization—for example, on the Charter 88 mechanisms; on others a polarization between the Conservatives and everyone else—for example, on devolution; on others, such as the banning of sensational crime stories, there is a (very weak) polarization between all those with party preferences and those without party preferences. Our issue-specific party-preference scales accommodate such differences. Contrast this approach with our earlier use of a fixed vote-preference scale which only and always modelled Conservative versus Labour polarization and thus failed to detect any effect of party preference when it was other aspects of party preference that influenced attitudes to issues.

Finally, since arguments differ in content and meaning from one issue to another, it is obvious that our scales of argument must be custom-built to the issue in question (Table 12.17).

Clearly the power of various influences upon attitudes towards issues of practice is variable. It depends upon the relevance of particular principles to particular issues, and the relevance and persuasiveness of the particular arguments or challenges which we used in our attempts to manipulate opinion. Earlier in this chapter we looked at opinion on ten issues without using explicit arguments or challenges. We have arranged them in sequence from those most influenced by principle rather than by party, to those most influenced by party rather than by principle. Only attitudes to parliamentary quotas provide an exception: they were most affected by whether the interviewee was a member of the public or a politician. For the rest, principle and/or party were the predominant influences.

Attitudes towards the right to strike, and towards devolution to regions within England were about equally affected by principle and by party. But support for more women and minority MPs, support for Charter 88 mechanisms, and willingness to permit potentially riotous political demonstrations or football matches were all much more affected by principle than by party. And, by contrast, attitudes towards devolution for Scotland, a ban on private medicine, and especially attitudes towards the Conservative Party mechanisms were all more affected by party than by principle, though principle still remained influential on all these issues.

TABLE 12.17. *The influence of principle, party, and being a politician on attitudes to practical issues*

	Principle	Party	Being a politician	Living in Scotland
	(path coefficients (×100) in the combined sample)			
More women/minority MPs	39	.	.	.
Charter 88 Mechanisms	37	14	+11	.
Allow political demonstration	29	13	.	−12
Allow football disorder	16	.	.	.
Parliamentary quotas	18	13	−27	.
Devolution within England	25	25	+11	.
Right to strike	24	26	.	.
Devolution for Scotland	24	31	.	.
Ban private medicine	17	25	.	.
Conservative Party mechanisms	32	45	.	.

Notes: Signs have no meaning when the path coefficients refer to composite measures. Entries for composite measures of principle and party preference therefore show magnitudes only.

Principle = a varying and optimal mix of liberty and equality (see text for details).

Party = a varying and optimal mix of preference for the Conservatives, Labour, Liberal Democrat, SNP, and no party (see text for details).

Path coefficients less than 0.10 have been replaced by full points.

There is nothing very obscure about this varying balance of influence between principle and party. On the issues where party proved more influential than principle, the parties had taken up clearly opposed positions and maintained them for a long time.[8] Party did not replace principle as an influence on these issues but its influence grew to the point where it exceeded that of principle (Table 12.18).

On five issues we deployed arguments, on one a challenge, and on another both arguments and challenges. Here we shall make no distinction between prior arguments and after-the-event challenges. Clearly the power of argument varied just like that of principle and party. On two issues our arguments failed to have much effect at all: attitudes towards the publication of government secrets were influenced primarily by principle, while attitudes to referendums were influenced primarily by whether the respondent was a politician or an ordinary member of the public. But the influence of our arguments outweighed that of principle on the issue of job quotas, equalled the influence of principle on the issue of conviction on confession, and rivalled that of principle on the free use of drugs. Conversely, the influence

TABLE 12.18. *The influence of arguments and other factors on attitudes to practical issues*

	Argument	Principle	Party	Being a politician	Living in Scotland
	(path coefficients (×100) in the combined sample)				
Job quotas	35	15	.	.	.
Convict on confession	18	18	.	.	.
Use any drugs they like	20	25	.	−14	.
Censor crime reports	17	29	.	.	.
Death penalty	19	36	.	−12	.
Censor government secrets	.	34	19	.	.
Referendums	.	10	18	−27	.

Notes: Signs have no meaning when the path coefficients refer to composite measures. Entries for composite measures of principle and party preference therefore show magnitudes only.

Principle = a varying and optimal mix of liberty and equality (see text for details).

Party = a varying and optimal mix of preference for the Conservatives, Labour, Liberal Democrat, SNP, and no party (see text for details).

Argument = a varying and optimal mix of arguments or challenges (see text for details).

Path coefficients less than 0.10 have been replaced by full points.

of principle outweighed that of our arguments and challenges on the censorship of sensational crime stories and the death penalty.

These findings cannot be separated from the quality of our arguments, of course. But there seems more of a substitutability pattern here than we found with the balance between principle and party: arguments seemed most effective when principles provided relatively weak or unclear signals. It was not just a matter of obscure or technical issues: job quotas for women and minorities are an easily understood and emotive issue but one on which principles of liberty and equality conflicted so much that there was scope for argument to have an unusually large influence.

CONCLUSION

Our analysis has shown that, although principles are crucial in shaping the practice of rights, the process is both complex and understandable. Fundamental commitment to the principles of liberty and equality clearly did affect people's attitudes to both the theory and practice of rights. But so did their prejudices in favour or against social and political claimants, on the one hand, and the judicial/political system, on the other. And, while these fundamental principles and sympathies interacted and influenced each other, they were also all powerfully shaped by people's social background and—in a difficult-to-quantify way—by their direct, personal experience of politics and civic life also.

However, as our analysis in this final chapter has shown, the impact that people's principles have on their attitudes towards the practice of rights can be influenced in three other important ways. Principles can—as we saw in the cases of strike action, devolution, private medicine, and Conservative party reforms—be mediated by partisanship. They can also be overridden—as they were in the case of parliamentary quotas and referendums—by the experience of political office. And on occasions, as we found in the responses to our questions on job quotas, principles can prove too weak an influence on people's attitudes towards the practice of rights, because their impact can be broken by a simple, clear, and intuitive counter-argument.

NOTES

1. Or −6, −3, 0, +6, as we described it in Ch. 9. It makes no difference to correlation coefficients or path coefficients, whichever we use.
2. See Ian Budge, Ivor Crewe, and Dennis Farlie (eds.), *Party Identification and Beyond* (London: Wiley, 1976), esp. the chapter by Ronald Inglehart and Hans Klingemann, 'Party Identification, Ideological Preference and the Left–Right Dimension among Western Mass Publics', 243–73. At pp. 269–70 they conclude 'among European publics one's sense of belonging to the left or right reflects party affiliations more than issue preferences. Left–right self-placement corresponds very closely to political party identification everywhere except in Ireland so it seems plausible to conclude . . . that *left–right orientations are derivative from party identification* . . . The classical view of the left–right dimension as primarily a super-issue seems largely untenable for Europe . . . The ideological component of [left–right self-images] tends to be greatly overshadowed by the partisan component everywhere except in the United States' (emphasis added). We could not disagree more: our findings show that principle was a far more important component of ideological self-images than that.
3. See William L. Miller, Harold D. Clarke, Martin Harrop, Lawrence LeDuc, and Paul F. Whiteley, *How Voters Change: The 1987 British Election Campaign in Perspective* (Oxford: Oxford University Press, 1990), 35.
4. See e.g. Robert Nozick, *Anarchy, State and Utopia* (Oxford: Blackwell, 1974).
5. See John L. Sullivan, James Pierson, and George E. Marcus, *Political Tolerance and American Democracy* (Chicago: University of Chicago Press, 1982, 1989), ch. 6 for an example of circularity in regression predictions which we drew attention to in our Ch. 8.

6. Colin Crouch, 'The Peculiar Relationship: The Party and the Unions', in Dennis Kavanagh (ed.), *The Politics of the Labour Party* (London: Allen & Unwin, 1982), 171–90.

7. All these arguments against the death penalty are from Thomas R. Dye and L. Harmon Zeigler, *American Politics in the Media Age* (Belmont, Calif.: Wadsworth, 1983), 404.

8. It is true that there was no official Labour policy to ban private medicine, but there can be no doubt that the Conservative Party policy was much more favourable to the concept of private, or privatized, medicine. The correlation between party and attitudes on this issue reflects massive Conservative opposition to such a ban, rather than massive Labour support for it. Our surveys show that a ban was opposed by 91% of Conservative politicians, 76% of Conservative voters in Britain as a whole, and 69% in Scotland; and it was supported by 63% of Labour politicians, 51% of Labour voters in Britain as a whole, and 57% in Scotland. Other parties had intermediate opinions.

APPENDIX I

Design and Sampling

Sampling

The survey consisted of four samples:

1. BRITPOP: 2,060 interviews with a random sample of the adult population of Great Britain;
2. SCOTPOP: 1,255 interviews with a random sample of the adult population of Scotland (212 of these also form part of the BRITPOP sample);
3. LEADERS: 1,244 interviews with a sample of political leaders in Great Britain;
4. INTERV: 109 self-interviews with interviewers.

Northern Ireland was excluded because of its particular circumstances which merit separate attention. Excluding the interviewers' self-interviews and counting each Scottish interview once only, the total number of interviews in the study was 4,347.

The BRITPOP and SCOTPOP Samples

For the BRITPOP sample we set out to interview approximately 2,000 adults, chosen to represent the electorate of Great Britain. We began by selecting approximately 2,000 telephone numbers from the ninety-eight British Telecom (BT) telephone directories. There are three problems with using British telephone directories as a sampling frame, however:

1. Some people do not have telephones, but according to the *1990 General Household Survey (GHS)* by the government's Office of Population Censuses and Surveys at least 88 per cent of adults were accessible by phone at the time of our survey.
2. Some of those who had phones were not listed in the BT directories. According to private communications from BT, approximately one quarter of all phones were not listed, and the percentage of unlisted numbers was much higher in some areas such as central London.
3. Some phone numbers were listed in two or more overlapping directories and BT did not follow any consistent nation-wide procedure on multiple listings.

Following inspection of very large-scale maps depicting the area covered by each directory, we withdrew four telephone directories from our sampling frame—Aylesbury and District (BT319), Banbury and District (BT321), Cambridge and District (BT337), and Glasgow (BT275)—to eliminate the worst overlaps and consequent duplication. We also excluded the Northern Ireland directory (BT241) to restrict our samples to Great Britain.

Directories for large cities were suitably divided into separate business and residential sections ('divided' directories), but others mixed business and residential numbers together ('undivided' directories). Some divided directories also had four columns of numbers on each page instead of the more usual three. Sampling procedures therefore had to be slightly different, depending upon the style of the directory.

For undivided directories (i.e. with business and residential numbers listed together, and three columns per page):

1. We selected one number from the same place on every twentieth page, from a random starting-point. The starting-point was defined by a random selection of one page in the first twenty pages, and a random choice of location (column and line number) within that page.
2. Then we discarded, without taking substitutes, any business number or advertisement selected. (It is important to avoid substitutes, because the presence of business numbers and advertisements inflates the number of pages in a directory. Our sampling procedure automatically compensates for this.)

For divided directories (i.e. with residential numbers listed separately):

1. We selected one number from every twentieth (if three columns) or fifteenth (if four columns) page of the domestic section.
2. It was unnecessary to discard any business numbers, but we discarded any selections that landed on advertisements—again without substitution.

Selected numbers were divided systematically into ten subsamples, and the sequence of numbers within each subsample randomly shuffled, before reassembling the subsamples and placing them in sequence. This guaranteed a random stream of attempted interviews which provided a continuously representative random sample as the survey developed, automatically protecting against two kinds of bias—interviewer bias, and space–time correlation bias, since the phone numbers assigned to each interviewer were a random subset of the full sample, and since interviews done at any particular time were also a random subset of the full sample. Both these biases occur routinely in conventional face-to-face surveys. In addition, our sample was completely unclustered, which makes it roughly equivalent in terms of random sampling errors to conventional face-to-face surveys (which are inevitably clustered) with about three times as many interviews.

This sampling procedure produced 2,124 'base' numbers. To cope with the problem of unlisted numbers we chose not to dial these base numbers themselves. Instead we increased the last digit of the base number by one and dialled the adjusted number. This version of random-digit dialling overcomes the problem of unlisted numbers but unfortunately reintroduces some business, fax, and unobtainable numbers.

If for any reason we failed to get an interview at the adjusted number, we readjusted the base number and tried again. Altogether five attempts were made to get an interview corresponding to each base number by using the following adjustments: increasing and decreasing the last digit by one, then increasing and decreasing the second last digit by one, then using the base number itself. Having dialled a number and made contact, we selected the resident adult (aged 18 or over) with the most recent birthday. This simple selection procedure, also used by our Canadian colleagues, is the simplest and fastest method of making a random selection at the phone number.

If the initial contact, or (much less frequently) the selected adult refused an interview, we waited for at least two weeks and tried again, but we took a second refusal as final to avoid accusations of harassment. If there was no reply when we dialled, or we were connected to a telephone-answering machine, we made three further attempts on non-consecutive evenings. With engaged numbers we tried again on the same evening and then on later evenings. If we met with a double refusal, or a persistently unanswered, business, fax, or unobtainable number, we moved to the next stage in the base-number-adjustment sequence. Using these procedures we came close to our target number of interviews, although a second set of base numbers had to be constructed to bring us fully up to target.

The SCOTPOP sample was constructed in the same way, but using a higher sampling frequency.

The LEADERS Sample

For our population of political leaders we designated the leaders of every political group on every local-government council in Great Britain. In those few councils where there were no political groups, not even a 'group' of Independents, we designated the Chair and Vice-Chair of the council.

We set out to obtain 1,000 interviews with these senior local government councillors to form a comparative data-set with the BRITPOP and SCOTPOP samples. In the event we exceeded our target and achieved so many interviews that our LEADERS sample is more of a population than a sample. Over 85 per cent of those we designated as political leaders gave interviews and more had agreed to do so if we had been willing to continue the survey past its closing date.

We began with a letter to the Chief Executives of all the County, District, Metropolitan, and Borough Councils in England and Wales plus the Regional and District Councils in Scotland, in which we asked the Chief Executives to supply names and home telephone numbers for the leaders of each political party or Independent group they recognized on the council. We also asked Chief Executives to bring our study to the attention of these named leaders. In those few cases where the Chief Executive did not recognize any political groups, we requested details of the council Chair and Vice-Chair. If necessary we followed up our letters with phone calls to complete our list of local political leaders.

Following the logic of the BRITPOP and SCOTPOP samples, we randomized the sequence in which we attempted to interview political leaders, but, to avoid too much discussion between those who had already been interviewed and those who had not, we attempted to interview all the leaders on any one council at approximately the same time. So the randomization was by council rather than by councillor.

When phoned, many councillors asked for further written information about the study before they would consent to an interview. We wrote to them. We also wrote to those few leaders who refused to take part, asking them to reconsider and pointing to the low rate of refusals amongst their colleagues.

In a year that included a parliamentary general election, and widespread local-government elections, political leaders proved to be very busy and elusive people, though cooperative enough if we could contact them at the right time. So, while all BRITPOP and SCOTPOP interviews were carried out after 6 p.m. in the evening to allow access to the working population and to take advantage of cheap telephone rates, we interviewed council group leaders whenever they were available, in evenings (81 per cent) or afternoons (19 per cent), at home or at council offices. And, in contrast to our procedures with the BRITPOP and SCOTPOP samples, we set no limit to the number of times we attempted to contact them.

The Interviews

To avoid basing our results upon transient opinion, over-influenced by the events of a particular time, the BRITPOP and LEADERS interviews were spread over the period from November 1991 to August 1992. The SCOTPOP interviews were spread over the period from November 1991 to November 1992, but with over half of them carried out in the months of October and November 1992. The difference in time scale between BRITPOP and SCOTPOP samples was the result of unavoidable funding inflexibilities.

Interviewers carried out self-interviews as part of their training programme and these provide the INTERV sample. We have not reported details of this sample but used it to classify the interviewers for special analyses where we suspected that the answers given by BRITPOP, SCOTPOP, and LEADERS respondents might have been affected by the characteristics of the interviewers. For example, the gender of interviewers might have influenced answers to questions about gender equality or gender quotas; and the nationality of interviewers might have influenced answers to questions about immigration or devolution. While telephone interviewing allows much greater anonymity by drawing a veil across the interviewer's visible characteristics, the respondent would usually be able to distinguish male from female interviewers, or Scots and American from English interviewers, and perhaps even identify minority ethnic interviewers.

On average, interviews took about forty-five minutes to complete, with only 10 per cent taking less than half an hour and another 10 per cent taking more than an hour. The table gives exact timing statistics for each of the three main samples. LEADERS interviews took about one minute longer, and SCOTPOP two minutes less, than the BRITPOP interviews (Table AI.1).

Within the BRITPOP sample there was no relationship between the length of interview and education, gender, nation (i.e. Scotland, England, Wales), region, or voting

TABLE AI.1. *Length of interview*

	Mean (mins.)	Lowest decile (mins.)	Median (mins.)	Highest decile (mins.)
LEADERS	46	34	43	62
BRITPOP	45	32	42	59
SCOTPOP	42	32	40	56

TABLE AI.2. *Length of interview, by age*

	<35 (mins.)	35–45 (mins.)	45–55 (mins.)	55–65 (mins.)	65–75 (mins.)	>75 (mins.)
BRITPOP	42	44	46	48	51	53

preference, and no trend during the year. However, council tenants took slightly longer than house owners (two minutes on average), and people with a job took slightly less than those without (three minutes on average), to complete their interviews. However, there was a stronger correlation with age: every ten years of age added at least another two minutes to the length of the interview. Not surprisingly, the over-75-year-olds took eleven minutes longer than the under-35s to complete the interview (Table AI.2). Checks suggest that the length of an interview was not an indicator of its quality: correlations between attitude questions were not consistently lower in short (or long) interviews, for example.

Refusals Analyses

Refusals in the LEADERS Sample

For the LEADERS sample we knew exactly which council group leaders failed to give an interview and we could categorize them by the type of party group they led (according to the Chief Executives' reports). Table AI.3 shows that 85 per cent of leaders gave interviews, 9 per cent refused, and we failed to contact the remaining 6 per cent. It also shows that our success rate was very much the same amongst Conservative, Labour, Scottish National, and Independent leaders, though substantially higher amongst the numerous Liberal Democrat group leaders and the very few Welsh Nationalist group leaders.

TABLE AI.3. *Refusal rates in the* LEADERS *sample*

	Interviewed (%)	Refused (%)	No contact (%)
Conservative	81	14	5
Labour	82	9	9
Liberal Democrat	92	5	3
Scottish Nationalist	83	17	0
Welsh Nationalist	100	0	0
Independent and other	84	11	5
All	85	9	6

Refusals in the BRITPOP *Sample*

The BRITPOP sample was based on 'cold-calling' to randomly selected telephone numbers. Consequently we had little information about who refused. None the less we had some. Interviewers were instructed to estimate the age (simply 'young' or 'old'—defined as under and over 45 years) and the gender of anyone who refused an interview. The gender estimate is probably quite accurate, the age estimate less so. According to our interviewers' estimates, a high proportion of refusals were by women, particularly by old women—as the last column of the table shows. That was in line with our expectations that elderly women, many living alone, would be specially reluctant to spend forty-five minutes speaking to a complete stranger. We also got slightly higher refusal rates amongst young women than young men, but we none the less got more interviews from young women than from young men because they proved more accessible by phone (Table AI.4).

Overall, we dialled 10,602 numbers to obtain 2,060 interviews. However, 4,101 numbers were unobtainable, business, or fax numbers. So our overall response rate was 32 per cent. While low compared to surveys in which potential respondents are contacted and screened before interview, this is comparable with the success rate in standard British market-research polls where potential respondents are contacted 'cold' (e.g. the quota polls of voting intentions published regularly in the press).[1] We could have achieved a much higher response rate by shortening the length of our interviews, since many potential respondents refused when told the interview would take thirty or forty minutes, but we judged it more important to achieve in-depth interviews than a high response rate.

By making some heroic assumptions, or tolerating a fair degree of inaccuracy, we can calculate a 'response rate' by age and gender. Some refusals were by people who answered the phone but who would not have been selected as the appropriate respondent to interview within the household. But if the age and gender pattern of those who refused approximated that of those we would have selected, and if we

TABLE AI.4. *Response rates in the* BRITPOP *sample*

	% of all numbers issued	% of all numbers contacted	% of all refusals where age and sex estimated
Unobtainable	39	n.a.	n.a.
Refusal by young men	6	10	17
Refusal by old men	7	11	19
Refusal by young women	9	15	26
Refusal by old women	14	23	38
Refusal but age/sex unknown	6	9	n.a.
Interview obtained	19	32	n.a.
TOTAL	100	100	100

Note: n.a. = not applicable.

count interviews with those aged under 45 as interviews with the 'young' and with those aged over 45 as interviews with the 'old', then we can calculate a 'response rate' as the number of successful interviews in an age/gender category divided by the number of interviews plus the number of refusals which interviewers assigned to that age/gender category. By that calculation—imperfect perhaps, but indicative none the less—the response rate was 46 per cent amongst young men, 39 per cent amongst young women, and 37 per cent amongst old men, but only 23 per cent amongst old women. Comparing the age/gender structure of the successful interviews with the estimated age/gender structure of all contacts and with government estimates of the population (from the *1991 GHS*) suggests that we under-contacted young men but got a high response rate amongst those we did contact, and over-contacted old women but got a very low response rate amongst them.

Apart from these age and gender estimates we can say nothing about the social background or political attitudes of those who ultimately refused to give us an interview. But we can classify our interviews on a three-point scale, according to how difficult they were to achieve:

1. interviews achieved on the first contact with that number;
2. interviews achieved only after first obtaining an engaged tone, or arranging a call-back at a more convenient time;
3. interviews achieved after an initial refusal followed by a second call a fortnight (or more) later.

Differences between those who gave an interview on the first call and those who initially refused, but were later persuaded to take part, were remarkably small, though usually in the expected direction. Initial refusals were 3 per cent more likely to be council tenants, 9 per cent less likely to have a university degree, and 10 per cent more likely to express no interest in politics. They were between 3 and 5 per cent less likely to be active in a wide range of organizations and activities and 9 per cent less likely to have signed a petition in recent years.

But their voting patterns were almost identical with those who gave an immediate interview and they were not consistently more, or less, liberal on civil-rights issues: 5 per cent less liberal on free speech, but 4 per cent more liberal on abortion, for example. In short, their backgrounds were more deviant than their opinions (Table AI.5).

The difference between the people who gave an interview immediately and those who initially refused but were later persuaded to do so gives some guide to the likely characteristics of those who ultimately refused. However, we need to remember that those who ultimately refused were likely to differ from those who never refused by a larger margin than those who only initially refused and later agreed to be interviewed. Initial refusals are unlikely to be exactly the same as ultimate refusals and cannot be used to provide exact correction factors to compensate for ultimate refusals.

Reactions to the Interview

Our interviews were long, searching, and, at times, even aggressive. But, although many of the people we 'cold-called' refused to give an interview at all, often because of the length, very few started an interview and then broke off before finishing it. And, despite a long, searching, and challenging interview, the vast majority indicated that they would be willing to undergo another interrogation by us 'in a year's time'. Although we did not, in the event, follow this up, 99 per cent of the LEADERS sample and 95 per cent of both the BRITPOP and SCOTPOP samples agreed to another interview, which seems to indicate that the experience of the interview was not, in retrospect, too daunting.

Although the length of interview clearly dissuaded many people from giving us an interview at all, there was no relationship between the actual length of a particular interview and the respondent's willingness to be reinterviewed: those who took a relatively long time over the interview did so because it suited them.

Weighting

Weighting the BRITPOP Sample

We would expect the unweighted BRITPOP sample to be biased, since we recorded a high rate of refusals and estimated a clear age/gender structure amongst these refusals. We also found weaker but noticeable differences between those who gave an interview on our first contact with them, and those who initially refused but later consented to an interview.

We calculated the net social bias caused by sampling and refusals by comparing our raw data with the *1991 GHS*. Similarly we calculated the net regional bias by first superimposing maps of parliamentary constituencies and BT regions to find the

TABLE AI.5. *Differences between first-contact interviews and
refusal–conversion interviews*

	First-contact interviews (%)	Refusal–conversion interviews (%)	Difference (%)
House tenure: % council (or housing assoc.)	12	15	+3
Education: % university/polytechnic	21	12	−9
Interest in politics: % none at all	23	33	+10
Watch TV current affairs: % yes	70	67	−3
Class self-image: % middle class	42	41	−1
Party supporter: % yes	52	53	+1
% vote at 1992 General Election			
Conservative	44	45	+1
Labour	32	33	+1
Liberal Democrat	18	19	+1
Other	7	3	−4
% Active in			
arts club/choir etc.	16	11	−5
school organization	18	14	−4
religious organization	20	16	−4
charity	33	30	−3
trade union	17	14	−3
community group	31	27	−4
signing petition	73	64	−9
demonstration/protest meeting	16	13	−3
Felt discrimination: % yes	32	26	−6
% Liberal on (i.e. disagree with):			
free speech not worth disorder	64	59	−5
should not tolerate morally wrong	48	43	−5
abortion morally wrong	48	52	+4
suspend civil rights	20	20	0
test cooks/surgeons for AIDS	33	27	−6
immigrants should be more like British	34	35	+1

TABLE AI.6. *Specification and evaluation of rim-weighting for* BRITPOP *sample*

	GHS target (%)	Unweighted BRITPOP (%)	Weighted BRITPOP (%)	Final bias (%)
Age/gender				
men under 45 years	25	27	24	−1
men over 45 years	23	20	23	0
women under 45 years	25	31	26	+1
women over 45 years	27	21	27	0
House tenure				
council tenants	25	12	25	0
private renters	6	6	6	0
owner occupiers and others	69	82	69	0
Educational qualifications				
none	37	27	37	0
school/college	55	53	55	0
university/polytechnic	8	20	8	0
Economic activity				
in work	58	64	57	−1
not in work	42	36	43	+1
BT region				
London	14	12	14	0
South	29	32	29	0
North	42	40	42	0
Scotland and Wales	16	16	16	0

Note: BT region = British Telecom areas aggregated as follows: South = East Anglia, South East, South West, Chilterns, and South Midlands; North = Rest of Midlands, North East, North West.

total electorate in each BT region, and then comparing these regional electorates with our raw data.

Using these comparisons as the basis for social and regional weights, we then applied a 5-component iterative rim-weighting scheme[2] with two iterations. Finally weights were truncated to ensure that no interview was up-weighted or down-weighted by a factor greater than three. This truncation had almost no effect upon the sample as a whole but guards against excessive weighting of individual interviews in some of the small subcategories of respondents required in complex or detailed analyses. Rim-weighting components, along with the *GHS* target percentages and the unweighted and weighted BRITPOP percentages, are shown in Table AI.6. Rim-weighting with only two iterations proved highly successful in bringing the BRITPOP sample into line with the *GHS*. The maximum bias in the table is reduced to 1 per cent.

As Table AI.6 shows, our unweighted sample contained too many interviews with university and polytechnic graduates and too few with council tenants and old people (especially old women). Paradoxically, over-representation in our raw data of those relatively few people with high levels of education was particularly fortunate because, while we could easily use weighting to eliminate the bias caused by it, at the same time we could take advantage of the disproportionately large number of interviews with the highly educated to obtain more reliable estimates of educated opinion than would be possible in a fully representative sample. Since the civil-rights attitudes of the highly educated are distinctive, this over-sampling of a small but distinctive and influential group was very fortunate. If it had not occurred naturally, we would have been tempted to design it into the sampling procedure.

Since we interviewed only one person at each selected household, we anticipated that we should have to weight our sample by the number of adults at each telephone number. In the event this proved unnecessary. People in larger households had a smaller probability of selection *if* we made contact with them and *if* they agreed to an interview. However, this potential bias was offset by the greater likelihood that a larger household would have a phone, plus the greater likelihood that someone in a larger household would be present to answer the phone, and possibly by a greater reluctance amongst those living alone to grant an interview to a stranger.

Weighting the SCOTPOP Sample

Since the *GHS* did not publish figures for Scotland, we obtained Scottish target percentages from the *Scottish Abstract of Statistics*, the *Labour Force Survey*, and *Regional Trends* (all government publications). We anticipated that it might be necessary to repeat the iterative rim-weighting procedure used for the BRITPOP sample. However, we found that, if weights calculated for the BRITPOP sample were applied to the SCOTPOP sample, only a regional adjustment was necessary to bring the SCOTPOP sample closely into line with the target percentages.

The advantage of doing this rather than carrying out a separate iterative rim-weighting exercise for Scotland is that the weights applied north and south of the Scottish border are the same. For example, interviews with council tenants are up-weighted by the same factor and interviews with university graduates are down-weighted by the same factor in the SCOTPOP sample as in the BRITPOP sample. The disadvantage is that applying weights calculated from the BRITPOP sample to the SCOTPOP sample means that the weighted SCOTPOP sample does not get quite as close to the target percentages as it would if we calculated separate Scottish weights. None the less the maximum social bias is only 3 per cent and the average bias only 1 per cent.

The Effect of Weighting the BRITPOP and SCOTPOP Samples

Given that our unweighted samples over-represented the highly educated, we should expect them to over-represent the liberal perspective on civil and human rights. The effect of weighting would then be to decrease support for liberal attitudes. And so it did, but the effect was small. On the range of attitudes shown in Table AI.7, the effect of weighting was very similar in the BRITPOP and SCOTPOP samples even when Scottish and British attitudes diverged as they did on abortion (where Scots were more conservative than Britons generally) and immigrants (where Scots were more liberal than Britons generally). Weighting decreased support for the liberal viewpoint by a maximum of 5 per cent and, at the other extreme, increased support for the liberal viewpoint by 1 per cent. On average, weighting reduced support for the liberal viewpoint by 3 per cent in both the BRITPOP and SCOTPOP samples.

Voting Behaviour in the BRITPOP and SCOTPOP Samples

We decided not to include party choice in our weighting schemes, but to use it as an independent test of the accuracy of our sampling and weighting procedures. The general election of 1992 was notable for the inaccuracy of opinion-poll predictions of the actual result both in Britain as a whole and in Scotland. On the weekend before the election, published opinion polls put the Labour Party 2 per cent ahead of the Conservatives though the Conservatives won the election by a margin of 8 per cent, partly, at least, because many voters changed their minds at the last moment. Such volatility means that voting *intentions* are not sufficiently stable to provide the basis for a check on sampling. By definition, voting *behaviour* in the 1992 general election cannot suffer from volatility but some voters refuse to say how they voted, others tell lies, and others fail to remember accurately.

Our survey ran from five months before the election to seven months after it. We have to discard interviews taken before the election when only voting *preferences* were available. After the election, respondents reported how they had actually voted, though as time passed their reports were likely to be less accurate, especially when the popular mood swung heavily against the government in the autumn. Since the SCOTPOP sample was interviewed mainly in the autumn of 1992, it was more likely to have been affected by this change in mood than the BRITPOP sample.

Table AI.8 shows that all reported votes in the BRITPOP sample were within 3 per cent of the actual votes before weighting and within 2 per cent after weighting. Weighting reduced the anti-Labour bias in our survey but did not quite eliminate it. Reported votes in the SCOTPOP sample were all within 3 per cent of the actual result both before and after weighting, and, in Scotland, weighting, replaced a small anti-Labour bias with a slightly smaller pro-Labour bias.

For a simple (unclustered) random sample equal in size to the number of voters interviewed after the election in the BRITPOP sample (764 voters) the sampling error (at the conventional 95 per cent confidence level and for a party with about the strength of Labour or the Conservatives—i.e. approximately 40 per cent) is 3.5 per cent; and for the SCOTPOP sample (911 voters) it is 3.2 per cent. Both samples, therefore, report voting percentages within conventional sampling-error limits. So while it would be easy to devise plausible non-random explanations for the residual

TABLE AI.7. *Effect of weighing on liberal attitudes to rights*

	BRITPOP			SCOTPOP		
	Unweighted (%)	Weighted (%)	Effect (%)	Unweighted (%)	Weighted (%)	Effect (%)
Liberal on (i.e. % disagree with)						
free speech not worth disorder	66	61	−5	67	62	−5
should not tolerate morally wrong	47	44	−3	52	47	−5
abortion morally wrong	51	49	−2	44	41	−3
suspend civil rights in emergency	20	21	+1	22	24	+2
test cooks/surgeons for AIDS	34	29	−5	34	29	−5
immigrants should be more like the British	36	33	−3	43	41	−2
AVERAGE EFFECT			−3			−3

TABLE AI.8. *Reported votes in 1992 British general election*

	BRITPOP (764 voters)			SCOTPOP (911 voters)		
	Actual (%)	Unweighted (%)	Weighted (Error) (%) (%)	Actual (%)	Unweighted (%)	Weighted (Error) (%) (%)
Conservative	43	45	44 (1)	26	27	23 (−3)
Labour	35	32	33 (−2)	39	36	42 (3)
Liberal Democrat	18	19	18 (0)	13	15	12 (−1)
Others	4	4	5 (1)	22	22	22 (0)

errors in the weighted BRITPOP and SCOTPOP samples, it would display more ingenuity than wisdom. If our samples have succeeded in describing the British culture of rights as accurately as they reported votes in the general election, we would be very well pleased indeed.

Weighting the LEADERS Sample

The LEADERS sample was weighted to correct for over- or under-representation of political groups. This compensated for the slight over-representation of Liberal Democrat and Welsh Nationalist leaders, but had no other significant effects. For this book, as we explained in Chapter 3, the LEADERS sample was further weighted to bring their voting preferences into line with those of the (weighted) BRITPOP sample, in order to ensure that differences of opinion between politicians and the public could not be attributed to partisan bias.

NOTES

1. Nick Moon, Market Research Society Seminar, Glasgow, Oct. 1992.
2. See Dave Elliot, *Weighting for Non-Response: A Survey Researcher's Guide* (London: OPCS, 1991), for a lucid description of these techniques and the reasons for using them—in particular the reasons for using rim-weighting rather than full interlocking weighting.

APPENDIX II

The Questionnaire

How to Read the Questionnaire

Alternative Wordings

This survey makes full use of Computer Assisted Telephone Interviewing (CATI) techniques. Since we are concerned to measure the pliability and conditionality of attitudes, many questions appear in several, differently worded forms. Each form was put to a randomly selected subset of respondents. For example, if there are two forms of wording, half the sample was asked each form; if there are three forms of wording, one third of the sample was asked each form; and so on. Alternative wordings are shown using square brackets thus: [wording A/wording B/wording C]. Where the square bracket contains '(null)', it indicates that one random subset of the sample was asked a question which had no additional words inserted at that point. Usually this occurs where some subsets were exposed to arguments, but one was not—for example, in [argument A/argument B/(null)] the third subset was not exposed to any argument at all. In some complex questions, several parts of the question may each have two or more alternative wordings. In that case, every possible combination of wordings was put to randomly selected subsets of respondents.

Conditional Questions

Sometimes supplementary questions were put to respondents depending upon their answers to the initial question. In these cases the condition for asking the supplementary is indicated by small capital letters, for example: IF YES.

Strength of Feeling

Many questions were framed as statements, often quite aggressive statements. In these cases respondents were asked to 'agree or disagree' and then to indicate their strength of feeling by answering a non-conditional supplementary: 'a lot or a little' or 'very strongly or not very strongly', although, as we explained in Chapter 2, the additional prompt was not repeated explicitly after each statement in a battery of agree/disagree questions. All questions that asked for a 'yes-or-no' answer had answer codes that included 'qualified yes', 'qualified no', but these were never offered explicitly.

'Don't Knows', etc.

Throughout the questionnaire, responses 'don't know', 'can't decide', and 'bit of both' were accepted and recorded when given spontaneously but never prompted by the interviewer.

Questionnaire Sections

The two main sections to this questionnaire are headed 'General Principles and Outlook' and 'Scenarios and Mechanisms'. The questions in these sections roughly correspond to the questions used in the text as indicators of, first, principle and, secondly, practical issues and mechanisms. However, alert readers will notice that this division is only approximate, and a few indicators of one type are included in a section mainly devoted to the other. In crafting the questionnaire we were concerned with the flow of the interview more than anything else.

Text Discussion

Answers to most—but not all—questions are discussed in the text.

The Questions

Opening Sequence

Q1. Do you read any *daily* morning newspaper *regularly*? Which?

    IF MORE THAN ONE: Which do you rely on most?

    (*Note: if asks, 'regularly' means 'at least three times a week'.*)

Q2. On television, do you regularly watch current-affairs programmes like *Panorama, World in Action*, or similar programmes?

    (*Note: if asks, 'regularly' means 'at least one current-affairs programme per week, though not necessarily the same one'.*)

Q3. We would like to know whether you pay much attention to politics from day to day, when there isn't an election campaign. Would you say you pay: a great deal of attention, quite a lot, some, or not much?

Q4. Can you tell me your age?

    (*Note: record age in years.*)

Q5. Sex of respondent.

    (*Note: code by interviewer without question; question only if in doubt.*)

General Principles and Outlook

Q6. Here are a number of things which many people think are very desirable goals but, at the same time, many people feel that it is not the responsibility of the government to provide them. Do *you* think each of the following should, or should not, be the *government*'s responsibility:

- a decent standard of living for everyone?
- that everyone who wants a job can have one?
- adequate housing for everyone?
- good education for everyone?
- good medical care for everyone?
- that citizens are safe from crime?
- that big business treats its customers with fairness and consideration?
- upholding morality?
- fighting pollution?
- evening out differences in wealth between people?
- equal opportunities for everyone?

Q7. Now, using a number from zero to ten, please tell me how important each of the following is to you. If it's one of the absolutely most important things to you, give it a *ten*. If it's one of the least important things, or you don't like it at all, give it a *zero*. But remember, you can use *any* mark between zero and ten. First:

- tolerating different beliefs and lifestyles?
- preserving traditional ideas of right and wrong?
- respect for authority?
- self-reliance, having everybody stand on their own two feet?
- following God's will?
- taking care of the needy?
- strengthening law and order?
- maintaining strong defence forces?
- emphasizing individual achievement?
- guaranteeing equality between men and women?
- protecting ethnic and racial minorities?
- providing help for the disabled?
- guaranteeing everyone the right to free speech?
- guaranteeing equal rights for homosexuals?
- cutting taxes?
- reducing unemployment?
- holding down inflation?
- achieving economic growth?

Now I'm going to read out a number of statements and ask you to say whether you *agree* or *disagree* with each of them. Please don't feel under any pressure to agree—we expect most people to agree with some statements but disagree with others. And if you have *strong* feelings about any of these statements, please just say that you agree or disagree *strongly*.

Q8. We [have gone too far/have not gone far enough] in pushing equal rights in this country . . . strongly or not?

Q9. On the whole, the [police/security services] [do more to harm our liberties than to protect them/protect our liberties more than they harm them].

Q10. In Britain today, there is too much emphasis on citizens' [rights and not enough on citizens' duties/duties and not enough on citizen's rights].

Q11. Free speech is just not worth it if it means we have to put up with the danger to society from extremist views.

Q12. Religious freedom should [apply to all religious groups, even those/not apply to religious groups] that the majority of people consider strange, fanatical, or weird.

Q13. On the whole, the rights and liberties enjoyed by British citizens are [less/greater] than those enjoyed by people who live in [America/West European countries like France and Germany/Scandinavian countries like Norway, Denmark, or Sweden].

Q14. A person charged with a crime should have the right to refuse to answer questions in court, without it being held against them.

Q15. By their nature, men are more suited than women to do senior jobs in business and government.

Q16. The majority is often wrong.

Q17. The only alternative to strong government is disorder and chaos.

Q18. It is very important to protect children and young people from wild and immoral ideas.

Q19. [If something is morally wrong, then it should be made illegal/Even though something may be morally wrong, it should not necessarily be made illegal.]

Q20. I'll put my trust in the practical experience of ordinary people rather than the theories of experts and intellectuals.

Q21. Social workers have too much power to interfere with people's lives.

Q22. [Television and the press should be more independent of government control/There should be more government control of television and the press.]

Q23. If people wish to protest against [something/a government action they strongly oppose/a law they feel is really unjust and harmful], they should have the right to hold protest marches and demonstrations.

Q24. Most politicians can be trusted to do what they think is best for the country.

Q25. [It is important for a government to be able to take decisive action without looking over its shoulder all the time/Constitutional checks and balances are important to make sure that a government doesn't become too dictatorial and ignore other viewpoints.]

Q26. To compromise with our political opponents is dangerous, because it usually leads to the betrayal of our own side.

Q27. Immigrants to Britain should try harder to be more like other British people.

Q28. We should not tolerate people whose ideas are morally wrong.

Q29. In Britain today, too much emphasis is placed on individual interests at the expense of the community's interest.

Q30. On balance, British governments have been [reducing/increasing] the rights and liberties of British citizens in recent years.

Q31. The poor are poor because [they don't try hard enough to get ahead/the wealthy and powerful keep them poor].

Q32. Government regulation of business usually does more harm than good.

Now some questions about choices.

Q33. Should people have a general *right to know* the facts about each of the following:
- information about themselves, for example, their own medical records and credit ratings?
- the government's plans?
- private business activities that might affect the health of people who live near the company's factory?

Q34. Should there be any religious teaching in publicly funded schools in Britain?

IF YES: Should it be mainly Christian, or should it treat all the major religions equally?

IF CHRISTIAN: And should it be mainly Christian, even in schools where the majority of children come from non-Christian families?

Q35. Which comes closer to your view? Our laws should aim to:
- enforce the community's standards of right and wrong;
- protect a citizen's right to live by any moral standard he or she chooses provided this does no harm to other people.

Q36. Which comes nearest to your view? Workers and management:
- will always have conflicting interests;
- share the same basic interests in the long run.

Q37. Ideally, society should be like:
- a unified body pursuing a common goal;
- a collection of people independently pursuing their own goals.

Q38. Which comes closer to your view? Women should be:
- satisfied to stay at home and have families;
- encouraged to have careers of their own.

(Note: an 'It's up to each woman to decide for herself' answer code was available if that answer was spontaneously given, but it was never prompted.)

Q39. In dealing with mugging and other serious street crime, which is more important:
- to protect the rights of suspects?
- to stop such crimes and make the streets safe even if we sometimes have to violate the suspects' rights?

Q40. Generally speaking, would you say that most people you come into contact with are:
- trustworthy or untrustworthy?
- helpful or unhelpful?
- selfish or unselfish?

Q41. Would you support or oppose giving greater powers of self-government to Scotland? Wales? Northern Ireland? London? and regions of England, such as the North-West or South-East?

(Note: answer codes included 'support it if the locals want it' if this was spontaneously given, but it was never prompted.)

Q42. Please give a mark out of ten to indicate how you would rate the fairness and impartiality of British judges. If you feel they are extremely fair give them a ten; if extremely unfair, give them zero; but remember, you can use *any* mark between zero and ten.
- Now, how would you rate British judges?
- And how would you rate the fairness and impartiality of the police?
- And the fairness and impartiality of social workers?

Now some Yes/No questions.
(Note: 'qualified yes or no' codes were available for all yes/no answers if spontaneously given, but never prompted.)

Q43. Suppose parliament passed a law you considered unjust, immoral, or cruel. Would you still be morally bound to obey it?

Q44. Should [all workers, even those in essential public services like the Ambulance Service or the Fire Brigade/workers who do not work in essential public services]:
- have the right to join a trade union if they wish?
- have the right to strike?

Q45. Should workers have the right to *refuse* to join a trade union if they do not want to join one?

Q46. Do you think the police need to be subject to strong external control in order to protect civil liberties?

Q47. I am going to read you a list of groups which some people like but others dislike. Please give a mark out of ten to show how much you like each group. If you like a group, give it a score above five; the more you like it, the higher the score. If you dislike a group, give it a score less than five; the less you like it, the lower the score. First, what number between zero and ten indicates how much you like:
- gays and lesbians?
- environmental campaigners like Greenpeace?
- animal-rights activists?
- communists?
- feminists?
- National Front supporters?
- Muslim activists?
- Militant Tendency supporters?
- IRA sympathizers?
- people who sympathize with Protestant terrorists in Northern Ireland?
- black activists?

(Note: computer calculates the 'Most Disliked Group' (MDG) with the lowest score, selecting randomly if several tie with equally low scores.)

Q48. IF MDG SCORE IS LESS THAN FIVE: Now I'm going to ask you whether you agree or disagree with some statements about one of the groups you dislike. *(In fact, the chosen group is always the MDG.)* Remember, if you feel strongly about any of these statements, please say you agree or disagree strongly.
- I would be unhappy if a [MDG] moved in next door to me.
- I would be unhappy if a child of mine became emotionally involved with a [MDG].
- [MDG]s should not be allowed to make public speeches in my locality.
- [MDG]s should not be allowed to teach in publicly funded schools.

Q49. Do you regard [MDG] as dangerous, or merely unpleasant?

IF DANGEROUS: Very dangerous or only a bit dangerous?

Scenarios and Mechanisms

Now some questions about how rights and duties might work out in practice.

Q50. Please give a mark out of ten to indicate how much you feel citizens' rights and liberties are protected by each of the following. Ten indicates something you feel is extremely important for protecting rights and liberties; while zero indicates something you feel does nothing at all to protect them. But remember, you can use *any* mark between zero and ten.

- tabloid newspapers, like the [*Sun/Daily Mirror*]?
- quality newspapers like the [*Telegraph/Guardian*]?
- television?
- back-bench MPs in parliament?
- local-government councils?
- trade unions?
- churches?
- bodies like the Equal Opportunities Commission or the Commission for Racial Equality?
- British courts?
- European courts?

And what marks would you give the following for their contribution to protecting citizens rights?

- the sale of council houses to sitting tenants?
- privatization of nationalized industries?
- recent changes in the way the NHS is organized?
- the introduction of elected school boards?

And now some things which have been proposed for Britain by some people, but are opposed by others. How much would our rights and liberties be protected and strengthened by each of the following? Use the same scale from zero to ten as before.

- a Bill of Rights, passed by parliament, and enforced by the courts?
- a Freedom of Information Act, giving more legal access to government information?
- a reformed House of Lords, whose members were elected?

Q51. Suppose we had a constitutional Bill of Rights, as some other countries do. If parliament passed a law but the courts said it was unconstitutional, who should have the final say, parliament or the courts?

Q52. Suppose someone in Britain objects to a law passed by parliament and takes the case to the European Court of Human Rights. Who should have the final say, the European court or the British parliament?

Q53. Suppose a local council wants to do something, and gets the support of local people by winning a local [election/referendum] on that issue, but the government is opposed to it. Who should have the final say, the local council, or the government?

Q54. Suppose [the majority of people in this country/parliament/the government] wanted to ban private medicine, in order to make health services the same for both rich and poor. Should they be able to do so even though the ban would reduce the freedom of individuals to do what they want? And would you, yourself, favour such a ban?

And suppose [the majority/parliament/the government] wanted to ban the ritual slaughter of animals by cruel methods, even if it was part of a religious tradition. Should they be able to do so? And do you, yourself, favour such a ban?

And suppose [the majority/parliament/the government] wanted to make homosexuality a crime. Should they be able to do so even though the ban would reduce the freedom of individuals to do what they want? And do you, yourself, favour such a ban?

(*Note: once chosen in a particular interview, the computer uses the same authority, i.e. 'majority', 'parliament', or 'government' throughout all three parts of this question.*)

Q55. Some people think that there should be no restrictions on what can be published in books and newspapers or screened on television, but others disagree. For each of the following please say whether you think it should be [*allowed* on television without any restrictions, or *restricted*, for example, to late night viewing, or *banned* from television altogether/*allowed* in newspapers without any restrictions, or *restricted*, for example, to books, or *banned* from publication altogether].

(*Note: use answer code 'restrictions' for* any *kind of restrictions, not just the examples given.*)

- pictures of extreme violence?
- abusive attacks on [the Christian religion/minority religions such as the Muslim or Hindu religion]?
- interviews with supporters of [IRA terrorists/Protestant terrorists in Northern Ireland]?
- stories that intrude into [ordinary people's/leading politicians'] private lives?
- lies and distortions of the truth?

Now I'm going to read some more statements and ask you to say whether you agree or disagree with each of them. If you have strong feelings about any of these statements, please just say that you agree or disagree strongly.

Q56. [Political organizations with extreme views should be banned/We should never ban any political organization whatever its views.]

IF AGREE: Would you still agree even if the political organization [did not support/supported] violence?

IF DISAGREE: Would you still disagree even if the political organization [supported/did not support] violence?

Q57. Courts should not convict people purely on the basis of a confession [(null)/because people sometimes confess to things they haven't done/because people are sometimes put under so much pressure they confess to things they have not done].

Q58. [Important political issues are too complex to be decided by everyone voting in a referendum, and should be left to parliament to decide/It would be better to let the people decide important political issues by everyone voting in a referendum, rather than leaving them to parliament as at present.]

Q59. If people don't like the government's decisions about [income tax or VAT/local-government taxes], they can vote against it at the next election, but they should *not* [refuse to pay a tax they don't like/hold disorderly demonstrations and riots to force the government to change its tax decisions/physically attack officials who are trying to collect the tax/hold protest rallies and demonstrations to oppose the tax].

Q60. Newspapers which get hold of confidential government documents about [defence/economic/health service] plans should *not* be allowed to publish them [(null)/because publication might damage our national interests].

Q61. Newspapers should be banned from publishing research showing very high rates of crime among blacks [(null)/because this may encourage prejudice against them].

Q62. Heavy television and press coverage of dramatic crimes like murders or terrorist incidents should be banned [(null)/because it may encourage others to commit more crimes/because, later on, it may prevent an accused person getting a fair trial].

Q63. State benefits like family allowances should only be paid to those who really need them.

Q64. People should be allowed to [take whatever drugs/drink as much as] they like [(null)/provided they do not harm or behave offensively to other people].

And now some Yes/No questions.

Q65. Should a [political protest group/religious group/group organizing a town's festival or gala] be allowed to hold a parade that blocks town-centre traffic for two hours?

Q66. Should social workers have the right to take a child away from its parents if [(null)/there are allegations that] the parents regularly ill treat their child?

Q67. In the case where there is concern about [illegal drug use/shoplifting] in a shopping centre, do you think that a [security guard/police officer/shop owner] should have the right to make random searches of the bags carried by [shoppers/people who work in that shopping centre]?

Q68. If a person consults a [journalist/clergyman] in confidence, and confesses to a crime, do you think that a court should be able to force the [journalist/clergyman] to reveal the name of that person?

Q69. Do you think it should be against the law to write or speak in a way that promotes [racial/religious] hatred?

IF YES: If this results in less freedom of speech about important public issues, would you feel differently about it being against the law?

IF NO: If this results in more [racial/religious] prejudice, would you feel differently about it not being against the law?

Q70. Should [citizens of/people from] Commonwealth countries like [Canada and Australia/Nigeria and India] be allowed to vote in British elections if they are living in Britain at the time? And how about people from European Community countries?

Q71. Should [people who cook for restaurants or schools/surgeons and dentists] be required to take a test to prove that they have not been infected by the virus which causes AIDS?

And now some questions of choice.

Q72. If there is a real possibility that a [political demonstration/football match] may lead to public disorder or even a riot, should it be banned in advance or should the authorities make special arrangements to deal with trouble but allow it to go ahead?

IF FOR BAN: Who should have the final say on whether to ban the [proposed demonstration/football match]: the local council, the government, or the police?

Q73. [Given that parliament has repeatedly voted against the death penalty/In order to clamp down on rising crime and violence], do you think Britain should reintroduce the death penalty for murder, or keep things as they are?

IF FOR DEATH PENALTY: If careful research showed that reintroducing the death penalty *would not* cut the number of murders in Britain, would you *still* be in favour of the death penalty?

IF AGAINST DEATH PENALTY: If careful research showed that reintroducing the death penalty *would* cut the number of murders in Britain, would you *then* be in favour of the death penalty?

Q74. If there is a genuine national emergency, is it all right to suspend some of our usual civil rights?

IF YES: Who should have the power to declare an emergency: parliament, or the government alone?

ALSO IF YES: Would [widespread terrorism/widespread public disorder/widespread attacks on minority ethnic or racial groups/an economic crisis caused by strikes in important industries] be sufficient to justify suspending some of our usual civil rights?

Q75. In order to combat [crime, should the police/terrorism, should the security services/the spread of dangerous and undemocratic ideas, should the security services] ever be allowed to [tap phones/inspect people's bank accounts]?

IF NO: Would you feel differently about that if you were convinced it would really help to combat [crime/terrorism /the spread of dangerous and undemocratic ideas]?

IF YES, or NO BUT FEEL DIFFERENTLY: Should the [police/security services/ security services] themselves decide when to do this, or should they get permission, each time from a judge?

ALSO IF YES, or NO BUT FEEL DIFFERENTLY: If you discovered the [police/ security services/security services] had done it to you, would you no longer feel it should be allowed, or would you feel it was just part of the price to be paid by law-abiding citizens for their protection?

Q76. Who should investigate complaints against the [security services/police] and monitor their activities: [the government/senior members from another police force] or [a committee of MPs/elected local councillors] or an independent outside body?

(*Note: wordings in answer codes depend upon whether question is about security services or about police.*)

Q77. Suppose that a woman decides to have an abortion for *no other reason* than that she does not wish to have the child. Then, in this particular case, would she be morally right or morally wrong to have an abortion?

IF MORALLY RIGHT: Should she be able to get an abortion free on the NHS, or should she have to pay for it?

IF MORALLY WRONG OR DON'T KNOW, ETC.: Irrespective of your personal views, do you think that the *law* should forbid such an abortion?

Q78. Is it important to have more [women/ethnic or racial minority] MPs in parliament?

IF IMPORTANT: Ideally, should the proportion of [women/ethnic or racial minority] MPs in parliament be as large as in the country as a whole?

ALSO IF IMPORTANT: Should the *law* be changed to ensure more [women/ethnic or racial minority] MPs?

Q79. Do you think the law should require [large private companies/the government and civil service] to hire a fixed percentage of [women/blacks and Asians/disabled people], or should [women/blacks and Asians/disabled people] get no special treatment?

IF FOR JOB QUOTAS: Would you feel the same even if this *frequently* means not hiring the best person for the job?

IF AGAINST JOB QUOTAS: Would you feel the same even if it means that [women/blacks and Asians/disabled people] remain economically *very* unequal?

Q80. Should [parents who live in Wales/Muslim parents] have the right to have their children educated in publicly funded [Welsh-speaking/Muslim religious] schools if they wish?

IF YES: Would you still feel that way even if it substantially increased the amount of taxes local people had to pay?

IF NO: Would you still feel that way even if, as a result, the continued existence of that [language/religion] was threatened?

Q81. Suppose [an NHS doctor or hospital/a private doctor, or private hospital, outside the NHS] makes a serious mistake in treating a patient. In these circumstances, should the patient get financial compensation, or just be regarded as unfortunate?

IF FOR COMPENSATION: Would you still feel that way if that meant that [taxes/private medical charges] had to be increased substantially to pay for compensation awards?

Q82. Suppose that [British Rail/British Gas/British Telecom/an Electricity Company] provides a particularly poor service to one of its customers by failing to meet its advertised standards. Should the customer get financial compensation, or just be regarded as unfortunate?

IF FOR COMPENSATION: Would you still feel that way if that meant that [rail fares/gas prices/telephone charges/electricity charges] had to be increased substantially to pay for compensation awards?

Now some questions about ways of ensuring fair competition between the three main parties, Conservative, Labour, and Liberal Democrat.

Q83. First, consider the amount of coverage these three parties get on television. Should it be *exactly the same* amount for each party, or should it reflect the *size of vote* each party got in the last election, or should it depend upon *how newsworthy* each party is at the time?

Q84. Next, consider how the electoral system affects these three parties. Should the proportion of seats for each party in the House of Commons be the same as its proportion of votes in the election, or should MPs be elected the way they are now?

Background/Analysis Variables

Finally a few questions to help us analyse the answers to this survey.

Q85. Were you born in England?

IF YES: In the north, Midlands, south, or in London?

IF NO: In what country were you born?

Q86. When you were growing up, did you live mainly in a big town or city, a small town, or a rural area?

Q87. What about now, do you live in a big town or city, a small town, or a rural area?

Q88. Are you now (*read list*): married and living with your spouse, living with a partner, widowed, divorced, separated, or have you never been married, or none of the above?

Q89. Do you have any children?

IF YES: Sons, daughters, or both?

Q90. Do you have any brothers or sisters?

IF YES: Brothers, sisters, or both?

Q91. Are you now self-employed, working for pay, or not working?

IF SELF-EMPLOYED: Do you have any employees? Does your company get most of its business from the public sector or from the private sector?

IF WORKING FOR PAY: In a full-time job, or a part-time job?

IF NOT WORKING: Are you looking after the home, retired, unemployed, a student, or disabled/unable to work, or something else?

IF UNEMPLOYED/LOOKING AFTER HOME/DISABLED, ETC./OTHER: Have you had a paid job at any time?

IF WORKING/RETIRED, UNEMPLOYED, ETC., BUT ONCE HAD A JOB: In your present/last job:

- are/were you in a trade union?
- do/did you supervise, or are/were you responsible for the work of any other people?
- would you say you were part of the management or part of the workforce?
- do/did you work for a private company; or in publicly funded education, health, or social services; or in the Civil Service or central government (excluding education, health, or social services); or in local government or for a local council (excluding education, health, or social services); or for a nationalized industry or public corporation; or in something else?

Q92. Most people say they belong either to the middle class or to the working class. If you had to make a choice, would you call yourself middle class or working class?

Q93. Would you say that most people living in your neighbourhood are middle class or working class? And when you were growing up, would you say your parents, at that time, were middle class or working class?

UNLESS 'MIDDLE' or 'WORKING': But if you had to choose, what would you say?

(*Note: answer codes included 'mixed/both' if this was spontaneously given, but it was never prompted.*)

Q94. How many adults aged over 18 are there living at this telephone number?

Q95. What is your own total annual income from all sources, before tax, to the nearest thousand pounds?

(*Note: if asks 'own or household', stress its their 'own' income.*)

Q96. Does anyone in your household have a car of their own, or the use of a company car?

IF YES: Altogether, how many cars are there in your household?

Q97. Does your household own or rent your house?

IF RENT: Is that from a private landlord, a local council, or a housing association?

IF OWN: Is that on a mortgage, or is it owned outright?

Q98. Was any of your schooling obtained:

- in a religious school?
    IF YES: Protestant, Catholic, Jewish, or Muslim?
- in a private, fee-paying school?

Q99. Do you have any school certificates or any other educational or training qualifications?

IF YES: Do you have a degree from a University or Polytechnic, including the Open University? In what subject?

IF NO TO UNIVERSITY: Do you have a certificate or a diploma from a college? In what subject?

Q100. What is your religion, if any?
(*Note: read list only if answer is unclear.*)

- Church of England (C. of E.)
- Church of Scotland (C. of S.)
- Protestant non-conformist (not C. of E. or C. of S. but other Protestant— including other Presbyterian, United Reformed, Congregational, Baptist, Unitarian, Methodist)
- Roman Catholic
- Greek, Russian, Romanian Orthodox
- other Christian
- Jewish
- Muslim
- Hindu
- Sikh
- other non-Christian
- not religious now

IF ANY RELIGION: About how often do you attend religious services?

IF CHRISTIAN: Would you describe yourself as an 'evangelical' Christian?

Q101. Were you brought up in any religion?

IF YES: What?

(*Note: read list, as above, only if answer is unclear.*)

Q102. To which of these groups do you consider you belong: black, Asian, or white? Would you say that the area you live in is mainly white, mainly black, or mainly Asian?

(*Note: answer codes included 'mixed' if this was spontaneously given, but it was never prompted.*)

Q103. Now in the last few years have you, or anyone in your household:

- received unemployment benefit or income support from the government?
- sent children to a private, fee-paying school?
- had any medical treatment as a private, fee-paying patient?

Q104. In politics, would you say that you are generally on the left, in the centre, or on the right?

IF CENTRE: Do you lean a little more towards the left or the right?

IF LEFT or RIGHT: Strongly or not very strongly?

Q105. Generally speaking, do you think of yourself as a *supporter* of any one political party?

IF YES: Which? And how strongly do you support that party: very strongly, or not very strongly?

IF NO/DON'T KNOW: Do you think of yourself as a little closer to one political party than to the others?

IF YES: Which?

Q106. If there were a general election tomorrow, which party do you think you would be most likely to vote for?

Q107. (*Note: After 9th April 1992 only.*) Thinking back to the general election *on 9 April*, when the main party leaders were John Major, Neil Kinnock, and Paddy Ashdown, do you remember whether you voted at that election?

IF VOTED: And which party did you vote for?

IF DON'T KNOW or DID NOT VOTE, ETC.: Which party did you prefer at that time?

Q108. Thinking back to the general election *in 1987*, when the party leaders were Mrs Thatcher, Neil Kinnock, David Steel, and David Owen, do you remember whether you voted at that election?

IF VOTED: And which party did you vote for?

IF DON'T KNOW or DID NOT VOTE, ETC.: Which party did you prefer at that time?

Q109. If the government found that it had a surplus of cash available, which should it do: cut taxes or increase spending on public services?

Q110. Now looking ahead to the next year:
  • do you think the British economy will get better or get worse?
  • and your household's economic circumstances: do you expect they will get better or get worse?

Q111. Would you say that once you have made up your mind on an important question, you are not likely to change it easily, or can you often be persuaded to change it if someone has a good argument?

Q112. When you work on something, do you like to take charge, or prefer to let others organize the tasks?

Q113. Have you personally ever felt discriminated against, in some important matter, on grounds of your sex, race, ethnic background, religion, age, disability, or political beliefs?

IF YES: And was that mainly because of sex, race, ethnic background, religion, age, disability, or political beliefs? And was that mainly by an employer, the police, a local or national government official, or someone else?

Q114. Have you personally been stopped and interviewed by the police about a traffic violation or anything else?

IF YES: And on balance did the police behave courteously or rudely towards you?

Q115. Have you personally ever been the victim of a crime such as having your house broken into, your car stolen, being assaulted, or anything else?

IF YES: And on balance did you find the police helpful or unhelpful?

(*Note: answer codes included 'no police contact' if this was spontaneously given, but it was never prompted.*)

Q116. Have you personally ever contacted a local councillor about some problem?

IF YES: And on balance did you find them helpful or unhelpful?

And your local council offices:

IF YES: Helpful or unhelpful?

And your MP?

IF YES: Helpful or unhelpful?

And an office of a government department, such as DHSS, DoT, DoE?

IF YES: Helpful or unhelpful?

(*Note: It was usually unnecessary to reiterate the full original question wording when asking about council offices, MPs, and government departments, though this was done where necessary.*)

Q117. In the last few years have you, or anyone in your household received treatment at an NHS hospital?

IF YES: Generally, were you satisfied or dissatisfied with the service provided by the NHS? A lot or a little? And was that mainly because of the staff or because of the resources they had available to them?

Q118. In the last few years, have you taken an *active* part in:

- a sports club?
- an arts organization, for example, a choir or a film club?
- a school board, parent–teacher association, or other school organization?
- a church or religious organization?
- a charity organization, like Oxfam, Barnardos, Sue Ryder, or Famine Relief?
- the affairs of a trade union or a professional association?

- a business organization, for example, a Chamber of Commerce, or a Round Table?
- an election campaign?
- any other political campaign?
- working with others in your community to solve some community problem?

And in the last few years, have you:

- signed a petition?
- taken part in a demonstration, picket, march, or protest meeting?

Special Questions for Politicians' Sample Only

Q119. When you last stood for election as a councillor, did you stand as a party candidate or as an Independent?

IF PARTY: Which party?

Q120. On the council, do you *now* sit as a councillor for a particular party or as an Independent?

IF PARTY: Which party? And are you the leader of that party on the council?

IF INDEPENDENT: Are you the leader of the Independent group on the council?

Q121. Do you chair your council or any of its committees?

IF NOT: Are you: Vice-Chairman? or Mayor?

(Note: code most significant office only: i.e. the one nearest the top of the list.)

- Chair or Convenor of Council/Mayor
- Vice-Chair or Vice-Convenor of Council
- Chair of Policy or Resources Committee
- Chair of other Committees
- none of the above

Q122. Does any one party or group have outright, majority control of the council?

IF YES: Which?

IF NO: Does any one party none the less exercise minority control?

IF YES: Which?

IF NO: Is there a cross-party coalition which controls the council?

IF YES: Does it include: the Conservatives? Labour? the Liberal Democrats? Independents? the Nationalists? other groups?

IF NO: So the council is a completely 'hung' council, or is it run on non-party-political lines?

Q123. So do you regard yourself as on the side of the parties or groups which control your council, or in opposition to the parties or groups which control your council, or neither?

Q124. How long have you been a councillor?

Q125. And how long have you been active in politics?

Closing Sequence

I hope you enjoyed the interview. Thank you very much for helping us with this survey.

Q126. If we wanted to contact you again in a year's time, to update our survey, would you be willing to answer a few more questions?

Constructed Variables

Q127. Nation (Scotland, England, Wales).

Q128. Region (13 category region).

Q129. Date of interview.

Special Constructed Variables for Politicians' Sample Only

Q130. Which party group led by interviewee, according to Chief Executive.

Q131. Council type.

Q132. Total seats on council.

Q133. Largest party on council (which).

Q134. Seats held by largest party (number).

Q135. Seats held by largest party (per cent).

Q136. Standard spending assessment (total).

Q137. Standard spending assessment (per capita).

Q138. Poll tax liable population.

Q139. Average population per council seat.

BIBLIOGRAPHY

ACTON, LORD, *Lectures in Modern History* (London: Fontana, 1960).

ALMOND, GABRIEL, and VERBA, SIDNEY, *The Civic Culture: Political Attitudes and Democracy in Five Nations* (Princeton: Princeton University Press, 1963).

—— (eds.), *The Civic Culture Revisited* (Boston: Little, Brown, 1980).

American Civil Liberties Union, 'Why Free Speech for Racists and Totalitarians', in Robert E. DiClerico and Allan S. Hammock (eds.), *Points of View: Readings in American Government and Politics* (Reading, Mass.: Addison Wesley, 1983), 286–90.

ANDREWS, GEOFF, 'Universal Principles', in Geoff Andrews (ed.), *Citizenship* (London: Lawrence & Wishart, 1991), 212–18.

—— (ed.) *Citizenship* (London: Lawrence & Wishart, 1991).

ANWAR, MUHAMMAD, *Race and Politics: Ethnic Minorities and the British Political System* (London: Tavistock, 1986).

ARMSTRONG, LORD, 'The Case for Confidentiality in Government', in William L. Miller (ed.), *Alternatives to Freedom: Arguments and Opinions* (London: Longman, 1995), 47–63.

ATTWOOLL, ELSPETH, 'The Right to be a Member of a Trade Union', in Tom Campbell, David Goldberg, Sheila McLean, and Tom Mullen (eds.), *Human Rights: From Rhetoric to Reality* (Oxford: Basil Blackwell, 1986), 223–49.

AVINERI, SHLOMO, and DE-SHALIT, AVNER (eds.), *Communitarianism and Individualism* (Oxford: Oxford University Press, 1992).

BACHRACH, PETER, *The Theory of Democratic Élitism: A Critique* (London: London University Press, 1967).

BARBER, BENJAMIN R., *Strong Democracy: Participatory Politics for a New Age* (Berkeley and Los Angeles: University of California Press, 1984).

BARNUM, DAVID G., and SULLIVAN, JOHN L., 'Attitudinal Tolerance and Political Freedom in Britain', *British Journal of Political Science*, 19 (1989) 136–46.

BARRETT, MICHÈLE, and PHILLIPS, ANNE (eds.), *Destabilizing Theory: Contemporary Feminist Debates* (Cambridge: Polity Press, 1992).

BARWISE, PATRICK, and EURENBERG, ANDREW, *Television and its Audience* (London: Sage, 1988).

BEETHAM, DAVID (ed.), *Defining and Measuring Democracy* (London: Sage, 1994).

BIRCH, ANTHONY H., *The British System of Government* (7th edn., London: Allen and Unwin, 1986).

—— *The Concepts and Theories of Modern Democracy* (London: Routledge, 1993).

BLAIR, TONY, Speech to the Labour Party Conference, Blackpool, 4 Oct. 1994.

—— article, *Herald*, 28 Apr. 1995, p. 15.

BLOCK, W. E., and WALKER M. A. (eds.), *Discrimination, Affirmative Action and Equal Opportunity: An Economic and Social Perspective* (Vancouver: The Fraser Institute, 1981).

BOLIVAR, SIMON, *Angostura Address Feb. 19th 1819*, trans. Lewis Bertrand, repr. in Arend Lijphart (ed.), *Parliamentary versus Presidential Government* (Oxford: Oxford University Press, 1992).

BRADLEY, A. W., BATES, T. St J. N., and HIMSWORTH, C. M. G., *E. C. S. Wade and A. W. Bradley's Constitutional and Administrative Law* (London: Longman, 1987).

BRAND, JACK, MITCHELL, JAMES, and SURRIDGE, PAULA, 'Will Scotland Come to the Aid of the Party?', in Anthony Heath, Roger Jowell, and John Curtice (eds.), *Labour's Last Chance? The 1992 Election and Beyond* (Aldershot: Dartmouth, 1994), 213–28.

BRODIE, JANINE, and JENSON, JANE, *Crisis, Challenge and Change: Party and Class in Canada Revisited* (Ottawa: Carleton University Press, 1988).

BUDGE, IAN, CREWE, IVOR, and FARLIE, DENNIS (eds.), *Party Indentification and Beyond* (London: Wiley, 1976).

BURROWS, NOREEN, 'International Law and Human Rights: The Case of Human Rights', in Tom Campbell, David Goldberg, Sheila McLean, and Tom Mullen (eds.), *Human Rights: From Rhetoric to Reality* (Oxford: Basil Blackwell, 1986), 80–98.

BUTLER, DAVID, and RANNEY, AUSTIN (eds.), *Referendums: A Comparative Study of Practice and Theory* (Washington: American Enterprise Institute, 1978).

—— (eds.), *Referendums around the World: The Growing Use of Direct Democracy* (London: Macmillan, 1994).

—— and STOKES, DONALD, *Political Change in Britain: The Evolution of Political Choice* (London: Macmillan, 1974).

BYRNE, TONY, *Local Government in Britain* (5th edn., London: Penguin, 1992).

CAMPBELL, TOM, GOLDBERG, DAVID, MCLEAN, SHEILA, and MULLEN, TOM (eds.), *Human Rights: From Rhetoric to Reality* (Oxford: Basil Blackwell, 1986).

Canada, Department of Justice, *The Role of the United Kingdom in the Amendment of the Canadian Constitution* (Ottawa: Publications Canada, 1981).

Canada, *Report of the Commission on Equality in Employment* (Ottawa: Minister of Supply and Services).

CLARKE, HAROLD D., JENSON, JANE, LEDUC, LAWRENCE, and PAMMETT, JOHN H., *Absent Mandate: The Politics of Discontent in Canada* (Toronto: Gage, 1984).

—— and STEWART, M. C., 'Political Culture and Political Economy: Canada and the United States in Comparative Perspective', a paper presented at the Canadian Politics in Comparative Perspective Conference, Center for Advanced Study in the Behavioral Sciences, Stanford, May 1993.

CLARKE, LINDA, *Discrimination* (London: Institute of Public Management, 1994).

CLARKSON, STEPHEN, and MCCALL, CHRISTINA, *Trudeau and our Times*, Vol I: *The Magnificent Obsession* (Toronto: McClelland & Stewart, 1990).

Cmnd 6218, *Committee on Criminal Procedure in Scotland* (London: HMSO, 1975).

Cmnd 8092, *Royal Commission on Criminal Procedure in England and Wales* (London: HMSO, 1981).

Cmnd 2918, *Privacy and Media Intrusion: The Government's Response* (London: HMSO, 1995).

Commission on Social Justice (Chair: Sir Gordon Borrie), *Social Justice—Strategies for National Renewal* (London: Vintage, 1994).

CONLON, GERRY, *Proved Innocent—The Story of Gerry Conlon and the Guildford Four* (London: Hamish Hamilton, 1990).

Conservative Research Department, *Civil Liberties* (London: Conservative Research Department, 17 May 1990).

Council of Europe, *European Convention on Human Rights: Collected Texts* (7th edn., Strasbourg: Council of Europe, 1971).

COXALL, BILL, and ROBINS, LYNTON, *Contemporary British Politics* (London: Macmillan, 1994).

CRANSTON, MAURICE, 'Human Rights, Real and Supposed' and 'Human Rights: A Reply to Professor Raphael', in D. D. Raphael (ed.), *Political Theory and the Rights of Man* (London: Macmillan, 1967), 43–53 and 95–100.

CREWE, IVOR, DAY, NEIL, and FOX, ANTHONY, *The British Electorate 1963–87* (Cambridge: Cambridge University Press, 1991).

CROUCH, COLIN, 'The Peculiar Relationship: The Party and the Unions', in Dennis Kavanagh (ed.), *The Politics of the Labour Party* (London: Allen & Unwin, 1982), 171–90.

DALYELL, TAM, *Misrule: How Mrs Thatcher has Misled Parliament from the Sinking of the Belgrano to the Wright Affair* (London: Hamish Hamilton, 1987).

DAVIS, JAMES A., 'British and American Attitudes: Similarities and Contrasts', in Roger Jowell, Sharon Witherspoon, and Lindsay Brook (eds.), *British Social Attitudes: The 1986 Report* (Aldershot: Gower, 1986), 89–114.

DE VAUS, D. A., *Surveys in Social Research* (London: Allen & Unwin, 1991).

DiCLERICO, ROBERT E., and HAMMOCK, ALLAN S. (eds.), *Points of View: Readings in American Government and Politics* (Reading, Mass.: Addison Wesley, 1983).

DOERN, G. BRUCE, 'The UK Citizen's Charter: Origins and Implementation in Three Agencies', *Policy and Politics*, 21 (1993), 17–20.

DOWNS, ANTHONY, *An Economic Theory of Democracy* (New York: Harper, 1957).

DYE, THOMAS R., and ZEIGLER, L. HARMON, *American Politics in the Media Age* (Belmont, Calif.: Wadsworth, 1983).

—— *The Irony of Democracy: An Uncommon Introduction to American Politics* (Belmont, Calif.: Wadsworth, 1970).

ELLIOT, DAVE, *Weighting for Non-Response: A Survey Researcher's Guide* (London: OPCS, 1991).

ELLIS, CAROLINE, 'Sisters and Citizens', in Geoff Andrews (ed.), *Citizenship* (London: Lawrence & Wishart, 1991), 235–42.

ELLIS, PETER BERRESFORD, and MAC A'GHOBHAINN, SEUMAS, *The Scottish Insurrection of 1820* (London: Pluto Press, 1989).

502   *Bibliography*

ELTON, DAVID, 'The Charlottetown Accord Senate: Effective or Emasculated?', in Kenneth McRoberts and Patrick Monahan (eds.), *The Charlottetown Accord and the Future of Canada* (Toronto: University of Toronto Press, 1993), 37–57.

ETZIONI, AMITAI, *The Spirit of Community: The Reinvention of American Society* (New York: Simon & Schuster, 1993).

EVETTS, JULIA (ed.), *Women and Career: Themes and Issues in Advanced Industrial Societies* (London: Longman, 1994).

EWING, K. D., and GEARTY, C. A., *Freedom under Thatcher: Civil Liberties in Modern Britain* (Oxford: Oxford University Press, 1990).

EYSENCK, H., *The Psychology of Politics* (London: Routledge & Kegan Paul, 1951).

FERNS, HENRY S., *The Disease of Government* (London: MauriceTemple Smith, 1978).

FLETCHER, JOSEPH F., 'Mass and Élite Attitudes about Wiretapping in Canada: Implications for Democratic Theory and Politics', *Public Opinion Quarterly*, 53 (1989), 225–45.

—— 'Participation and Attitudes towards Civil Liberties: Is there an "Educative" Effect?', *International Political Science Review*, 11 (1990), 439–59.

FOOT, PAUL, *Murder at the Farm: Who Killed Carl Bridgewater* (London: Penguin, 1988).

FRIEDMAN, MILTON, with the assistance of FRIEDMAN, ROSE D., *Capitalism and Freedom* (Chicago: University of Chicago Press, 1962; updated edn., 1982).

GIFFORD, TONY, *Where's the Justice: A Manifesto for Law Reform* (London: Penguin, 1986).

GIRVIN, BRIAN, 'Varieties of Conservatism', in Brian Girvin (ed.), *The Transformation of Contemporary Conservatism* (London: Sage, 1988), 1–12.

—— (ed.), *The Transformation of Contemporary Conservatism* (London: Sage, 1988).

GLENDON, MARY ANN, *Rights Talk: The Impoverishment of Political Discourse* (New York: The Free Press, 1991).

GOODIN, ROBERT E., and LE GRAND, JULIAN, *Not Only the Poor* (London: Allen & Unwin, 1987).

GRIGOR, IAIN FRASER, *Mightier than a Lord* (Stornoway: Acair, 1979).

GUTMAN, AMY, 'Communitarian Critics of Liberalism', in Shlomo Avineri and Avner de-Shalit (eds.), *Communitarianism and Individualism* (Oxford: Oxford University Press, 1992), 120–36.

—— (ed.), *Multiculturalism and 'The Politics of Recognition'* (Princeton: Princeton University Press, 1992).

HAILSHAM, LORD, *The Dilemma of Democracy: Diagnosis and Prescription* (London: Collins, 1978).

HALSEY, A. H., *Change in British Society* (2nd edn., Oxford: Oxford University Press, 1981).

HART, VIVIEN, *Distrust and Democracy: Political Distrust in Britain and America* (Cambridge: Cambridge University Press, 1978).

—— 'The Right to a Fair Wage: American Experience and the European Social Charter', in Vivien Hart and Shannon C. Stimson (eds.), *Writing a National Identity:*

Political, Economic and Cultural Perspectives on the Written Constitution (Manchester: Manchester University Press, 1993).

—— and STIMSON, SHANNON C. (eds.), *Writing a National Identity: Political, Economic and Cultural Perspectives on the Written Constitution* (Manchester: Manchester University Press, 1993).

HATTERSLEY, ROY, *Choose Freedom: The Future for Democratic Socialism* (London: Michael Joseph, 1987).

—— 'Though Equality to Liberty', in William L. Miller (ed.), *Alternatives to Feedom: Arguments and Opinions* (London: Longman, 1995), 133–50.

HAYWARD, JACK (ed.), *Elitism, Populism and European Politics* (Oxford: Oxford University Press, 1996).

HEATH, ANTHONY, 'Do People have Consistent Attitudes?', in Roger Jowell, Sharon Witherspoon, and Lindsay Brook (eds.), *British Social Attitudes: The 1986 Report* (Aldershot: Gower, 1986), 1–16.

—— and TOPF, RICHARD, 'Political Culture', in Roger Jowell, Sharon Witherspoon, and Lindsay Brook (eds.), *British Social Attitudes: The 1987 Report* (Aldershot: Gower, 1987), 51–70.

—— JOWELL, ROGER, and CURTICE, JOHN, *How Britain Votes* (Oxford: Pergamon, 1985).

—— —— —— (eds.), *Labour's Last Chance? The 1992 Election and Beyond* (Aldershot: Dartmouth, 1994).

—— CURTICE, JOHN, JOWELL, ROGER, EVANS, GEOFF, FIELD, JULIA, and WITHERSPOON, SHARON, *Understanding Political Change: The British Voter 1964–87* (Oxford: Pergamon Press, 1991).

HEATHERINGTON, PETER, 'Social Workers Failed to Stop and Think about Raid', *Guardian*, 28 October 1992, p. 3.

HELD, DAVID, *Models of Democracy* (Oxford: Blackwell, 1987).

HILLYARD, PADDY, and PERCY-SMITH, JANIE, *The Coercive State: The Decline of Democracy in Britain* (London: Fontana, 1988).

HOBBES, THOMAS, *Leviathan* (London: Penguin, 1974).

HOHFELD, WESLEY, *Fundamental Legal Conceptions* (New Haven: Yale University Press, 1923).

HONDERICH, TED, *Conservatism* (London: Hamish Hamilton, 1990; Penguin, 1991).

HOOPER, DAVID, *Official Secrets: The Use and Abuse of the Act* (London: Secker & Warburg, 1987).

HOOVER, KENNETH, and PLANT, RAYMOND, *Conservative Capitalism in Britain and the United States* (London: Routledge, 1989).

HOROWITZ, GAD, 'Conservatism, Liberalism and Socialism in Canada: An Interpretation', *Canadian Journal of Economics and Political Science*, 32 (1966), repr. in Hugh G. Thorburn (ed.), *Party Politics in Canada* (5th edn., Scarborough: Prentice Hall, 1985), 41–59.

House of Commons, *British North America Acts: The Role of Parliament* (London: Her Majesty's Stationery Office, 1981).

Hucko, Elmar M., *The Democratic Tradition: Four German Constitutions* (Oxford: Berg, 1987).

Hurwitt, Malcolm, and Thornton, Peter, *Civil Liberty: The Liberty/NCCL Guide* (4th edn., London: Penguin, 1989).

Inglehart, Ronald, and Klingemann, Hans, 'Party Identification, Ideological Preference and the Left–Right Dimension among Western Mass Publics', in Ian Budge, Ivor Crewe, and Dennis Farlie (eds.), *Party Identification and Beyond* (London: Wiley, 1976), 243–73.

Jackman, Robert, 'Political Élites, Mass Publics and Support for Democratic Principles', *Journal of Politics*, 34 (1972), 753–73.

Jenkins, Lord, 'The Case for a People's Bill of Rights', in William L. Miller (ed.), *Alternatives to Freedom: Arguments and Opinions* (London: Longman, 1995), 21–30.

Jowell, Roger, Witherspoon, Sharon, and Brook, Lindsay (eds.), *British Social Attitudes: The 1986 Report* (Aldershot: Gower, 1986).

—— —— —— (eds.), *British Social Attitudes: The 1987 Report* (Aldershot: Gower, 1987).

Kavanagh, Dennis (ed.), *The Politics of the Labour Party* (London: Allen & Unwin, 1982).

—— *British Politics: Continuities and Change* (Oxford: Oxford University Press, 1989).

Kellas, James G., *The Scottish Political System* (4th edn., Cambridge: Cambridge University Press, 1989).

Kilbourn, William, *Canada: A Guide to the Peaceable Kingdom* (New York: St Martin's Press, 1970).

King, Desmond S., *The New Right: Politics, Markets and Citizenship* (London: Macmillan, 1987).

Lessnoff, Michael, *Social Contract* (London: Macmillan, 1986).

Lijphart, Arend (ed.), *Parliamentary versus Presidential Government* (Oxford: Oxford University Press, 1992).

Lipset, Seymour Martin, *Political Man* (London: Heinemann, 1983).

—— *Continental Divide: The Values and Institutions of the United States and Canada* (New York: Routledge, 1990).

Lipsitz, Lewis, 'Working Class Authoritarianism: A Re-Evaluation', *American Sociological Review*, 30 (1965), 103–9.

Lister, Ruth, 'Tracing the Contours of Women's Citizenship', *Policy and Politics*, 21 (1993), 3–16.

Locke, John, *A Letter Concerning Toleration*, ed. J. Tully (Indianapolis: Hackett, 1983).

—— *Essay Concerning Civil Government*, in *Locke's Two Treatises of Government*, ed. Peter Lazlett (Cambridge: Cambridge University Press, 1988), 265–428.

Lovenduski, Joni, *Women and European Politics* (Brighton: Wheatsheaf, 1986).

McClosky, Herbert, 'Consensus and Ideology in American Politics', *American Political Science Review*, 58 (1964), 361–82.

—— and BRILL, ALIDA, *Dimensions of Tolerance: What Americans Believe about Civil Liberties* (New York: Russell Sage Foundation, 1983).

McCRONE, DAVID, 'Scottish Culture', in David McCrone, *Understanding Scotland: The Sociology of a Stateless Nation* (London: Routledge, 1992), ch. 7, 174–96.

McELROY, WENDY, 'Preferential Treatment of Women in Employment', in Caroline Quest (ed.), *Equal Opportunities: A Feminist Fallacy* (London: Institute for Economic Affairs, 1992), 101–14.

McLELLAN, DAVID, and SAYERS, SEAN (eds.), *Socialism and Democracy* (London: Macmillan, 1991).

MacPHAIL, I. M. M., *The Crofters' War* (Stornoway: Acair, 1989).

McROBERTS, KENNETH, 'Quebec: Province, Nation or "Distinct Society"?', in Michael Whittington and Glen Williams (eds.), *Canadian Politics in the 1990s* (Scarborough: Nelson, 1990), 98–117.

—— and MONAHAN, PATRICK (eds.), *The Charlottetown Accord and the Future of Canada* (Toronto: University of Toronto Press, 1993).

MADISON, JAMES, 'Number X: The Same Subject Continued', in James Madison, Alexander Hamilton, and John Jay, *The Federalist Papers* (London: Penguin, 1987), 122–8.

MAHER, GERRY, 'Human Rights and the Criminal Process', in Tom Campbell, David Goldberg, Sheila McLean, and Tom Mullen (eds.), *Human Rights: From Rhetoric to Reality* (Oxford: Basil Blackwell, 1986), 197–222.

MARSH, ALAN, *Protest and Political Consciousness* (London: Sage, 1977).

MARSHALL, THURGOOD, Justice of the Supreme Court, 'The Case for Racial Quotas, in Robert E. DiClerico and Allan S. Hammock (eds.), *Points of View: Readings in American Government and Politics* (Reading, Mass.: Addison Wesley, 1983), 308–14.

MARSHALL, T. H., and BOTTOMORE, TOM, *Citizenship and Social Class* (London: Pluto Press, 1992).

MAY, TIM, *Social Research: Issues, Methods and Process* (Buckingham: Open University Press, 1993).

MEEHAN, ELIZABETH M., *Women's Rights at Work: Campaigns and Policies in Britain and the United States* (London: Macmillan, 1985).

—— and SEVENHUIJSEN, SELMA, *Equality Politics and Gender* (London: Sage, 1991).

MENDUS, SUSAN, *Toleration and the Limits of Liberalism* (London: Macmillan, 1989).

MILL, JOHN STUART, *On Liberty*, ed. G. Himmmelfarb (London: Penguin, 1978).

—— *Representative Government* (Everyman Edition; London: Dent, 1972).

MILLER, WILLIAM L., *The End of British Politics? Scots and English Political Behaviour in the Seventies* (Oxford: Oxford University Press, 1981).

—— *Irrelevant Elections? The Quality of Local Democracy in Britain* (Oxford: Oxford University Press, 1988).

—— *Media and Voters: The Audience, Content, and Influence of Press and Television at the 1987 General Election* (Oxford: Oxford University Press, 1991).

—— 'Local Elections in Britain', in Lourdes Lopez Nieto (ed.), *Local Elections in Europe* (Barcelona: Institut de Ciencies Politiques i Socials, 1994), 59–84.

MILLER, WILLIAM L., (ed.), *Alternatives to Freedom: Arguments and Opinions* (London: Longman, 1995).

—— CLARKE, HAROLD D., HARROP, MARTIN, LEDUC, LAWRENCE, and WHITELEY, PAUL F., *How Voters Change: The 1987 British Election Campaign in Perspective* (Oxford: Oxford University Press, 1990).

—— TIMPSON, ANNIS MAY, and LESSNOFF, MICHAEL, 'Public Tolerance of Private Freedom', in William L. Miller (ed.), *Alternatives to Freedom: Arguments and Opinions* (London: Longman, 1995), 185–208.

—— —— —— 'Public Opposition to Parliamentary Sovereignty', in William L. Miller (ed.), *Alternatives to Freedom: Arguments and Opinions* (London: Longman, 1995), 31–46.

—— —— —— 'Freedom from the Press', in Jack Hayward (ed.), *Elitism, Populism and European Politics* (Oxford: Oxford University Press, 1996), 67–87.

—— WHITE, STEPHEN, and HEYWOOD, PAUL, 'The Locus of Democratic Values', paper presented at the ESRC Conference on Mass Response to the Transformation of Post-Communist Societies, St Antony's College, Oxford, 1995.

—— —— —— *Values and Political Change in Post-Communist Europe* (London: Macmillan, forthcoming).

—— —— —— and WYMAN, MATTHEW, 'Democratic, Market and Nationalist Values in Russia and East Europe: December 1993', paper presented at the Political Studies Association Annual Conference, Swansea, 1994.

—— —— —— —— 'Parties and Democratic Values in Russia and East-Central Europe: December 1993', paper presented at the XVI World Congress of IPSA, Berlin, 1994.

MONTESQUIEU, BARON DE, 'Of the Laws which Establish Political Liberty with Regard to the Constitution', in Philip Norton (ed.), *Legislatures* (Oxford: Oxford University Press, 1990), 23–35.

MOYNIHAN, DANIEL PATRICK, 'Defining Deviancy Down', in William L. Miller (ed.), *Alternatives to Freedom: Arguments and Opinions* (London: Longman, 1995), 171–84.

MULLEN, JOHN, TRAVIS, ALAN, and NORTON, RICHARD, 'Nudge-Nudge, Wink-Wink Game after a Muzzling Injunction in the High Court', *Guardian*, 6 Feb. 1992, p. 2.

MULLEN, TOM, 'Constitutional Protection of Human Rights', in Tom Campbell, David Goldberg, Sheila McLean, and Tom Mullen (eds.), *Human Rights: From Rhetoric to Reality* (Oxford: Basil Blackwell, 1986), 15–36.

MURDOCH, JIM, 'The Rights of Public Assembly and Procession', in Tom Campbell, David Goldberg, Sheila McLean, and Tom Mullen (eds.), *Human Rights: From Rhetoric to Reality* (Oxford: Basil Blackwell, 1986), 173–96.

MURRAY, CHARLES, *The Emerging British Underclass* (London: Institute of Economic Affairs, 1990).

NEMETZ, PETER N., STANBURY, W. T., and THOMPSON, FRED, 'Social Regulation in

Canada: An Overview and Comparison with the American Model', *Policy Studies Journal*, 14 (1986), 588–602.

NIE, N., VERBA, S., BRADY, H., SCHLOZMAN, K., and LUNN, J., 'Participation in America: Continuity and Change', paper presented at the Midwest Political Science Association Annual Meeting, Chicago, Illinois, 1988.

NIETO, LOURDES LOPEZ (ed.), *Local Elections in Europe* (Barcelona: Institut de Ciencies Politiques i Socials, 1994).

NORTON, PHILIP, *The British Polity* (London: Longman, 1984).

—— (ed.), *Legislatures* (Oxford: Oxford University Press, 1990).

NOZICK, ROBERT, *Anarchy, State and Utopia* (Oxford: Blackwell, 1974).

Office of Population Censuses and Surveys (OPCS), *1991 Census Monitor for Parliamentary Constituencies* (London: OPCS, 1994).

—— *1991 Census Monitor for Parliamentary Constituencies in Scotland* (Edinburgh: General Register House; London: OPCS, 1994).

OPPENHEIM, A. N., *Questionnaire Design and Attitude Measurement* (New York: Pinter, 1992).

OWRAM, DOUG, *The Government Generation: Canadian Intellectuals and the State 1900–1945* (Toronto: University of Toronto Press, 1986).

PAREKH, BHIKHU, 'British Citizenship and Cultural Difference', in Geoff Andrews (ed.), *Citizenship* (London: Lawrence & Wishart, 1991), 183–204.

—— 'Cultural Diversity and Liberal Democracy', in David Beetham (ed.), *Defining and Measuring Democracy* (London: Sage, 1994), 199–221.

PARIZEAU, JACQUES, 'Modern Quebec and its Quest for Sovereignty', lecture presented to the Royal Institute of International Affairs, Chatham House, London, 5 July 1995.

PARRY, GERAINT, MOYSER, GEORGE, and DAY, NEIL, *Political Participation and Democracy in Britain* (Cambridge: Cambridge University Press, 1992).

PATEMAN, CAROL, *Participation and Democratic Theory* (Cambridge: Cambridge University Press, 1970).

PAUL, ELLEN FRANKEL, MILLER, FRED D., JR., and PAUL, JEFFREY, *Reassessing Civil Rights* (Oxford: Blackwell, 1991).

PAXMAN, JEREMY, 'The Moral Catch', *Guardian*, 23 Feb. 1995, pp. 2–3.

PERCY, LORD, *The Heresy of Democracy* (London: Eyre & Spottiswood, 1954).

PHILLIPS, ANNE, 'Universal Pretensions in Political Thought', in Michèle Barrett, and Anne Phillips (eds.), *Destabilizing Theory: Contemporary Feminist Debates* (Cambridge: Polity Press, 1992), ch. 2, 10–30.

PLANT, RAYMOND, 'Social Rights and the Reconstruction of Welfare', in Geoff Andrews (ed.), *Citizenship* (London: Lawrence & Wishart, 1991), 50–64.

QUEST, CAROLINE (ed.), *Equal Opportunities: A Feminist Fallacy* (London: Institute for Economic Affairs, 1992).

RANDALL, VICKI, *Women and Politics* (London: Macmillan, 1982).

RAPHAEL, D. D. (ed.), *Political Theory and the Rights of Man* (London: Macmillan, 1967).

ROKEACH, M., *The Nature of Human Values* (New York: Free Press, 1973).

ROMANOW, ROY, WHYTE, JOHN, and LEESON, HOWARD, *Canada . . . Notwithstanding: The Making of the Constitution* (Toronto: Carswell/Methuen, 1984).

ROSE, RICHARD, *Politics in England Today* (London: Faber & Faber, 1974).

—— *Understanding the United Kingdom: The Territorial Dimension in Government* (London: Longman, 1982).

ROTHENBERG, STUART, and NEWPORT, FRANK, *The Evangelical Voter: Religion and Politics in America* (Washington: Free Congress Research and Education Foundation, 1984).

RUSSELL, PETER H., *Constitutional Odyssey: Can Canadians be a Sovereign People?* (Toronto: University of Toronto Press, 1992; 2nd edn., 1993).

SARTORI, GIOVANNI, *The Theory of Democracy Revisited* (Chatham, NJ: Chatham House, 1987).

SCHUMPETER, JOSEPH A., *Capitalism, Socialism and Democracy* (London: Allen & Unwin, 1942).

SEDLEY, STEPHEN, 'Charter 88: Rights and Wrongs', in Geoff Andrews (ed.), *Citizenship* (London: Lawrence & Wishart, 1991), 219–27.

SEYD, PATRICK, and WHITELEY, PAUL, *Labour's Grass Roots: The Politics of Party Membership* (Oxford: Oxford University Press, 1992).

SHULGIN, VASILII V., *The Years: Memoirs of a Member of the Russian Duma*, trans. Tanya Davis (New York: Hippocrene Books, 1984).

SIIM, BERTE, 'Welfare State, Gender Politics and Equality Policies: Women's Citizenship in the Scandinavian Welfare States', in Elizabeth Meehan and Selma Sevenhuijsen (eds.), *Equality Politics and Gender* (London: Sage, 1991), 175–92.

SILVERSTONE, ROGER, *Television and Everyday Life* (London: Routledge, 1994).

SNIDERMAN, PAUL M., BRODY, RICHARD A., and TETLOCK, PHILIP E., *Reasoning and Choice: Explorations in Political Psychology* (Cambridge: Cambridge University Press, 1991).

—— FLETCHER, JOSEPH F., RUSSELL, PETER H., and TETLOCK, PHILIP E., *The Clash of Rights: Liberty, Equality and Legitimacy in Pluralist Democracy* (New Haven: Yale University Press, 1996).

—— —— —— —— and GAINES, BRIAN J., 'The Fallacy of Democratic Élitism: Élite Competition and Commitment to Civil Liberties', *British Journal of Political Science*, 21 (1991), 349–70.

—— TETLOCK, PHILIP E., GLOVER, JAMES M., GREEN, DONALD PHILIP, and HOUT, MICHAEL, 'Principle, Tolerance and the American Mass Public', *British Journal of Political Science*, 19 (1989), 25–45.

SOWELL, THOMAS, 'Weber and Bakke, and the Presumptions of Affirmative Action', in W. E. Block and M. A. Walker (eds.), *Discrimination, Affirmative Action and Equal Opportunity: An Economic and Social Perspective* (Vancouver: The Fraser Institute, 1981), 37–63.

STAMMERS, NEIL, *Civil Liberties in Britain during the Second World War* (Beckenham: Croom Helm, 1983).

STOKER, GERRY, *The Politics of Local Government* (2nd edn., London: Macmillan, 1991).

STOUFFER, S., *Communism, Conformism and Civil Liberties* (New York: Wiley, 1955).

SULLIVAN, JOHN L., PIERSON, JAMES, and MARCUS, GEORGE E., *Political Tolerance and American Democracy* (Chicago: University of Chicago Press, 1982, 1989).

SYPNOWICH, CHRISTINE, 'Rights, Community and the Charter', *British Journal of Canadian Studies*, 6 (1991), 39–59.

TANNEN, DEBORAH, *You Just Don't Understand: Women and Men in Conversation* (New York: Ballantine, 1991).

TAYLOR, CHARLES, 'The Politics of Recognition', in Amy Gutman (ed.), *Multiculturalism and 'The Politics of Recognition'* (Princeton: Princeton University Press, 1992).

TAYLOR-GOOBY, PETER, 'Citizenship and Welfare', in Roger Jowell, Sharon Witherspoon, and Lindsay Brook (eds.), *British Social Attitudes: The 1987 Report* (Aldershot: Gower, 1987), 1–28.

THORBURN, HUGH G., 'Interpretations of the Canadian Party System', in Hugh G. Thorburn (ed.), *Party Politics in Canada* (5th edn., Scarborough: Prentice Hall, 1985), 20–40.

—— (ed.), *Party Politics in Canada* (5th edn., Scarborough: Prentice Hall, 1985).

THORNTON, PETER, *Decade of Decline: Civil Liberties in the Thatcher Years* (London: National Council for Civil Liberties, 1989).

TIMPSON, ANNIS MAY, 'Between the Royal Commissions: Women's Employment Opportunities in Canada 1966–86', *London Journal of Canadian Studies*, 4 (1987), 68–81.

—— 'Rejection Slip for Unused Accord', *Times Higher Education Supplement*, 6 Nov. 1992, p. 17.

—— 'Canada's Electoral Earthquake', *The World Today*, 50 (1994), 6–7.

—— 'The Politics of Employment Inequality in Canada: Gender and the Public Sector', in Julia Evetts (ed.), *Women and Career: Themes and Issues in Advanced Industrial Societies* (London: Longman, 1994), 44–57.

TREVOR-ROPER, HUGH, 'Introduction', to *Lord Acton's Lectures in Modern History* (London: Fontana, 1960).

VERBA, SIDNEY, and NIE, NORMAN, *Participation in America: Political Democracy and Social Equality* (New York: Harper & Row, 1972).

WAINWRIGHT, HILARY, 'New Forms of Democracy for Socialist Renewal', in David McLellan and Sean Sayers (eds.), *Socialism and Democracy* (London: Macmillan, 1991), 70–86.

WHITE, STEPHEN, GILL, GRAEME, and SLIDER, DARRELL, *The Politics of Transition: Shaping a Post-Soviet Future* (Cambridge: Cambridge University Press, 1993).

WHITELEY, PAUL, SEYD, PATRICK, and RICHARDSON, JEREMY, *True Blues: The Politics of Conservative Party Membership* (Oxford: Oxford University Press, 1994).

WHITTINGTON, MICHAEL, and WILLIAMS, GLEN (eds.), *Canadian Politics in the 1990s* (Scarborough: Nelson, 1990).

WILL, GEORGE F., 'Nazis: Outside the Constitution', in Robert E. DiClerico and Allan S. Hammock (eds.), *Points of View: Readings in American Government and Politics* (Reading, Mass.: Addison Wesley, 1983), 291–3.

WINCH, DONALD, *Adam Smith's Politics: An Essay in Historiographic Revision* (Cambridge: Cambridge University Press, 1979).

ZINN, HOWARD, 'How Democratic is America?', in Robert E. DiClerico and Allan S. Hammock (eds.), *Points of View: Readings in American Government and Politics* (Reading, Mass.: Addison Wesley, 1983), 2–14.

INDEX

Note—Bold face figures indicate the information is found only in the table. The notes have been indexed for items not directly accessible from the text or the bibliography.

Church of England 246–7, **248**, 250, 328
Church of Scotland 247, 328, 366
churches (civil institution):
  confidence in 48, 70, **71**, 107, 113;
    influences on 247, 249, 395, **396**
  as practical mechanism 185, **186**, 187, 197,
    198, **199**, 204
  as socio-political organization 342–6, **347**,
    348, 350–4
citizen groups, sympathy for (micro-sympathy)
    44–5, 68, **69**
  see also under individual groups
Citizens' Charters 4, 30–1, 375
citizens' rights, *see* rights
civil and political rights 3, 6–9, 10–13,
    27–34, 55, 122, 178–9, 183
  and overview 417
civil institutions, confidence in (micro-
    sympathy) 48, 70, **71**
  and coherence 107, 109–11, **112**, 113, 118
  and practice 178, 183, 185–7, 191, 197,
    198, **199**, 394–6
  Scottish sample **371**
  and social background 240, **241**, 247, **305**
civil liberties/rights (US) 136–7, 303–4, 365
class, *see* social background
clergy 127, 155–7, **159**
Clyde, Lord 53–4 n. 35
coherence:
  dimensions of principle and sympathy
    79–118
  external coherence 81
  internal coherence 81, 83–95
  mechanism 183–204
  practice of principle 121–79
'Combination Acts' 133
Commission for Racial Equality 50, 71–2,
    108, 327, 360, 395, **396**
  as mechanism 185, 186, 187, 197–8, **199**
Commission on Social Justice 189
Committee on Criminal Procedure in Scotland
    29
Commonwealth countries:
  vote in Britain 164, 166, **167**
communists, sympathy for 44, **45**, 68, **69**,
    104–5
  as MDG 123, 389, **391**
  and social background 244, 250, 262, 270
communitarianism 169
community:
  interest 5, 39, 41, 65–6, 93, 381
  standards 37, 51, 64, **65**, **90**, 150–5
compensation:
  business 174, **175**, **176**, 223, 224, 231
  medical 174, **175**, **176**, 223–4, 231

Concise Oxford Dictionary 255
confession, conviction on, *see* suspects' rights
confidentiality of sources 155–7, 158, **159**
conservatism, contemporary 296
Conservative Party:
  mechanisms for reform 184, **187**, 188–9,
    196–7, 198, **200**, 202, 204, 315–17;
    Canada and Britain 395, **396**; and
    overview 419–20, 440–3, 444, 459, **460**,
    462, 463 n. 8
  and partisanship and ideology 58, **300**,
    301–3, 306, 308, 312–17, 358; and party
    preference 430, 431, **432**, 433–8
  and personal experience 341–2
  and practice 286, 446, **447**, 455–61
  and sample groups 55, 60
  Scottish support for 368–9
Conservative Research Department 188
Conspiracy and Protection of Property Act
    (1875) 133
constitution:
  demand for British 3–4, 5–6, 9, 15–16,
    184, 364–6, 377
  Canadian model 373–406
  and parliamentary sovereignty 191–2
  US 5, 28–9, 451
  see also Bill of Rights (British)
conviction on confession, *see under* suspects'
    rights
council house sales, *see* Conservative Party
    mechanisms for reform
Council of Europe 9, 15, 376, 377
councillors, local-government, *see* local
    government councils
courts, *see* British courts; European courts
Craig, Malcolm 319 n. 1
Cranston, Maurice 6, 7, 8–9, 14, 27
Crick, Bernard 35
crime:
  black crime rates **147**, 148, **149**, 150, 220,
    221, 230
  personal experience as victim of 332, 333,
    336, **337**, 360
  protection from, *see* protection
  sensational coverage of **128**, 129–30,
    138–9, 140, **142**, 178; and argument 220,
    221, 230, 447–9, 457, **458**, 459, 460–1
  see also judicial system; police; surveillance
Criminal Justice and Public Order Act (1994)
    11, 12, 30
Criminal Procedure, Royal Commission on
    (1981) 30, 220–1
Criminal Procedure in Scotland, Royal
    Committee on (1975) 29
Curtice, John 96–7

Index